Nursing Law and Ethics

Second Edition

Edited by

John Tingle and Alan Cribb

© 1995, 2002 by Blackwell Science Ltd,
a Blackwell Publishing Company
Editorial Offices:
Osney Mead, Oxford OX2 0EL, UK
  Tel: +44 (0)1865 206206
Blackwell Science, Inc., 350 Main Street, Malden,
MA 02148-5018, USA
  Tel: +1 781 388 8250
Iowa State Press, a Blackwell Publishing
Company, 2121 State Avenue, Ames,
Iowa 50014-8300, USA
  Tel: +1 515 292 0140
Blackwell Science Asia Pty, 54 University Street,
Carlton, Victoria 3053, Australia
  Tel: +61 (0)3 9347 0300
Blackwell Wissenschafts Verlag,
Kurfürstendamm 57, 10707 Berlin, Germany
  Tel: +49 (0)30 32 79 060

First Edition published 1995 by Blackwell
Science Ltd
Reprinted 1996, 1998, 1999, 2000, 2001
Second Edition published 2002

Library of Congress
Cataloging-in-Publication Data
is available

ISBN 0-632-055073

A catalogue record for this title is available from
the British Library

Set in 10/12pt Berkeley Old Style
by DP Photosetting
Printed and bound in Great Britain by
MPG Books Ltd, Bodmin, Cornwall

For further information on
Blackwell Science, visit our website:
www.blackwell-science.com

Nursing Law and Ethics

Contents

Preface to the First Edition

One of the key indicators of the maturation of nursing as a profession and as a discipline is the growing importance of nursing law and ethics. A profession which seeks not only to maintain, and improve on, high standards but also to hold each of its individual members accountable for an increasing range of responsibilities is inevitably concerned with legal and ethical matters. It is not surprising that these matters have come to prominence in nurse education, and to enjoy a central place along with clinical and social sciences in the disciplinary bases of nursing. There is now a substantial body of literature devoted to nursing law and to nursing ethics.

This book is distinctive because it is about both law *and* ethics. We believe it is of practical benefit, and academic value, to consider these two subjects together. Put simply we need to be able to discuss 'what the law requires' and 'what is right', and to decide, amongst other things, whether these two are always the same.

The book is divided into two parts. The first part is designed to be an overview of the whole subject and includes introductions to the legal, ethical and professional dimensions of nursing, as well as a special chapter on patient complaints. The second part looks at a selection of issues in greater depth. These chapters contain two parts or perspectives – one legal and one ethical. The legal perspectives take the lead – the authors were invited to introduce the law relating to the subject at hand. The ethics authors were invited to write a complementary (and typically shorter) piece in which they took up some of the issues but then went on to make any points they wished. Thus the terms of invitation for the ethics authors were different, and more flexible, than those for the lawyers. This difference in treatment of the two perspectives is quite deliberate.

The essential difference is this: it makes good sense to ask lawyers for an authoritative account of the law, but it is not sensible to ask authors for an authoritative account of what is good or right – which is the subject matter of ethics. An account of the law will not simply be factual; it will inevitably include some discussion of the complexity and uncertainties involved in identifying and interpreting the implications of the law. But it is in the nature of the law that lawyers should be able to give expert guidance about legal judgments. There are no equivalent authorities on ethical judgement. Instead some nurses with an interest in ethics and some philosophers with an interest in nursing ethics were invited to discuss some of the issues and/or cases raised in the first part of the chapter.

Clearly these responses are of different styles and are written from different standpoints. Each author is responsible for his or her piece and any of the views or opinions expressed within them. This difference between the two sets of perspectives is indicated (indeed rather exaggerated) by giving the former the definite, and the latter an indefinite, article – 'The Legal Perspective' but 'An Ethical Perspective'!

These differences in presentation reflect deeper differences between the two subjects. In short, law and ethics are concerned with two contrasting kinds of 'finality' – in principle ethics is final but in practice law is final. It is important to appreciate the need for both open-ended debate and for practical closure. When it comes to making judgements about what is right and wrong, acceptable or unacceptable, the law is not the end of the matter. Although it is reasonable to expect a considerable convergence of the legal and the ethical, it is perfectly possible to criticise laws or legal judgments as unethical (this is the central impetus behind legal reform). On the other hand society cannot organise itself as if it were a never-ending philosophy seminar. There are many situations in which we need some authoritative system for decision making, and mechanisms for closing debate and implementing decisions – this is the role of the law. Any such system will be less than perfect but a society without such a system will be less perfect still.

Of course there are also areas in which there is little or no role for the law. The way in which nurses routinely talk to their patients raises ethical issues, and may also raise legal issues (e.g. informed consent, negligence) but unless some significant harm is involved these ethical issues can fall outside the scope of the law. For example, it is a reasonable ideal for a nurse to aim to empathise with someone she is advising or counselling; she might even feel guilty for failing to meet this ideal, but she could hardly be held legally guilty. Laws which cannot be enforced, or which are unnecessary, could be harmful in a number of ways. They could detract from respect for the law and its legitimate role, and they could create an oppressive and inflexible climate in which no-one benefited. So even if we are clear that a certain practice is ethically unacceptable it does not follow that it should be made illegal. However, the opposite can also be true. The overall consequences of legalising something which many people regard as ethically acceptable (e.g. voluntary euthanasia) may be judged, *by these same people*, to be unacceptable – as raising too many serious ethical and legal complications. Both lawyers and ethicists have to consider the proper boundaries of the law.

Even these few examples show that the relationship between the law and ethics is complicated. Professional values, such as those represented in the UKCC Code of Conduct, act as a half-way house between the two. They provide a means of enabling public discussion of public standards. They address the individual conscience but, where necessary, they are enforceable by disciplinary measures. We hope that this book will illustrate the importance of considering all of these matters together, and will help to provide nurses with insight into what is expected of them, and the skills to reflect on what they expect of themselves.

Alan Cribb and John Tingle

Preface to the Second Edition

We are, of course, pleased that the first edition of this book was so well received; and we are delighted to have had the chance to update and revise it. There is comparatively little to add to the Preface produced for the first edition; this sets out the rationale for, and the structure of, the book, and these remain the same. But there are many changes to the content of the book. The last six years have seen an extraordinary amount of change in many aspects of health care law and ethics, in the regulation and management of health services, and in conceptions of health professional accountability. The contributors to this new edition have sought to reflect and illuminate these changes and also to provide clear overviews of their subject matter.

There is a new chapter in the first part of the book which summarises the changing policy context and legal environment of nursing; and in the second part there is a new 'pair' of chapters on clinical governance. We are grateful to all the authors who have updated their work and/or written material for the first time in this edition. We very much hope that this new edition will prove to be of practical benefit – and theoretical interest – to the nursing community.

Acknowledgements

We would like to thank Professor Jean McHale, Faculty of Law, University of Leicester and Mr Harry Lesser, Centre for Philosophy, University of Manchester, for acting as editorial advisers.

Alan Cribb and John Tingle

List of Contributors

Dr Richard Ashcroft   Head of Medical Ethics Unit, Imperial College, School of Medicine, Department of Primary Health Care, Norfolk Place, London W2 1PG

Professor Robert Campbell   Bolton Institute, Chadwick Street, Bolton BL2 1JW

Dr Alan Cribb   Director, Centre for Public Policy Research, King's College London, Cornwall House, London SE1 8WA

Linda Delany   Principal Lecturer in Law, School of Law, The Manchester Metropolitan University, Elizabeth Gaskell Campus, Hathersage Road, Manchester M13 0JA

Dr Bobbie Farsides   Senior Lecturer, Centre for Medical Law & Ethics, King's College London, Strand, London WC2R 2LS

Charles Foster   6 Pump Court, Temple, London EC4Y 7AR

Marie B. Fox   Senior Lecturer, Faculty of Law, University of Manchester, Oxford Road, Manchester

Lucy Frith   Lecturer in Health Care & Ethics, Department of Primary Care, Whelan Building (2nd floor), Liverpool L69 3BX

Professor Michael Gunn   Head of Department of Academic Legal Studies and Associate Dean of Nottingham Law School, Nottingham Trent Unversity, Burton Street, Nottingham NG1 4BG

John Hodgson   Principal Lecturer, Nottingham Law School, Nottingham Trent University, Burton Street, Nottingham NG1 4BU

Professor Robert Lee   Cardiff Law School, University of Wales, PO Box 427, Museum Avenue, Cardiff

Harry Lesser   Senior Lecturer, Faculty of Economic & Social Studies, University of Manchester, Oxford Road, Manchester

Professor Jean McHale   Faculty of Law, University of Leicester, Leicester LE1 7RH

Reg Pyne   Welwyn Garden City, Hertfordshire

M. E. Rodgers   Senior Lecturer in Law, Nottingham Law School, Nottingham Trent University, Burton Street, Nottingham NG1 4BU

Professor David Seedhouse   Director, Centre for Health & Social Ethics, Faculty of Health Studies, Auckland University of Technology, Private Bag 92006, Auckland, New Zealand

Arnold Simanowitz   Chief Executive, Action for Victims of Medical Accidents, 44 High Street, Croydon, CR0 1YB

John Tingle   Reader in Health Law, Nottingham Law School, Nottingham Trent University, Burton Street, Nottingham NG1 4BU

Jo Wilson   Director, Clinical Service, Marsh Risk Consulting, Newcastle upon Tyne

Part One
The Dimensions

Chapter 1

The Legal Dimension: Legal System and Method

John Hodgson

We live in a society dominated to an increasing, some would say excessive, extent by legal rules and processes. Many of these apply to all of us, for instance the rules relating to use of the road as driver, passenger, cyclist or pedestrian, while others apply only to specific groups. In this chapter we will concentrate on the law as it affects the provision of health care. It is easier to do this than to look at the law relating to nurses or nursing, since for many purposes there is no legal distinction between different health care professionals and their contributions to the overall health care system. Before we do this, however, it is necessary to look briefly at the main features of the legal system in which health care operates. This system is the English and Welsh one. Scotland and Northern Ireland have their own systems and rules, although there are some common areas. It is also possible to draw valuable illustrations and guidance from other countries, although these are influential but not decisive.

1.1 The law and its interpretation

In this section we will look briefly at the various sources of law operating in England and Wales and at some of the methods used by judges when they have to interpret and apply the law [1].

1.1.1 Statute law

Most English law is in the form of statutes. These are made by the Crown in Parliament. Since 1688 the Crown in Parliament has been the supreme legislative body in England, and subsequently in the United Kingdom. A statute, or Act of Parliament, results from a bill or proposal for a statute. The bill may be proposed by the Government or by any individual MP or member of the House of Lords. It is debated and approved, with or without amendment, in both Houses [2]. Once approved in Parliament the bill then receives formal Royal Assent. Statutes have been passed on almost any topic imaginable. Among those of direct relevance to the health care professions are:

- The series of statutes establishing the NHS and subsequently modifying its structure and organisation. The original Act was the National Health Service Act 1946 which carried through Nye Bevan's project to secure a national, public, health service. Today the principal Act is the National Health Service Act 1977, but this has been amended and supplemented many times, most extensively by the National Health Service and Community Care Act 1990 which introduced NHS Trusts and the internal market, and most recently by the Health Act 1999 which introduced Primary Care Trusts and the Commission for Health Improvement.
- The Acts regulating the health care professions, such as the Medical Act 1983 for doctors and the Nurses, Midwives and Health Visitors Act 1997 [3].

Statutes generally provide the broad framework of rules. Thus section 1 (1) of the National Health Service Act 1977 provides:

'It is the Secretary of State's duty to continue the promotion in England and Wales of a comprehensive health service designed to secure improvement – (a) in the physical and mental health of the people of those countries, and (b) in the prevention, diagnosis and treatment of illness, and for that purpose to provide or secure the effective provision of services in accordance with this Act.'

This is called 'primary legislation' because it sets out basic rules. More detailed regulations are contained in statutory instruments, which are made by ministers (or in practice by their civil servants) under powers conferred by a relevant statute. This is called 'secondary legislation' because it deals with matters of detail dependent on the general powers given by primary legislation. So, for instance, the provision of GP services is governed by Part II of the National Health Service Act 1977, and this provides for regulations on a variety of topics, including the qualifications and experience required to be a GP. The Welsh Assembly has powers to make secondary legislation of this kind for Wales, but no powers to pass primary legislation [4].

In theory the Crown in Parliament can pass a statute on any subject whatever, and may also repeal any existing legislation. In theory parliament can accordingly legislate for the execution of people on some arbitrary ground, such as having red hair. This is subject to three very different qualifications:

(1) Parliament can only operate within the scope of what is politically and socially acceptable. This not only means that the Red-haired Persons (Compulsory Slaughter) Act will never see the light of day, but more importantly means that legislation on such contentious issues as abortion or euthanasia is not undertaken lightly.
(2) By virtue of the European Communities Act 1972, Parliament has granted supremacy to the legislation of the European Community and Union in those areas covered by the Treaty of Rome and the Treaty of the European Union. This can mean that existing Parliamentary legislation can be found to be incompatible with EC law, although the courts will always try to interpret the two pieces of legislation consistently with each other, and can even mean that new legislation must be disregarded [5]. In practice EC law does not really have much specific bearing on medico-legal and ethical issues, although

since it does deal with recognition of qualifications and many equal pay and equal opportunity issues in employment law, it may have an impact on the professional life of many nurses. EC free trade and competition rules apply to drugs and medicines as to any other products, and they feature in much of the case law.

(3) The Human Rights Act 1998 came into full effect on 2nd October 2000. This Act is designed to give effect in English law to the rights conferred by the European Convention on Human Rights and Fundamental Freedoms. This has been in effect since 1954, and has been binding on the UK internationally, but not as part of our own legal system. So even if rules of English law, whether in statutes or otherwise, have been inconsistent with the Convention, the English rule prevails, although the UK may then be held to be in default by the European Court of Human Rights. This will now change:

- English law must be construed so far as possible as compatible with the Act. Each new bill must be certified to comply, or an explanation given. If an Act is found to be incompatible, the judges will make a declaration to that effect and it will be up to the Government to invite Parliament to make the necessary changes.
- The courts will have regard to decisions of the European Court of Human Rights when interpreting English law.
- All public bodies must act in accordance with the Convention. This will include the health service.

The Convention confers a number of rights on people. Some of them are substantive in nature, such as the right to life and the right to freedom of expression, while others are procedural, such as the guarantee of a fair trial. This applies to disciplinary proceedings and requires that there be an independent and impartial tribunal. This may be problematic for bodies such as the UKCC which have been responsible for the investigation and adjudication of complaints and do not seem to provide for the necessary degree of independence. It is too soon to predict exactly how the Act will operate, but some areas of medico-legal significance are likely to be affected. One example is the detention of the mentally impaired. This is permitted in principle under Article 5 where it is necessary for the protection of the patient or others and there is the safeguard of an appeal to an independent judicial body independent of the executive government [6]. It is likely that it will be difficult to justify under the Human Rights Act informal measures to keep 'compliant' patients in hospital without using powers under the Mental Health Act which were approved by the House of Lords in 1998 in the case of *L* v. *Bournewood NHS Trust* (1998) [7].

The right to life would appear to be of direct concern to the health care community, but in practice it focuses on negative aspects (preventing officially sanctioned killing), rather than positive ones (requiring states to provide resources and facilities to cure the sick) [8]. In *D* v. *United Kingdom* (1997) it was held that, while deporting an HIV+ prisoner to St Kitts, where treatment was not available, amounted to inhuman and degrading treatment, it was not necessary to consider whether the state was failing to ensure the right to life. The Convention, and therefore the Act, is concerned with civil and political rather than social rights. It is however clear as a result of one of the first cases under the Act that withdrawal of hydration and nutrition from a patient in PVS does not entail a breach of the right to life (*NHS Trust A* v. *Mrs M., NHS Trust B* v. *Mrs H.* (2000)).

1.1.2   Common law

The rules of the common law predate statute. However there are now so many statutes in so many areas of law that the common law rules are of secondary importance. These rules are legal principles laid down over the centuries by the judges in deciding the cases that came before them. In theory the judges were simply isolating the relevant principles from a body of law which already existed and which represented the common view of the English people as to what was right, but in practice the judges were really developing a coherent and technical set of rules based on their own understanding of legal principle. We will look at the techniques the judges currently use later. For the moment it is important to recognise that there are some areas where, despite the rise of statute, the common law remains of considerable importance:

- Substantive law areas where statute has intervened only to a limited extent. The best example is tort, in particular negligence. This is important to nurses, as this branch of the law deals with whether a patient who has suffered harm while being treated will be able to recover compensation because the treatment he received was faulty.
- The judges have the task of interpreting statutes and statutory instruments and giving effect to them. They have developed their own techniques and principles for this task, which are themselves part of the common law.
- An important function of the judges today is controlling the activity of central and local government and other public bodies by means of judicial review. This is now the responsibility of the Administrative Court, which is part of the High Court. Judicial review is essentially a means of ensuring that decisions and policies are made lawfully and by the correct procedures. The judges themselves have developed the rules on which decisions can be challenged and what grounds of challenge are available [9]. In principle, the judges accept that they have not been given responsibility for making the decisions in question, and so do not consider the merits. In *R* v. *Central Birmingham Health Authority ex parte Walker* (1987) the court had to consider a failure to provide treatment to a particular patient, as a result of decisions not to allocate funds to this particular aspect of the Authority's operations. It was held that the Authority was responsible for planning and delivering health care with a given budget and the resulting decisions on priorities. The court could not substitute its own, inexpert, judgment, particularly as it would only hear detailed arguments about the needs of this one patient, and not about the whole range of demands. The issue of health care resources is more fully discussed in Chapter 8.

1.1.3 European Union/Community Law

Throughout the post World War II period, the states of Western Europe have been engaged in a complex and long-term project of economic co-operation and integration. The first major stage in this was the Treaty of Rome which established the European Economic Community in the 1950s. The United Kingdom joined this Community in 1974. The initial objective was the establishment of a common market, an area within which there was to be free movement of the various factors of production of goods and provision of services, namely goods, labour, management skills and capital. Initially this meant the removal of obvious barriers, such as customs duties, immigration controls, exchange controls on money and other restrictions. Subsequently other objectives, such as environmental protection, have been added, although the main impact of the Community is still on economic affairs.

Free movement of workers, guaranteed by Article 39 of the European Community Treaty, implied many additional social policies, as workers would not, in practice, move around the community unless their social security entitlements were ensured and they were allowed to bring their families with them. Genuine freedom of movement also required a common approach to qualifications, with no discrimination on grounds of nationality, and also equal opportunity, at least between men and women. This has resulted in much legislation and many decisions of the European Court of Justice. Article 47 of the Treaty specifically gives power to regulate mutual recognition of diplomas and qualifications. Directives 77/452 and 80/154 have made provision for general nurses and midwives respectively, and there are also general frameworks for the recognition of degree level and other vocational qualifications (covering a number of professions allied to medicine) in Directives 89/48 and 92/51 respectively. The case of *Marshall* v. *Southampton and SW Hants AHA* (1986) established that UK law permitting differential retirement ages as between men and women in the health service was incompatible with EC law requiring equal treatment, and as a result the UK law had to be disregarded.

The member states of the Community have agreed, in effect, to transfer their sovereign rights to make and apply laws to the Community institutions in those areas for which the Community is to be responsible. The European Union, introduced in the Maastricht Treaty of 1992, operates somewhat differently. It is an agreement by the member states to co-operate and collaborate in relation to foreign affairs and aspects of criminal justice and home affairs, but action is by the states acting through the European Council and no rights are transferred to the institutions.

The European Council, which comprises the heads of Government of the member states together with the president of the European Commission, is the principal policy-making and legislative body for the Community. In some cases it can legislate itself, after consultation with the European Parliament. In most cases however the legislation is made jointly by the Council and the Parliament. In many cases the Council can act by a majority, and thus legislate against the wishes of a member state. The majority is usually a 'qualified' or weighted majority designed to ensure that there is very substantial support for the measure. In practice great efforts are made to ensure a consensus of opinion.

The Parliament does not initiate legislation, but as noted above does have to approve and join in making most important legislation, so it has at least a blocking power. The Parliament must also approve the Community budget and also the members of the Commission. It may also remove the whole Commission, and although it has never voted to do so, the likelihood of this occurring led to the resignation of the Commission in 1999 as a result of allegations of financial irregularities.

The Commission is the administrative arm of the Community. It implements policies and proposes legislation, and can itself make detailed regulations, particularly in relation to the Common Agricultural Policy. It also makes decisions on alleged infringements of Community law, for example in relation to competition law. It is also responsible as 'guardian of the treaties' for ensuring that member states comply with their Community obligations.

The European Court of Justice, assisted by the Court of First Instance, is responsible for interpreting EC law; it does so by means of rulings on points of law referred by national courts (Article 234 of the Treaty), deciding cases brought against the member states by the Commission (Articles 226 and 228-9) and by judicial review of the validity of acts of the institutions (decisions on particular cases or regulations and directives) on the application of other institutions, the member states and others directly affected (Article 230).

There are two forms of act which amount to secondary legislation. These are Regulations and Directives; both are governed by Article 249 of the Treaty.

Regulations, which may be made by the Council, with or without the Parliament or by the Commission, are directly effective rules of Community law which must be obeyed by all persons and companies within the EC and will be enforced by national courts.

Directives, which are normally made by the Council and Parliament, are used where the EC wishes to ensure that national law in all member states achieves the same results, but it is not appropriate to do this by way of regulation. One example is in relation to company law, where the law of the states is very variable in its form and terminology, so regulations would be meaningless.

Community law applies not only to states but also to individuals. This was not clear from the beginning, but the Court of Justice ruled in *van Gend & Loos* (1962) that an individual could rely on a treaty provision which was clear and complete and capable of conferring direct rights (in this case a prohibition on new customs duties) to defeat a claim by a state based on its own incompatible legislation. In *Defrenne* v. *Sabena* (1976) it was held that a treaty provision meeting these requirements (in this case the right to equal pay for women) could be relied on against a person or company, notwithstanding incompatible national legislation. The position with regard to directives is more complex:

- They normally provide for an implementation period; while this is running they have no legal effect (*Pubblico Ministero* v. *Ratti* (1979))
- After the implementation date they are binding on the state [10], so the state is prevented from relying on its own incompatible law [11]. In addition, the state

can be obliged to act in accordance with them (*Marshall* v. *Southampton and SW Hants AHA* (1986)).

- This binding effect applies to the courts, which must interpret national legislation 'as far as possible' in accordance with the directive, even in cases involving two private litigants with no state involvement (*Marleasing* (1992)). This applies particularly to rules relating to remedies, which must be effective (*von Colson* (1986). However, where the two cannot be reconciled, national law will prevail (*Wagner Miret* (1993)).
- A directive cannot be relied on as such against a private individual or company (*Faccini-Dori* v. *Recreb* (1995)), although the court can be asked to interpret national law as above.
- Where an individual or company suffers loss as the result of the failure of the state to implement a directive properly or at all, as a last resort the state may be held liable in damages (*Francovich* (1993)) providing that the breach is sufficiently grave (*Brasserie du Pêcheur/Factortame (No. 3)* (1996)).

English courts have been willing to apply very radical interpretative methods to English legislation introduced specifically to give effect to EC requirements, even to the extent of reversing the apparent meaning of the English legislation. The reasoning behind this is that it was the primary intention of Parliament to comply with the EC requirement, and the words used were believed to achieve this, so any reinterpretation meets that underlying purpose, even if it is not the obvious interpretation of the particular passage (*Pickstone* v. *Freemans* (1989); *Litster* v. *Forth Dry Dock* (1990)). After considerable uncertainty it seems that the same will apply to other legislation not passed specifically to meet EC requirements (*Webb* v. *EMO Air Cargo* (No. 2) (1995)) although there is some suggestion that the English courts are happier to see damages claims for non-implementation, rather than radical interpretation (*Kirklees MBC* v. *Wickes* (1993)).

1.2   The English legal system

This system has developed over many centuries and although there have been piecemeal reforms, many old procedures and systems remain in place. This applies particularly to titles. Why should the principal judge of the civil side of the Court of Appeal be called the Master of the Rolls? He has nothing to do with either baking or gymnastics. What actually happened was that an official responsible for keeping the official records or rolls of the Chancery was gradually given a judicial role and by the nineteenth century, when the Court of Appeal in its modern form was established, he had become a senior judge and was therefore the right person to be appointed to preside over the Court of Appeal.

Effectively there are two court systems in England. The criminal courts concentrate on crime, and the civil courts deal with everything else. There are some exceptions, where specialised tribunals have been set up. The most important of these are probably the Employment Tribunals [12] and the Employment Appeal Tribunal, which deal with most employment related issues, including equal opportunities, although the various tribunals within the social security system deal with more cases. There are also separate tribunals for income tax and VAT.

1.2.1 Criminal justice system

All cases start with an appearance in the magistrates court. Usually, the case will have been investigated by the police, and will be prosecuted by the Crown Prosecution Service, but other government departments and agencies, local authorities and bodies such as the RSPCA also prosecute cases. Private individuals may prosecute, but rarely do. There are a total of some 2,000,000 cases each year [13] of which 75% are purely summary offences (motoring offences such as speeding, careless driving and defective vehicles, and other minor offences of drunkenness, vandalism, assault, etc.). These must be dealt with in the magistrates court. The great majority of defendants plead guilty or do not contest the case. The remaining more serious offences fall into two groups. The most serious offences, such as murder, rape and robbery can only be tried at the Crown Court, 'on indictment'. The magistrates court only deals with bail and legal aid. These are actually a small proportion of the total. The others are the middle range of offences (e.g. most assaults, theft, fraud and burglary). These are said to be triable 'either way'. At present this means that if the defendant admits the charge when it is put to him in the magistrates court he is convicted there, although he may be committed to the Crown court for sentence if the magistrates' powers of sentence [14] are inadequate. If he does not admit the offence the magistrates must decide whether they have power to hear the case, having regard to its seriousness and complexity. If they decline to hear it the case must go to the Crown Court. If they agree to hear the case the defendant may still elect trial at the Crown Court. Current proposals will change this procedure and give the decision to the magistrates, although they will have to consider the effect of the case on the defendant [15].

Where a case is heard by the magistrates the defendant may appeal against sentence (and if he pleaded not guilty, conviction) to the Crown Court. These appeals are heard by a judge sitting with magistrates. Although an appeal against conviction is a full rehearing it will not be before a jury.

Both prosecution and defence may appeal to the Queens Bench Division of the High Court [16] where they consider that the final decision is wrong on a point of law (as opposed to a wrong decision on the facts). They may also apply to the same court for judicial review of any preliminary decision (e.g. on bail or legal aid).

The Crown Court deals with about 80,000 cases a year, of which about 20,000 are contested trials. About 40% of these result in acquittals. These trials are before a judge and jury, with the judge responsible for decisions on matters of law, evidence and procedure, and the jury responsible for matters of fact and the final verdict.

The defendant may appeal to the Court of Appeal (Criminal Division) on the ground that the verdict is unsafe. The Court considers whether the defendant was prejudiced by irregularities at the trial such as rulings of the judge on law, or the admissibility of evidence, or errors in the judge's summing up. In effect the Court is asking, 'Can we rely on the jury's verdict, or do we feel that they would have decided otherwise if the irregularity had not occurred?'. The prosecution may not appeal against an acquittal, although they may ask the Court of Appeal to consider the point of law involved in an acquittal on a hypothetical basis by an Attorney-General's reference. The defendant may, with leave, appeal against sentence, and the prosecution may appeal against an unduly lenient sentence. There is an appeal to the House of Lords for both prosecutor and defendant from the Court of Appeal where the case raises a point of law of public importance.

A review of the criminal justice system under Lord Justice Auld is currently underway, and is likely to lead to considerable changes in the system described above.

Although nurses may commit crimes, there is usually no direct connection with their professional activities. The availability of controlled drugs in a hospital environment may lead nurses into temptation, and there may be cases of deliberate harm to patients, which will be prosecuted as assaults under the Offences Against the Person Act 1861, or in extreme cases as murder, as in the notorious case of Beverley Allitt, a children's nurse at Grantham hospital, who in the 1990s murdered or seriously harmed a number of children in her care. Nurses have no general privileges in relation to the physical management of patients, but most actions undertaken reasonably and in good faith will be protected by the ordinary law of self defence, actions taken to prevent crime (restraining one patient to prevent an attack on another) and necessity. Restraint is also specifically authorised in some circumstances under the Mental Health Act. Prosecutions usually result from actions which go well beyond normal practice, for which there is no apparent explanation, and which are clear abuses of the nurse's professional responsibilities. In extreme cases health professionals may find themselves facing criminal charges arising from decisions made and actions taken within normal professional parameters:

- Manslaughter by gross negligence. Where one person owes another a duty of care (and a nurse owes this duty to a patient), there may be criminal liability where there is a clear and obvious breach of this duty which obviously exposes the victim to a specific risk of death, and the victim dies (*R* v. *Adomako* (1994)).
- 'Mercy killing' or active euthanasia. Any action which results in the shortening of life, and which is undertaken with that intent, is murder. It is irrelevant that the victim is terminally ill and in acute distress or severely disabled, whether or not the victim or the next of kin consent. Juries are notoriously unwilling to convict [17], and reliance is often placed on 'double effect' which legitimises the use of strong pain control, even if life is incidentally shortened.

1.2.2 Civil justice system

The general system has, in the late 1990s, been significantly reformed by the introduction of new Civil Procedure Rules [18]. These create a new overriding objective of dealing with cases justly, having regard to ensuring that the parties are on an equal footing, expense and proportionality to the importance and complexity of the case. In practice this means that all cases are allocated either to the small claims track for speedy and informal disposal of small-scale disputes, to the 'fast track' for routine cases requiring limited court time or to a 'multi track' which allows for more complex cases to be handled as they deserve. Procedural judges take charge of the timetable of the case and the parties have to comply with the standard timetable of the fast track, or the agreed timetable in the multi track. In the process the distinction between the County Court and the High Court has been blurred. Most cases will actually be tried in the County Court, including many high value claims, but High Court judges will continue to hear the most complex cases. A decision of a procedural judge may be appealed to a circuit judge, and an appeal from the decision at a trial may be made to the Court of Appeal. There are special arrangements for family law cases.

Much of the work of the High Court is now judicial review. This is, in effect, a review of the legality and propriety of decisions by government departments and other public bodies while exercising statutory powers. The main grounds of review are illegality, where the decision is outside the powers given; procedural impropriety, e.g. a failure to give the applicant notice of the allegations against him; and irrationality, or reaching a decision which no reasonable body, carefully considering all relevant considerations, could have reached.

There is an appeal from the County Court or High Court to the Court of Appeal, provided that the leave of either court is obtained. There is an appeal from the Court of Appeal to the House of Lords, but as in criminal cases there must be an issue of public importance.

The aspect of civil law which impinges directly on the health care profession is negligence. This is dealt with in depth in Chapter 6. At this stage it is important to note that liability for negligence is essentially liability for failure to reach a proper standard of care in dealing with someone to whom a legal duty is owed. In many cases this duty is imposed by the law in general terms, but in others it arises from a prior contractual agreement.

- Since the eighteenth century it has been established that a physician or surgeon (and by extension any health care professional who takes responsibility for a patient) owes a duty to that patient. This general duty covers all NHS patients. It does not extend to practitioners who are 'off duty' so as to require them to intervene, if, for example, they come upon an accident victim in the street.
- In private medicine there is a contract between the practitioner and the patient. Ordinarily, this contract will merely require the practitioner to use reasonable care and skill [19] and this is the same standard as under the general law. However in some circumstances the patient may have greater rights under the contract. The contract may specify a particular model of artificial hip, and failure to provide this is a breach. There would be liability to an NHS patient only if the device fitted was one which was not regarded as suitable by a responsible body of opinion. Normally a practitioner undertakes to use proper care and skill, but does not guarantee a cure. However a contract may include a warranty of a cure, although this would be unusual (*Thake* v. *Maurice* (1986)).

1.3   Legal method

Judges have two roles. Firstly they are responsible for ensuring that the facts of the particular case are ascertained. They do this directly in civil cases, and supervise the jury in criminal cases. This is an important task, and vital for the parties to the case. It is not, however, the more legally significant of the two roles. The crucial role is in ascertaining the law, so that it can be applied to the facts of the case. The facts are usually quite specific, and affect only the parties [20], but the legal principle is of general application. As indicated above, ascertaining the law may involve a review of existing common law rules or an interpretation of statute, Community law or the European Convention on Human Rights.

In English law, judges have the power to state the law. In this they differ from judges in most Continental European systems, who have no status to declare the law but merely a duty to interpret and apply the law which is to be found in the national legal codes. Of course these interpretations are entitled to respect and are usually followed for the sake of consistency and because they reflect a learned opinion on the meaning of the texts. However, if judges can state the law, it is necessary to have rules as to which statements are authoritative and must be followed (whether later judges agree with them or not).

Binding authority. The following statements of law, forming the basis in legal principle on which a case was decided, are binding on later judges:

- Decisions of the European Court of Justice bind all English courts.
- Subject to the above, decisions of the House of Lords bind all other English courts. The House itself may, if it is persuaded that there is good reason to do so (either because there is a strong case that the earlier decision was wrong, or because the earlier decision is no longer appropriate to modern social and economic conditions) depart from an earlier decision and restate the law.
- Decisions of the Court of Appeal bind the Court of Appeal and all lower courts.
- Decisions of the Divisional Court bind magistrates courts.

Judges may consider any other material; this will however merely be persuasive. This can include *obiter dicta* or comments in a judgment which do not form part of the basis of the decision [21], statements in dissenting judgments [22], statements by more junior judges [23], decisions in other jurisdictions and academic comments. Decisions of the European Court [24] of Human Rights come into this category [25].

An earlier statement of law will only be binding if the present case raises the same legal issue. It is possible to distinguish cases by explaining how, while similar, they do not raise the same legal issues. It is also possible to cheat by claiming to distinguish cases where the judge does not want to follow the earlier ruling, or vice versa, and it is often difficult to be sure whether judges are using this technique properly or not. Applying the law is an art not a mechanical process.

In practice judges need to go beyond earlier statements of the law. New issues arise and new social and economic conditions arise. In the past judges were very coy about admitting that they did make new rules rather than reinterpreting old ones, but they now accept that they do. They are usually very conservative, preferring to go no further than strictly necessary. When in *Airedale NHS Trust* v. *Bland* (1993) the House of Lords was asked to rule on whether treatment could be withheld from a patient in an irreversible persistent vegetative state, they did so on the narrow basis that there was no justification for intrusive treatment as it did not serve the patient's best interests, and expressly stated that they could not consider general arguments based on the legality or desirability of general rules on euthanasia. That was a matter for Parliament.

Interpreting statutes (and Community law). The law has been laid down here by Parliament (or the Community institutions). The judges may or may not approve, but in principle they must apply the law as passed. Unfortunately not all law is clear. There may be inconsistencies or ambiguities, or there may be situations which Parliament did not foresee and therefore did not cover.

Over the years the judges have worked out an approach to interpretation which allows some flexibility but stays as close as possible to the words actually enacted by Parliament. The approach will depend to some extent on the type of legislation. Criminal and tax legislation is always interpreted against the state in cases of doubt, while legislation intended to meet a Community law requirement will be interpreted to achieve that purpose.

The priority is to give effect to the words of the statute if they have a plain and unambiguous meaning. This will be applied even if it is not what Parliament 'meant', as in the case of *Fisher* v. *Bell* (1961) where Parliament had clearly introduced legislation designed to prohibit trading in flick-knives. However, it created an offence of 'offering' such a knife for sale, and when a shop-keeper was prosecuted because she had one on display in the window the court ruled that, since it had already been decided that it was the customer who made an offer for goods on display, she was not guilty of the offence. The words used were clear, and it was wrong to look back at what the underlying intention was as this was a criminal case and the statute had to be interpreted in favour of the defendant anyway. Where wording is ambiguous various approaches may be used:

- Preferring a sensible meaning to an absurd meaning. So the word 'marry' in the definition of the crime of bigamy was interpreted in *R* v. *Allen* (1872) as 'go through a form of marriage' rather than 'contract a [valid] marriage' which would have made the offence impossible to commit, as someone already married cannot validly marry again.
- Consider the underlying intention of the statute. In *Kruhlak* v. *Kruhlak* (1958) the expression 'single woman' in the context of affiliation proceedings was interpreted to mean any woman not living with her husband or supported by him, i.e. it could include a divorcee or widow. The mischief was the need to ensure financial support for illegitimate children, whatever the marital status of the mother. Similarly in *Knowles* v. *Liverpool Council* (1993) a broad interpretation was given to the expression 'equipment' in the Employers Liability (Defective Equipment) Act 1969, in order to give effect to the broad aims of the legislation in the light of the known mischief.
- Refer to any authoritative statement by the sponsoring minister on the meaning of the particular provision, in Hansard (*Pepper* v. *Hart* (1993)).

The main danger in interpretation is that the greater the leeway the judges allow themselves, the more likely it is that they will be accused of interpreting to suit their own notions of what is right and proper. As most such cases either involve issues of political controversy or raise contentious ethical issues, and this will increasingly be the case under the Human Rights Act, there is increasing concentration on the judges, and questions are increasingly being asked about their qualifications to adjudicate on these controversial issues as opposed to technical legal matters, where their expertise is acknowledged.

1.4   The legal context of nursing

Nurses are governed by three separate sets of legal rules [26], quite apart from the law which establishes the framework of the NHS and the general law of the land.

- There are legal obligations to patients, normally arising in the context of allegations of negligence.
- There are professional obligations, imposed in the case of nurses by the United Kingdom Central Council for Nursing, Midwifery and Health Visiting (UKCC), which is responsible for education, registration, professional standards and discipline. The essence of the professional standards [27] established by the UKCC in its Code of Practice are that each nurse must:

  - safeguard and promote the interests of individual patients and clients;
  - serve the interests of society;
  - justify public trust and confidence and
  - uphold and enhance the good standing and reputation of the professions.

  Specific obligations in the Code of Practice require the nurse to respect the right of the patient to be involved in the planning of care, to work co-operatively with colleagues and to report anything which adversely affects the standard of care being provided.

- The large majority of nurses work as employees in the NHS or the private health sector and thus have a legal employment relationship. Despite the reforms of the 1980s which were intended to create an internal market of independent NHS Trusts, each establishing its own terms and conditions of employment to replace the earlier national Whitley Council arrangements, in practice terms and conditions have remained relatively uniform. The employer is entitled to a professional standard of performance of the duties assigned, and the employee is entitled to be treated properly. Three aspects of employment law appear to be particularly relevant to the nursing profession:

  - Equal opportunity, both between the sexes and in relation to ethnicity, has been a major issue for many years. The latter is a purely English matter, regulated by the Race Relations Acts, while the former is regulated by the Equal Pay Act and the Sex Discrimination Act, both supplemented by Community law. Direct discrimination is rare, and most difficulties concern disguised discrimination. Disadvantageous treatment of part-time workers may amount to indirect discrimination because these part-time workers are predominantly female (*R* v. *Secretary of State for Employment ex parte EOC* (1995)). The salary scale for a particular group may be depressed because the profession or group is largely female, and this may constitute indirect discrimination (*Enderby* v. *Frenchay Health Authority* (1993)) although it is important that the two groups are actually comparable, and where one is objectively rated as more demanding, the case will fail [28]. The law will seek to deal with historical anomalies based on gender specific recruitment, but cannot resolve complaints about the relative valuation of different jobs.

- Psychological and stress-related industrial illness. Employers are increasingly being held liable for such illness where it arises from the way in which work is organised and allocated. In *Lancaster* v. *Birmingham City Council* (1999) the employer transferred an administrative employee to a new post in a significantly different area with a promise of training and support which did not materialise. The employer admitted liability for the resultant disabling stress. In *Walker* v. *Northumberland CC* (1995) the employee, a social work manager, became ill with work related stress. On his return to work he received no support and his workload increased. The employer was held liable when he suffered a recurrence. In *Johnstone* v. *Bloomsbury Health Authority* (1990) the Court of Appeal held that a junior doctor had an arguable case that the conditions under which he was obliged to work constituted a reasonably foreseeable risk to his health. Since much of the work in some areas of the NHS, in particular A&E departments and ICUs, is inherently highly stressful, and other work can easily become so if poorly managed or short-staffed, this is clearly a significant area.

- 'Whistle blowing' has been problematic. Nurses are under a professional duty to report circumstances which may adversely affect patient care. They may also be under a duty to the patient. Some employers, including NHS Trusts, place greater weight on the management of information and resent adverse publicity, whether or not it is justified. Nurses who have publicised matters of concern have in the past attracted considerable attention and suffered serious consequences, like Graham Pink, a nurse at Stepping Hill Hospital, who became frustrated at what he considered to be managerial indifference to his complaints over staffing levels and in the early 1990s drew these to public notice, attracting disciplinary action from his employers as a result. Some protection is now given by the Public Interest Disclosure Act 1998. This protects an employee from dismissal or other retaliatory action if he discloses information relating to circumstances which disclose an apparent breach of legal duties or a threat to the health and safety of any person. The disclosure must be to the employer, to the Secretary of State if the employee is in the public sector (including NHS Trusts, but not GP practices) or to the press or public where the employer has not taken action on an earlier report to him.

Most of the time these three duties do not cut across each other. Most of the time employers and employees have a common interest in promoting the welfare of patients in an efficient and professional manner. There are problems however. The employee may feel professionally obligated to report deficiencies in the employer's services to patients or may feel that other professionals are not respecting the patient's autonomy, or allowing the nurse to act as an effective patient advocate [29]. In these circumstances the law is, at best, an imperfect instrument. Balancing the three duties is difficult, and a legal process which focuses on which of two cases has the better basis in law and in fact, is not well adapted to weigh more complex issues.

1.5   Notes and references

1. We only have time for a brief consideration of these matters; for a more detailed treatment see either Terence Ingman, *The English Legal Process*, Blackstone Press, London, 2000, or Michael Zander, *The Law-Making Process*, Butterworths, London, 1999.
2. A bill may be voted down. This often happens to bills proposed by individuals (private members' bills) but rarely to Government bills because the Government can usually guarantee that its MPs will support it. The Lords is less predictable even after the recent reforms, but cannot block financial and tax bills, will not block bills which are part of the manifesto on which the Government was elected and can in any event only delay bills for one year.
3. There are over 1400 references to 'medical practitioner' in statutes ranging from obvious ones such as the Mental Health Act to others such as the Deregulation and Contracting Out Act and the House of Commons (Disqualification) Act.
4. The position in Scotland is different. The Scottish Parliament can pass primary legislation on a large range of issues, including the health service.
5. As occurred in the *Factortame (No 2)* case [1991] 1 AC 603.
6. The European Court of Human Rights (ECtHR) case of *X v. UK* (Case 7215/75, judgment 5.11.81) established that the original advisory role of the Mental Health Review Tribunal did not meet this requirement. As a result the MHRT now makes the decision itself.
7. A reference has been made to the European Court of Human Rights.
8. There may be a positive obligation on the police authorities where an individual is under specific threat: *Osman v. United Kingdom* (1998) ECtHR Reports 1998-VIII. In *LCB v. United Kingdom* (1998) ECtHR Reports 1998-III the court considered 'that the first sentence of article 2 § 1 enjoins the State not only to refrain from the intentional and unlawful taking of life, but also to take appropriate steps to safeguard the lives of those within its jurisdiction,' but this was again in the context of non-health related government action (exposure to radiation during nuclear tests).
9. These are, essentially, that the decision was illegal because it was made without power to act, was irrational or was in breach of procedural fairness.
10. Which includes state agencies such as the NHS.
11. Which includes state agencies such as the NHS.
12. Formerly Industrial Tribunals.
13. This excludes some 7,000,000 fixed penalties for motoring and parking offences. Source: *Home Office Digest* 4: http/www.homeoffice.gov.uk/rds/digest4/digest4.pdf
14. Up to six months (or in some cases 12 months) custody and usually fines of £5000 per offence).
15. Criminal Justice (Mode of Trial) Bill.
16. Additionally, the defendant may do this after he has exercised his right of appeal to the Crown Court.

17. *R* v. *Arthur*, The Times 5.11.81, was a case where nutrition was withheld from a severely disabled neonate, who died. There was some evidence of acute ailments other than those initially identified, and which might have led to death. The doctor appeared to have decided, with the parents, that they did not want the child to survive, but was nevertheless acquitted by the jury. In *R* v. *Cox* [1993] 2 All ER 19 the jury were in tears as they convicted of attempted murder relating to an elderly terminal patient who had repeatedly asked for release from her intractable pain.
18. The so-called 'Woolf Reforms' following a report by Lord Woolf.
19. Section 13, Supply of Goods and Services Act 1982.
20. There are of course important cases where the facts affect many different people, such as industrial disease and drug defect claims, but these are in the minority.
21. The so-called 'neighbour principle' expounded by Lord Atkin in *Donoghue* v. *Stevenson* in 1932 has been extremely influential in the development of liability for negligence over the past 30 years.
22. A dissent by Lord Justice Denning in *Candler* v. *Crane Christmas* in 1949 ([1951] 2 KB 164) formed the basis of the decision of the House of Lords in *Hedley Byrne* v. *Heller* in 1964 ([1964] AC 465).
23. The so-called *Bolam* test for medical negligence was laid down by Mr Justice McNair, but has been endorsed by many senior judges in the Court of Appeal and House of Lords.
24. Also decisions of the European Commission on Human Rights and of the Council of Ministers of the Council of Europe, both of which formerly had a role in the application of the European convention.
25. Human Rights Act 1998, section 2.
26. Those working in mental health are also governed by the Mental Health Act, making four in all.
27. See http://www.ukcc.org.uk/index.html
28. As in *Southampton & District HA* v. *Worsfold* (1999) LTL 15.9.99, where a female speech therapist's work was rated at 55 and a male clinical psychologist's at 56.5.
29. UKCC Guidelines for Professional Practice 1996, pp. 9–11.

Chapter 2

The Ethical Dimension: Nursing Practice, Nursing Philosophy and Nursing Ethics

Alan Cribb

What are the values that shape nursing practice? This is a much debated question. In fact most of the debate that takes place in nursing and academic nursing literature is about values. The only exception is debate about purely factual or technical matters. Value debates take place about the nature of professional–patient relationships, and ideas like empowerment, partnership and advocacy. More specifically there are a host of particular debates about such things as how midwives can best protect the interests of pregnant women, or how far the work of health visitors should be dictated by public health targets. Set alongside these are discussions about the professional standards of nursing, the framework of which is reviewed in the next chapter. All these debates should be seen as continuous with nursing ethics, because they all involve making value judgements about the means or ends of nursing care; in short they all ask 'What is good nursing?'. Anyone who has an interest in, and some grasp of, these issues is already 'inside' nursing ethics although they may not have thought about their concerns in these terms.

This is not meant to imply that nursing ethics is easy – far from it: all of these issues are complex. In any case even if someone was very good at debating the nature of 'good nursing' this would not make them 'a good nurse'. If nursing ethics is to be of more than academic interest it should have something to say about how people might become good nurses. I will return to this question later but notice that there is some apparent ambiguity in it. If we talk about a nurse being 'a good nurse' are we talking about her professional or technical skills or are we making an ethical judgement about her character, or perhaps both? It would certainly seem odd to call someone a good nurse if she could demonstrate many 'competences' but she lacked any concern or commitment for her clients or colleagues. In this respect it seems very different from calling someone a good mathematician – a set of skills which is, on the face of it, compatible with being lazy, insensitive, and self-centred!

All nursing practice is necessarily informed, partly implicitly, by some nursing philosophy. Such a philosophy embodies answers to a range of questions which are faced by any nurse. These include questions about the aims of care, professional–client relationships, working in teams and with colleagues, and wider questions about institutional, local or national policies. Although nursing involves activities other than patient or client care, such as health care research and management, it seems reasonable to view care as central, and to see the other activities as supporting this central one. But 'care' is too broad a notion to be of much help in clarifying the aims of nursing; care is the focus, but what are the aims of care?

One example of the debate about nursing philosophy and the aims of nursing is what has been called the shift 'from sick nursing to health nursing' [1]. The shift – which is dramatic in some areas of practice and incremental in others – is from doing things *to* patients towards working *with* them; from an approach which is 'disease based' and expert centred to one which is 'health based' and patient centred. This shift follows from and reflects many things including changing patterns of ill-health, emerging professional roles, an increase in consumerism, and developing ideas about health promotion. But at its heart is what might be called an ethical shift, a shift in values which has two inter-related components. Firstly, and rather crudely put, there is a move from treating people as passive towards treating them with respect as equals. This is not only because individuals have an important role to play in their own care, but also because individuals 'deserve' to be treated with respect, whether or not to do so is useful to professionals. Secondly, there is a move from equating the best interests of patients with being 'disease free' towards an acceptance that there is much more to well-being. Quality of life, peace of mind, and self respect, for example, are legitimate concerns for a nurse, as well as disease management. These two components are closely related because one aspect of well-being, an aspect which many see as fundamental, is being able to make choices and have them treated with respect. These issues will be discussed more fully in the next section.

This example of a cultural shift shows the importance of what can be called 'habitual ethics' [2, 3]: the ethical judgements that individuals make as a matter of course, the values that are built into ways of working. Any shift in the philosophy or culture of nursing, which entails that normal practice and expectations are changed, has enormous impact. Practice can be enhanced (or made worse) for literally thousands of people. Generally speaking much less rests upon the prolonged agonising about particular cases however difficult they are. Of course these sorts of shifts in normal practice are difficult to implement: they involve reform of policies, institutions, and so on. To reformers they might seem an overwhelming task, like trying to get the earth to spin on a different axis, yet they are the bedrock for any practical ethic.

2.1 Promoting welfare and well-being

Let us say, to use a piece of shorthand, that nursing is about the promotion of well-being. This seems a useful phrase yet, at the same time, it throws up a lot of questions. Many of the key ethical issues faced by nurses, and other health care workers, can be identified and clarified by working through some of these questions.

Is this formulation of the nurse's role not too broad? There are many aspects of well-being; someone's well-being may be increased by a tour of the Mediterranean, by acquiring a new friend, or by learning Latin. None of these things, nor many others like them, seem to be the function of nursing. So perhaps it would be better to say that nursing is about the promotion of certain elements of well-being. One version of this, for example, is to equate nursing with the promotion of health. This is only an improvement if we can give a meaning to health which is less all-encompassing than well-being, and yet less narrow than the idea of absence of disease, which fails to capture all of the work of nurses. A number of authors have advocated such a 'middle-order' conception of health, with the intention that such a conception would help clarify the central objectives and priorities of health workers [4, 5]. Broadly speaking these conceptions identify health with what others would call 'welfare', i.e. someone is healthy to the extent that they have the resources to pursue and achieve well-being or fulfilment. In practical terms this would mean that nursing is about helping to ensure that individuals are in a position to travel, or to learn languages etc. This is not the place to review all of the discussions that have taken place on the theme. But it is possible to make a few comments on the central issues.

Although it is useful to try and clarify the aims of nursing there is no reason to suppose that a single phrase or formula will capture everything which nurses aim at. It is reasonable to assert that the central or overall aim of nursing is to con-tribute to welfare, but this simple formula needs to be qualified otherwise it is arguably both too broad and too narrow. First, the way in which welfare is pro-moted is, in the main, based around the management (including prevention) of suffering or risk rather than wider aspects of welfare promotion such as financial assistance or education, although there is a place for these within health care. That is to say that nurses rightly do not regard the promotion of all aspects of all people's welfare as within their remit. They respond to the suffering of individuals, or to the risks faced by certain populations. Second, once in a relationship with a client they need to have regard to all aspects of well-being that might be relevant to caring for that person. This is part of what is meant by holistic care, but it also follows from a concern with the promotion of welfare; for how can you know whether you are contributing to someone's welfare if you do not see what you do in the context of their whole life? Only by having regard to the whole can nurses ensure that their work is in the interest of their clients.

It is not possible to promote welfare, for example, without having regard to both the costs and the benefits of proposed interventions. Any intervention is likely to have some 'cost' or risk for the client which has to be weighed against the expected benefit; and there will be wider costs and benefits for others affected directly or indirectly. (We will return to this below.) Neither can welfare be promoted without having regard to the wishes or preferences of clients. This is because an important part of my welfare consists in having my wishes respected. So even if a nurse is clear about her aims, and has a clear view of what is in the interest of her client, she faces a number of potential problems of fundamental importance. What if the client disagrees about what is in his or her interest? What if the client agrees that in some respects the nurse's preferred intervention is in his or her interest but for some reason does not wish the intervention to take place? What if the client is not in a position to express an opinion? Under all of these sets of circumstances an appeal to 'promoting welfare' is not sufficient. A well intentioned intervention is not necessarily in the best interest of clients, and, even in those cases where it is, that is not sufficient to justify unwanted 'interference' in people's lives.

The possible tension between 'welfare' and 'wishes' is one of the key issues in health care ethics. Many of the contributions in this book discuss it in one form or another. How should nurses balance promoting the welfare and respecting the wishes of their clients? This is, for example, the background against which the importance of informed consent is discussed. This issue is so important in health care contexts because these typically involve, on the one hand, a patient who is in some distress and in a relatively powerless state and, on the other hand, a group of health professionals in relatively powerful positions and who are charged with looking after the patient. This creates a constant temptation to 'take over' in one way or another for the sake of the patient, without proper regard for the patient's wishes. The ideal circumstances are those in which a client is able to discuss and understand the options facing him, and able to negotiate care and freely assent to any intervention. This assumes that the client is conscious, of sufficient maturity, mentally well and in an open and non-pressurised environment. When one or another of these conditions is not met then there is scope for ethical debate about how best to act. It is usually relevant to consider what the client would wish if they were able to express themselves freely. This might entail imaginatively 'putting ourselves in their shoes', or consulting their family and friends about their views. Sometimes health professionals or family members may be able to make an informed judgement based upon the wishes previously expressed by the client.

2.2   Respect for persons and respect for autonomy

Although it is certainly essential to take into account the views or wishes of clients it should not be assumed that it is always right for these wishes to prevail. What is needed is an ethical account of why 'wishes' are of such importance, and when, if ever, they can be overridden. The intuitions which lie behind this judgement are so basic that it is difficult to produce an account. But the idea of 'respect for persons' helps to articulate it. In brief this is the idea that each of us has an intrinsic value which, if we are to recognise one another properly, cannot be ignored or 'traded off' for some other end. To treat someone only as an object, or only as a tool or resource, is to fail to treat them as a person. This way of expressing the value of persons is derived from part of Kant's moral philosophy, and for many modern thinkers it is close to the essence of ethics. One way in which respect can be exercised is by taking seriously the autonomous choices which people make and by not ignoring or overriding them. Hence the importance of consultation, part-nership, and informed consent.

However, respect for persons does not involve only autonomous choices. Parents may recognise the choices of their teenage children as autonomous, and may choose to override some of their children's wishes without necessarily being guilty of treating them as 'objects'. Indeed they may be treating them with great respect and love, and they may be motivated purely by concern for their children's welfare. Acting in what you judge to be the best interests of someone else, in a way that overrides or limits the exercise of their autonomy is called paternalism (or sometimes parentalism). As we have seen, paternalism is a constant temptation in health care, and if we are to respect autonomy there should be a presumption against it, but are there occasions on which it might be justified?

There are two reasons why nurses may, from time to time, be justified in acting paternalistically. First, autonomy is partly a matter of degree. How autonomous a choice is depends upon a number of factors including the level of understanding and reasoning of the chooser. A choice made by a client may be judged autonomous at a minimum level, and as worthy of respect and serious consideration. Yet judged against a more demanding standard the same choice may not be seen as sufficiently autonomous to decisively settle the matter. Second, it is often difficult to assess the degree of autonomy of a choice. Sometimes we cannot be clear what lies behind a decision or action, in particular how far it rests upon a misperception, a whim, a disturbed temperament, or external pressure. Under these conditions it might be justified to postpone a decision, or even override an apparently autonomous choice, in order to assess how far a choice is really autonomous. Both of these reasons are more likely to come into play if the risk to welfare is great (a suicide attempt is the paradigm case here).

Paternalism involves limiting a person's exercise of autonomy for his or her own sake, but there are, of course, other reasons to limit the extent of what an individual wants. Respect for persons means taking into account the interests and wishes of all those affected. Normally this means that the client concerned has the overriding voice, but this is subject to important qualifications. A patient or client, even if we assume they are 'fully' autonomous, cannot merely demand any intervention whatever the cost to other people, or regardless of the views of health professionals. If we are to respect persons then nurses cannot merely be used as objects or tools to meet other people's demands – doctors or patients. This will happen unless they are involved in appropriate decision making, and allowed to withdraw in a responsible fashion from involvement when they strongly object to what is decided. Also there is sometimes more than one client. A nurse may, for example, be supporting a bereaved family. Here respect for autonomy necessarily entails balancing the wishes of different individuals together, and having regard for the well-being of the family as a whole. Finally a nurse acting as a budget holder or policy maker has to consider the overall implications of decisions for the general population.

2.3   Utilitarianism and the public interest

This takes us on to a second cluster of problems concerning the promotion of welfare. How are nurses supposed to balance together the interests of different individuals, and how are they to consider both the needs of their immediate clients and a commitment to the general welfare or the public interest? A large number of practical dilemmas turn upon these two questions. Dramatic examples of the first kind include those cases where individuals donate organs to others, or cases in which the interests of pregnant women and fetuses can come into conflict. Dramatic examples of the second kind arise when clients are a potential danger to the health or safety of others. If someone has a highly infectious and serious condition, or is seriously mentally disturbed, under what circumstances should they be able to determine their own lifestyle in the community?

One way of thinking about these dilemmas is to see them as about considering the expected costs and benefits of alternative courses of action in order to see which produces the best overall outcome. This way of thinking is called utilitarian, and there is a tradition of moral philosophy called utilitarianism in which it is defended as the basis of ethics. There are many debates about utilitarianism, and within utilitarianism, which cannot be summarised here. But it is possible to indicate both the plausibility, and some of the difficulties, of the central idea.

Its plausibility arises because it seems odd to see ethics as simply about following rules for their own sake. Surely what we are interested in is bringing about better, rather than worse, states of affairs. A nurse who is asked to adopt 'ethical standards' will expect to see how they are connected to protecting or promoting welfare, how they make the world 'a better place'. Yet a rule or guideline which seems to work well most of the time may, on occasions, seem to do more harm than good. For example, it seems important to have rules to protect the confidentiality of clients, but it also seems that there are circumstances where the risks or costs of silence may be so grave that confidentiality could justifiably be broken. It appears that in this kind of example a more fundamental, and utilitarian, ethic is being appealed to.

However, there are some problems with this way of thinking. There is no exact ethical accountancy by which the different sorts of costs and benefits can be optimised, and different individuals are likely to disagree about when a guideline is unhelpful and can be broken. At the extreme this could lead not only to a climate of uncertainty about policy, but to a nurse's idiosyncratic conception of what counts as a cost or benefit having undue influence.

More generally a concern about utilitarian thinking is that it can involve sacrificing some people's interests for the sake of others, and that this could amount to treating people merely as objects or resources. There is, on the face of it, a tension between certain examples of utilitarian thinking and the idea of respect for persons.

For example, consider resource allocation as an ethical issue which, on the face of things, lends itself to utilitarian thinking. A nurse manager might have to decide how to divide a budget between a number of patients and the professionals who work with them. It is plausible to suppose that she should use her experience, and research evidence, to determine which pattern of distribution would 'do the most good' (although note the complexity and uncertainty inherent in this), and opt for this. This sounds fine in the abstract, but in the real world it would probably involve overriding the views and wishes of the patients and professionals involved. Certainly any decision which entailed not treating certain sick individuals at all because money 'wasted' on them might be better spent elsewhere would appear to treat the former with less than respect. For this reason many people react against utilitarian thinking, seeing it as amoral or even 'immoral'. Yet health professionals, including nurses, have some responsibility to the general welfare or the public interest, as well as to the individuals in front of them, and need to explore ways of balancing these responsibilities. This is merely one illustration of the ways in which our basic approach to ethical thinking shapes the day-to-day practical decisions we might make.

2.4   Principles of health care ethics

One approach to health care ethics which has gained widespread currency is to set out fundamental principles, each of which needs to be taken into account when we make ethical judgements. This approach, and the so-called 'four principles' have been made famous by the work of Beauchamp and Childress [6] and Raanon Gillon [7, 8]. The four principles are:

(1)   the principle of respect for autonomy;
(2)   the principle of nonmaleficence;
(3)   the principle of beneficence;
(4)   the principle of justice.

In short, this means that in deciding how to act, health professionals ought to respect autonomy, avoid harming, where possible benefit, and consider (fairly) the interests of all those affected. This is not a formula for ethical decision making, rather it is a broad framework which can be used as a basis for organising ethical deliberation and discussion.

There is no substitute for reading about this approach in the source texts referred to above. These make quite clear the difficulties in interpreting and applying these principles, and the ways in which they tend to conflict with one another in practice. We have already seen that the idea of autonomy, and the ideas of costs and benefits, are open to different interpretations, and the idea of justice is, if anything, even more controversial. For example, some people would argue that a health care system in which health care is distributed by an open market, in which everyone has an opportunity to buy care, is perfectly just. Whereas others would see this as profoundly unjust, arguing perhaps that health care ought to be distributed according to need.

This 'four principles' approach has come under criticism for being too superficial or too limited. Some of this criticism can be dismissed because it is based on false assumptions about the proponents of this approach. They are not arguing that all ethical thinking can be reduced to a few key words, or that the four principles provide a quick and easy method for solving ethical dilemmas. They are arguing that the principles provide a reminder of the key dimensions of ethical thinking, and that they can provide a common vocabulary and framework for individuals with different outlooks or philosophies. Although its proponents have produced sophisticated replies to critics, this approach is, in part, designed to avoid the paralysis of endless theoretical debate, and to be of practical help in real cases.

Leaving aside the question of its ultimate validity, the practice of applying the principles to cases provides important lessons for nursing ethics. Although the principles supply 'rules of thumb' we cannot assess what we ought to do in a specific case without considering the particular circumstances of the case. Ethical judgement depends crucially on questions of fact as well as questions of principle, and it is worth noting in passing that a good deal of apparent ethical disagreement stems from disagreements about the facts. Also, because so much ethical thinking involves weighing together the conflicting demands of different principles, it is possible for a small difference between two similar cases to result in apparently contradictory conclusions. We have already seen, for instance, how a decision to act paternalistically can rest upon very fine judgements about a client's degree of autonomy. Hence not only abstract reasoning but also sensitivity and attention to detail are an essential part of ethical thinking.

2.5   Philosophical ethics – its value and limitations

Philosophy students study 'Ethics' as an academic subject, albeit one which is normally seen to have an applied element. The questions typically considered in this context vary in their level of abstraction. The most abstract or general ones include, for example: What is the basis of ethics? Is it possible to have ethical knowledge? What is the meaning and the uses of the concept 'good'? Then there are middle order questions which raise matters of practical substance but at a considerable level of generality, for example: What are the various conceptions of a fair society? Under what circumstances is it permissible to break promises? Finally there are the most applied questions in which philosophers analyse the 'rights and wrongs' of specific policies or actions. In relation to health care this might include consideration of specific cases in which it is asked if nurse X was right to Y (e.g. breach of confidentiality) in circumstances Z (where these could be spelled out in some detail). Nurses who are also philosophers, or nurses who are interested in philosophy – and there are increasing numbers of both – will be interested in all of these questions, but what is their relevance to nurses with other interests?

Philosophers who wanted to 'sell' their subject could offer the following argument: every nurse has to answer the applied or practical questions, and it is impossible to avoid answering them even if only by default (i.e. faced with circumstances Z you either do or do not breach confidentiality; you cannot fail to 'answer' the question merely by not thinking about it). But, it could be argued, answers to the applied questions lower down the list depend upon having or assuming answers to the sort of questions higher up the list. Therefore, if you want to answer the practical questions responsibly you must address the more philosophical questions. This is a very plausible argument. It takes the same form as all sales talk – 'You cannot do what you want to, or have to, without my product'. For this reason we should be suspicious of it; however I would suggest that in essence it conveys a truth. The only way in which we can appraise specific circumstances is by standing back and comparing them with others. In so doing we will also find ourselves asking what kind of yardsticks, if any, we have. Are there some general standards we can apply, or does it vary from case to case, or from person to person?

Philosophical ethics is a discipline which is commited to this process of 'standing back' and systematic reflection and argument. There are a number of competing theoretical traditions which attempt to organise ethical reflection into systems of thought. At their most ambitious they attempt to produce a single theory (or a unified set of theories) to account for all our ethical judgements. Given such an overarching theory we could identify any particular decision, action, policy or person to be right or wrong, or good or bad, in specified respects. Philosophers disagree about the extent to which it is possible or desirable to aim for such general accounts, or whether they should be satisfied with the 'untidyness' of competing or complementary accounts. They also disagree about the extent to which ethics lends itself to rational analysis, and the extent to which it is rooted in conventional codes and customs (note that these two things are not necessarily incompatible). However, anyone with an interest in applied ethics is interested in seeing how far systematic thinking can be of help in making or evaluating ethical decisions.

Hence one of the benefits of philosophical ethics is that it allows us to reflect in more depth about such things as utilitarianism, the idea of respect for persons, or the idea of principles of health care ethics: What are the different versions of utilitarianism? How far are utilitarian ways of thinking inevitable, how far are they useful? etc. We can ask this sort of question in the hope that we might arrive at a definitive overview of the basis and nature of ethics, or merely in the hope that we will illuminate some of the complexity of the subject. Although there is a danger that health professionals may see these philosophical questions as irrelevant traps (and something like the four principles approach may be preferred as a 'working model'), it is important for everyone to recognise that these basic questions are hotly disputed – i.e. that there is no definitive 'knowledge base' in nursing ethics.

For example, in the health care ethics literature there is frequent mention of the value of 'autonomy', and there are many references to 'informed consent'. It would not be unreasonable for someone coming to the subject for the first time to assume that, in relation to such basic building blocks, there was a clear consensus as to their meaning and role. Thus it might easily be supposed that each time an author uses such an expression he or she is making use of a shared technical vocabulary; that, for example, 'autonomy' always means precisely the same thing, that it is always valued for the same reason, and that its relative importance to other values is agreed. In reality there are commonalities and differences in the way these terms are used, and this is not a product of poor 'co-ordination' but a function of the inherent contestability of ethics. (Incidentally some of these commonalities and differences are illustrated by the ethical perspectives in the second part of this book, and some disagreements about the meaning and value of autonomy are discussed explicitly in the ethical discussions of consent.)

There are a number of other things which the philosophical tradition can offer to nursing ethics. First, there is a considerable literature in which the terms and issues of ethics are clarified and debated. So much has been written over centuries, and over recent years, about well-being and justice and so on. Second, there are conventions for debate, based upon ideals such as disinterested and reasoned discussion, which can serve as useful models for people entering the subject. Third, there are many issues of health care ethics which have philosophical problems built into them. For example, questions about abortion and euthanasia do not only turn upon factual matters but also upon intrinsically philosophical matters to do with the nature and value of life. In these cases it is impossible to treat these issues seriously without some consideration of philosophical questions.

Finally, and paradoxically, one of the benefits of philosophical ethics is an awareness of its own limitations. Being philosophically skilled is not the same as being a good person. There may be some philosophers who believe that a full ethical theory would be sufficient to determine what should be done in every set of circumstances, but no-one could think that this would be enough to make it happen. How would this perfect knowledge become embodied in practice? We all know that it is possible, sometimes all too easy, not to do what we regard as the right thing. For these reasons philosophers have to take an interest in character as well as in actions. What is it that makes people more or less likely to understand ethical demands, and to be inclined or disposed to meet them?

2.6   Being a good nurse

One tradition of philosophical ethics, which is concerned with 'the virtues', sees these questions about character as being at the heart of ethics. The tradition is usually associated with Aristotle's ethical writings but it is a thread that runs through all of ethics. The idea of 'virtues' may seem old fashioned but it is a useful name for good qualities of character, in particular for admirable or desirable dispositions. To encourage children to do 'the right thing' we need not only to help them know what the right thing is but also to enable them to want to do it; preferably for it to become a habit or 'second nature'. The same goes for all of us.

It would be no exaggeration to say that nurse education and development is about the cultivation of desirable dispositions as well as the transmission of clinical skills. Some of these dispositions relate to professional attitudes and behaviour – such as research awareness – but underpinning them all is a disposition to care for patients or clients, the habit of paying attention to and responding to needs. Unless a nurse has this quality she cannot be, except in very restricted circumstances, a good nurse. And this 'skill' of caring is intrinsic to ethics, it is not like other skills which may be used in good or bad ways. In fact caring is viewed by some as the pivotal concept of feminist ethics [9]. Caring does not necessarily mean a self-conscious emotional empathy or identification; there may be many instances where nurses are too tired or stressed to *feel* caring. The whole point of talking about a desirable *disposition* is to make clear that an attitude which is rooted in feelings will persist even when the requisite feelings are absent.

It would be an interesting, and perhaps useful, exercise to ask a group of experienced nurses to list the virtues necessary for nursing. At one time the Christian virtues of faith, hope and charity might have headed the list. Nowadays most people are likely to think of ideas like honesty or integrity, whereas ideas like patience or loyalty might be more controversial. One thing is clear – as the conditions of nursing change a different balance of virtues is called for. No doubt humility is a good quality but as the pressures of individual accountability increase it needs to be tempered by courage and resolution. We all have some conception of what it is to be a good nurse. We can look at role models and try to identify which aspects of their character we admire. In this way we can set ourselves standards.

It is essential to note the difference between 'setting standards' for ourselves as individuals and the public kinds of standard setting which have become increasingly important in health care – in the form of evidence based guidelines, clinical governance, performance management and so on. Certainly the good nurse must take the latter into account and will, by and large, be happy to work towards publicly defined standards. But a nurse who has not only a sense of his or her personal accountability as a professional but also a strong sense of ethical integrity, and embodies nursing virtues such as courage, will want to 'aim above' public standards and – where necessary – critique, challenge or expose them. A number of the ethics authors in the second half of this book point to ways in which ethics can be personally more demanding than the requirements of the law or of professional norms.

Hence, in the end, a serious engagement with ethics highlights some of the tensions between nursing as an ethical role and nursing as a professional or legal or institutional role – between the individual nurse and the nurse as part of the system. It is plausible to suggest that in the few years since the first edition of this book was published there has been a substantial increase in these kinds of tensions, and hence a heightening of importance for nursing ethics. On the one hand more and more emphasis is given to personal accountability in an ever growing range of health care agendas and settings. On the other hand there is a development and consolidation of both national and institutional policies, frameworks and guidelines. In many respects nurses are expected to 'do everything' – including to be both personally responsible and to jump through other people's hoops!

This suggests that as well as cultivating courage nurses increasingly need to cultivate a form of constructive scepticism. They need, for example, to engage constructively with the systems of clinical governance that are put in place within their institution. Many things depend upon institutional systems and standards being in place. However, if they see aspects of these systems as misguided or ineffective – or if they find that they seem to be expressed only in apparently meaningless and self-referential jargon – they ought to explore means of saying so. In the health service the emperor is often quite naked and real standards sometimes depend upon people pointing this out!

So developing one's own personal standards is essential, but it is not a sufficient basis for establishing good nursing. Individual nurses cannot be expected to pull themselves up by their own boot straps. Only the exceptional few could achieve high ethical standards in an unethical environment. It is essential that the cultures and institutions of nursing foster the virtues of nursing. This is why it is important to continue the shift towards a philosophy of nursing founded upon ethical commitments. This is why it is important to have professional values and standards articulated in public documents and policies. This is why it is important for nurses to be able to debate the underlying principles and the particulars of ethics.

2.7   Notes and references

1. Macleod Clark, J. (1993) From sick nursing to health nursing: evolution or revolution? In *Research in Health Promotion and Nursing* (eds Wilson-Barnett, J. & Macleod Clark, J. Macmillan, Basingstoke.
2. Oakeshott, M. (1962) The Tower of Babel. In *Rationalism in Politics*. Methuen, London.

3. Peters, R.S. (1981) Reason and Habit: The Paradox of Moral Education. In *Moral Development and Moral Education*. Allen and Unwin, London.
4. Seedhouse, D. (2001) *Health: the foundations for achievement*. John Wiley and Sons, Chichester.
5. Nordenfelt, L. (1987) *On the Nature of Health*. Reidal, Dordrecht.
6. Beauchamp, T.L. & Childress, J.F. (2001) *Principles of Biomedical Ethics*. Oxford University Press, New York.
7. Gillon, R. (1986) *Philosophical Medical Ethics*. John Wiley and Sons, Chichester.
8. Gillon, R. (1994) *Principles of Health Care Ethics*. John Wiley and Sons, Chichester.
9 Gilligan, C. (1982) *In a Different Voice*. Harvard University Press, Cambridge, Mass.

Chapter 3

The Professional Dimension: Professional Regulation in Nursing, Midwifery and Health Visiting

Reg Pyne

In one sense, the preparation of this chapter for a new edition of this book was ill-timed. Examination of the previous edition reveals that the legislative system it describes and the regulatory processes that flow from them remain in place. So also do the associated statements about the statutory regulatory body's expectations of its registered practitioners and guidance on aspects of professional practice to which reference was made The only change in the law since 1995 to have become operative has been the simple consolidation of the Nurses, Midwives and Health Visitors Acts of 1979 and 1992 into the 1997 Act of the same name. During the same period the United Kingdom Central Council for Nursing, Midwifery and Health Visiting (UKCC) has added to the range of documents providing guidance for its registered practitioners and seeking to enhance standards of professional practice. The temptation is therefore simply to refer the reader to the first edition for a description of the system as it currently operates.

Conversely, however, the timing was opportune, since it provides an opportunity to refer to the challenges to that system, to the measures taken and still being taken to replace it with something that the Government intends to be more effective, and to offer some proposals for an eventual form of regulation of not only nursing, midwifery and health visiting but of all the health professions, that would be constructed so as to genuinely serve the interests of the public.

It is, perhaps, not without significance that, unlike some other countries that have introduced regulation of health professions more recently, the laws establishing organisations for the purpose of regulating the various health professions in the United Kingdom do not commence with an unequivocal statement of the purpose to be served. It is left to be inferred that it has something to do with serving the public interest and allows the regulatory bodies to claim that this is what they are doing. But the absence of a statement to that effect has possibly contributed historically to those bodies operating in such a way that their role has sometimes been perceived as that of enhancing the status of the persons on the register and providing some protection of what they regard as their professional territory.

3.1   The present nursing regulatory system summarised

What currently exists for nursing, midwifery and health visiting, is, in essence, a statutory system that:

- requires the maintenance of a register of nurses, midwives and health visitors;
- requires that admission to that register be controlled;
- makes it a criminal offence for a person to falsely represent themself to be on the register;
- provides a system whereby persons may be removed from the register 'for misconduct or otherwise';
- establishes the principal functions of the regulatory Council as 'to establish and improve standards of training and professional conduct' of the persons included in the register; *and*
- empowers that Council to provide advice on standards of professional conduct for its registrants.

Since 1983, every person who, following appropriate preparation, becomes a registered nurse, midwife or health visitor in the United Kingdom, is placed on the professional register maintained by the UKCC. The Council's power and responsibility derive from the Nurses, Midwives and Health Visitors Act 1997. It is not the purpose of this chapter to examine the subject of education and training for admission to the register. The chapter does, however, provide outline information about the process by which registration can be removed or suspended, or those decisions reversed, since much of the criticism to which the UKCC has been subjected is associated with this aspect of its work.

3.2   Constitution of the UKCC

The Council's constitution provides for a membership of up to 60 persons, two thirds of whom are to be registered nurses, midwives or health visitors elected by their peers, the remainder being persons appointed by Government ministers. Since 1992 the UKCC has chosen to be of the maximum permitted size. The law also permits the Council to include in its committees some persons who are not Council members.

3.2.1   The Council's expectations of registered practitioners

Section 2(1) of the Act describes an end that has to be achieved: 'The principal functions of the Central Council shall be to establish and improve standards of training and professional conduct' for, respectively, admission to the register and conduct once on the register. Section 2(5) offers at least one of the means by which the latter can be done, stating that 'The powers of the Council shall include that of providing, in such manner as it thinks fit, advice for nurses, midwives and health visitors on standards of professional conduct'.

Given the responsibility and authority described, the UKCC has provided, since its birth in 1983, to each registrant, a statement of its expectations of them and, coincidentally, a template against which they can be judged if they are the subject of a complaint alleging misconduct. This is provided through the Code of Professional Conduct for the Nurse, Midwife and Health Visitor. The Code is also of value to the public and those who employ the practitioners, since it is a means by which they are made aware of the Council's standards. This brief but immensely important document has been supplemented over subsequent years by a number of other documents that offer guidance generally or promote standards in respect of specific aspects of professional practice.

3.2.2 Proceedings concerning the registration of individuals

Section 12 of the Nurses, Midwives and Health Visitors Act requires the Council to 'determine the circumstances in which and the means by which . . . a person may, for misconduct or otherwise, be removed from the register'. A related passage of text provides the Council with the power formally to caution a practitioner or to suspend their registration. These powers are a natural and logical consequence of an Act of Parliament which (even if it does not state as much in explicit terms) is concerned with the interests of members of the public who depend on professional practitioners, often when those members of the public are at their most vulnerable. Those words 'or otherwise' in the quotation above, provided the basis in primary legislation for the development (in 1983) of procedures whereby, in the public interest, it is possible to suspend or remove a person's registration on the grounds of their unfitness to practise due to illness. It is surprising, given that this power has been used effectively and without legal challenge for several years, that the 'or otherwise' opportunity has not been used by the Council to develop procedures to protect the public from intractably incompetent practitioners.

It is important to provide practitioners with guidance and a statement of expectations, but without specific sanctions underpinned by law the degree of protection provided for the public would be frail.

The procedures that must be followed to consider allegations of either misconduct or unfitness to practise due to illness are set out in subordinate legislation in the Professional Conduct Rules [1]. These procedures provide for consideration of a complaint alleging misconduct, by a committee of the Council named the Preliminary Proceedings Committee. This committee, after considering the documentary evidence, can:

- decline to proceed and close the case;
- issue a formal caution;
- refer the case for hearing by the Professional Conduct Committee with a view to removal from the register;
- refer the case to the panel of professional screeners where it believes that the conduct complained of is indicative of illness.

It is also open to the committee, where it considers it necessary as an urgent measure in the public interest, to order the 'interim suspension' of a person's registration pending completion of the investigation and bringing the case urgently to the Professional Conduct Committee (PCC). This power has been used to good effect since it was made available.

The PCC, meeting in public, considers cases referred to it by the Preliminary Proceedings Committee. The procedures by which it operates are prescribed in the Professional Conduct Rules. The standard of evidence that must be satisfied is the same as that which applies in criminal courts: the committee must be satisfied so that it is sure. Given the enormity of the committee's weightiest sanction – removal from a person of their registration status thus preventing them from practising in their chosen profession – this seems only right.

Where the PCC finds the facts alleged proved, applying that high standard of proof, it must then consider whether the proven facts amount to misconduct in a professional sense. In doing so it is likely to be mindful of the Council's principal template for conduct, the Code of Professional Conduct. If it labels the proven facts 'misconduct', having heard evidence as to the practitioner's previous history and in mitigation and set the case in its context, the committee must decide whether:

- to remove or suspend a person's name from the register with immediate effect;
- to administer a formal caution;
- to postpone its judgment for a stated period (leaving open the possibility of removal) and state the evidence it requires for a resumed hearing; *or*
- to take no further action on the proven misconduct.

The PCC also considers applications for restoration to the register of persons previously removed for misconduct. Just as there is nothing in law that requires the committee to remove the registration of persons found guilty of specific acts of misconduct (whether by action or omission), nothing requires restoration after a specific period of time. The decisions lie entirely in the hands of the committees. Regrettably, in the view of this author, the law does not require them to give the reasons for their decisions.

The one constraint of which those serving on the PCC are aware, and about which they are sometimes reminded by the legal assessor who sits with them (not to participate in the decision but to advise on matters of law and admissibility of evidence), is the right of persons who feel aggrieved by a decision to remove them from the register to appeal against that decision to the High Court. That right has been exercised on a significant number of occasions since 1983, sometimes with success. In addition the growing area of law that allows persons to seek judicial review of a finding of misconduct, even if it was not followed by a decision to remove from the register, has been exploited on a number of occasions.

Operating in parallel with this process is another which provides the UKCC with the means to consider those cases where the allegation is not that the person concerned is guilty of misconduct, but rather that their fitness to practise is seriously impaired by reason of illness that is not of a transient form.

That, in essence, is how the system operates at present. It has to be recognised, however, that in common with the comparable system for the medical profession and those for other registered health professions, it no longer enjoys significant public confidence. Why this is so and what alternatives might serve the public interest better are points that need to be explored. In order to do that it is necessary to examine the origins of professional regulation in the United Kingdom, and that means first looking at the medical profession.

3.3   Regulating British medicine

Margaret Stacey, in *Regulating British Medicine* [2], sets out the historical background in great and fascinating detail. In a particularly telling paragraph, she concludes that:

> 'Looking back on the establishment of the [General Medical] Council in 1858 it seems clear that the impetus came from medicine – it was a desire to create circumstances in which their income and status could be improved that led medical men to press for reform of medical regulation. Whatever their differences, all were agreed on the importance of regulation for the help it would be to them in controlling who could practise, thereby reducing competition. Contrary to the beliefs of many, the interests of the public were a secondary, not a primary consideration.'

Stacey also quotes the minutes of the General Medical Council (GMC) of 1973 [3] as stating that the 1858 Act:

> 'was passed largely as a result of an initiative within the profession, and the establishment of the Council was desired as much for the protection of the duly qualified medical practitioner from the competition of unqualified practitioners as for the protection of the public.'

That minute formed part of the GMC's evidence to the Merrison Committee, established to conduct a review of its functions and operations at a time when the Council was under significant attack from within the ranks of medicine. That minute emphasises Stacey's 'protection and privilege' conclusion.

It is interesting, in the context of debate now taking place about the regulation of the health professions generally, that, prior to the 1858 Act being passed, one proposal had been that a body of laymen should regulate medicine, rather than the Council entirely composed of members of the profession that emerged. Needless to say it did not find favour.

The regulatory body that emerged would, in the course of time, be used as the basic model for the establishment of professional regulatory bodies for other health professions. With adjustments made over the years through amending legislation, not least related to increases in its membership and enhancement of its powers – and from 1950 even the inclusion of the first 'lay' member – the GMC model remains. Not only medicine but other regulatory bodies, with the consent of Parliament through the legislation that it approves, perpetuate systems whereby a substantial majority of their members are drawn from within the professional group regulated.

It is worthy of note that the Merrison Report of 1975 (The Report of the Committee of Inquiry into the Regulation of the Medical Profession [4]) appeared to accept the appropriateness of that, at least as far as medicine was concerned, stating:

> 'An instructive way of looking at professional self-regulation is to see it as a contract between public and professions, by which the public go to the profession for medical treatment because the profession has made sure it will provide satisfactory treatment.'

It also stated as crucial, for the self-respect of professionals, that they should regulate themselves.

Is it any wonder that Celia Davies [5], earnestly grappling with the need to introduce radical change in matters of regulation, describes the modest changes (modest in that they did not challenge the fundamental structures) leaving us with 'A Nineteenth Century Idea in a Twenty First Century Setting'. She also makes a valuable contribution to the debate about professional regulation now taking place, contending that:

> 'As each professional group seeks a more secure and respected place, so it has developed institutions that mirror or mimic those of medicine – something that has the potential as much to pull the care delivery team apart as to bring its members together.'

Truly effective reform of the regulation of the health professions cannot therefore be achieved unless they are also considered as part of the same reform package. It is, after all, the same people who depend on their practitioners' competence and conduct.

3.3.1   The challenge to systems of professional regulation

It was only after Parliament, through amending legislation in 1969, had granted to the GMC the power to levy an annual fee on all persons on its register, precipitating a professional revolt that brought a threat to the medical staffing of the National Health Service, that any UK Government seemed to take the issue of professional regulation seriously. Even then, in 1972, in announcing the establishment of a committee of enquiry, the then Secretary of State, Sir Keith Joseph, effectively limited its impact at the outset by stating that, 'The General Medical Council is a body with a notable record of service to the public and the profession. It is not contemplated that the profession should be regulated other than by a predominantly professional body' [6].

In other words, professional regulation itself was not to be called into question. Twenty years later, when taking legislation (the Nurses, Midwives and Health Visitors Bill) to revise the regulatory structure for nursing through the House of Commons, another Secretary of State, Virginia Bottomley, said that the principle of professional self-regulation was not in question. She reinforced this, once the legislation had received the Royal Assent, by appointing only two genuinely lay persons to the 60 member Council.

The years subsequent to 1975 have faced the GMC with criticism and challenges of a different sort and principally from outside the profession. In 1988, through the organisation Health Rights, Jean Robinson – at the time one of the lay members of the GMC – published a critique, *A Patient Voice at the GMC*, of the Council's style, operation and the effect of some of its decisions in professional disciplinary cases [7], generating a very defensive response from the Council in *The Lancet*. The years that followed have seen further complaints, serious expressions of dissatisfaction and evidence of a much greater willingness on the part of the public to challenge and question. These have culminated, during 1999–2000, in outbursts of anger over the doctors from the Bristol Childrens Hospital who became the subject of a belated and much publicised hearing, and the case of Dr Harold Shipman – a General Practitioner working in a single practitioner practice – who was convicted for the murder of a number of his patients. These are simply the most widely publicised examples of cases that have generated much public disquiet.

3.3.2   The UKCC subject to challenge

Expressed dissatisfaction with the UKCC has not been as great as that on record about the GMC. It did, however, reach a crescendo during the latter part of the 1990s in response to several remarkably perverse decisions by the PCC to restore to the register some persons who had previously been removed for extremely serious criminal offences involving vulnerable patients. One of these decisions, in a case concerning a convicted rapist, was taken to the courts by the Royal College of Nursing for judicial review, and the decision overturned.

There was nothing in the law that prevented the committee members from making these decisions, but equally nothing that required them to decide as they did. The law simply requires them to consider any application for restoration and, after due consideration, to decide to accept it or reject it. The decision lies with the members serving on the day. Would they have made the decisions they did if they were required to state their reasons in public, or would the discipline of having to articulate their reasons mean their decisions would have been different?

In the aftermath of these much publicised and criticised decisions the new Government chose in August 1997 to bring forward the periodic review of the operation of the Nurses, Midwives and Health Visitors Act 1979 (as amended by the 1992 Act and consolidated in the 1997 Act) and commissioned a firm of management consultants to undertake this task. The previous review, by other management consultants conducted in a very short time in 1991, had led to the amendments contained in the 1992 Act.

The consultants engaged were J.M. Consulting Ltd who, at the time, had recently completed a comparable review of the much older legislation concerning the Council for the Professions Supplementary to Medicine. Given that fact, and noting the turbulence surrounding the General Medical Council at the time and indications from Government that it was minded to legislate in that direction as well, it has to be regarded as extraordinary that neither the J.M. Consulting report nor the Government's response to it in February 1999 [8], contained any indication that the fundamental principle of the regulatory bodies maintaining a majority membership from within the profession regulated might be open to challenge. J.M. Consulting recommend a new Nursing and Midwifery Council with between 24 and 27 members with a professional majority and a minimum of one third lay members. The Government stated its acceptance of the recommendation.

Similarly, neither document contained anything to suggest that more radical thinking had been undertaken – thinking that might possibly result in a suggestion that professional practitioners (albeit from different occupational groups) who work together as members of the same team might be regulated by the same regulatory body.

3.3.3 A new approach to the law

In its response to the J.M. Consulting recommendations, the Government confirmed its intention to include a clause in the new Health Bill enabling it to effect changes to primary legislation concerning the health professions by Order, thus avoiding the need for Parliamentary time and reducing delay in bringing about the changes the Government of the day consider important. The prospect of such a radical change as the various health professions being joined in some form of shared regulatory structure even being considered was confirmed as remote by the wording of the relevant clauses in what became the Health Act 1999.

This Act, in its 'Miscellaneous' section, under the heading 'Regulation of health care and associated professions', declares that:

> 'Her Majesty may by Order in Council make provision (a) modifying the regulation of any profession to which subsection 2 applies so far as appears to Her to be necessary or expedient for the purpose of securing or improving the regulation of the profession or the services which the profession provides or to which it contributes; and (b) regulating any other profession which appears to Her to be concerned (wholly or partly) with the physical or mental health of individuals and to require regulation in pursuance of this section.'

This would seem to herald the prospect of something potentially radical. It certainly opens the door to regulation which is no longer quite as 'arm's length' from Government as has been the case, and is more exposed to the risk of intervention. While the use of the word 'necessary' in the passage quoted is logical, the inclusion of 'expedient' is worrying. Might this, for example, lead to ill considered and rushed changes in legislation by Order in response to press reports that the Government finds unhelpful in an election year?

The Act, having declared the new position concerning modifying professional regulation, then clarifies that the professions it is referring to are those regulated by the Pharmacy Act 1954, the Medical Act 1983, the Dentists Act 1984, the Opticians Act 1989, the Osteopaths Act 1993, the Chiropractors Act 1994, the Nurses, Midwives and Health Visitors Act 1997, the Professions Supplementary to Medicine Act 1960 and any other professional groups that may, in the future, be brought within the regulated circle by Order in Council. It goes on to make it clear, however, that the latter two Acts are (from dates to be determined) 'to cease to have effect', to be replaced by new regulatory bodies established by Order for those respective groups.

Since the Act also indicates [9] that it will not be permissible by Order to abolish the regulatory body of any profession named, whether it exists by virtue of continuing primary legislation or the Orders creating the new bodies referred to above, the regulation of the several related groups is set to continue in a fragmented and unco-ordinated manner until that situation is changed by a new Act of Parliament at some future stage. It seems that the 'joined up government' philosophy has yet to reach this part of Government's thinking.

3.4   Regulation of nursing – the short term prospect

From all of that it would seem that the immediate prospect for the regulation of the nursing, midwifery and health visiting professions, when an Order in Council establishing a new body for that purpose has been approved, is for a new Council much as described by J.M. Consulting; that is, a Council of no more than 27 members, with a majority drawn from the professions and at least one third of lay members. Once again 'lay' is not explained, sustaining the prospect that many of the places so defined will be filled by persons who are only 'lay' in the sense that they are not nurses, midwives or health visitors. The other J.M. Consulting recommendations, and the Government's response to them, relate to functions, structures and style. They do not address the fundamental point of whether 'professional self-regulation' in the form it has existed since the creation of the General Medical Council in 1858 is sustainable or to be preferred in the twenty-first century. I could only hope that the Government, through the future Order in Council, in spite of the constraints it had imposed upon itself, would do more than simply tamper around the edges of the existing system.

3.4.1   An international contribution

In this context it seems wise for those who draft the proposed Order to look beyond our own shores. While, particularly since 1997, the intention to 'strengthen the existing systems of professional self-regulation' [10] has been expressed, the subject of professional regulation has been under review elsewhere.

In 1997 the International Council of Nurses (ICN) published the result of its work to review its position statement on regulation. This document, *ICN on Regulation: Towards 21st Century Models* [11], restates the twelve principles enunciated in the previous version of the statement, but supports them with fresh narrative. Several of these principles have particular relevance to the UK debate and could usefully be used as a template against which to assess the contents first of a proposed draft Order (perhaps even the preparation of that draft), and subsequently of the procedures and processes that the UKCC's replacement adopts.

The first of these principles might be regarded as a statement of the glaringly obvious, but the obvious does sometimes need stating. It reads 'Regulation should be directed towards an explicit purpose'. The text that follows opens by contending that 'The overriding purpose of the statutory regulation of nursing is that of service to and protection of the public'. Later it asserts that 'Benefits to the profession and individual practitioners are secondary and, although they can be significant, do not of themselves provide justification for statutory regulation'.

The next principle – equally obvious, but equally important – states that 'Since the overriding purpose of statutory regulation is service to and protection of the public, the regulatory system should be designed to satisfy this intent in a comprehensive manner'. The text explores the implications this has for individual practitioners, for the settings in which they work and for the process of setting and reviewing standards for education and practice.

The third principle is concerned with definitions of professional scope and accountability. The supportive text includes this statement:

'ICN's clear preference, and therefore its strong recommendation, is that legislation adopt a flexible approach to *scope of practice* issues. ICN recognises and accepts that benefits in service delivery can result from overlapping scopes of practice among different health professions and that a dynamic approach to professional practice will enable greater public service.'

The full set of principles and the supplementary text reward study, but for the purposes of this chapter I restrict myself to referring to just one more.

Principle V states that:

'Regulatory systems should recognise and incorporate the legitimate roles and responsibilities of interested parties – public, profession and its members, employers and other professions – in various aspects of standard-setting and administration.'

The role of each of these parties, and the way in which they can come together to form the whole, is then explored in a passage of text too long to reproduce. I select a few passages only.

The section concerning the role of the professions contends that:

'... the profession, through its culture and ethic and its regulatory mechanisms, must promote the personal growth of its individual members. It must promote vigorously that component of professional regulation that the individual practitioner imposes on himself or herself as a matter of personal professional accountability.'

In respect of related professions it contends that:

'Related professions have the right to participate in nursing's external governance processes to promote complementarity of the professions in the public interest.'

But also the contention that 'The nursing profession should expect reciprocal arrangements to exist'.

On the subject of the role the public could play, the document states that:

'Members of the public ... should be encouraged to participate in the regulatory processes. This helps to increase the visibility of the profession's collective accountability for its practice.'

It later adds:

'They should be invited to join health professionals to participate in public policy development to ensure that the essential purpose of the health care system and the role of health professions are observed.'

Although I did not arrive at this conclusion when I was serving as the consultant for ICN's expert group whose work resulted in this text, it now seems to me that this offers the essence of a case and even part of a formula for a single regulatory body for all the professions whose members provide health services.

Celia Davies [12] has argued that a key idea for the future is a form of stake-holder regulation. That would seem to resonate well with much of what can be found in the ICN text and would create the prospect, if only the key people and organisations are unblinkered enough to engage in constructive debate, for creating an effective twenty-first century model of professional regulation. Davies contends that:

'... these questions about standard-setting and the maintenance of standards, and the way they are given effect through the register, need to be placed at the centre of a modern understanding of professional regulation.'

To this she adds that

'... since safeguarding professional standards is an activity in which a number of parties have an interest and which each of them can promote or undermine, they all need to be involved. The question of standards thus needs to be addressed through a dialogue in which there is space for the voices of patients, employers, educators, professional associations and trade unions as well as government. There needs to be a credible process of balanced decision-making, which precludes the possibility of domination by any one of the parties.'

That is the principal idea around which she proposes a stakeholder model of regulation. That expression of the idea alone is adequate to use as a litmus test for the future Order.

3.5   The new context for professional regulation

Much has changed, not only since the Medical Act of 1858 provided the legislation that became the model for professional regulatory systems in the United Kingdom (and many other countries), but also since the current Acts of Parliament for the various health professions came into effect. This has been explored in some detail by Dingwall, Rafferty and Webster [13]. The speed of change to which they refer has accelerated in the last decade.

The regulation of the health professions now has to operate in a situation in which members of the public are more inclined to challenge and question, and much less deferential. They have higher expectations of the health professions. They are better informed about issues that affect their lives and better equipped to express their concerns. In these circumstances the time must surely have come to engage both public and professions in major debate aimed at creating a valid twenty-first century system of professional regulation. The powers the Government has taken to itself in the Health Act 1999 to influence professional regulation fall short of what will be needed to achieve true root and branch reform. It will require primary legislation of some magnitude that, unless it is preceded by a process of major education and debate leading to some winning of professional hearts, minds and confidence will encounter massive opposition. Surely the time has come to initiate that debate, and for the Government to take the lead.

Perhaps a window of opportunity has opened. In March 2000 the National Health Service Executive released for consultation a document entitled *Modernising Medical Regulation: Interim Strengthening of the GMC's Fitness to Practice Procedures* [14]. It can presumably be inferred from the use of the word 'interim' that something more definitive and permanent is to follow within a reasonably short time. Could this opportunity be used to take the radical step that I now believe to be necessary? I do not pretend that it would be easy, and along the way there is no doubt that some 'turf wars' would become apparent. But the longer a radical change is deferred the greater will become the need for it, and the level of public disenchantment with the current system will grow.

When I was serving as the UKCC's Director for Professional Conduct it was sometimes the case that, as the Council's solicitors investigated allegations against some registered nurses, it became apparent that other registered health professionals – usually but not invariably doctors – had been involved in the same allegedly culpable conduct. It was sometimes a matter of grievance to the nurses involved that while they were the subject of complaint to the UKCC, no comparable complaints in respect of the doctors had reached the General Medical Council. Where, however, both parties were the subject of complaint alleging misconduct, the regulatory processes that then applied (and still apply) meant that the evidence in support of the allegations would be heard at separate times by two entirely separate groups of people and often result in distinctly different conclusions. How can this be regarded as either right or efficient?

3.5.1 Professional defensiveness

Why do members of the health professions feel so anxious and insecure about the wider involvement of articulate members of the public, and appear so reluctant to see them playing a more significant role in the regulation of their professions? Has it, perhaps, something to do with the negative connotations that associate with the word 'lay' when used by some health professionals?

Margaret Stacey has stated her position on what she describes as 'Professional knowledge and people knowledge' [15] She contends:

'On the whole I prefer to speak of "people knowledge" rather than "lay knowledge". This is because "lay" (even though it originally comes from a Greek word meaning "of the people") tends to be used for those people who do not belong to a specific profession... In referring to people who lack particular qualifications, "lay" suggests the absence of something valuable or prestigious, and may imply less competence, or even less moral worth. Thus it underlines the very distinction I wish to argue is false except in a limited technical sense.'

Later she adds:

> 'It can also be helpful to remember that while each health worker may be an expert in their own area, faced with expertise of another kind they are just one of the people.'

3.5.2   A personal journey

The latter years of my professional career were spent in senior positions with the statutory bodies charged with the regulation of the nursing, midwifery and health visiting professions. In 1998 – three years after my retirement from the last of those posts, and by then the Chairman of a Community Health Council and Vice Chairman of the Association of Community Health Councils for England and Wales – I wrote a chapter entitled 'How does it look from the outside?' [16]. (The 'it' was the way in which the regulatory body for my profession addressed the performance of its statutory functions.) I opened that chapter by quoting a letter by Leo Haynes published in *The Independent* in 1996. He took to task the then President of The Law Society who had recently declared that the role of a professional regulatory body was to identify and then serve the interests of the profession. Mr Haynes corrected him, pointing out that its primary duty was to serve the interests of the public.

From that beginning, looking at my own profession, I argued the case for greater openness, critical self-appraisal, vigilance and competence. I still hold the view expressed in the chapter's final sentence: 'We must always remember that this cachet of professional regulation is not for adornment – it is for application.'

Although, when writing those words, I had already made sufficient of a journey to comment in a constructively critical manner about the regulatory system for my profession, I had not reached the conclusion that the perpetuation of a panoply of regulatory bodies was no longer the right way to serve the public interest. A further three years on, having not only completed the work with the ICN to which I have referred, but having also served as the chairman of a National Health Service Trust and come to grapple with its clinical governance agenda, I have almost completed the journey.

I now see no grounds and can no longer find any justification for the existence of eight separate regulatory bodies for the health professions. I no longer see a use for that term 'professional self-regulation', beyond it meaning '… that component of professional regulation that the individual practitioner imposes on himself or herself as a matter of personal professional accountability' [17]. Given the purpose of the whole professional regulatory process, I no longer argue for or seek to justify the existence of a regulatory body (whether for a single profession or many) in which the profession's members outnumber those who can be seen as better able to represent a 'public' view.

I continue my journey, keen to co-operate with any person or organisation interested in creating a twenty-first century model of professional regulation. In doing so, however, I have to record my concern that neither the relevant passages in the NHS Plan (*The NHS Plan: A plan for investment; A plan for reform*) [18], or the wording of the consultation documents *Modernising Regulation: The New Nursing and Midwifery Council* [19] or *Modernising Regulation: The New Health Professions Council* [20] appear to have addressed what I see as the fundamental issues.

One passage in the NHS Plan holds out what I regard as some modest hope. Paragraph 10.15 states that:

'There also needs to be formal coordination between the health regulatory bodies. For this reason a UK Council of Health Regulators will be established including ...'

It then names the eight existing health regulatory bodies or their intended successors. It then adds, in a sentence on which I hang my limited hopes of more radical change:

'In the first instance the new body would help co-ordinate and act as a forum in which common approaches across the professions could be developed for dealing with matters such as complaints against practitioners. Were concerns to remain about the individual regulatory bodies its role could evolve.'

But that statement, intended no doubt to be reassuring, begs more questions than it answers. How will it be composed? Will it be an overarching body with real authority? Will it have a genuinely lay majority? Will it have sufficient independence of the constituent bodies to bring to ministers the recommendation that its role should evolve, possibly to replace them? Until these questions are answered the prospect remains of a revised system that is more an expedient response than a genuine solution to a matter of genuine public interest.

3.5.3   The draft Nursing and Midwifery Order 2001

And now, just as my final deadline for submission of this chapter is reached, from the Department of Health there has emerged the document *Establishing the new Nursing and Midwifery Council* [21] This text, open for consultation until 1 June 2001, introduces and explains the draft Nursing and Midwifery Order that fills most of its pages. So how does it look, measured against my own views and the opinions of others I have quoted? I feel that the best I can say is that it makes some significant gestures towards these concerns, but still falls well short of achieving a satisfactory outcome and still reflects an unwillingness to really grasp the regulation nettle. Limitations of space allow me to comment on only a few aspects of the draft Order.

Does the text make clear the purpose of the intended legislation? Not, regrettably, with a clear statement of purpose. It does, however, (at clause 3 (4)(a)) state that:

'In performing its functions the Council shall treat the health and well-being of persons using or needing the services of registrants as paramount.'

Does it at least edge towards the 'stakeholder' concept? Perhaps it does a little, but in a very cautious way. Clause 3(4)(c) will require the new Council to:

'cooperate wherever reasonably practical with
(i) employers of prospective registrants,
(ii) persons who provide, assess or fund education or training for registrants or prospective registrants, or who propose to do so,
(iii) persons who are responsible for regulating or coordinating the regulation of other health and social care professionals, or of those carrying out activities in connection with the services provided by those professions or the professions regulated under this Order.'

Not, you will notice, users of the services of the Council's registrants. They do, at least, get a mention in clause 3(13). This requires that:

'Before establishing any standards or giving any guidance under this Order the Council shall consult representatives of any group of persons it considers appropriate including, as it sees fit. . .'.

The list of examples of those to be consulted as the Council sees fit, places registrants first, their employers second, and only then do users of services find mention. I accept that it is not presented in a ranking order, but it perpetuates an unfortunate image of precedence to be given to those within the profession. I find that disappointing.

And what of the intended membership profile? The limitation in the size of the Council membership, allied to its capacity to engage persons who are not members in various aspects of its work, is to be welcomed. Much less welcome, however, is the determination to hold on to an arrangement that places the 'lay' members of Council in a minority of one in a 23 member Council. The means by which these lay members will be appointed is set out in Clause 4 of Schedule 1 of the Order. This states:

'Having consulted such persons as it considers appropriate, the Privy Council shall appoint lay members from among persons who are not and never have been on the register and who have such qualifications and experience as, in the opinion of the Privy Council will be of value to the Council in the performance of its functions.'

It therefore remains possible, for example, to appoint medical practitioners as lay members. I hope that the Privy Council do not travel that road.

The draft Order is silent about the means by which the Privy Council will identify persons for appointment in this category. Since, with effect from April 2001, chairmen and non-executive directors of Health Authorities and NHS Trusts are to be appointed, following personal application and a rigorous process, by the new publicly accountable NHS Appointments Commission, it would surely have been logical for the Government that introduced that process to adopt similar procedures for lay members of statutory regulatory bodies.

What about the expressed concern that reasons should be give for decisions by committees empowered to remove registration? The fact that the person who made the allegations that have been heard in public must be notified of the decision and the reasons for it is welcome. Since the committee will have to be clear about its reasons to do that, surely those reasons should be stated publicly when the decision is announced. The decision to introduce an Appeal Tribunal as a first stage in the process of appealing against decisions of the same committees is also welcomed. Sadly the right to appeal, both to this level and the courts, is provided for the aggrieved practitioner only – not the aggrieved complainant.

These are some of my negative reactions. Unequivocally good, however, is the introduction of an overt authority to deal with the practitioner who puts vulnerable members of the public at risk by being incompetent.

Earlier I expressed the hope that, notwithstanding the constraints it had imposed on itself, the Government would do more than tamper around the edges of the existing system. I have to concede that my worst fears have not proved justified – it is not all bad, though I feel it creates a system of fiendish complexity. I must, however, record my disappointment that the approach taken has not been truly radical and fundamental. I suspect that, before many more years pass, another Government, faced with further waves of public dissatisfaction about the health professions, will find it necessary to revisit the subject of regulation.

Perhaps – just perhaps at this stage – the prospect of real progress becomes more likely as a consequence of Recommendations 39 and 71–74 of the Final Report of the Bristol Royal Infirmary Inquiry [22]. The first of these recommends that the 'Council of Healthcare Regulators' referred to in the NHS Plan [18] should instead become a 'Council for the Regulation of Healthcare Professionals'. Although leaving in existence the range of separate regulatory bodies that the NHS Plan lists, and seeing the addition of an additional one for managers, this 'overarching' Council would have some genuine authority and the opportunity to create a more unified system of regulation. Specifically, it would be required to '... ensure that there is an integrated and coordinated approach to setting standards, monitoring performance, and inspection and validation'. That, if accepted in principle and implemented in practice by the Government and its agents, would present the prospect of a twenty-first century model of professional regulation becoming a reality. The big question is, will what emerges from Government and Parliament match this template?

3.6   Notes and references

1. Professional Conduct Rules, Statutory Instruments No. 893, 1998 No. 1103 and 2001 No. 536.
2. Stacey, M. (1992) *Regulating British Medicine*. John Wiley & Sons Ltd, Chichester.
3. GMC Minutes, CX (1973) p. 179.
4. *Report of the Committee of Inquiry into the Regulation of British Medicine*, 1975 Cmnd.6018. HMSO, London.
5. Davies, C. (2000) *Is Professional Self-Regulation Sufficient?*. Web publication http://www.humanvalues.swan.ac.uk
6. Hansard. House of Commons, 28 November 1972, Vol. 846, pp. 464–5.
7. Robinson, J. (1988) *A Patient Voice at the GMC: a lay member's view of the GMC*. Health Rights, London.
8. Government response to the Review of the Nurses, Midwives & Health Visitors Act. *Health Service Circular* HSC 1999/030.
9. Health Act 1999, Schedule 3, clause 7.

10. The New NHS – Modern, Dependable. Department of Health, London, 1997.
11. *International Council of Nurses on Regulation: Towards 21st Century Models.* ICN, Geneva, 1997.
12. Davies, C. Unpublished paper presented to an Invitation Seminar convened by the Royal College of Nursing, 19 January 2000.
13. Dingwall, R., Rafferty, A.M. & Webster, C. (1988) *An Introduction to the Social History of Nursing.* Routledge, London.
14. *Modernising Medical Regulation: Interim Strengthening of the GMC's Fitness to Practise Procedures.* NHS Consultation Document. March 2000.
15. Stacey, M. (1994) Chapter 5, 'The Power of Lay Knowledge' in *Researching the People's Health* (eds Popay, J. & Williams, G.) Routledge, London.
16. Pyne, R. (1998) *Professional Discipline in Nursing, Midwifery and Health Visiting,* 3rd edn. Blackwell Science, Oxford.
17. *International Council of Nurses on Regulation: Towards 21st Century Models.* ICN, Geneva, 1999.
18. *The NHS Plan: A plan for investment; A plan for reform,* Cmnd 4818-1. July 2000.
19. *Modernising Regulation: The New Nursing & Midwifery Council.* NHS Executive Consultation Document. August 2000.
20. *Modernising Regulation: The New Health Professions Council.* NHS Executive Consultation Document. August 2000.
21. *Establishing the new Nursing and Midwifery Council.* Department of Health. April 2001.
22. *The Bristol Royal Infirmary Inquiry – Final Report.* July 2001.

Chapter 4

The Complaints Dimension: Patient Complaints in Health Care Provision

Arnold Simanowitz

There has probably been more fundamental change in the area of complaints since this chapter was written for the first edition of this book six years ago, than in any other aspect of the ethical side of health care provision. This change has affected the legal side to some extent as well.

On the face of it that might appear to be an extravagant claim. There have been major developments, if not advances, on all fronts in the ethical and legal spheres of health care, as the other chapters of this book demonstrate, some of an extremely far-reaching nature. In those areas, however, the developments have related to specific areas or specific issues such as the critically ill patient and declining and withdrawing treatment.

Insofar as complaints are concerned, however, the change has been of a more fundamental kind. Indeed, whilst the issue of complaints was quite properly included in a book about law and ethics, when the first edition was written, at that time complaints were not really seen as an ethical matter at all and had very little impact on or involvement with the law. With regard to ethics, on the one hand complaints were simply regarded by health care providers as an attack on the institution or individual involved, to be rejected if possible or diverted if not; on the other hand, patients believed, partly because of that very attitude of the providers, that if they complained, they were doing something somewhat frowned upon by society and possibly harmful to the NHS. As a result complaints were not seen as an ethical issue at all.

It was because of this that the original steps taken to introduce procedures to enable patients to complain, satisfied neither patients nor health carers. On the providers side they were introduced grudgingly as a minimum that might satisfy the 'difficult' patient; on the other they did not begin to satisfy the first principle of a complaints procedure which is to look at the problem from the patient's point of view. If someone of negative intent had sat down to create a system for patients to complain about health care they would have been unlikely to have come up with anything as unhelpful as the system that operated before the changes brought in following the Wilson enquiry in 1994 [1].

Firstly there was an entirely different procedure depending on where the treatment had taken place. If it had taken place in a hospital then the procedure under Health Circular (81) 5 applied. This could lead to an 'independent' professional review by consultants from outside the region in which the care had taken place. Whilst that procedure was described as independent, patients did not see it as such. Although the consultants carrying out the review were from outside the region, nevertheless they were seen as part of the health service and therefore likely to support their colleagues. A further problem was that if there was an allegation of negligence which might have been the subject of litigation, then the complaint could not proceed.

On the other hand, where the care complained of had taken place in a General Practitioner's surgery then the complaint had to be made to the Family Health Services Authority where the procedure was totally different. Here, unlike with hospital complaints, even if the complaint involved an allegation of negligence it would still be dealt with.

Secondly there was yet another distinction between types of complaint. If the complaint was about administration then it could be made to the Health Service Commissioner – but not if it related to primary care services in respect of which the Commissioner had no jurisdiction.

Thirdly, if the complaint related to the conduct of a clinician, it might amount to professional misconduct and would therefore have to be made to the General Medical Council or the UKCC where the doctor or nurse could be disciplined. The burden of proof of professional misconduct was, however, so heavy for the complainant that the vast majority of such complaints were rejected out of hand. But that was not the only way in which a hospital doctor working in the NHS could be disciplined. His or her employer, the hospital Trust, could itself implement disciplinary proceedings the result of which could lead to dismissal but not to removal from the register which was the purview of the General Medical Council alone.

Finally, if the complaint concerned damage to the patient who consequently wished for compensation, then the only recourse was to the courts.

It can be seen, therefore, that any patient wishing to complain was faced with a bewildering array of procedures any or all of which were mutually exclusive. Any one of them could involve a process of such length and complication that patients often did not have the stamina either to commence it, or once they had commenced, to last the course.

Now, however, there is an awareness on the part of the providers that there are two ethical aspects to the question of complaints. Firstly there is a recognition that how a complaint is dealt with can have an important effect on a patient and his or her family. It can be seen as part of the care of a patient and as such the obligation to deal with it properly comes within the duty of care of all health care providers. The Chief Medical Officer recognised this in his seminal report on learning from adverse events in the NHS *An organisation with a memory* [2]:

> 'The processes of dealing with adverse events which lead to litigation are often themselves perceived by patients as further elements of poor care.'

Although this recognition is not yet universal, certainly among the leaders in the professions the concept, if not its consequences, is a reality and is accepted as applying not only to those events which lead to litigation but to those which elicit a complaint as well.

Secondly, there is a recognition that complaints have a major role to play in the improvement of health care; that they are 'jewels to be treasured' – they show, more than anything else, the shortfalls in the system.

At the same time, patients have at last come to recognise that the provision of health care is a service which, if not exactly the same as any other service such as the provision of electricity, is nevertheless something they are entitled to receive at a reasonable standard. If that standard is not attained they are far more prepared to complain without feeling that they are undermining the NHS.

Insofar as the law is concerned the complaints procedure has started to become an integral part of the legal process. It features both in the pre-action protocol (discussed in Chapter 5) where it is something that should be considered before a claimant is advised to take legal action [3]; and it features strongly in the Legal Service Commission's guidance in clinical negligence cases where public funding may not be granted if resort has not been made first to the NHS complaints procedure.

There is little doubt that since the first edition of this book complaints have come centre stage in the National Health Service and have even begun to make an impact in the independent sector. It is not within the scope of this chapter to describe in detail all the reasons for this. Nevertheless it would not be appropriate to ignore entirely the three main causes. The first is the approach of the government. It is government policy to insist that the citizen is entitled to expect a good service in all public areas and to complain if they do not get it. It is the government itself that has insisted that the Health Service should in this respect be treated like any other service.

The second is the high profile disasters that have received such prominent reporting in the media, above all the Bristol Royal Infirmary tragedy. That disaster involved the avoidable deaths of about 35 babies and led to a public inquiry that lasted more than two years. The *BMJ* editorial in June 1998, commenting on the tragedy, started with the words 'All changed, changed utterly'. [4] To the extent that that brought realisation to the wider public that doctors could be challenged, that statement was absolutely correct and this has influenced attitudes towards complaints ever since. It is an irony that, whilst Action for Victims of Medical Accidents (AVMA) had by then dealt with over 25,000 adverse events, some equally devastating for the families concerned and involving at least as bad behaviour on the part of the doctors concerned, it was only after Bristol, which involved only 24 incidents, albeit of the most distressing kind, that the public, the media, the healthcare providers and the government began to take the matter of adverse incidents really seriously.

The third reason for the increased importance of complaints is the change in approach that was recommended by the Wilson report. Whilst fundamental problems remain with the way complaints are dealt with, nevertheless both the underlying principles for a proper complaints procedure proposed by Wilson [1] and the new procedure itself have led to changes in the way complaints are perceived.

It will be seen below that the new procedures introduced as a result of the

Wilson recommendations have addressed a number of the complaints about the previous procedure, but many remain.

4.1 The 'new' complaints systems

At the heart of the mechanisms for patients to complain about the service they have received from health care providers within the NHS is the complaints procedure which came into effect on 1 April 1996 following the report of the Wilson Inquiry [1]. This replaced all existing hospital, community health service and family health service complaints procedures with a two stage procedure: local resolution and independent review.

4.1.2 Local resolution

The whole idea behind the new procedure is that complaints should be dealt with as close as possible to the point where the service was provided. The majority of complaints are investigated by the Trust or the general practitioner's practice itself. One of the major complaints made by patients about the previous procedures was the interminable time complaints could take. The guidance to the new procedure recommends specific timetables for dealing with the complaint in an attempt to ensure that the patient receives a full response within a reasonable time [5].

The procedure should, as recommended by the Wilson Report be:

- accessible for complainants;
- simple;
- separate from disciplinary procedures;
- able to provide lessons about the quality of service delivery;
- fair;
- rapid and open;
- honest and thorough with the prime aim of resolving problems and satisfying the concerns of the complainant.

Whilst there remains considerable dissatisfaction on the part of many patients about the way local resolution is conducted, this revolves largely around implementation by many of the Trusts and GPs and their personnel rather than the procedure itself. By and large the procedure is an improvement on what took place before, mainly because it has concentrated the minds of those responsible for dealing with complaints on their responsibilities to patients.

Unfortunately the same cannot be said for the independent review.

4.1.3 Independent review

The major complaint by patients' organisations about the review procedure for hospital complaints that existed before the Wilson Inquiry was that notwithstanding its title, the Independent Professional Review was not really independent. Two consultants from outside the region would be appointed by the Regional Medical Officer; there would be no input into the review by the patient who would have no knowledge of what investigations were made nor see the statements made by other parties. (See the evidence of AVMA to the enquiry and their comments on the recommendations made by the Review Committee.)

Furthermore, there was no opportunity for the complainant to hear the explanation of the clinician, let alone cross-examine him or her. The consultants were at liberty to obtain the information they required in whatsoever way they considered appropriate and the complainant would have no way of testing or challenging that information. At the conclusion of the 'review' the patient would simply be told what had been decided. If the decision was unsatisfactory there was no appeal. While on the face of it the review might seem independent because clinicians from outside the hospital concerned were making the decision, to the complainant it could not appear to be anything other than the doctors, or the NHS itself, 'sticking together'. If the aim of the complaints procedure is to satisfy complainants, which it is self-evident it should be, then it can clearly be seen that such a situation was unacceptable.

What is more, even if the complaint were upheld the complainant would not necessarily be told what action had been taken to ensure that similar incidents would not be repeated for other patients. In particular, if the complaint was against an individual clinician or other employee of the Trust, no information would be given to the complainant as to what action, disciplinary or otherwise, had been taken against that individual.

It is the experience of all those involved in dealing with complaints on behalf of patients that few are motivated by feelings of revenge. It is widely recognised that one of the major considerations on the part of those complaining about care, particularly where that care led to considerable distress for the patient or their family, is to ensure that others do not have to suffer in the same way. In many complaints, therefore, failure to inform the complainant of what action had been taken remained a cause of great dissatisfaction and resulted in the complainant feeling that the complaint had been a waste of time.

It is recognised that this is not a straightforward issue as matters of employment law and, now, human rights are involved. Nevertheless the health care provider must provide the complainant with reassurance that appropriate action has been taken if the whole complaints procedure is not to be undermined.

As far as complaints against General Practitioners were concerned the problem was a different one. The actual procedure was far more open, with the patient able to confront the doctor and ask him or her questions before a tribunal. The basic flaw with that procedure, however, was that it was not a system aimed at dealing with dissatisfied patients but with the relationship between the doctor and the Family Health Services Authority as employee and employer. Patients were therefore misled into believing that their grievances were going to be addressed whereas in fact the enquiry was simply to establish whether there had been a breach of the doctor's terms of service.

Nevertheless there were major advantages to this procedure over that for hospital complaints. In the first place the tribunal included a number of lay people including a lay chair; secondly the proceedings were open, with the doctor subject to cross-examination – although not by lawyers as they were not allowed to represent either party – and often findings that a doctor had been in breach of terms of service did amount to a vindication of the patient's complaint. Most importantly, the patient had the opportunity of seeing the person whom they considered responsible for the problem, being required to account for his or her actions.

How much of the dissatisfaction with the old procedure was satisfactorily dealt with by the Wilson reforms? Under the 'Wilson' system, if patients are not satisfied with the result of Local Resolution they make a written request for an Independent Review. There is no automatic right to such a review. The decision as to whether a review should take place is taken by the convenor who is usually a non-executive director of the relevant Health Authority or Trust Board. If the convenor agrees, a review panel will be convened. Membership of the panel will comprise:

- an independent lay chair;
- the convenor;
- in the case of a Trust, a representative of the purchaser;
- in the case of a primary care complaint, for a health authority panel, another independent lay person.

The panel will, in the case of clinical complaints, be advised by at least two clinical assessors nominated by the regional office, from a list compiled on advice from relevant professional bodies.

The procedure adopted by the panel is decided by the chair on an ad hoc basis and there is no obligation to hold a hearing. Indeed the thrust of inquiries is to avoid a confrontation between the patient and those who might be the cause of the complaint.

It will be seen that from the patient's point of view they will be confronted by a panel that, apart from the chair, is not independent, comprising, and being advised by, representatives of the very discipline about which they are complaining. The problem of lack of independence was therefore, from the patient's point of view, not satisfactorily addressed; the patient is still left without the right to hear the evidence of the clinician or to test it, although it is common for the chair to agree to a hearing of sorts but no legal representation is allowed; there remains no right of appeal; and the patient will never be informed as to what action has been taken with regard to any practitioner who may have been found to have acted inappropriately.

A report published by the Public Law Project [6] following extensive research into the working of the new procedure concluded that:

> 'In the course of our analysis, certain key characteristics of panel hearings emerged which raised serious questions about their independence, fairness and ability to achieve satisfactory outcomes for complainants.'

4.2   The Health Service Commissioner (Ombudsman)

The role of the Ombudsman, too, has changed considerably. Until 1996 his remit extended only to complaints about administrative matters and did not include issues of clinical judgement. This often caused considerable frustration for both patients and the Ombudsman himself. The Ombudsman had built up an impressive reputation for objective and fair adjudication on complaints referred to him. Yet in the area in which the most distress was caused to patients, that of clinical complaints, he was not permitted to intervene. In latter years such was the frustration of the Ombudsman with this state of affairs, and the pressure of patients' representatives, that when the nature of a complaint, though relating to clinical issues included even a hint of administrative matters as well, he would often be prepared to consider it.

Now, following the Health Service Commissioner (Amendment) Act 1996, the Ombudsman is able to look at the whole of a complaint including clinical care. His remit is also extended to complaints about Family Health Services from which he was previously excluded. A particularly helpful aspect of his role is that if the convenor refuses or fails to set up an independent review the complainant can complain to the Ombudsman who can then require that a review be implemented.

There is major scope for the Ombudsman to perform a role that would come close to the truly independent and objective system that patients require. Unfortunately that role is not permitted. He does not investigate complaints unless they have exhausted the rest of the complaints procedure and then only if he, in his wisdom, considers that maladministration is involved. He is often seen as someone to whom an appeal lies in the case of dissatisfaction with the result of a complaint. Although application to the Ombudsman can sometimes have the effect of an appeal that is not his role. His role is still confined to ensuring that the process takes place in accordance with the rules and spirit of the procedure.

As a result only a tiny number of patients who remain dissatisfied with the results of the complaints procedure have their complaints further investigated. Furthermore his procedures are not regulated in any way and, whilst painstaking, they still rely on medical experts who do not necessarily have the trust of patients.

4.3   Complaints in the independent health care sector

Until recently, patients who were unhappy with any aspect of care within the independent sector had no recourse to any formal complaints procedure. They were left to take up their complaint with the hospital administration or the clinician direct. Furthermore, there was no support system available to them as the remit of the Community Health Councils did not extend to the independent sector.

The attitude of successive governments appeared to be that as they were not responsible for treatment outside the National Health Service, problems within that service were not their concern. This left patients with problems with no redress and often they were driven to litigate as the only way in which they could ensure that their complaint was taken seriously. The numerous problems that arose with independent care and a number of high profile disasters within that system led to an inquiry by the Health Select Committee. In its report in October 1999 the Committee stated, *inter alia* [7], 'We consider that it is vital that the NHS complaints procedure is made more open and transparent and that the system is seen to be fair and independent'.

At last, in 2000 the Independent Healthcare Association introduced a pilot complaints procedure for the sector. Although some consultation with interested parties had taken place before its introduction the procedure was not in a form acceptable to a number of patients' organisations. It remains to be seen whether, once the pilot comes to an end, the independent sector will be prepared to introduce and enforce a patient-friendly complaints procedure

4.4   Disciplinary issues

For patients, the most disappointing aspect of the whole system for complaining about a doctor has been the General Medical Council. Most people have little or no knowledge of the system for complaining about doctors generally and only learn about it when they come to have need of it. There is a vague awareness, however, that doctors are subject to some control and that if something goes wrong there is a body that will discipline the doctor.

What they discovered, when something did go wrong however, was that that body was reluctant to address their problem, confining itself only to what appeared to them to be the most arcane complaints; that it was extremely difficult to persuade it to investigate a complaint; that the procedures were complex, lengthy and did not involve the patient to any meaningful degree; and that the entire system was heavily weighed in favour of the doctor.

In recent years the GMC has taken major steps to try and address these problems:

- It has extended its remit so that it can deal not only with complaints involving serious professional misconduct but also with issues of poor performance. That has meant that it can at least consider a complaint by a patient that a doctor has treated him or her badly. If the complaint discloses a serious defect in the doctor's performance then the GMC will deal with it.
- It is far more prepared than in the past to investigate any complaint, not hiding behind difficult issues of definition.
- Patients are seen much more as part of the process and are given more support.
- By including many more lay people both on the Council and in the disciplinary process it appears less biased in favour of the doctor.

Nevertheless two facets of the GMC's procedures tend to leave patients suspicious of those procedures. Firstly, the GMC remains in the position of both prosecutor and judge. It is the GMC, through its Preliminary Proceedings Committee, that decides whether a complaint should go forward; it is then the GMC that collects the evidence and prosecutes the complaint against the doctor; and then it is the GMC through its Professional Conduct Committee that decides whether the complaint has been proved and what sanction, if any, should be imposed.

The second area of major dissatisfaction is the standard of proof that the GMC demands in order to uphold a complaint. It is not that which applies in all civil cases, but rather that applied in criminal cases. The case must be proved 'beyond reasonable doubt' which makes it extraordinarily difficult to prove complaints.

Both these issues are currently under review.

4.5   Help for complainants

Given the difficulties facing patients who wish to make a complaint of any kind, it would be helpful if there were some statutory body to whom they could turn for help. Unfortunately that is not the case. The only statutory bodies that do deal with complaints are, at the time of writing this chapter, the Community Health Councils. As they are the 'patients' watchdogs' many of them have taken on that role notwithstanding that it is not specifically included in their remit. That has meant, in the first place, that not all Councils do undertake this work, and secondly that there is great discrepancy in the skills and effectiveness of those Councils who are prepared to deal with complaints.

Nevertheless, as independent bodies committed to the welfare of patients, they have, notwithstanding limited resources and lack of statutory backing, been able to assist a large number of patients in achieving a just outcome to their complaint. There is some doubt as to whether this help will continue. The Government in its NHS Plan published in 2000 stated its intention to abolish Community Health Councils. In its place it plans to establish a Patient Liaison and Advocacy Service (PALS) situated within each Trust *inter alia* to assist patients with their complaints. Various other bodies were to be established to deal with the other tasks at present undertaken by the CHCs.

The proposals attracted a great deal of criticism. First and foremost the objection was to the lack of independence of the PALS. In addition it was argued that dealing with complaints was not something that could be isolated from CHCs' other work. Their vast knowledge of the operation of the Health Service in their area gave them the background to deal far more effectively with the complaint of an individual patient about the service that had been provided.

As a result of these criticisms the Government modified their proposals and insofar as complaints are concerned proposed an independent advocacy service where patients were unhappy with the assistance given by the PALS. In addition they agreed to set up Patients' Councils which would be responsible for that service. It remains to be seen whether any further modification to the government's plans will take place and whether these plans will give a better service to complainants than CHCs have been able to give.

4.6   Complaints and litigation

One of the major defects in the system for dealing with complaints is the fact that these are corralled into rigidly separate compartments. The Ombudsman will not deal with a complaint 'where the complainant can seek a remedy in the courts' unless 'he is satisfied that in the particular circumstances it is not reasonable to expect the complainant to resort to a legal remedy'.

On the other hand, if a patient makes a complaint but before the investigation is complete the patient 'explicitly indicates an intention to take legal action' (which is not necessarily the same as wanting to make a claim for compensation) the National Health Service Executive guidance says that the complaints process has to cease, particularly if the patient has requested an independent review [5]. Some health care providers interpret this requirement very narrowly – an approach from a solicitor, a request for medical records with a possible claim in mind, a brief reference to compensation or legal remedy in a letter – and the work on the complaint immediately stops.

But most patients only know, or suspect, something has gone wrong. They may want compensation but often that is not in the forefront of their minds and in any event it is only one part of what they are seeking. More commonly, and today this is generally recognised, what they seek is an opportunity to air their concerns; if appropriate, further treatment to resolve the medical problem; a full and open explanation of what has happened and why; and, if there has been a mistake or unacceptable service, an apology and assurances that lessons will be learned for the future. Compensation is often only an issue if the other remedies are not provided, or not quickly enough, or the damage suffered by the patient is very serious.

Most patients have no previous experience of making complaints or claims, and have little or no knowledge of the complaints or legal system, or of the cost, stress and difficulty of pursuing a legal claim in particular.

Many of those who seek advice from a solicitor only do so out of frustration at the NHS body's seeming inability to understand and try to resolve the problem. Yet the system obliges dissatisfied patients to choose, often artificially and too soon, which route to follow. Pushing patients into litigation which they do not really want makes very little sense from any perspective. But patients need incredible stamina to follow first the complaints procedure, and possibly all three stages of it, and then, if they want or need compensation, to go down the legal route.

Both the Health Service Commissioner and the Health Select Committee have strongly criticised the system. The former noted that 'when people did complain, it appeared they often became even more dissatisfied with the process and the outcome of the complaint and confused by a regulatory system which gave them a number of options for taking action' [8]. The Ombudsman has referred to patients' 'complaint fatigue' [9].

Best practice in the NHS has given a strong pointer as to how complaints should be handled. Enlightened claims managers will identify quickly what the patient is after and will not only ensure that the complaint is adequately and expeditiously dealt with but will also ensure that if she is entitled to a small amount of compensation, that this is paid. The provision that all claims or complaints managers adopt a similar course and that if the unresolved complaint proceeds to an independent review an award of limited compensation can be part of the remit of that review, would have a dramatic effect for patients and the health service providers alike. Patients would be satisfied that all their grievances had been dealt with within a reasonable time; both patients and clinicians involved would be spared the distress of protracted legal proceedings and the NHS itself would save the considerable costs of litigation.

4.6.1   A case study

The case of Mrs B clearly illustrates how the system fails patients. It also demonstrates how that failure results in unnecessary litigation.

Mrs B was expecting twins in 1994. The first baby was born with little difficulty. The second baby became stuck and after twenty minutes the registrar appeared to panic and an emergency Caesarean section was carried out. The baby suffered severe brain damage and died after the life support machine was switched off with the consent of the parents. The mother was full of praise for the treatment received at the hospital to which the baby had been transferred for specialist treatment. She wrote: 'The hospital staff at … were brilliant, so sensitive helping us through every step of the whole terrible business…'

Nevertheless the parents were not happy about the reasons for the death of their son. They carried out their own research and discovered that the medical records showed clearly that the CTG tracings had disclosed foetal distress and the delay in delivery. They visited the original hospital on a number of occasions and spoke to the various members of the obstetric team. All denied that there had been foetal distress and insisted that everything had been properly done. They were treated in a patronising manner and no allowance was made for the fact that they were grieving parents. Their last meeting was with a number of maternity staff and a consumers affairs manager when they met with the same 'brick wall'.

In November 1995 Mrs B contacted AVMA. After they had read the notes they referred her to a solicitor. She was advised by the solicitor that her case was one of the strongest he had seen. Mrs B said that 'the three years of her case were extremely stressful on many levels but at least we got some answers'. Three weeks before the trial the Trust offered a settlement which she was advised to accept.

Even after this settlement the parents wrote to the Trust 'pleading for a full explanation and admittance of errors'. The Chief Executive replied that because of the legal case he was not obliged to comment. Both parents are adamant that if the Trust had given them a full explanation and apology in the first place they would not have embarked on litigation.

4.7   The ethical aspect

As will have been seen, there have been many changes and not a few advances in the patient's situation with regard to complaints. We have seen that it is now recognised that a complaint can be dealt with as part of the care of a patient and as such the obligation to deal with it properly comes within the duty of care of all health care providers. There remains, however, a fundamental flaw in the approach by the health service when there is a breach in that duty. It should not be an issue of complaint, blaming someone, some institution or even a system. A complaint exposes a defect in care. That should be recognised by those providing the care when it happens, not when the patient draws attention to it. But if the health care provider has waited until the patient draws attention to it then that is how it should be seen and categorised – not as a complaint but as an issue of care to be dealt with.

One major advance in dealing with complaints along these lines would be for the body complained against to obtain an independent medical report. At present clinical advice is obtained internally. It is the experience of many representing patients that this advice often results in a false approach to the complaint. The issue may eventually be resolved, often by litigation, but after compounded distress to the patient, lengthy delays and unnecessary costs. If advice were to be sought from a clinician accepted as independent by the patient, that would be consistent with looking at the issue as one of care rather than complaint and would lead to far greater patient satisfaction whatever the outcome.

The Department of Health commissioned an evaluation of the whole complaints procedure. Following publication of the evaluation report the DoH published in September 2001 'a listening document' setting out a number of options for reform.[10] Responses were required by 12th October, and the Department will make its decision during 2002.

4.8   Notes and references

1. *Being Heard*, report of the Review Committee on NHS complaints procedures, chaired by Professor Alan Wilson. May 1994.
2. Report of an expert group on learning from adverse events in the NHS, chaired by the Chief Medical Officer. May 2000, p. 58 para. 4.33.
3. Pre-action Protocol for the Resolution of Clinical Disputes. Civil Procedure Rules Practice Direction.
4. *BMJ* Vol. 316, p. 1917.
5. *Guidance on implementation of the NHS Complaints Procedure*. NHS Executive March 1996.
6. *Cause for Complaint?* An evaluation of the effectiveness of the NHS complaints procedure paragraph 4.58 published by the Public Law Project.
7. Health Committee Session 1998–99 Sixth Report: *Procedures Related to Adverse Clinical Incidents and Outcomes in Medical Care*; para. 88.
8. Health Committee Report, para. 20.
9. In an address to the UKCC on 7th June 1999.
10. For the evaluation see www.doh.gov.uk/nhscomplaintsreform/evaluationreport
    For the listening document see www.doh.gov.uk/nhscomplaintsreform

Chapter 5

The Policy Dimension: the Legal Environment of the New NHS

John Tingle

As the previous chapters have indicated, the legal and health policy contexts of nursing have changed significantly since the first edition of this book was published in 1995. This chapter summarises and illustrates the ways in which these policy changes have impacted upon the legal environment of nursing care. The summary given here is a broad ranging one, although most emphasis is given to illustrating these processes through a discussion of the changing management of health litigation. At the end of the chapter some general trends in policy change are identified and pulled together.

The Woolf Civil Litigation Reforms and the Clinical Negligence Pre-Action Protocol, discussed in more detail later in this chapter, were early products of a national recognition that the ever present high levels of clinical negligence litigation could no longer be tolerated and had to be reduced and health care quality improved. Trusts, health bodies and the Government are now taking the issue of health litigation and avoiding patient injury much more seriously. Avoiding health litigation has become a national priority and quite rightly so. At the same time nurses are expanding their professional role and are doing more. This is all taking place within an increasingly litigious working environment. Hence a knowledge of the legal aspects of the health care environment has become very important as nurses try to understand their professional and legal accountabilities.

The well publicised case of Dr Shipman and the Bristol heart surgery revelations and subsequent inquiry have given the Government and the health care professions a forceful push in the direction of health care quality improvement, accountability and care management. And, as we saw in the opening chapter, the Human Rights Act 1998 is a relevant addition and a further springboard for change. Human rights has now become an essential part of the language and environment of nursing (and the importance of the Act to nursing practice will be discussed in a number of the following chapters).

Clinical risk and litigation management strategies have also been developed nationally, along with a number of other health quality initiatives, which have introduced a whole new set of 'buzz phrases' such as clinical governance, controls assurance, clinical risk management, patient empowerment, reflective practice, evidenced based healthcare and life long learning.

The overall result of these factors is a major impetus for change; this change is already proceeding at a fast rate and is gaining momentum.

5.1   The Government's health policy agenda

Concepts underpinning practice in nursing and health care come and go as times, and governments, change and as new opportunities and challenges arise. Nurses and others in the NHS now have a new health policy concept to understand, work with and to apply – patient empowerment. This concept sits alongside those mentioned above and, as we will see, it has important legal implications.

5.1.1   Patient empowerment

The concept of patient empowerment is built into the central government's new health service policy agenda, the NHS National Plan [1] and the Health and Social Care Act 2001. It can be regarded as the key NHS buzz phrase and has quickly become the main driver of change in today's NHS. The concept is essentially linked to health litigation and nursing law and ethics, and the agenda – of patient cent- redness – that it embodies is explored in other chapters of the book but can be summarised here: the NHS, according to the NHS National Plan, exists for the benefit of patients, and their interests are to be regarded as paramount. The patient is the recognised weaker party in the care equation but now moves to take centre stage.

Where health policy is being developed, for example in relation to clinical risk or litigation management, it can now be argued that in keeping with the spirit of the plan, patients' interests should weigh more heavily in the policy making process and in the balancing of competing interests. Also patients have under the Plan more formal mechanisms to make their voices heard in the NHS.

Initiatives have come into effect under the NHS Plan and the NHS Act to put the patient empowerment concept fully into place. For example, consent to treatment practices have been reviewed with a new *Reference Guide to Consent for Examina- tion or Treatment* produced by the Department of Health in June 2001. New Patient Forums are to be established in every NHS Trust and Primary Care Trust, to provide direct input from patients into how local NHS services are run. Further changes to the clinical negligence system are also mooted as a possibility in the NHS Plan. As the quality of health care rises, so do patient expectations. The NHS National Plan should help ensure that patients are alert to their rights and to the duties of nurses and others. This book hopefully sheds light on where these rights and duties lie in the context of the forever developing NHS and the law.

5.1.2   New organisations for new needs

A number of new organisations have been set up to achieve the Government's goals of NHS care quality improvement and litigation management; these are introduced in this chapter and some of them are further discussed in subsequent chapters. They are: NICE (National Institute of Clinical Excellence), CHI

(Commission for Health Improvement), NHSLA (National Health Service Litigation Authority), NPSA (National Patient Safety Agency). These organisations can all affect the care environment through their activities such as litigation case management, guideline creation and identifying and investigating bad care practices and adverse incident reporting.

5.2   Focus on health litigation

More patients are suing their health carers than ever before. The NAO (National Audit Office) in 2001 [2] noted an increase in clinical negligence litigation:

'The rate of new claims per thousand finished consultant episodes rose by 72 per cent between 1990 and 1998 ... The estimated net present value of outstanding claims at 31 March 2000 was £2.6 billion (up from £1.3 billion at 31 March 1997). In addition, there is an estimated liability of a further £1.3 billion where negligent episodes are likely to have occurred but where claims have not yet been received.'

In Finance Directorate Letter (FDL) (96) 39, the Department of Health clearly acknowledge a rise in clinical negligence litigation [3] as does the Lord Chancellor's Department [4]. The Department of Health estimated in 1996 that the total cost of NHS clinical negligence was likely to grow at nearly 25 per cent per annum for the next five years [5]. The cost of clinical negligence to the Department of Health in 1996–97 was £300 million [6].

It is now generally accepted by the Department of Health and by all those concerned with the provision of health services, that health litigation is on the increase and that strategies to deal with this identified trend need to be developed. The Clinical Disputes Forum [7] identify the problem and some corrective strategies:

'The number of complaints and claims against hospitals, GPs, dentists and private healthcare providers is growing as patients become more prepared to question the treatment they are given, to seek explanations of what happened, and to seek appropriate redress. Patients may require further treatment, an apology, assurances about future action, or compensation.'

Statistics on litigation claims are helpful but they can be distorted. Charles Lewis [8] argues that 'statistics for medical negligence litigation are constantly being distorted by those with an axe to grind'. The Lord Chancellor's Department produced a consultation paper on conditional fees [9] which contained some financial statistics on the cost of clinical negligence litigation to the tax payer:

'However, the Government does need to tackle the problem of the high number of cases that recover nothing or next to nothing. The net cost of medical negligence cases to the taxpayer last year was £27 million. Looking at the cases closed by the Legal Aid Board in 1996/97, 32 cases recovered £500,000 or more. Leaving these cases aside, the average cost of cases was £4,122 to recover average damages of £4,107. In only 17 per cent of cases was £50 or more recovered (and 1996/97 was a good year: closed case data from previous years shows recovery rates between 13 per cent and 17 per cent).

... The Government believes that part of the reasons for the high failure rate is that cases are being pursued by lawyers who are insufficiently experienced in this area of litigation.' (p.19)

The message coming from this statement is that most clinical negligence cases do not succeed and that inexperienced lawyers are bringing weak cases. Charles Lewis explains these figures, arguing [8]:

'... we can accept a success rate of about 17 per cent in respect of *all* legal aid certificates issued for proposed medical negligence claims. That is because most cases do not appear, upon investigation, to stand a good chance of success, and therefore the legal aid certificate is discharged upon the advice of the patient's lawyers, and no claim is commenced.'

Lewis argues that most medical negligence claims in which proceedings are actually commenced do succeed and that a distinction has to be made between proposed claims for which a legal aid certificate is granted and claims that are pursued beyond the stage of investigation.

The debate and positioning of the parties continues and different perceptions on the issues are apparent. Arising from the consultation paper [9] has been the notion of the experienced specialist health lawyer and that it is in the public's interest to ensure that claimants only have access to experienced clinical negligence legal practitioners.

5.2.1 Improving the quality of health lawyers

From 1 February 1999 clinical negligence legal aid franchises form the basis for exclusive provision of legal aid in this area. To apply for membership practitioners must be a member of either the Law Society or the AVMA (Action for Victims of Medical Accidents) panel. [10]. A quality threshold has therefore been created for legal advice to claimants who wish to be legally aided. A solicitor who wishes to practice in the clinical negligence field must now seek membership of one of the panels and satisfy their quality criteria. Clinical negligence is now seen by the Government and the Legal Aid Board (now replaced by the Legal Services Commission) as a highly specialised legal practice area.

The Government's view can be seen to be that the public interest needs safeguarding and that this can only be achieved by ensuring that only competent firms of solicitors practice in clinical negligence litigation. This action is designed to protect scarce public resources and to ensure public protection. A line between conflicting and competing interests has been drawn and the product is a more central form of control over professional legal practice. This type of legal advice quality control exercise has also been carried out in relation to the solicitors who advise NHS Trusts and Health Authorities by the Special Health Authority which manages NHS litigation, the National Health Service Litigation Authority (NHSLA).

5.2.2   The NHSLA

The NHSLA was set up under section 11 of the NHS Act 1977 and its principal task is to administer schemes set up under section 21 of the National Health Service and Community Care Act 1990, which have been mentioned above [11]. There are a number of schemes which are managed by the NHSLA to control clinical risk, personal injury, property, etc. The Clinical Negligence Scheme for Trusts (CNST) and the ELS (Existing Liability Scheme) are the two main schemes for our purposes. The CNST was introduced in 1995 as a voluntary scheme to limit the liability of member Trusts for clinical negligence claims where the incident occurred after March 1995. Trusts fund the scheme by paying the equivalent of premiums, and in return receive assistance with costs of cases above a certain amount – their 'excess'. The ELS covers all NHS bodies' liabilities for claims for incidents that occurred before April 1995, and is funded by the Department of Health. Up to 1 April 2000 it covered only those claims with a settlement value of over £10,000 [2]. A condition of entering the CNST scheme is that NHS Trusts have regard to principles of good clinical risk management [3]. Two other schemes managed by the NHSLA are the Liabilities to Third Parties Scheme and the Property Expenses Scheme [12].

The NHSLA in April 1998 appointed a panel of 18 defence solicitors to handle litigation claims brought against NHS bodies. Previously the NHSLA had to work with nearly 100 defence firms. The rationale for the reduction was to enable the NHSLA to manage defence litigation practices more effectively by having a smaller number of firms. Quality of advice and service was also a motivating factor. The NHSLA chief executive, Stephen Walker, has stated:

> 'In addition to volume, it must be said that the range of quality across those practices was also an issue' [13].

Quality of NHS advice provision and value for money can again be seen as the central issue. The NHSLA centralist perception of the quality of legal services that Trusts receive differs from that of NHS Trusts generally. A research report published by the Health Services Management Centre at the University of Birmingham reveals that, when asked directly about the quality of clinical negligence legal services they receive from their legal advisers, most NHS Trusts think they get a good service. The authors of the report [14], however, argue that Trusts are not particularly well equipped to judge the quality of advice they receive. The report overall found the actual standards of service to be very variable. Solicitors could make improvements in their standards of communication, consultation and reporting requirements to NHS Trusts.

The NHSLA stated in its 1999 Report and Accounts [15] that it was optimistic that it is moving in the right direction in respect of CNST clinical negligence claims and its panel of approved solicitors:

> 'Direct instruction of solicitors through the medium of the panel has begun to suggest that it will prove very successful . . . The panel understands that its role is to support the NHS in the round; not to litigate for the sake of litigation.'

5.2.3 Centralist control

The freedom and autonomy of NHS bodies to select their legal advisors has been seriously restricted. The firms of solicitors who were not selected to the panel and who previously had a large amount of health authority work will have to reassign staff and no doubt will have suffered financially. The firms who are on the panel will wish to stay there and know that their practices will be scrutinised by the NHSLA. Loss of panel membership for them will have dire financial consequences.

The balance of power in defending NHS bodies has changed. Defendant solicitor firms are accountable to the NHSLA and the NHSLA is in a very powerful position to impose agendas. These agendas can be directed by the NHS Executive, or may come from within the NHSLA management structure itself.

A clear recent trend of centralist control of clinical negligence legal advice services is emerging. The Government and the NHSLA have intervened in who can act for the parties in a clinical negligence litigation dispute. Those seeking legal advice have to approach approved firms of solicitors. In the case of defendant solicitors, they must be acceptable to the NHSLA as well as the Trust they advise. There is no free market for the provision of legal services to NHS bodies and claimants. Solicitor firms are subject to new pressures which vary according to whether they act for defendants or claimants. On balance those who act for claimants appear to have more control of their professional practices once they qualify for panel membership as they are not managed by the NHSLA and do not have that element of direct accountability. The trend of centralisation and to some extent, standardisation, of the conduct of clinical negligence litigation is perhaps best illustrated by the Clinical Negligence Pre-Action Protocol.

5.2.4 The Clinical Negligence Pre-Action Protocol

The Clinical Negligence Pre-Action Protocol arose from a review of civil litigation by Lord Woolf [16] and subsequently the work of the Clinical Disputes Forum (CDF), a multi-disciplinary group formed in 1997 as a result of the Woolf Civil Justice Inquiry. The Protocol [7] is now part of a Practice Direction which accompanies the Civil Procedure Rules. Parties to a clinical negligence dispute will be penalised by sanctions, including cost penalties, if they do not follow the protocol. The protocol covers two central areas – commitments and steps.

The commitments section gives guiding principles which health care providers, patients and their advisers are invited to subscribe to when dealing with patient dissatisfaction with treatment, and with complaints and potential claims. The steps section sets out in a prescriptive form a recommended action sequence to be followed if litigation is a prospect [7]. Issues covered include patients reporting any concerns and dissatisfactions to the health care provider as soon as is reasonably possible. Health care providers should ensure that key staff, including claims and litigation managers, are appropriately trained and have some knowledge of health care law, complaints procedures and civil litigation practices and procedures. Health service provider response times to key events such as record requests are stated.

The emotion aspect of the Protocol

The Protocol was a product of consensus opinion of all the main interested parties in clinical negligence litigation. Its implementation should result in a more caring and efficient handling of clinical negligence cases and complaints.

What is clearly apparent from reading the Protocol is the extent to which regard has been had to the emotional aspects of clinical negligence litigation: how clinicians and patients can *feel* about the litigation process has been taken into account in the Protocol. The good practice commitments address many of the concerns Lord Woolf raised in his final report [16]. Legal education for health carers, patient communication strategies and reflective clinical practice are all discussed. So often in legal procedures, the 'how parties feel' aspect of proceedings appears to have been neglected. The adversarial nature of our procedures and legal system has resulted in a combative and competitive approach to litigation. The Woolf Report [16] and subsequently the Clinical Disputes Forum seem to have paused and taken a step back and have taken into account the emotional aspect of clinical negligence proceedings.

The Woolf reform themes

Lord Woolf [16] set the focus and theme for the procedural reforms in clinical negligence litigation when he gave his reasons for looking at medical negligence:

'The answer is that early in the Inquiry it became increasingly obvious that it was in the area of medical negligence that the civil justice system was failing most conspicuously to meet the needs of litigants in a number of respects.
(a) The disproportion between costs and damages in medical negligence is particularly excessive, especially in lower value cases.
(b) The delay in resolving claims is more often unacceptable.
(c) Unmeritorious cases are often pursued, and clear-cut claims defended, for too long.
(d) The success rate is lower than in other personal injury litigation.
(e) The suspicion between the parties is more intense and the lack of co-operation frequently greater than in many other areas of litigation.'

Factor (e) is particularly noteworthy because it singles out clinical negligence litigation from other areas and draws attention to its special emotive nature. Lord Woolf further considered this aspect and responded to it in his report when he called for a change of culture in clinical negligence litigation. He noted the mistrust that can sometimes exists between the parties and stated:

'If that mistrust is to be removed, the medical profession and the NHS administration must demonstrate their commitment to patient's well-being by adopting a constructive approach to claim handling.
It must be clearly accepted that injured patients are entitled to redress, and that professional solidarity or individual self-esteem are not sufficient reasons for resisting or obstructing valid claims.'

Lord Woolf also considered the doctors' perspective on clinical litigation:

'... The fear of litigation among so many doctors is often based on ignorance of the legal system. I have heard, for example, of doctors who are unclear about the difference between civil and criminal proceedings, and afraid they might be sent to prison if they were "found guilty" of medical negligence.'

He also made a call for more legal education for doctors to help demystify the legal process.

The Clinical Negligence Pre-Action Protocol combines Lord Woolf's sentiments as expressed in his report. The Protocol, however, represents another centralist shift in health litigation management. The parties to a clinical negligence claim are subject to the Protocol and it represents another layer of control. Control and regulation must by definition reduce the exercise of professional discretion and creativity. The exercise of discretion and creativity are the hallmarks of a professional role; in this instance that of the lawyers who advise the patient and the health body.

The ideas behind the Protocol are very laudable. Everybody can agree that saving money and time by avoiding unnecessary litigation is a good idea. The NHSLA state the aims as being [17, 18]:

'Savings in costs, both Plaintiff's costs and the Trust's own costs;
Disposal of unsubstantiated claims at an earlier stage;
Improved risk management and encouragement of good practice;
Improved claims handling standards pre-litigation;
Plaintiffs with meritorious claims will be compensated earlier.'

Again a balance had to be struck, and has been struck, between professional legal practice autonomy and the perceived public interest.

Is the Protocol working?

There is no detailed empirical research yet on the success of the Woolf reforms in the clinical negligence area. The Law Society [19] produced the first survey on the impact of the changes with a small survey of 30 solicitors throughout England and Wales, who are co-ordinating feedback on the civil justice changes to the Law Society. The report reveals that the respondents felt that despite the fact that it was early on in the changes the Civil Procedure Rules seemed to be working quite well. Respondents were asked to comment on the personal injury and clinical negligence pre-action protocols:

'The vast majority of respondents believe that the pre-action protocols are working either very well or quite well. Again, however, it was thought by some too early to tell, not least as some solicitors have stopped issuing at present. Some insurance companies are apparently demonstrating a reluctance to follow the Protocols.'

Research also needs to be done on NHS Trust managers' perceptions of the Protocol in order to achieve a balanced view. The Law Society's small respondent cohort makes conclusions difficult to draw; a much larger and professionally diverse sample needs to be taken.

5.3   Law and health policy: changing the balance of power

In short a new balance between professional legal practice autonomy and the perceived public interest can be seen to have been drawn in the delivery of health care legal services. This has been achieved by a new emphasis on centralisation. Similarly doctors, nurses and other health carers are also facing centralist pressures that are impacting on their own professional practice. As we have seen, the concept of a quality driven, patient centered NHS firmly underpins this Labour Government's NHS policy, and the NHS Plan [1].

In order to understand how the legal environment of nursing care operates, it is important to have some understanding of the policy concepts and initiatives that are driving changes in clinical practice in the NHS. These changes have an impact on legal practices and they must all be considered together in order to see the full picture. The NHS White Paper [20] which set out the Government's programme for a ten year modernisation programme of the NHS stated six guiding principles which included:

> '... Patients will get fair access to consistently high quality, prompt and accessible services right across the country
> ... to shift the focus onto quality of care so that EXCELLENCE is guaranteed to all patients, and quality becomes the driving force for decision-making at every level of the service ...
> ... to rebuild PUBLIC CONFIDENCE in the NHS as a public service, accountable to patients, open to the public and shaped by their views.' (p. 11)

More details on the reform framework followed the publication of a consultation document, *A First Class Service: Quality in the New NHS* which set out the main elements of the Government's health quality reform programme [21].The main elements are:

> 'Clear national standards for services and treatments, through National Service Frameworks;
> The creation of a new National Institute for Clinical Excellence;
> Local delivery of high quality health care, through clinical governance under-pinned by modernised professional self-regulation;
> Extended lifelong learning;
> Effective monitoring of progress through a new Commission for Health Improvement, NHS Performance Assessment Framework and a new national survey of patient and user experience.'

The NHS National Plan [1], discussed above, and subsequently the Health and Social Care Act 2001, take these issues further and focus on the empowerment of the patient and improving health quality.

5.3.1   The reforms: CHI and NICE

Key health reforms are now enacted in the Health Act 1999. Section 18 places a new duty of quality on NHS Trusts, Primary Care Trusts and Health Authorities in addition to their common law duty of care. Section 18 (1) provides that it is the duty of each Health Authority, Primary Care Trust and NHS Trust to put and keep in place arrangements for the purpose of monitoring and improving the quality of health care which it provides to individuals.

Section 19 and Schedule 2 create a new Commission for Health Improvement (CHI) with functions stated in section 20 (1):

'(a) the function of providing advice or information with respect to arrange-ments by Primary Care Trusts or NHS trusts for the purpose of monitoring and improving the quality of health care for which they have responsibility.

(b) the function of conducting reviews of, and making reports on, arrangements by Primary Care Trusts or NHS trusts for the purpose of monitoring and improving the quality of health care for which they have responsibility.

(c) the function of carrying out investigations into, and making reports on, the management, provision or quality of health care for which Health Authorities, Primary Care Trusts or NHS trusts have responsibility.

(d) the function of conducting reviews of, and making reports on, the man-agement, provision or quality of, or access to or availability of, particular types of health care for which NHS bodies or service providers have responsibility.'

CHI operates with another NHS body, The National Institute for Clinical Excel-lence (NICE), which has been established as a Special Health Authority, (National Institute for Clinical Excellence (Establishment and Constitution) Order 1999, SI 1999/220).

NICE's role [22] is to establish a coherent programme of activity to develop guidance on clinical and cost effectiveness. NICE helps ensure uniformly high care standards across the NHS. Clinical guidelines are issued on individual treatments, products and clinical interventions. Lifestyle advice is also to be given. Guidance is appraised and disseminated.

CHI looks at how the NICE guidance is being implemented across the NHS and it has used its powers to review, investigate and report on these matters, high-lighting failures. NHS health bodies have to establish arrangements which show how these initiatives are being implemented. NICE, to date, has been very active and a number of national guidelines have been issued.

CHI and NICE are central features of the Government's health improvement and monitoring programme along with the concepts discussed earlier, clinical governance, controls assurance, clinical risk management, patient empowerment, etc. They are also central to the efficient execution of the NHS National Plan. Some of these terms will be discussed further in later chapters.

5.3.2   Clinical governance, controls assurance and risk management

Clinical governance provides a framework, 'within which local organisations can work to improve and assure the quality of clinical services for patients' [23]. It is:

'A framework through which NHS organisations are accountable for continuously improving the quality of their services and safeguarding high standards of care by creating an environment in which excellence in clinical care will flourish.'

Clinical governance is underpinned by the statutory duty contained in section 18 and includes the following components which health bodies must ensure they satisfy:

- clear lines of responsibility and accountability for the overall quality of care;
- a comprehensive programme of quality improvement activities;
- clear policies aimed at managing risk;
- procedures for all professional groups to identify and remedy poor performance [23].

The NHS controls assurance project operates alongside the clinical governance initiative and is more directed at ensuring that organisational controls are in place to ensure proper management. It is defined as:

'. . . a holistic concept based on best governance practice. It is a process designed to provide evidence that NHS organisations are doing their "reasonable best" to manage themselves so as to meet their objectives and protect patients, staff, the public and other stakeholders against risks of all kinds.' [24]

Risk management is seen as the 'common thread' linking controls assurance and clinical governance [24].

5.4   The cumulative effect of the reforms

The cumulative effect of all these initiatives should be to bring more effective control of the management of untoward incidents in the NHS. Health lawyers for claimants and defendants will need to be aware of the claims reporting, complaint systems and the general quality controls environment that exists in order to effectively manage the presentation of their case. Effective legal disclosure will be dependent on lawyers' knowledge of these systems. Clinicians' professional practice will be subject to these systems from reporting procedures of incidents to the adoption of set clinical practice guidelines. Already there are defined standards which must be met under the Clinical Negligence Scheme for Trusts (CNST) and these have been revised [25].

'Standard 1: Clinical Risk Management – Strategy and Organisation. The board has a written strategy in place that makes their commitment to managing risk explicit. Responsibility for this strategy and its implementation is clear.'

The centrally orchestrated initiatives of clinical governance, controls assurance, clinical risk management and patient empowerment, and CHI and NICE, will directly influence the practice of nurses and others. Professional discretion can be seen to be compromised but this is being done for the laudable public interest motives of quality and accountability.

The centre, in terms of the Department of Health and its component bodies, NHS Executive, NICE, CHI, NHSLA and the (to be formed) NPSA, will have increasing practical control over the delivery of health care services and over the management and resolution of disputes. The concept of patient empowerment will be seen to dominate health quality and other NHS initiatives for some considerable time to come. In the care equation, when interests are being balanced, patients' should be paramount. We will all have to see whether this actually works out in the reality of the new NHS. The chapters in the second part of this book – which focus on more specific themes in law and nursing care – will provide further illustration of what the changes in the policy climate, reviewed in this chapter, will entail in practice.

5.5   Notes and references

1. *The NHS Plan: A Plan for Investment: A Plan for Reform*, Cmnd. 4818. July 2000. The Stationery Office, London, see http://www.doh.gov/uk/nhsplan/nhsplan.htm
2. National Audit Office. Handling clinical negligence claims in England, HC403 Session 2000–2001, 3 May 2001, www.nao.gov.uk
3. Clinical Negligence Costs, FDL (96) 39, October 1996. NHS Executive, Department of Health, Leeds.
4. *Access to Justice with Conditional Fees:* A Consultation Paper. Lord Chancellor's Department, March 1998, London.
5. Clinical Negligence and Personal Injury Litigation: Claims Handling. EL (Executive Letter) (96) 11, 1 April 1996. NHS Executive Leeds.
6. House of Commons, Hansard Debates for 24 March 1998, (Pt.2) Column 165, Dr Tony Wright, Ms Tessa Jowell.
7. Civil Procedure Pre-Action Protocol, Clinical Negligence. Lord Chancellor's Department, 1999, London.
8. Charles Lewis, 'Claims for medical compensation', *The Times*, 18 June 1999.
9. *Access to Justice with Conditional Fees:* A Consultation Paper, March 1998. Lord Chancellor's Department, London.
10. Do you deal with clinical negligence cases? *Focus Issue*, 25 December 1998. Legal Aid Board, London.
11. The National Health Service Litigation Authority (NHSLA) framework document, 96, FP0046, September 1996. NHS Executive, London.
12. 'NHSLA launches non-clinical risk schemes for NHS Trusts.' *NHSLA Review*, Issue 15, p. 1, 1999. NHSLA London.
13. Stephen Walker (1998) Litigation Authority announces panel of approved legal firms. *CNST Review*, Issue 12, Spring, p. 1. CNST, Bristol.
14. Maria Dineen & Kieran Walshe (1999) Clinical Negligence Litigation and the NHS: An Evaluation of the Nature and Quality of Legal Advice and Support on Clinical Negligence to NHS Trusts in England. Project Report 7, Health Services Management Unit, University of Birmingham.
15. The National Health Service Litigation Authority Report and Accounts 1999. NHSLA, London.
16. Access to Justice: Final Report by Lord Woolf, Master of the Rolls, July 1996. The Stationery Office, London.
17. HSC (1998) 183, Handling Clinical Negligence Claims, 16 October, 1998, NHS Executive, Leeds.
18. NHSLA Circular 99/C1, The Woolf Report, 11 February 1999.
19. Responses to Woolf Network Questionnaire, No.1. The Law Society, London, September 1999.
20. The New NHS, Modern, Dependable, Cmnd. 3807. December 1997. The Stationery Office, London.

21. A First Class Service: Quality in the New NHS. June 1998. Department of Health, London.
22. Faster Access to Modern Treatment: How NICE Appraisal Will Work: A Discussion Paper. February 1999. NHS Executive, Leeds.
23. Clinical Governance: Quality in the New NHS, HSC(1999)065, 16 March. NHS Executive, Leeds.
24. Governance in the New NHS, Controls Assurance Statements, 1999/2000: Risk Management and Organisational Controls, HSC (1999)123, 21 May 1999. NHS Executive, Leeds.
25. CNST Risk Management Standards, June 2000, NHSLA, London, CNST Bristol, at http://tap.ccta.gov.uk/doh/rm5.nsf/AdminDocs/CNSTReview?OpenDocument

Part Two

The Perspectives

Chapter 6
Negligence
A   The Legal Perspective

Charles Foster

Lawyers use the word 'negligence', confusingly, in two ways. First, they use it to describe a particular type of fault – a fault whose characteristics are defined by a number of legal decisions. Negligence in this respect can be either criminal (leading to prosecution) or civil (leading to an action in the civil courts for money). And second, they use it to describe that which must be proved in order for a claimant to succeed in recovering money ('damages') in respect of damage which is caused by that fault. When used in this second sense, they are referring to the tort of negligence. A tort is simply a legal wrong which does not involve a breach of contract.

This chapter is concerned mostly with the tort of negligence. But criminal negligence is important too. Medical manslaughter features commonly in the newspapers. When a doctor is charged with killing a patient accidentally, he will be convicted by the Crown Court of manslaughter if the jury finds that he has been grossly negligent – so negligent that his action or inaction deserves the penalty of criminal conviction [1]. This definition of gross negligence is of course circular: it comes down to saying someone should be convicted if he should be convicted. Precisely the same principles apply to the liability of a nurse for manslaughter, but as yet there are no reported English cases in which a nurse has been successfully prosecuted for manslaughter arising out of a breach of her professional duty to a patient.

The vast majority of medico-legal cases concern the civil law of negligence. They are tried in the County Court or the High Court (depending on their value and/or their complexity) by a judge sitting alone, without a jury. Only a tiny proportion will ever get to court. Most are settled or abandoned long before trial. Of those which do get to trial, most are decided in the defendant's favour. Clinical negligence cases are notoriously difficult for claimants to win. Some of the reasons for this will appear in this chapter.

It is very rare for nurses to be sued individually. If a nurse has been negligent, generally the employing Health Authority, NHS Trust, private hospital or clinic will be sued. This is a consequence of the doctrine of vicarious liability, which states that employers are liable for the torts of their employees when the act or omission which constitutes the tort occurred in the course of the employment. This doctrine does not absolve the employee from responsibility: the claimant can sue the employee instead of or as well as the employer, but generally it would be foolish for a claimant to do so when the claimant knows that the issues in the action against the employer will be identical to those in the action against the employee, and that the employer will certainly be able to pay damages, whereas the employee may well not be able to.

Where an employee has been negligent, and the employer is successfully sued in relation to that negligence, the employer can sue the employee for an indemnity (*Lister* v. *Romford Ice and Cold Storage Co Ltd* (1956) but in practice this is almost unheard of in nursing cases. With the rapid expansion of private medicine, however, it may become a contractual requirement of employment at a private hospital that the nurse has a policy of professional indemnity insurance which could pay an indemnity in the event of the hospital's liability. That fact, rather than any change in the substantive law of negligence, is likely in the future to lead to more actions against individual nurses.

6.1   The elements of the tort of negligence

To succeed in an action for clinical negligence, a claimant must show:

(1)   That the defendant owed the claimant a duty of care (i.e. a duty to do something which should have been done, or a duty not to do something which has been done); *and*
(2)   That the defendant has breached the duty; *and*
(3)   That the breach of duty has caused some injury, loss or damage to the claimant of a type which the law acknowledges.

6.2   The existence of a duty of care

A duty of care between a claimant and a defendant will exist if the following three criteria are satisfied (*Caparo Industries plc* v. *Dickman* (1990)):

(1)   The relevant damage was foreseeable; *and*
(2)   The relationship between the claimant and the defendant is sufficiently 'proximate'; *and*
(3)   It is 'fair, just and reasonable' to impose such a duty.

Foreseeability of damage is rarely an issue in clinical negligence cases, but the proximity of the relationship between the claimant and the defendant often is. The courts have been reluctant, in cases involving doctors, to say that the necessary proximity exists beyond the confines of the ordinary doctor–patient relationship, and have defined that relationship fairly narrowly. A good example is *Kapfunde* v. *Abbey National* (1998). Here the claimant applied for a job with the first defendant. The first defendant employed a doctor, the second defendant, to take a medical view of applicants, based on completed medical questionnaires. The second defendant told the first defendant that the claimant was, because of her history of sickle cell anaemia, likely to have unusually long absences from work. The court held that there was no doctor–patient relationship between the claimant and the second defendant, and that accordingly no duty of care existed.

Another example is *Goodwill* v. *BPAS* (1996), in which the defendant performed a vasectomy on his patient, and then advised him that he was sterile. Three years later the patient met the claimant, and he told her that he was sterile. They had unprotected sexual intercourse, and the claimant became pregnant. She sued the defendant for the cost of upkeep of the child [2]. The court held that the action must fail. There was no sufficiently proximate relationship between the relevant doctor and the claimant because the doctor could not know that his advice would be passed onto and relied on by the claimant.

A number of the cases on proximity were decided alternatively on the grounds of 'just, fair and reasonable'. It may now be that the question 'is it just, fair and reasonable to impose a duty?' should be expanded to read: 'Is it just, fair and reasonable to impose a duty to pay damages as big as those claimed?', and that in order for damages to be recoverable, there has to be reasonable proportion between the damages claimed and the duty assumed.

6.3   Breach of duty

6.3.1   The general principles

A clinical professional will have discharged his duty to the patient if what that professional has done would be endorsed by a responsible body of practitioners in the relevant specialty at the material time. This is the famous and ubiquitous *Bolam* test [4].

The *Bolam* test is a rule not only of substantive law (defining what amounts to adequate care), but also a rule of evidence (indicating how a court determines whether adequate care has been given). Thus in *Maynard* v. *West Midlands RHA* (1985) Lord Scarman said:

> '... a judge's "preference" for one body of distinguished professional opinion to another also professionally distinguished is not sufficient to establish negligence in a practitioner whose actions have received the approval of those whose opinions, truthfully expressed, honestly held, were not preferred... In the realm of diagnosis and treatment, negligence is not established by preferring one respectable body of professional opinion to another.' (p. 639)

In the past the *Bolam* test has been caricatured as asserting that a professional escapes liability if he can get someone who at some stage has qualified in the relevant specialty and avoided utter professional disgrace to stagger into the witness box and say that he or some of his (unspecified) friends would have acted as the defendant did. This was never the case in theory, although it may, in some more outlandish county courts, have worked like that.

That caricature was laid finally to rest in a case before the House of Lords called *Bolitho* v. *City & Hackney Health Authority* (1997). *Bolitho* underlined the word 'responsible' in the *Bolam* test. The central passage reads:

'. . . in cases of diagnosis and treatment there are cases where, despite a body of professional opinion sanctioning the defendant's conduct, the defendant can properly be held liable for negligence. . . In my judgment that is because, in some cases, it cannot be demonstrated to the judge's satisfaction that the body of opinion relied upon is reasonable or responsible. In the vast majority of cases the fact that distinguished experts in the field are of a particular opinion will demonstrate the reasonableness of that opinion. In particular, where there are questions of assessment of the relative risks and benefits of adopting a particular medical practice, a reasonable view necessarily presupposes that the relative risks and benefits have been weighed by the experts in forming their opinions. But if, in a rare case, it can be demonstrated that the professional opinion is not capable of withstanding logical analysis, the judge is entitled to hold that the body of opinion is not reasonable or responsible. I emphasise that in my view it will very seldom be right for a judge to reach the conclusion that views genuinely held by a competent medical expert are unreasonable. The assessment of medical risks and benefits is a matter of clinical judgement which a judge would not normally be able to make without expert evidence. . . it would be wrong to allow such assessment to deteriorate into seeking to persuade the judge to prefer one of two views both of which are capable of being logically supported. It is only where a judge can be satisfied that the body of expert opinion cannot be logically supported at all that such opinion will not provide the bench mark by reference to which the defendant's conduct falls to be assessed. . .' (p. 243)

Bolitho said nothing new, but caused a lot of unnecessary hysteria [5]. It was dubbed 'a claimant's charter'. It was feared that it would encourage medically illiterate judges to substitute their own uninformed views of what was medically reasonable for the views of distinguished practitioners. It is unlikely, as the cited passage clearly states, to have that effect in many cases. But it will have the effect of making experts look more critically at the practices they are defending. It will not lead to a proliferation of litigation, but it might lead to a proliferation of footnotes in expert reports.

The requirement that practice, to be defensible, has to be 'responsible', begs the question of whether, in a clinical world increasingly dominated by evidence based medicine, a practice which the literature clearly shows leads to statistically worse results than another economically comparable practice, can sensibly be said to be 'responsible'. It is likely to be found irresponsible not to adopt an evidence based approach, and irresponsible not to adopt an intelligent strategy in deciding which evidence based approach to use. It may be that the clinical negligence cases of the future will be battles between statisticians, with the issue to be decided by the judge being whether the published results which are said to justify a particular clinical approach really do justify it.

The standard which the law expects of practitioners is the standard which is appropriate to a person undertaking the relevant task. Thus a nurse undertaking the work which normally (and appropriately) a senior house officer would do undertakes to do it as well as a senior house officer would [6] and cannot complain if she is judged by that standard [7].

The standard of care expected is decided by reference to the post occupied by the person giving the care, rather than to the rank or status of that person or to the individual characteristics or training of that person. Thus, for instance, where the performance of work of a type which is reasonably done by staff nurses is criticised, the question of whether the work has been done negligently will be answered by reference to the standard expected of responsible staff nurses, not by reference to the standard which might normally be expected of that particular staff nurse with her particular experience [8].

Liability for negligent prescribing by nurses is likely to be approached by the courts, at least for the next few years, by reference to the standard of prescribing expected of those doctors who originally performed the task which the nurse has taken on. Public policy considerations make it inconceivable that nurses will have less expected of them.

There is a legal duty to keep reasonably up to date [9], but the courts do not expect practitioners to read every relevant article which appears in the professional press [10]. Of course the duty to keep up to date includes a duty to know about guidelines affecting the profession: it is far less excusable not to know of a relevant NICE guideline than it is not to have read an editorial in an immensely obscure specialist journal.

It is clear that one does not decide that a particular practice is or is not responsible by counting the numbers of practitioners who do or do not do it. This principle is important in cases involving super-specialists doing pioneering work (*De Freitas* v. *O'Brien* (1995)).

6.3.2   Obtaining properly informed consent

In the past the *Bolam* test has been held to apply to the issue of obtaining consent from patients. Thus a clinician would not be negligent if what he had told a patient about a procedure would be what a responsible body of practitioners in the relevant specialty would have told that patient (*Sidaway* v. *Board of Governors of the Bethlem Hospital and the Maudsley Hospital* (1985)).

This extension of *Bolam* to the realm of consent has recently been doubted by some commentators, although the *Sidaway* case which asserted it (a House of Lords case), has certainly not been overruled. The doubts arise from an off-the-cuff comment in *Bolitho* to the effect that the remarks there about the *Bolam* principle were made in the context of '... cases of diagnosis and treatment' [11], not in the context of consent to treatment. In inserting this caveat the House of Lords might have had in mind the Senate of Surgery's document *The surgeon's duty of care* [12], which has subsequently been extended to all registered medical practitioners by the GMC's guidelines: *Seeking patients' consent: the ethical considerations* [13]. The details of these guidelines do not matter for present purposes. It is enough to say that they state categorically how consent must be obtained. If the ruling body of medical practitioners states that particular procedures must be followed, can it seriously be argued that there is a responsible body of medical practitioners which would not follow those procedures? The point is a moot one: it has yet to be tested in the courts.

The relevant guidelines on consent for nurses are in the UKCC's 1996 publication *Guidelines for Professional Practice*. They are much more sensible and general, and far less prescriptive than those imposed by the Senate of Surgery and the GMC, and nurses are unlikely to find that these guidelines deprive them of their *Sidaway* shield (*Sidaway* is discussed in Chapter 7). The relevant sections, clauses 27 and 28, say:

'... it is important that you give the information in a sensitive and understandable way and that you give the patient or client enough time to consider it and ask questions if they wish. It is not safe to assume that the patient or client has enough knowledge, even about basic treatment, for them to make an informed choice without any explanation... It is essential that you give the patient or client adequate information so that he or she can make a meaningful decision...'

6.3.3   The relevance of protocols to civil liability

The points above about guidelines raise the general question, important to nurse practitioners, of the relevance of protocols to issues of breach of duty. Clinicians from all medical and nursing specialities worry about protocols because they think that failure to follow them will necessarily connote negligence. In legal theory, of course, this is nonsense: *Bolam* does not cease to apply simply because a protocol has been drafted.

In the context of nurses failing to follow protocols, two situations have to be distinguished. The first is where a nurse has carelessly failed to do what the protocol says. An example might be failure to give the prescribed regime of post-operative antibiotics because of forgetfulness or ignorance of the regime. Here, *Bolam* will not protect, because *Bolam* never applied: there is no responsible body of nursing opinion which forgets or is ignorant of protocols. The second situation is where a nurse has failed to do what a protocol says because she exercised her own independent clinical judgement and decided to do something other than what the protocol says. Here, *Bolam* would excuse the nurse if there were a responsible body of nursing opinion which would, in the relevant circumstances, have acted in the way that the nurse did.

As a general rule, adherence to local or national protocols is likely to protect, because the courts are likely to find that those protocols represent responsible practice (if not embodying the only responsible practice) [14]. Departure from local protocols may be *Bolam*-justifiable if the departure was made in the exercise of clinical judgement for responsible clinical reasons. Departure from national protocols, such as those imposed by NICE, may create problems, even if the departure is endorsed by other members of the same profession, because the courts will tend to think that nationally endorsed protocols definitively circumscribe acceptable practice.

Note that *Bolitho*'s endorsement of the propriety of looking at the reasoning which leads to clinical decisions is likely to bring greater judicial readiness to look at the research and consultation which led to the formulation of the relevant guidelines. It is therefore important that the formulation process is well documented.

6.4   Causation

6.4.1   The conventional rule

The claimant has to show that but for the defendant's negligence he would probably have avoided the injury and loss claimed. Thus lawyers often talk about the '51% test' or 'proof on the balance of probabilities'. In the context of causation they simply mean that the claimant will succeed if he shows that it is more likely than not that the defendant's default caused the injury/loss.

Causation is an essential element of the tort of negligence. Beware of confusing questions about whether causation has been established with questions about how much the judgment should be for.

6.4.2   Loss of a chance

It is often asserted that damages for loss of a chance are not recoverable in the English law of tort. This is untrue. In some commercial fields such damages are regularly recovered [15]. But whether they can be or should be recoverable in clinical negligence cases is contentious. The authority generally cited for the proposition that such damages are not recoverable in tort is *Hotson* v. *East Berkshire Health Authority* (1987). But *Hotson* says nothing of the sort. The Court of Appeal in *Hotson* decided that loss of a chance was damage which the law recognised, and that accordingly to prove that one had lost a chance was to prove causation. The Court of Appeal was anxious to avoid treating claimants who sued in tort and in contract differently. Damages are uncontroversially recoverable for loss of a chance in contract [16]. Why, the Court of Appeal said, should an NHS patient who is deprived by a doctor's negligence of a chance of recovery, be unable to recover damages, whereas the same patient, treated identically but privately (and therefore under a contract) by the same doctor, be successful? The court said that such an anomaly would be monstrous. The House of Lords never decided the question of recoverability of damages for loss of a chance: it merely decided that on the facts of that case it did not need to decide. The question is still open.

Opponents of the extension to clinical negligence litigation of damages for loss of a chance either rest their arguments on simple policy, or try to assert that in the commercial field damages for lost chances are awarded when what has been lost is the chance of obtaining a benefit rather than avoiding a detriment. This latter assertion is difficult to sustain. Any half competent barrister can convincingly frame the injury or loss in a clinical negligence claim as a lost benefit, and it is no more difficult to prove a lost chance of avoiding a detriment than it is to prove a lost chance of gaining a benefit.

It is arguable that in cancer cases the courts have been awarding damages for loss of a chance [17]. But probably the better view is that these are not really loss of chance cases at all.

Where damages for loss of a chance are recoverable, the lost chance does not have to be greater than 50%: it simply has to be 'real and substantial' [18].

6.4.3 Causation: material contribution

Sometimes it will be impossible for the experts to say that the defendant's default has, on the balance of probabilities, caused the damage, but they may be able to say on the balance of probabilities that the default has materially contributed to the damage. Where this is the case, the claimant is entitled to succeed in full.

An example is *Bonnington Castings* v. *Wardlaw* (1956). The claimant there was a steel dresser. In the course of his work he was exposed to silica dust from two sources. The exposure to dust from one source was a consequence of the defendant's breach of statutory duty; the exposure to dust from the other was not. He developed pneumoconiosis. It was impossible to determine the contribution which the 'guilty dust' and the 'innocent dust' had made to his disease. All that could be said was that the contribution made by the 'guilty dust' was not *de minimis*. Those facts, said the House of Lords, meant that the claimant was entitled to judgment for damages representing all his illness and its financial consequences. Lord Reid said:

> '... I cannot agree that the question is: which was the most probable source of the [claimant's] disease, the ['innocent dust'] or the ['guilty dust']? It appears to me that the source of his disease was the dust from both sources, and the real question is whether the ['guilty dust'] materially contributed to the disease. What is a material contribution must be a question of degree. A contribution which comes within the exception *de minimis non curat lex* is not material, but I think that any contribution which does not fall within that exception must be material. I do not see how there can be something too large to come within the *de minimis* principle but yet too small to be material.' (p. 621)

The House of Lords appeared to extend this principle in *McGhee* v. *National Coal Board* (1972). They said there that where the defendant's default had materially increased the risk of the injury which in fact occurred, the claimant succeeded in full. This case produced uproar among practitioners and academics. It was pointed out that if all you could do was to prove a material contribution to risk, you had failed to prove that there was anything causative about the defendant's default at all. Judges were extremely reluctant to follow *McGhee*, but it haunted the law of tort until it was exorcised by the House of Lords in *Wilsher* v. *Essex AHA* (1986). In *Wilsher* Lord Bridge said:

> '*McGhee* ... laid down no new principle of law whatever. On the contrary, it affirmed the principle that the onus of proving causation lies on the [claimant]. Adopting a robust and pragmatic approach to the undisputed primary facts of the case, the majority concluded that it was a legitimate inference of fact that the [defendant's] negligence had materially contributed to the [claimant's] injury. The decision, in my opinion, is of no greater significance than that...' (pp. 881–2)

Whenever the House of Lords describes the decision of a differently constituted House as 'robust and pragmatic' it is clear that there is deep intellectual embarrassment. The fact is that *McGhee* was plainly wrong.

It is surprising how seldom the *Bonnington Castings* principle is wielded in clinical negligence litigation. It is potentially extremely helpful to claimants in cases where experts cannot be pressed to agree with the artificial speculations about biological processes which lawyers love so much [19].

6.4.4 Causation: multiple competing causes

Often in clinical negligence cases there will be a number of candidates for the post of 'cause' of the injury. That was the case in *Wilsher*. The claimant there suffered from retrolental fibroplasia. It was said that this was a result of the negligent administration of hyperbaric oxygen. But there were several alternative explanations, and it could not be said that the negligent explanation was probably correct. Accordingly the claimant failed to establish causation.

6.4.5 The requirement that the loss is legally recoverable

Not everything which a claimant might justifiably complain of is recognised by the law as 'loss or damage' sufficient to ground liability. The most obvious examples relate to psychiatric harm. If the only harm suffered is psychiatric, the claimant will have to show, in order to obtain judgment, that a recognisable psychiatric illness has been suffered. Mere distress and shaking up is not enough [20]. A good example was *Reilly* v. *Merseyside RHA* (1994). The claimants were trapped in a hospital lift for one hour twenty minutes. They suffered fear and claustrophobia but no physical injury. They were not entitled to any damages.

6.4.6 The assessment of quantum

General

'Quantum' is simply the value of a case. There are a number of possible 'heads of claim' in clinical negligence cases. They are divided up as follows:

- pain, suffering and loss of amenity;
- special damage;
- future loss;
- hybrid heads of claim.

Damages in negligence cases are almost always intended to be simply compensatory – to put the claimant into the position he would have been in had the defendant not been negligent insofar as money can do that. In rare circumstances damages can be awarded which are intended to represent the court's disapproval of the defendant's oppressive or otherwise immoral conduct. These are referred to as aggravated damages. A good example of aggravated damages in a clinical negligence case was *Appleton* v. *Garrett* (1995). There, a dentist who was sued in negligence and trespass for doing unnecessary dental work on patients in order to enrich himself, was ordered to pay aggravated damages, calculated as 15% of the compensatory damages for pain, suffering and loss of amenity which he also had to pay.

The claimant is under a duty to 'mitigate' his loss. That means that he has to take reasonable steps to reduce the total sum of damages payable. Thus he is not entitled to buy in extravagantly priced care, or go to his hospital appointments in a chauffeur-driven Rolls Royce. If non-dangerous medical treatment would alleviate his condition, he may be obliged to have it: if he does not, he may forfeit that part of his claim which relates to the difference between the condition he is in fact in and the condition which he would have been in had he had the treatment. All the comments below about damages have to be read subject to this caveat about mitigation.

Damages for pain, suffering and loss of amenity

These are exactly what they say. They are inevitably quantifications of the intrinsically unquantifiable. In trying to assess this head of claim, lawyers rely on guidelines which prescribe broad brackets of awards for particular types of injury and disability [21], and on reported cases.

The Law Commission has recently criticised awards of damages for pain, suffering and loss of amenity as being too low. That is a common complaint. Certainly the disparity between such awards and awards of damages in libel cases for injury to reputation can often be insulting to claimants who have suffered personal injuries. In *Heil* v. *Rankin and Others* (2000) the Court of Appeal decided that where the conventional award of damages for pain, suffering and loss of amenity was £10,000 or under, there should be no change, and that above that, there should be a gradual tapering up of awards so that the largest awards would be about one third higher than they had previously been. Insurers were generally happy with this decision, since the vast number of cases they face attract awards of less than £10,000. The National Health Service will be hit particularly hard, since damages for pain, suffering and loss of amenity in clinical negligence cases are very often over the £10,000 threshold.

Special damages

These, broadly, are the financial losses which have accrued between the time of the negligence and the time of the trial. They can only be described broadly this way because they include heads of claim (for instance the cost of care) which relate to work which has been done free for the claimant, and it is rather artificial to describe these as 'financial losses'.

They typically include the cost of travel to and from hospital (both of the claimant and of visiting relatives), prescription and other medical expenses, the cost of care, lost earnings and the cost of equipment needed to cope with disability. In relation to each claim, the court will ask itself:

- whether the claimant has proved that the loss has in fact occurred;
- whether the loss was caused by the negligence; *and*
- in relation to expenditure, whether it was reasonable in principle to spend money on whatever the head of claim is, and if so, whether it was reasonable to spend the amount of money which is claimed.

If care has been given free by relatives or friends, the court values the cost of buying in that care and then reduces this sum by about 25–33% to take account of the fact that no tax or National Insurance has been paid, as it would have been had the care been bought.

In practice, special damages are often agreed. Judges rightly shout at barristers who ask them to decide whether the travelling expenses were £250 or £275.

Future loss

Because this involves speculation about future events, it is much more difficult to calculate. The basic system used is the multiplier–multiplicand system. The multiplier relates to the number of years over which the particular loss runs. The multiplicand represents the annual loss under that head.

Obviously the multiplier cannot simply be the number of years over which the loss runs. If a claimant will lose £1,000 per year for 10 years, he would be over-compensated if the court were to award him £10,000, because it has to be presumed that he will invest the award of damages. The amount of investment income has to be taken into account if the award is to represent the actual loss. The court in fact presumes that the award will be invested in index-linked government securities (*Wells* v. *Wells* (1998)). Exactly what the discount to take account of this presumption should be is controversial. Defendants said that it should be 3% per annum; claimants pointed out that the rate of return on these securities has fallen over the last couple of years, and often contended for a rate of around 2%. There is a statutory power to fix the discount rate [22]. Since 28 June 2001 it has been fixed at 2.5%.

The multiplier also needs to take into account future contingencies such as the possibility that the claimant would in any event have died, or (in the case of a future loss of earnings claim), have been unable to work in any event. The calculation of multipliers is becoming a sophisticated science in its own right – a science led by actuaries.

Significant heads of future loss often include future loss of earnings, future care, future accommodation requirements and the cost of equipment. Obviously in relation to equipment costs there needs to be expert evidence about the lifetime of each item of equipment. In the case of accommodation costs, claimants are given the costs of any necessary conversion and the costs associated with moving to the required accommodation, plus the court's valuation of the financial disadvantage resulting from the additional money tied up in the new property being unavailable. This is calculated, very roughly, by relation to the income which would have been earned had that sum been available for investment (*Roberts* v. *Johnstone* (1988)).

Sometimes it will be impossible to use the multiplier–multiplicand system to calculate future loss. It may be, for instance, that because of an injury a claimant would be at a disadvantage on the labour market were he to be made unemployed, but at the time of trial he is employed and that employment is expected to continue. Here, the court may make a (rather arbitrary) award to represent the disadvantage, and will assess in doing so the prospects of that claimant finding himself adrift on the labour market as well as the level of disadvantage once he is adrift (*Smith* v. *Manchester Corporation* (1974).

Hybrid heads of claim

Some heads of claim do not fall neatly within the above categories. The best example is damages for loss of congenial employment – an award to compensate the claimant for not being able to continue doing a particularly satisfying job (*Hale* v. *London Underground Ltd* (1992)). Nursing is one of the classically cited examples of satisfying employment.

Structured settlements

The court generally awards, or the defendant agrees to pay, a lump sum of damages [23]. That lump sum or part of it may then be invested in such a way that it produces an annuity which meets the claimant's assessed needs at various stages through his life. This form of investment is called a structured settlement. This may have tax advantages or be otherwise advantageous – for instance if there are concerns that a claimant, or whoever would be managing the money, might fritter it away.

6.4.7   Proving the case

General

It is for the claimant to prove the case. Proof is on the balance of probabilities. The general rule is that things are proved by adducing evidence or by getting the other side to agree them. If something is blindingly obvious and common knowledge, the judge may 'take judicial notice' of it, thus dispensing with the formal requirement of proof or agreement. But this is an extremely limited and in practice unimportant exception to the general rule.

Evidence is a highly technical branch of the law in its own right, and cannot be dealt with in this chapter. It is important to remember that evidence includes evidence not only of fact, but also of opinion from appropriately qualified experts.

The maxim *res ipsa loquitur*

Although Lord Woolf does not like Latin tags, lawyers still use them because they are convenient shorthand. One of the most common is *Res ipsa loquitur*: the thing speaks for itself. It refers to the situation where the mere facts of a case shout loudly and unequivocally 'Negligence, and nothing but negligence'.

A lot of mystique has sprung up around this maxim. It has at various times been suggested that where the maxim applies, the burden of proof shifts from the claimant to the defendant. It has now been established that this is wrong: the burden of proof never moves [24].

6.5 Clinical negligence: the future

Clinical negligence claims are big business. The numbers of claims brought has increased very rapidly over the last few years. The loss of legal aid for clinical negligence claims might stop the trend. Such claims are now increasingly funded by 'no win, no fee' type arrangements, and obviously such arrangements concentrate the mind of the claimant's lawyers harder on the merits than an unlimited legal aid certificate previously did.

Comparisons are often drawn between the rise in clinical negligence cases in England and the situation in the litigation-mad USA. The comparison is not a good one. In the USA juries generally assess damages, and are much less scientific, much more generous, and much less strictly compensatory about it than are the professional judges who assess damages in England. If irrationally large awards of damages are not going to become available, irrationally large numbers of clinical negligence actions are unlikely. In England, too, contingency fee arrangements for legal funding (whereby the lawyers get a percentage of the damages recovered – a clear incentive to push the damages as high as possible) are illegal. They should remain so. They are an invitation to sharp practice.

It is sometimes said that a lot of litigation is launched by litigants wanting an apology and an explanation rather than damages. This is true. Increasingly, procedures for investigation (and, if appropriate, compensation) which bypass the courts are available. These include informal mediation. Few clinical negligence cases have yet been arbitrated or mediated, but there seems no reason why these methods should not work in some cases.

It may seem unfair that a claimant's entitlement to damages should depend on him proving fault. The claimant's need for compensation is just as great whether or not fault can be proved. This consideration has led some to advocate no-fault liability schemes for clinical negligence. The basic problem is cost, and it seems highly unlikely that any British government in the foreseeable future will be prepared to finance such an initiative. In the case of National Health patients injured by National Health negligence, it is arguable that there is a de facto no-fault liability scheme in place anyway in relation to many of the costs which are claimed in clinical negligence actions. This is because much of the medical treatment and nursing care and many of the appliances which NHS negligence makes necessary are themselves provided by the NHS.

For the moment, then, it seems likely that the liability of NHS bodies and of individual practitioners will remain governed by the principles set out above.

6.6 Notes and references

1. See *R* v. *Adamako* [1994] 5 Med LR 277.
2. For actions in relation to the birth of an unwanted child now, see *Macfarlane* v. *Tayside Health Board* (HL) [2000] 1 Lloyds Rep. Med. 1.
3. See *Macfarlane* v. *Tayside Health Board (HL)* [2000] 1 Lloyd's Rep. Med. 1.
4. Arising from Mr Justice MacNair's direction to the jury in *Bolam* v. *Friern Hospital Management Committee* [1957] 1 WLR 582.

5. For a discussion of this issue, see Foster, Charles, (1997) 'Medical negligence: The new cornerstone (*Bolitho* v. *City & Hackney HA*)'. *Solicitors' Journal*, 5 December 1997, p. 1150; Foster, Charles (1998) 'Bolam: Consolidation and Clarification'. *Health Care Risk Report*, 4 (5) 5.

6. The UKCC Code of Professional Conduct, clause 4, emphasises that someone subject to the Code must 'acknowledge any limitations in your knowledge and competence and decline any duties or responsibilities unless able to perform them in a safe and skilled manner'. This is emphasised by *The Scope of Professional Practice* (UKCC, June 1992), which notes, at clause 9.4, that the registered nurse (etc.) '... must ensure that any enlargement or adjustment of the scope of personal professional practice must be achieved without compromising or fragmenting existing aspects of professional practice and care and that the requirements of the Council's Code of Professional Conduct are satisfied throughout the whole area of practice'. See too the UKCC's publication: *Perceptions of the Scope of Professional Practice* (January 2000).

7. See *Wilsher* v. *Essex Area Health Authority* [1986] 3 All ER 801; *Djemal* v. *Bexley Health Authority* [1995] 6 Med LR 269; and *Nettleship* v. *Weston* [1971] 2 QB 691.

8. See *Wilsher* v. *Essex Area Health Authority* [1986] 3 All ER 801, per Lord Justice Mustill at pp. 810–813.

9. There is also a professional obligation: The UKCC Code of Professional Conduct, clause 3, requires persons subject to the Code to '... maintain and improve your professional knowledge and competence'. Further, *The Scope of Professional Practice*, (UKCC, June 1992), provides that each registered nurse (etc.) '... must endeavour always to achieve, maintain and develop knowledge, skill and competence to respond to [the interests of the patient or client] ... (clause 9.2), and '... must honestly acknowledge any limits of personal knowledge and skill and take steps to remedy any relevant deficits in order effectively and appropriately to meet the needs of patients and clients' (clause 9.3). For further comments on the professional obligation to keep up to date, see the UKCC's publications: *PREP and you* (October 1997) and *Perceptions of the Scope of Professional Practice* (January 2000).

10. See *Crawford* v. *Charing Cross Hospital* (1953) *The Times*, 8 December; *Gascoine* v. *Ian Sheridan and Co* [1994] 5 Med LR 437.

11. *Bolitho* v. *City & Hackney Health Authority* [1998] AC 232, per Lord-Browne-Wilkinson at p. 243.

12. The Senate of Surgery, October 1997.

13. GMC, February 1999. Available on the GMC web-site at http://www.gmcuk.org/n_hance/good/consent.htm.

14. See *Re. C (a minor) (medical treatment)* [1998] Lloyds Rep Med 1: *Airedale NHS Trust* v. *Bland* [1993] 4 Med LR 39: *Early* v. *Newham HA* [1994] 5 Med LR 214: *Penney, Palmer and Cannon* v. *East Kent Health Authority* [2000] 1 Lloyds Rep. Med. 41.

15. See, for instance, *First Interstate Bank of California* v. *Cohen Arnold & Co* [1996] 1 PNLR 17: *Allied Maples Group Ltd* v. *Simmons & Simmons (a firm)* [1995] 1 WLR 1602.

16. See, for instance, *Chaplin* v. *Hicks* [1911] 2 KB 786.

17. See, for instance *Judge* v. *Huntingdon Health Authority* [1995] 6 Med LR 223.

18. *First Interstate Bank of California* v. *Cohen Arnold & Co.* [1996] 1 PNLR 17, per Lord Justice Stuart-Smith at 1611–12. For recent comments on loss of a chance, see *Smith* v. *NHSLA* (2000) [2001] Lloyd's Rep. Med. 90 and *Webb* v. *Barclays Bank Plc* (2001) [2001] Lloyds Rep. Med. 500.

19. Note, though, *Tahir* v. *Haringey HA* [1998] Lloyds Rep Med 105, in which the court laid down guidelines indicating when the *Bonnington Castings* analysis would be the correct one in a clinical negligence context.

20. See *Nicholls* v. *Rushton, The Times*, 19 June 1992.

21. *The Judicial Studies Board Guidelines for the Assessment of General Damages in Personal Injury Cases*, 4th edn, 1999. Blackstone Press, London.
22. Damages Act 1996 s. 1.
23. The court has, however, a power under the Damages Act 1996, s. 2, if the parties consent, to make an order under which the damages are wholly or partly in the form of periodical payments.
24. See *Ratcliffe* v. *Plymouth & Torbay HA and Exeter & North Devon HA* [1998] PIQR P170.

B An Ethical Perspective – Negligence and Moral Obligations

Harry Lesser

It is fairly clear that in a broad sense the legal and ethical uses of the term 'negligence' are the same. Negligence is, roughly, failure to exercise the appropriate level of care. Nevertheless, there are a number of important differences between what is appropriate legally and what is appropriate ethically. These may be summed up briefly by saying that the ethical standard – the level of care required to be doing what one ought to do – is higher than the level required by the law. But there are at least five ways in which legal and ethical duties of care are different; and one way of improving our understanding of the ethical duty to avoid negligence and its implications is to consider all five in turn.

6.7 Harm and risk

First – and this is made very clear in part A of this chapter – the courts come into operation only if harm has been done. There is a legal duty of care, as well as an ethical one, incumbent on, for example, nurses, health visitors and midwives. But failure to meet this duty will concern the law only if some harm or damage results. The law has to decide such things as whether harm has been done, who is to be held responsible for the harm and in what ways compensation for the harm should be calculated, and, sometimes, whether the negligence was so serious as to be criminal. But if no harm has been done, there is no place for the law. Ethics, though, is different: a professional who exposes a patient or client to serious and unnecessary risk by, for example, failing to take standard precautions is still morally to blame, even if by good fortune no harm is done. The law is concerned essentially with redressing, and sometimes with punishing, the harm done by negligence; ethics is concerned with the obligation to avoid negligence, whether harm in fact results or not. To make a very obvious point, a professional who has subjected a patient to unnecessary risk of this kind but without any harm resulting is in no danger of legal action, but ought nevertheless to have a 'bad conscience' and (more importantly) to resolve that this should not happen again.

6.8   The Code of Professional Conduct

Moreover, the standard of care required by ethics is higher than that needed to avoid the danger of litigation. The law is, again by its nature, concerned with maintaining the minimum that patients or clients are entitled to expect and with dealing with failures to maintain that minimum. Ethics has to go beyond this in a number of ways. To begin with, the professional codes themselves set a higher standard than the law. Thus the UKCC Code of Professional Conduct for the Nurse, Midwife and Health Visitor (1992) sets a standard of care that in both its negative and positive requirements goes well beyond the requirement to avoid negligence in the legal sense. Three passages may be used to illustrate this.

The first is the second clause of the Code, which is a version of what is often called the principle of non-maleficence, the principle that all health care workers have a duty not to harm patients or clients:

'As a registered nurse, midwife or health visitor … you must ensure that no action or omission on your part, or within your sphere of responsibility, is detrimental to the interests, condition or safety of patients and clients.'

On the positive side, with regard to beneficence – to positively helping the patient or client – the Code says twice, both in the brief preamble and the first clause, that the nurse, midwife or health visitor must 'act always in such a manner as to promote and safeguard the interests and well-being of patients and clients' (clause 1). (The preamble is similarly worded but refers to 'individual patients'.)

In these passages, even the negative one, the Code goes well beyond what is required by the law. The section on legal negligence says (clause 2.1):

'To succeed in an action for clinical negligence, a claimant must show … c) that the breach of duty has caused some injury, loss or damage to the claimant of a type which the law acknowledges.'

This sets a limit (admittedly not defined at this point) to the kinds of harm one has a legal duty to guard against, whereas the Code has no such restriction. Not only this, but the Code requires the professional to go beyond doing no harm and beyond merely safeguarding the 'interests and well-being' of patients and clients, and in addition to actively promote their interests and well-being.

6.9   Personal ethics

The Code sets a high standard, but ethics seems to require still more. It would seem that even a minimal standard of personal ethics would in some ways go beyond not only the legal requirements but also the requirements of the Code. To take just one example, the Code could be read as not absolutely requiring the nurse to be unduly concerned for the patient's comfort, if the discomfort was of a kind that did not affect their recovery. It could be seen as compatible with the attitude of the fictional matron played by the actress, the late Hattie Jacques, who informed the patients, 'You are not here to enjoy yourselves. You are here to get better. And better you are going to get.' But nursing ethics seems to require either that 'interests and well-being' are given a very wide interpretation, or that the nurse's ethical obligations go beyond observing the Code and include, where possible, safeguarding and promoting the patient's comfort and dignity, so that to imperil either of these would be ethically negligent.

There is here a further problem. Both the Code and (if I am right) the higher standard required by personal ethics involve an obligation to promote the interests of the patient or client and an obligation to do nothing detrimental to those interests. At first glance these look fully compatible – one positive, one negative, but involving the same purpose. But matters are not so simple. Not to care for a patient would very often result in harm or the risk of harm, but most, perhaps even all, forms of care themselves involve some degree of discomfort, harm or risk; there may be no way of absolutely safeguarding the interests of the patient, and it may be a matter of judging what is most in their long-term interests. Often this may be straightforward. The likelihood of a cure may be very high, for example, and the side-effects of the medication a short-term discomfort clearly worth enduring for the sake of the cure; the nurse administering the medication is in this case fairly clearly acting in the patient's interest. But sometimes matters are much less simple, and it is by no means clear how to balance the risks and possible benefits of a particular type of treatment, and how to decide what is or is not in the patient's interest. Even if the sphere of authority of the doctor and the nurse can be distinguished (which is far from certain), these problems arise, sometimes for the nurse as well as the doctor, and they do not arise only over general decisions as to a line of treatment.

Ethically, three things seem to be required. One is always, if possible, to consult the patient, so that risks are run and discomfort or pain endured with their understanding and consent. The others are to avoid unnecessary risks, not required for the sake of a likely benefit, and not to inflict harm greater than the benefit to the patient or client. All these arise essentially because of a difference between a legal and an ethical duty. Although, as the section on legal negligence makes clear, the legal obligations of a nurse are not something about which there is total clarity or precision, there is, rightly, an attempt to provide guidelines of such a nature that a nurse who acts according to those guidelines will not be guilty of legal negligence. But the UKCC Code of Professional Conduct is different. As the preceding discussion shows, one cannot simply 'act according to them' or 'act within them'; one is forced, whether or not one is conscious of this, to balance them against each other and to use intelligence and flexibility in translating them into action.

The reason for this complexity is one which lies at the base of many problems in health care ethics. Medicine – here taken to include the activities of nurses, doctors and other health care professionals – has three major aims: to cure or alleviate illness, disease and injury; to prolong life; and to relieve suffering. Very often these three aims coincide, and the same treatment will contribute to all three. But when they do not, problems arise about what should be done, and these problems are made worse by the fact that one is often dealing with probable or possible rather than certain consequences, so that it is not, for example, a matter of trading discomfort for cure, but of trading likely discomfort for a possible cure. Sometimes this can be dealt with by being left to the patient; some-times it is not in the nurse's hands, but a matter for the doctor or the doctor and patient; sometimes the answer is obvious. But there is a residue of situations where the task of weighing up the pros and cons is going to fall on the nurse. And here the legal position is different from the ethical one. Legally, if things are balanced in this way, the nurse is probably covered whichever course of action they take. Ethically, they are still obliged to consider carefully (in so far as time permits) what is the best thing to do.

It is perhaps worth pointing out – though this is largely drawing attention to the obvious – that these problems cannot be solved by a demarcation of the duties of the nurse and the doctor. There has been a tradition of seeing medicine and nursing as clearly divided, with the functions of the nurse being, for example, to keep the patient as comfortable as possible and to carry out the doctor's instruc-tions. It may be questioned whether this ever corresponded to what went on in practice; but it seems now to be agreed that no such exact demarcation of duties is either possible or desirable.

One may sum all this up by saying that ethics differs from law, in this field, by the fact that it operates all the time, and is concerned with avoiding potential harm and not only redressing actual harm; by the fact that ethics is more complex than law, and may require not simply doing one's duty but working out the best thing to do; and by the fact that ethical standards are, so to speak, two levels higher than legal ones: the Code is more exacting than the law, and the personal ethics of the nurse ought to be more exacting than the Code. This last point needs a bit more consideration. Personal ethics needs to be concerned not only with meeting standards but also with pursuing ideals. So the point needs to be made that individual professionals, such as nurses, need to be concerned not only with maintaining a level of care a bit above the minimum required by the law and the Code but also, where possible, with raising their standard above this, with remembering that in one sense duty is never completely done.

However, as soon as one says this, one must at once use common sense to qualify it. On the one hand, one needs an ethics that goes beyond duty; on the other, one must remember that nurses, like other people, have been issued with one pair of hands and live through days with 24 hours in them, that hospitals are under-staffed, and that even meeting the standards of the Code can take all the time available. Not only would it be unjust to nurses to expect too much – more than is possible or even more than is reasonable – if the standards are set too high, the practical result will be worse rather than better. What seems to be required here is a combination of a resolution to maintain a standard of care at least a little above the minimum required by the law and the Code, with an aspiration to achieve still more when time, energy and opportunity permit. What is also required is a sensible use of one's personal feelings, so that they maintain the standard rather than weakening it. To recognise that one sometimes fails in one's duty and to resolve not to repeat those failures are both useful, but guilt feelings which are inappropriate (for example, at a failure of aspiration which is not an actual failure of duty) or excessive (for example, which persist after the resolution not to repeat the failure has been made) often have the effect, like excessively high standards, of making actual practice worse rather than better.

6.10   The ethical duty of care

Three of the five issues have now been raised, if sketchily: the concern of ethics with potential consequences; the higher standard and greater complexity of the Code of Ethics when compared with the law; the way in which the personal ethics of individual nurses needs to be at least a little higher and more complex than either, and also needs to take in aspirations as well as strict duty and consider the role of personal feelings, as an internal sanction and an encouragement to maintain standards – all this needing to be tempered by a common-sense awareness of what is reasonable and possible. Much of this applies to other areas besides the avoidance of negligence, but this area affords a particularly clear example of the differences between legal and ethical obligation.

However, we now come to something that applies particularly to negligence: the extent to which there can be a specific ethical duty of care even when there is no legal duty. There are three cases where this may arise. The first is the case where a nurse happens to be on the scene of an accident. Legally, there is no obligation to help the victims; nurses, midwives and health visitors are under no obligation to stop and assist, unless they are already under a duty to help the person in question because of their contract of employment. But if one holds that one ought to help those in need if one can, then there is a moral obligation. Indeed, it might be argued that the obligation on health professionals to stop and help is greater than that on other people, because they have the relevant knowledge and skills; if there is a general obligation on anyone able to help to do so, there must be a special obligation, over and above this, on those with the relevant skills. It is true that there is one particular problem here: although there is no legal obligation to offer care, once it is offered it is subject to legal obligations, and the victim has a legal claim if they suffer harm. I would suggest, however, that the existence of this paradox, that a nurse could not be sued for not offering care but could be sued for offering it negligently, is not a sufficient ground for saying there is no moral obligation to offer care. But it is to be hoped that the law of negligence will not develop, as it has in some countries, in such a way that the legal risk of offering help becomes so great that people become afraid to offer it.

Secondly, there are the moral and legal responsibilities of the head of a team, or of the named nurse given overall responsibility for a patient's care. The named nurse (or other practitioner) is legally responsible for the negligence of other members of the team only if that negligence is the result of their own acts or omissions – if, for example, they fail to give clear instructions or to communicate properly information about the patient or fail generally to make sure that all those to whom care of the patient has been delegated were both adequately informed of their responsibilities and competent to carry them out.

This is the legal position. But clause 2 of the Code of Professional Conduct requires the nurse, midwife or health visitor to 'ensure that no action or omission on your part, or *within your sphere of responsibility*, is detrimental to the interests, condition or safety of patients and clients' (author's emphasis). Paragraph 20 of the position statement, *The Scope of Professional Practice*, amplifies this with special reference to the 'identified' practitioners, responsible for 'co-ordinating and supervising the delivery of care'. This would seem to require more than the law does: the use of the phrase 'within your sphere of responsibility' makes named practitioners and team leaders generally responsible, morally and professionally, for the standard of care given by those to whom they delegate it. Ethically, therefore, they are obliged, obviously only in ways consistent with good working relationships, not only to make sure that other members of the team are appropriately competent and fully and clearly informed and/or instructed, but also to maintain a check that standards of care are being maintained.

The third area where moral duty goes beyond legal duty concerns unborn children. Midwives and other health professionals have no legal duty to care for unborn children, and are not liable for pre-natal injuries to the child provided they have cared properly for the mother. But ethically, it would seem that as long as the interests of mother and child are compatible the duty of nurse or midwife must be to both, so that whatever benefits the child should be done, even if it is of no direct benefit to the mother. (In any case, this would normally 'benefit' the mother by being strongly in accordance with her wishes.) There is a technical problem of ethical language and ethical concepts here: it is a disputed matter whether a fetus/unborn child is a kind of being to which duties can be owed. But this seems to be genuinely a purely linguistic problem with no practical effects (unlike many issues in ethics which seem linguistic but turn out to be substantive). One can simply rephrase by saying that the legal duty of the nurse or midwife is to care for the mother, but there is a moral duty also to care for the unborn child even if this goes beyond caring for the mother. For example, if doing, or refraining from doing, certain things will benefit the child but have no effect on the health of the mother, there seems to be no legal duty on the nurse or midwife either to inform the mother of this or to recommend it. But there seems to be a moral duty to do both.

6.11   Conflicts between law and ethics

So far, we have been dealing with various ways in which the moral duty to 'promote and safeguard the interests and well-being of patients and clients' goes beyond the legal duty to avoid negligence, but is not incompatible with it. But there are two areas in which there may be an actual conflict between legal and ethical duty. One concerns the mother and unborn child: if the legal duty is to the mother, but the moral duty is to both, then a conflict is at least possible. Very often, of course, either the interests coincide or the mother strongly wants to put the child's interests first. In the main instance where they do not, that in which the mother is having an abortion, the law specifically allows a nurse with conscientious objections not to take part. One can conceive of a very determined opponent of abortion raising the question whether it could be the duty of a nurse or midwife not merely to refuse to take part but actually to try to sabotage the whole process; but I think that, given that there seems to be no possible way of doing this successfully, to say nothing of how ethically dubious it would be, one can dismiss this as not a serious suggestion.

But a problem remains. It seems clear that it is possible, though hopefully rare in practice, for a health care professional to consider on reasonable grounds when faced with a situation in which the interests of the mother and the child are in conflict, that the interests of the child ought ethically to prevail (in their judgement), and they cannot simply withdraw from the case on grounds of conscience. For example, suppose, as sometimes happens, that a caesarean section would be very advisable to prevent harm to the child, but the mother is refusing to have the operation. Legally, it seems, the midwife should support the mother's decision and not encourage her to expose herself to the risk of the operation; ethically, she might well feel that she should bring all reasonable pressure to bear in order to get the mother to agree. What she should do is a disputed matter; it might for example be argued that, since the mother, however she feels now, does not want a brain-damaged child, the duty to both mother and child is to bring the pressure to bear. But it is important to point out that it is possible, though hopefully very rare in practice, for health professionals to decide that they have an ethical duty to the child which conflicts with their legal duty to the mother. What they should then do – and different courses of action may be appropriate in different circumstances, depending on the exact possibilities and likely consequences – is a matter for the person involved rather than the academic theorist.

The second case of conflict between law and ethics concerns a health care professional who is given instructions that they believe to be wrong or mistaken. Under such circumstances the nurse, for example, is legally required to question the orders, and advised by the UKCC, if they are still in doubt, to demand that the doctor administer the treatment (e.g. the drugs). But if the orders are confirmed by the doctor or higher authority before being acted on, the nurse is not regarded as negligent, whereas in contrast failure to follow established hospital or national policy, unless there are good reasons in a particular case, may be regarded as evidence of negligence.

So the law will support a nurse who, under appropriate circumstances, questions an order or policy, or demands that a doctor carry it out personally, or for good clinical reasons exempts a particular patient from the established hospital policy. Paragraphs 11 and 12 of the Code of Practice go beyond this and require the nurse, midwife or health visitor to:

> 'report to an appropriate person or authority ... any circumstances in the environment of care which could jeopardise standards of practice ... any circumstances in which safe and appropriate care for patients and clients cannot be provided.'

(This incidentally provides a fourth example of a duty not required by the law, but required by ethics.) But ethically this may not be enough. If the consequences of, for example, administering a drug were sufficiently terrible, it would seem that there could be a moral duty not only to refuse to give the drug but also to prevent the doctor from administering it.

For while it is entirely reasonable that nurses, midwives and health visitors should comply with doctors' orders (if the orders relate to medical practice), nevertheless if in their professional judgement those orders are likely to result in harm to the patient or client, they have a clear moral and professional duty to question them and even to refuse to carry them out or, if this is practicable, to prevent their being carried out. The preamble to the UKCC Code makes each health care professional 'personally accountable', and following orders does not remove this personal accountability. Benjamin and Curtis [1] put the point very clearly:

> 'In so far as a nurse has an obligation to follow a doctor's orders, it is only a prima facie obligation, and may be overridden in certain circumstances by other factors. A nurse must be careful not to confuse a well-grounded prima facie obligation with blind faith.'

Similarly, hospital policy, or the policy of one's employer, whether in a private nursing agency, for example, or in industry, does not remove personal accountability. There is again a prima facie duty to comply with the rules and policies of one's employer or organisation, but this needs to be overridden if the policy does not meet agreed professional standards or fails to serve the best interests of the patient. Although this seems ethically clear, it is supported by the law only up to a point. Questioning the law or policy is positively required; refusing on professional grounds to carry out the policy has legal backing. But refusing on any other moral grounds is supported by the law only in the case of abortion; and trying to prevent an order being carried out has no support at all, as far as one can see. Reporting to the appropriate authority what is going on – 'whistleblowing' – is not required by the law, but is required, as we have seen, by the Code and is safeguarded by the law.

There is a real problem here. On the one hand, the running of any institution requires that individuals make some sacrifice of their personal judgement of what is best to the judgement of those in charge; life would be impossible if individuals constantly prevented decisions from being carried out, and even the questioning of orders – which is, up to a point, a good thing – has to be kept within limits if activities are not to grind to a halt. It is also important to remember that anyone taking the drastic step of trying to prevent an order from being complied with may well face disciplinary action and find that, however morally right they may be, the law and the Code do not protect them. Even 'whistleblowers', who if they are reporting genuine instances of unsatisfactory practice are precisely obeying the Code, may find that, whatever the theory, they are in fact in serious trouble. But on the other hand, despite the need to keep the institution running, and despite the importance of not encouraging people to put themselves on the line when it is not necessary, one must always remember the harm, sometimes terrible, that can be done if people take no steps to prevent wicked actions or policies, or even well-meant but mistaken actions or policies.

In the end, each health professional must decide for themselves when the moment has come to put themselves on the line; one hopes most will be spared ever having to make such a decision. The only guideline one might suggest is that this should be considered only if the alternative is something widely agreed to be seriously harmful. It remains important to acknowledge that one's moral duty can conflict with one's legal duty. Which should be given precedence, in these unfortunate situations, has to be a matter of individual conscience, and with awareness that there may be a price to pay.

6.12   Conclusion

A carer has both a legal and an ethical duty to avoid negligence. The ethical duty differs from the legal one primarily in the following ways:

(1) It operates whether or not any harm actually follows from the negligence, since it applies to actions, and failures to act, themselves, and not only to their *actual* consequences, but also to their *potential* ones.

(2) Both with regard to not doing harm and to doing good, the UKCC Code of Practice requires a higher standard than the law, and also requires that the carer be able to weigh up likely harms and benefits in order to decide what it is best to do.

(3) Time and energy permitting, the carer should have a personal ethical standard at least a little higher than that of the Code, and should also have an ethics of ideals as well as duties, again in line with what is reasonably possible.

(4) Ethics goes beyond the law in requiring a direct duty of care for unborn children; a duty towards accident victims if one can help them; a general duty to make sure that those whose work one is responsible for co-ordinating and supervising carry out their duties properly; and a duty to report circumstances in which care is endangered. (The first two of these are general moral obligations; the last two are specifically required by the Code.)

(5) Ethics may occasionally require someone to actively prevent an order or policy from being carried out, even though this may conflict with their legal duty, or to uphold the claims of someone they are not legally obliged to care for in preference to the claims of someone for whom they are legally obliged to care. (These situations are rare but not impossible.)

6.13   Notes and references

1. Benjamin, M. & Curtis, J. (1992) *Ethics in Nursing*. Oxford University Press, Oxford.

Chapter 7

Consent and the Capable Adult Patient

A   The Legal Perspective

Jean McHale

Obtaining the consent of a patient to treatment is a crucial part of health care practice. It fosters the bond of trust between practitioner and patient by according the patient respect for her autonomy of decision making. Obtaining consent before undertaking treatment is also part of the health professional's legal obligation [1]. If treatment is given without consent she runs the risk of being sued for damages in the civil law courts or prosecuted in criminal law.

The nurse has two main roles in the consent process. First, when she is acting as the primary carer, providing the patient with treatment, she has the task of obtaining the patient's consent. The expansion in the role of the nurse means increasingly that it is the nurse herself who will be taking on this role. Secondly, even if a doctor obtains the patient's consent a patient may be confused or uncertain about her treatment choice and may turn to the nurse for clarification. When complying with her legal obligations in relation to consent to treatment the registered nurse needs also to be aware of her professional ethical obligations including her role as advocate for her patient. Here, as in other areas of her practice, the nurse may find herself torn between what she believes are the obligations required of her under the UKCC professional code and her obligations under the contract of employment.

Consent to treatment is one area of health care practice in which the courts may be invited to consider the application of the European Convention of Human Rights [2] through the Human Rights Act 1998. Issues which concern consent to treatment can be found in relation to the debates concerning many areas of health care and this is reflected in many of the other chapters of this book [3]. This chapter discusses consent to treatment and the competent adult patient. In section one the general nature of consent in law and capacity to consent to treatment is discussed. Section two considers the liability of the nurse in civil and in criminal law if she fails to provide the patient with information regarding her treatment. Section three examines the situation in which a nurse believes that the doctor has provided her patient with insufficient information with which to make a treatment decision. Some of the difficulties which can face the nurse in attempting to act as an advocate for her patient are examined, particularly in the context of inter-professional conflicts of disclosure. The nurse should note clause 5 of the UKCC code which states that he or she should:

> 'work in an open and co-operative manner with patients, clients and their families, foster their independence and recognise and respect their involvement in the planning and delivery of care.'

It should be noted that while this chapter does give an introduction to the issues it is obviously not possible to explore the full breadth and range of complex issues which arise consequent upon consent to treatment; for a fuller exploration readers are referred to other sources [4].

7.1   Consent to treatment – some general issues

7.1.1   The consent form

One of the most frequent cries to be heard in a hospital is 'have you got her consent form?'. All nurses are familiar with the consent forms given to patients to sign before they go in for an operation. But the fact that the patient has signed a consent form does not by itself make that consent legally binding – oral consent may be perfectly valid. However, while it is not strictly required, written consent has the advantage of drawing a patient's attention to the fact that she is consenting to a clinical procedure and it may provide some evidence of her consent should there be any future dispute as to whether consent was given.

7.1.2   Express and implied consent

While consent may be given expressly, whether in writing or orally, in some situations even express oral consent is not required. If a patient proffers her arm for a bandage to be applied, although she may say nothing her actions imply that she has consented to the procedure. But there are dangers in too readily assuming that a patient has given implied consent. For example, particular difficulties can arise in relation to blood tests. When blood samples are taken, a number of tests are usually performed on the samples. It has been argued that by giving general consent to a blood sample being taken a patient is consenting to all those tests being performed which the doctor considers to be necessary [5]. But what if one of those tests is to determine a patient's HIV status? Is this a test of a different nature? It is clear that the implications for a patient if an HIV test is taken are considerable. For example, it may inhibit their ability to obtain insurance and employment. The precise legal position as to whether blood can be tested for HIV without consent remains uncertain. Different legal opinions have been expressed on this point [6]. The General Medical Council have stated in their 1997 guidance that consent must be obtained from patients before testing for a serious communicable disease [7]. This guidance goes on to state that:

> 'Some conditions such as HIV, have serious social, financial, as well as medical implications. In such situations the nurse must make sure that the patient is

given appropriate information about the implications of the test, and appropriate time to consider and discuss them.'

It is submitted that this is the appropriate approach to take and that testing should not be undertaken without the patient being made clearly aware of the consequences.

7.1.3 Capacity to consent

In order for consent to be valid in law a patient must be capable of making that treatment decision. Adult patients are presumed to have capacity to consent or to refuse consent to a particular treatment but this refusal can be rebutted (*Re T (adult: refusal of treatment)* (1992)). But what is meant by 'capacity'? [8] Obviously the patient will require some understanding of the implications of the decision which he or she is to make, but how much? In *Re C (adult: refusal of treatment)* (1994) the court upheld the right of a 68 year old paranoid schizophrenic who had developed gangrene in his foot to prevent his foot being amputated in the future without his express written consent. Mr Justice Thorpe suggested a three-part test to detemine capacity:

'... first, comprehending and retaining treatment information, secondly, believing it and thirdly, weighing it in the balance to arrive at a choice.'

At the hearing it was claimed that C was not competent because of his delusions that he was a doctor and that whatever treatment was given to him was calculated to destroy his body. But despite these claims Mr Justice Thorpe held that he was satisfied that C was capable of giving or refusing consent because he understood and had retained the relevant treatment information and believed it and had arrived at a clear choice.

One potential problem with the test in *Re C* is that it makes capacity dependent on the information which the patient is actually given. If the nurse provides a patient with a great deal of complex information she may be unable to understand it and as a result lack capacity. In contrast, if a basic explanation is given to that very same patient she may possess capacity to consent [9].

This approach was followed in 1995 by the Law Commission in their report *Mental Incapacity* concerning the care and treatment of those patients with mental incapacity [10]. They stated that the test should be decision-relative. They proposed that legislation should provide that a person should be deemed to lack capacity if at the material time he or she is:

(1) unable by reason of mental disability to make a decision on the matter in question;
(2) unable to communicate a decision on the matter because he or she is unconscious or for any other reason.

The Law Commission defined 'mental disability' as being 'any disability or disorder of the mind or brain, whether permanent or temporary which results in an impairment or disturbance of mental functioning'. They proposed that a person should be unable to make a decision on the basis of mental disability:

'if the disability is such that, at the time when the decision needs to be made he or she is unable to understand or to retain the information relevant to the decision, including information about the reasonably foreseeable consequences of failing to make that decision.'

They recommended that the patient should have a basic comprehension of information where this was given 'in broad terms and simple language'.

Judicial approval of the approach of the Law Commission and of *Re C* was given in *Re MB (medical treatment) (1997)*. Here a woman with a needle phobia, while agreeing to a caesarean section which was clinically required, repeatedly refused the anaesthetic prior to the caesarean section. Lady Butler Sloss held that a person is not capable of making a decision where:

'(a) the person is unable to comprehend and retain the information which is material to the decision, especially as to the likely consequences of having or not having the treatment in question: and
(b) the patient is unable to use the information and weigh it in the balance as of the process of arriving at a decision.'

The Court of Appeal in this case went on to consider the scope of capacity and the extent to which an individual may be regarded as incapable where the decision which is made can be regarded by some as irrational. This is discussed further below in the context of consent and refusal in relation to enforced caesarean sections.

The Law Commission's proposals were far more extensive than simply setting out one test and constituted a comprehensive review of capacity over the whole area of care and treatment of the mentally incompetent adult including such issues as advance directives (see Chapter 10A) and powers of attorney. After a period in which the Law Commission's report was left in abeyance the Government finally undertook consultations on the report in their document *Who Decides?* in 1997 [11] and in October 1999 issued a Green Paper, the document *Making Decisions* [12]. The ultimate proposals are considered in greater detail in other chapters in this book. While the Law Commission proposed a radical revision of the law the Government took a more limited approach, although *Making Decisions* did accept the need for a statutory definition of capacity [13]. It is to be hoped that the Law Commission's recommendations clarifying the position are taken forward in the near future.

7.1.4 Fluctuating capacity

In a situation in which a patient has a fluctuating mental state it may be acutely difficult to decide whether she is capable of giving consent. In such a situation it is tempting to say that she lacks capacity to make treatment decisions. This is because English law allows the incapacitated patient to be given such treatment as those treating her believe to be in her best interest (*Re F (mental patient sterilisation) (1989)*). In *Re R (a minor: wardship: consent to medical treatment) (1991)* the Court of Appeal held that a child with fluctuating mental capacity was to be regarded as totally incapable of making a decision to consent or refuse consent. However, in the later case of *Re T* (1992) the Court of Appeal held that the capacity of an adult patient is to be judged by reference to the particular decision to be made. This is surely right. If a patient is capable today of understanding what treatment is proposed the fact that yesterday she was not capable of understanding should not affect her right to make a decision. This approach is confirmed by *Re MB* (1997).

7.1.5   Criminal law and consent to treatment

As a general rule if a patient gives consent to a medical procedure being undertaken then no criminal liability will result. But the fact that consent has been given does not automatically mean that the treatment itself is lawful. The individual does not have absolute freedom in English law to do what he or she wishes with his or her body [14]. Some medical procedures such as female circumcision are expressly prohibited by statute [15]. Uncertainties surround the legality of certain other medical procedures [16]. For example, while it appears that as long as organ transplant operations do not constitute an unjustified risk to the life of the donor they will not be held to be unlawful [17], the lawfulness of animal to human transplantations is still to be resolved [18].

Where a major operation is undertaken without consent there is the possibility of a prosecution under section 18 of the Offences Against the Person Act 1861. This section makes it an offence to 'unlawfully and maliciously' cause grievous bodily harm to a person with the intention of causing grievous bodily harm. However it is more likely that a nurse who has given treatment without the patient's consent will be prosecuted for the less serious crime of battery. This makes unlawful any non-consensual touching [19].

7.2   Civil law liability

7.2.1   Battery

While treating without obtaining the patient's consent may lead to a criminal prosecution, it is far more likely that absence of consent will lead to an action in the civil courts. First, an action may be brought in the tort of battery. An action in battery arises if a patient is touched without her consent. Not every touching will lead to liability, for example an action is unlikely to result from the nurse accidentally brushing a patient's shoulder as she passes in a corridor. There is no need to prove that the touching caused damage – the fact that it took place is sufficient for an action to be brought.

In *Chatterton* v. *Gerson* (1981) Mr Justice Bristow held that no liability would arise as long as the patient was informed and understood in broad terms the nature of the procedure which it was proposed to undertake, and she had given consent. If a broad general consent is given then any further claim that a patient has been given inadequate information should be brought not in battery but in negligence [20].

7.2.2   Treating in an emergency where no consent can be obtained

There may be some situations in which it is lawful for the nurse to go ahead and treat a patient without obtaining her consent, most notably in an emergency situation as in the patient brought bleeding and unconscious into casualty. In such situations treatment can be given on the basis of necessity. In addition, if a patient has given initial consent to an operation but then, later, during the operation it is discovered that she is suffering, for example, from a life-threatening condition such as a cancerous tumour then this may be removed. But while necessity may justify the performance of a medical procedure in an emergency, exactly what is necessary is a matter of degree (*Devi* v. *West Midlands HA* (1981)). The nurse should ask herself if this particular procedure is immediately necessary or could it be postponed until the patient recovers consciousness and can make her own decision.

7.2.3   Consent and refusal

The patient has the right both to consent and to refuse medical treatment. An action in battery may be brought if treatment is given in the face of an explicit refusal of consent. A well known case often quoted as a warning to those who may be tempted to treat in the face of refusal is the Canadian case of *Malette* v. *Schumann* (1988). The claimant was brought into hospital following a road accident. A nurse found a card in her pocket which identified her as being a Jehovah's Witness and which requested that she was never to be given a blood transfusion. Despite the card the doctor performed the transfusion. On recovering her health the patient brought an action in battery. She succeeded and was awarded $20 000 damages. A further reason why a patient may argue that their decision to refuse treatment should be upheld is because this is a fundamental human right, one which is now safeguarded under the Human Rights Act 1998. A number of the rights contained in the European Convention of Human Rights may be relevant in this context; for example, Article 3, because imposition of treatment upon a competent patient against their wishes may be held to constitute inhuman or degrading treatment or punishment. In addition, Article 8 which concerns the right to respect for privacy of home and family life may be applicable – but as this right is not absolute it can be argued that there will not be an infringement of Article 8 where the patient is not in a position to give informed consent [21]. Article 9 of the Convention – freedom of religion – may also be used to support the refusal of treatment in a situation in which the reason why the individual is refusing treatment is because of a tenet of their particular religious belief. In the past in a number of cases refusal of treatment on religious grounds has been overruled by the courts, particularly in the context of refusal by child patients [22]. It will be interesting to see how these issues are considered in the future.

Overruling a refusal of treatment

While a clear refusal should be respected, there are situations in which a patient's refusal may be overridden. In *St George's NHS Trust* v. *S* (1998), the Court of

Appeal set out guidance concerning cases in which patients refused treatment (case discussed further at p. 109 below). Where a patient possesses capacity then they may refuse therapy; where a patient lacks capacity treatment may be given where it is in the patient's best interests. If there is a question mark over the patient's capacity then a proper assessment should be undertaken by an independent psychiatrist. If there is a serious doubt as to the patient's competence and a declaration is sought, the patient's solicitor should be informed. Where the patient is incapable of instructing a solicitor then the official solicitor should be involved. The guidance notes that in a situation of acute urgency an application to the court may be inappropriate due to time constraints. Nonetheless, it remains the case that judicial guidance may have advantages in such difficult cases.

7.2.4 Particular problems in overriding refusal of consent

Free not forced consent

A patient must reach her decision whether to consent or refuse treatment, freely and without pressure being applied by relatives or by carers. In *Re T* in 1992 (discussed above) an important factor in the decision to authorise a transfusion was that T's refusal came after she had spent time alone with her mother, a confirmed Jehovah's Witness. Ensuring that a patient gives free and full consent may be practically very difficult for a nurse working on a busy ward. Inevitably the amount of time that can be spent with a patient discussing the implications of a decision is subject to the time constraints of practice, but the patient must not be browbeaten by relatives or by medical staff into making the decision. In determining whether consent has been given in a particular situation the court will look to the circumstances. The fact that a patient is, for example, a prisoner does not mean that she is unable to give free consent. In *Freeman* v. *Home Office* (1984) the court held that whether the prisoner/patient had, in fact, consented was a question of fact for each individual case. But in this type of situation it is of particular importance that when information is given to the patient it is made clear to her that she has a free choice.

7.2.5 Pregnant women refusing care

A midwife is faced with a pregnant woman in difficulties in labour but who is refusing even to contemplate a caesarean section. By rejecting treatment she is placing her life and that of the fetus in jeopardy. Should her refusal of treatment be respected? This issue came before the English courts in a series of cases during the 1990s. In *Re S* (1992) the case concerned a woman six days overdue giving birth where the medical team sought to undertake a caesarean section. To attempt a normal birth would have caused a very grave risk of rupture to the uterus because the fetus was in transverse lie, placing the lives of mother and child in grave danger. S, a born again Christian, refused the operation because it was against her religious beliefs. The hospital went to court to obtain a declaration which was controversially granted by Sir Stephen Brown. The judge made reference to the rights of the fetus, but English courts have in the past consistently rejected claims that the fetus has such rights [24]. Second, Sir Stephen Brown placed some emphasis on a US case *Re AC* (1990). In a number of cases courts in the USA were prepared to order pregnant women to be given a caesarean section despite their refusal of treatment [25]. In *Re AC* the court initially ordered a caesarean section on a woman dying of cancer. This order was overturned on appeal after AC had died. The court said that in 'virtually all cases' a refusal could not be overridden. They did admit there may be exceptional circumstances in which a caesarean may be ordered. An example given in discussion in the case was very similar to the facts in *Re S*. Nevertheless *Re AC* is widely seen as the case which curtailed judicially ordered caesarean sections in the USA [26].

In many ways *Re S* can be regarded as an exceptional case – an aberration [27]. After the decision the Royal College of Obstetricians and Gynaecologists (RCOG) published a consultation paper stating that:

> 'It is inappropriate and unlikely to be helpful or necessary to invoke judicial intervention to overrule an informed and competent woman's refusal of a proposed medical treatment even though her refusal may place her life and that of her foetus at risk'. [28]

Despite this, in a number of subsequent cases judicial intervention was sought and the courts authorised the performance of caesarean sections upon women who had refused such procedures (*Rochdale NHS Trust* v. *C* (1996), *Norfolk & Norwich NHS Trust* v. *W* (1996)). The Court of Appeal were given an opportunity to rule on this issue in *Re MB* (1997). MB had a fear of needles. This had led her to refuse to have blood samples taken during pregnancy. In the late stages of pregnancy it was discovered that the fetus was in the breach position. A caesarean section was proposed. MB initially agreed; however she was opposed to administration of anaesthetic by needles. MB then went into labour. She agreed to a caesarean section and the administration of anaesthetic by mask, but at the last moment refused the anaesthetic [29]. The hospital then sought a court order, which was given by Mr Justice Hollis. He found that MB was incompetent because of the effects of the needle phobia on her decision-making powers. She asked her lawyer to appeal. She then herself agreed to the caesarean section and the operation was carried out the following day.

MB challenged the legality of the procedure. On appeal to the Court of Appeal the right of the competent patient to refuse treatment was confirmed [30]. However it was also recognised that, in an emergency, treatment could be given where a patient lacks capacity, as long as this was on the basis of necessity, the procedure not extending beyond what was reasonably required by the patient. Lady Butler Sloss noted the judgment of Lord Donaldson in *Re T* where he stated that the doctor must assess carefully whether in that case the patient had the capacity 'commensurate with the gravity of the decision' she purported to make. The Court of Appeal referred to the three-stage test for capacity set out by Mr Justice Thorpe in *Re C* discussed above. Lady Butler Sloss commented that:

> 'A competent woman who has the capacity to decide may, for religious reasons, other reasons, for rational or irrational reasons or for no reason at all, choose not to have medical intervention, even though the consequence may be the death or serious handicap of the child she bears, or her own death. In that event the

courts do not have the jurisdiction to declare medical intervention lawful and the question of her own best interests objectively considered, does not arise.'[31]

She went on to state that:

'Irrationality is here used to connote a decision which is so outrageous in its defiance of logic or of accepted moral standards that no sensible person who has applied his mind to the question to be decided could have arrived at it... Although it might be thought that irrationality sits uneasily with competence to decide, panic, indecisiveness and irrationality in themselves do not as such amount to incompetence, but they may be symptoms or evidence of incompetence. The graver the consequences of the decision the commensurately greater the level of competence is required to take the decision.'[32]

Capacity may be eroded due to temporary incompetence as indicated by Lord Donaldson in the earlier case of *Re T* as 'confusion, shock, pain and drugs'. The Court of Appeal on the facts of this particular case upheld the decision of the judge at first instance that MB had lacked capacity. She was competent to consent to the caesarean section. However she did not have competence to refuse as she was 'at that moment suffering an impairment of her mental functioning which disabled her. She was temporarily incompetent [33].' Her phobia of needles impaired her ability to decide. Two points arise here: first, the extent to which the circumstances of pregnancy itself served to erode the woman's capacity. In view of the fact that temporary factors may erode capacity, Kennedy is surely right to argue that '...there is an urgent need to establish the boundaries of the permissible', in this area [34]. Secondly, Butler Sloss makes an important statement confirming that the law sanctions 'irrational' refusals. Nonetheless the judgment leaves unclear where the boundary can be drawn between 'acceptable' irrationality which will not impact on respect for the patient's right to decide, and an 'irrational' decision which may impact on capacity such that an individual's competence to make that decision is affected.

Having found MB to be temporarily incompetent the Court of Appeal then considered whether the procedure itself could be authorised. The House of Lords in *Re F* (1988) confirmed that medical procedures may be undertaken on an incompetent adult where it is in his or her best interests to do so. The House of Lords indicated that best interests were to be determined with reference to the *Bolam* test [35], what a responsible body of professional practice would authorise in such a situation − a medically based test. The difficulties with the application of such a test have been noted by academic commentators [36]. It is questionable how far such a test formulated to determine issues of clinical judgement is appropriate in a broader context of determining the authorisation of treatment decisions [37]. A further point is that of the interrelationship of the 'best interests' test which applies in the case of the mentally incompetent adult, to the operation of the welfare principle in cases concerning the treatment of children. In *Re MB* Lady Butler Sloss stated that:

'In considering the scope of best interests, it seems to us that they have to be treated on similar principles to the welfare of a child since the court and the doctors are concerned with a person unable to make the necessary decision for himself.' [38]

These observations of Lady Butler Sloss are interesting. However, is it the case that one overarching principle should be applied or do different considerations apply in the context of the incompetent adult to those that apply in relation to a child patient? There has been much cross-reference between cases concerning children and mentally incompetent adults at the end of life [39]. However, treatment decisions regarding vulnerable adults were notably the subject of considerable separate (and indeed extensive) consideration by the Law Commission in their report on mental incapacity. The complexities of such issues are excellently highlighted in that report. It is suggested that before the application of the best interest tests are further conflated the whole question of the interrelationship between treatment decisions of incompetent minors and adults requires reconsideration.

The Court of Appeal held that the treatment was in MB's best interests in this emergency situation. But in whose best interests was this procedure? The Court of Appeal took into consideration the fact that agreement had initially been given by MB for the caesarean section. Furthermore, evidence from the consultant psychiatrist was to the effect that if the child had been born handicapped or had died, MB herself would have suffered long-term harm. In contrast little harm would be caused by the administration of the anaesthetic against her wishes.

What of the interrelationship between the best interests of both the fetus and the woman? The Court of Appeal upheld earlier cases such as *Re F (in utero)* (1988), *Paton* v. *British Pregnancy Advisory Service* (1978) in confirming that the fetus has no independent status in English law. They were of the view that Sir Stephen Brown in *Re S* had reached an incorrect conclusion. The Court of Appeal stated that:

> 'Although it may seem illogical that a child capable of being born alive is protected by the criminal law from intentional destruction, and by the Abortion Act from termination otherwise than as permitted by the Act, but is not protected from the (irrational) decision of a competent mother not to allow medical intervention to avert the risk of death, this appears to be the present state of the law.' [40]

Thus even at the point of birth itself the court could not intervene in the face of refusal of medical intervention by a competent woman with the aim of safeguarding the position of the fetus. The English courts may consider such future decisions in the light of Article 2 of the European Convention of Human Rights. However, the weight of authority makes it questionable whether a different approach will be taken.

Re MB also recognises that there may be circumstances (beyond the Mental Health Act 1983) when the use of forcible treatment may be justifiable. Lady Butler Sloss stated that:

> 'The extent of force or compulsion which may be necessary can only be judged in each individual case and by the health professionals. It may become for them a balance between continuing treatment which is forcibly opposed and deciding

not to continue with it. This is a difficult issue which may need to be considered in depth on another occasion.' [41]

One of the most important aspects of the decision in *Re MB* is that it provides guidance for future cases in this area by setting out procedures which should be undertaken. This includes the requirement that the woman should be represented in all cases save where, in exceptional circumstances, she does not wish to be so [42]. This recommendation goes some way to meet concerns as to the manner in which such proceedings have been brought [43]. This guidance has been subsequently incorporated into an NHS circular [44], and considered further in *St George's NHS Trust* v. *S* discussed below.

7.2.6   Caesarean sections and the Mental Health Act

There have also been a number of cases in which the Mental Health Act 1983 was used to sanction the performance of caesarean sections upon mentally incompetent women. Section 63 of the Act provides that:

> 'The consent of a patient shall not be required for any medical treatment given to him for the mental disorder from which he is suffering.'

The boundaries of section 63 – what amounted to medical treatment for mental disorder – came before the courts in *Tameside and Glossop Acute Hospital Trust* v. *CH* (1996) [45]. CH was detained under section 3 of the Mental Health Act 1983. She was suffering from paranoid schizophrenia. She was then discovered to be pregnant. It was held that as she lacked capacity to consent or refuse treatment a caesarean section could be authorised as the performance of a caesarean section was treatment for 'mental disorder' and thus fell within the scope of section 63 of the Mental Health Act 1983. This was because if a stillbirth had occurred her health would have deteriorated and she needed strong anti-psychotic medication which could not be given to her when she was pregnant. The court followed the approach in *B* v. *Croydon HA* (1994), that section 63 of the 1983 Act encompassed matters which related to the 'core treatment' (in that case including force feeding). Such a broad interpretation of this provision has been criticised [46]. For example, as Grubb has argued, section 63 does not cover any physical condition which impedes treatment of mental disorder. As he notes:

> 'The Government saw section 63 in far more limited terms covering perfectly routine, sensible treatment' [47].

A contrasting approach was taken by the Court of Appeal in the case of *St George's NHS Trust* v. *S* (1998). S was diagnosed as suffering from severe pre-eclampsia. She was advised that she should have an early delivery. S, who had intended a home delivery, refused treatment. She asserted that nature should take its course although she was informed as to the risk of death and disability to herself and the fetus. Her GP initiated steps which led to her detention in hospital under section 2 of the Mental Health Act 1983. She was subsequently transferred to another hospital. While she persistently refused treatment and sought legal advice, the hospital authority, without her knowledge, made an *ex parte* application to the

High Court for a declaration to the effect that it would be lawful to undertake treatment, including a caesarean section. Meanwhile S had been in touch with solicitors with the intention of making an application to a Mental Health Review Tribunal. The declaration was granted. It appears that the judge was under an incorrect impression that S had been in labour for 24 hours. S gave birth to a daughter. The detention under the Mental Health Act was terminated. S discharged herself. While detained in hospital S was not offered treatment for her mental disorder. An action was subsequently brought for judicial review to challenge the legality of the action taken.

The Court of Appeal again emphasised the fact that the competent adult is entitled to refuse treatment [48]. Lord Justice Judge stated that:

'In our judgment while pregnancy increases the personal responsibilities of a woman it does not diminish her entitlement to decide whether or not to undergo medical treatment. Although human and protected by the law in a number of different ways as set out in the judgment in *In re MB* . . . an unborn child is not a separate person from its mother. Its need for medical assistance does not prevail over her rights.'

These words are indicative of the tensions in drawing the boundaries between moral acceptability and legal enforcement in this area [50]. While some may regard a pregnant woman as possessing moral responsibilities to the fetus in the latter stages of pregnancy, this still does not limit her legal rights. The orthodoxy of *Paton* and subsequent cases was again confirmed by the court.

The court held that a battery had been committed on S. Lord Justice Judge stated that:

'. . . how can an enforced invasion of a competent adult's body against her will even for the most laudable of motives (the preservation of life) be ordered without irredeemably damaging the principle of self-determination.' [51]

The court examined the provisions of section 2(2) which provide that:

'An application for admission for assessment may be made in respect of a patient on the grounds that
(a) he is suffering from a mental disorder of a nature or degree which warrants the detention of the patient in a hospital for assessment (or for assessment followed by medical treatment) for at least a limited period; and
(b) he ought to be so detained in the interests of his own health and safety or with a view to the protection of other persons.'

The Court of Appeal emphasised that the criteria for detention under the section were cumulative. In this case the doctors had been justified in their assessment that the woman was suffering from depression which constituted 'mental disorder'. However, S was not being detained in order that treatment be given for her mental disorder. It was stated that:

'For the purposes of section 2(2)A such detention must be related to or linked with the mental disorder. Treatment for the effects of pregnancy does not provide the necessary warrant.'

Thus the courts have affirmed that for treatment to be lawful under section 63 it must be crucial to the mental disorder. While here the treatment was not treatment for mental disorder within the provisions of the statute, as Bailey Harris notes, questions regarding the connection between the disorder and the treatment proposed are likely to arise in the future [52]. Finally, there had been irregularities in the documentation used by the hospital. Forms had not been completed when the woman was transferred between hospitals, as was required by regulations made under section 19 of the Mental Health Act. This would, in any event, have entitled S to discharge herself from hospital. While some might regard her decision as unjustifiable or even irrational, this did not mean that it was of no legal validity. The Mental Health Act cannot be used as a means of circumventing the competent woman's right to refuse a caesarean section. Finally, the Court of Appeal criticised the procedure adopted in the case of the *ex parte* application; the application was made without the knowledge of S and her legal advisors, and as in *Re MB* they set out guidelines regarding the conduct of proceedings for a declaration.

The decisions of the Court of Appeal in *Re MB* and *St George's NHS Trust* v. *S* are in many respects welcome. The autonomy of the patient is confirmed. Judicial guidance is also given as to the correct procedures which should be adopted when making an application for a declaration and the need for pregnant women and their advisors to be provided with adequate information. Referring what appear to be insurmountable differences between the parties to the courts constitutes recognition that there are certain decisions which, because of their inherently difficult nature, may not be suitable for resolution by the parties alone because of their multi-faceted nature and because there are broader issues of public policy which may arise. A conflict between the patient and her midwife or doctor over the conduct of childbirth may in fact be well suited to the involvement of an independent arbiter. It also provides safeguards for the patient. There are dangers in low visibility of 'hard case' treatment decisions as evidenced by the concern of the courts, for example, to be involved in sanctioning certain invasive procedures on mentally incompetent adults such as sterilisation procedures or decisions at the end of life [53].

Nonetheless these controversial Court of Appeal decisions leave many issues to be resolved, in particular around the interpretation of 'capacity' to decide [54]. The test for capacity is decision-relative. The graver the consequences of the ultimate decision, the more careful the scrutiny given to the capacity of the patient to make that decision. This is inevitable. The more serious the consequences of the refusal, the more important it is to ensure that the patient possesses the necessary competence to make the treatment decision. It is also the case that as temporary incompetence may invalidate capacity, it is important to ensure that the notion of capacity is not manipulated to deny individual autonomy. Nurses and midwives as patient advocates are likely to play important roles in this process.

7.2.7   Consent and civil law liability negligence

For a general discussion of the law of negligence see Chapter 6. Obtaining a broad general consent to medical procedures being performed is sufficient to avoid liability in battery. But in addition, for a patient to give full and effective consent she must have some appreciation of the risks that the medical procedure in question may go wrong. If a patient is not informed of the risk of complications and if one or more of these complications arises, then she may bring an action in negligence. The basis of her claim is first that those who are treating her are under a duty to provide her with information about the risks of the treatment, secondly that this duty has been broken, and thirdly that she has suffered harm as had she known of the risk (which did in fact materialise) she would not have consented to the treatment.

The leading case is *Sidaway* v. *Bethlem Royal Hospital Governors* (1985). Mrs Sidaway underwent an operation after having suffered for some time from a recurring pain in her neck, right shoulder and arm. The operation was performed by a senior neurosurgeon at the Bethlem Royal Hospital. Even if the operation had been carried out with all due care and skill there was a 1–2% risk of damage to the nerve root and the spinal column. Although the risk of damage to the spinal column was less than to the nerve root, the consequences were more severe. The plaintiff was left severely disabled after the operation. She brought an action in negligence claiming that she had not been given adequate warning of the risks of the operation. During the hearing it was revealed that while the surgeon had told her of the risks of damage to the nerve root he had not told her of the risks of damage to the spinal column. In acting in this way he was conforming to what in 1974 would have been accepted as standard medical practice by a responsible and skilled body of neurosurgeons. The House of Lords rejected the claim that the surgeon had acted negligently. An 'informed consent' approach was rejected by all the Law Lords – except Lord Scarman. Some support was given to the suggestion that the test which a court should use in deciding whether the advice given was negligent was the same as that used in deciding whether medical treatment was negligent – the *Bolam* test [55]. This test provides that a health care practitioner:

'is not guilty of negligence if he has acted in accordance with a practice accepted as proper by a responsible body of medical men.'

This approach was followed by Lord Diplock in the House of Lords. This obligation of disclosure applies to all types of medical procedure. A broader approach was taken by Lord Bridge who said that a judge could disagree with the evidence given to him:

'I am of the opinion that the judge might in certain circumstances come to the conclusion that disclosure of a particular risk was so obviously necessary to an informed choice on the part of the patient that no reasonably prudent medical man would fail to make it.'

He commented that:

'The kind of case I have in mind would be an operation involving a substantial risk of grave adverse consequences, as for example, [a] 10 per cent risk of stroke from the operation... In such a case, in the absence of some cogent clinical reason why the patient should not be informed, a doctor ... could hardly fail to appreciate the necessity for an appropriate warning.'

Where the risk of an adverse effect was slight or insignificant, the information could be withheld where this was an accepted practice within the community of medicine. The risks disclosed must be reasonably foreseeable. Lord Templeman distinguished between general risks which would normally be known to the patient and special risks which may be required to be disclosed. Lord Templeman stressed that it was for the court to decide whether the practitioner had acted negligently or not. No distinction is drawn between therapeutic and non-therapeutic forms of care (*Gold* v. *Haringey Health Authority* (1987)). While the courts have traditionally been hesitant to scrutinise the responsible body of professional practice, one example of a case in which they did do so was *Smith* v. *Tunbridge Wells* (1994). Mr Smith, a 28 year old married man with two children, suffered a rectal prolapse. Surgery was proposed and was undertaken. While the operation was successful, the plaintiff suffered nerve damage during surgery and was left impotent. He brought an action claiming that he should have been informed of the risk of impotence. His claim was upheld by Mr Justice Morland who stated that:

'In my judgment by 1988, although some surgeons may still not have been warning patients similar in situation to the plaintiff of the risk of impotence, that omission was neither reasonable nor responsible.'

Until relatively recently this case could be regarded as very much the abberation. However, the House of Lords in *Bolitho* v. *City and Hackney HA* (1997) signalled a different approach (see Chapter 6). In this case Lord Browne Wilkinson stated that:

'if in a rare case, it can be demonstrated that professional opinion is not capable of withstanding logical analysis, the judge is entitled to hold that the body of opinion is not reasonable or responsible.' [56]

Admittedly this judgment is limited in scope and, despite some suggestions made at the time, it does not at all mean that the *Bolam* standard in negligence – the standard of the responsible body of professional practice – is dead. In addition, these comments relate to diagnosis and treatment. *Bolitho* itself did not address the question of disclosure of risk. However it may be indicative of an increasing judicial willingness to take a 'hard look' at the view expressed by a body of professional opinion in the future. The application of *Bolitho* to diagnosis and treatment was considered in the decision of *Pearce* v. *United Bristol NHS Trust* (1999). Here the Court of Appeal looked at the decisions in *Bolitho* and in *Sidaway*. Lord Woolf held that:

'if there is a significant risk which would affect the judgement of a reasonable patient then in the normal course it is the responsibility of a doctor to inform the patient of that significant risk, if the information is needed so that the patient can determine for him or herself as to what course that she should adopt.'

On the facts of the case the woman was advised against a caesarean section and the child was delivered still born. There was a small risk of between one to two in a thousand that the child would be stillborn. The claimant was unable to establish that this was 'significant'. Nonetheless, although the claimant was unsuccessful in this particular case the judgment itself can be seen as another step away from a clinical judgement based on a patient-based approach to consent to treatment [57].

While in the majority of cases, providing a patient with information about her treatment can be seen as a positive step enhancing her autonomy, there may be some situations in which those caring for her believe that information may be withheld under what is known as the 'therapeutic privilege' where this is in the best interests of the patient. In *Sidaway* Lord Templeman said:

> 'some information may confuse, other information may alarm a particular patient... the doctor must decide in the light of his training and experience and the light of knowledge of the patient what should be said and how it should be said.'

The application of this principle may be questioned in the light of recent medical practice with the movement towards providing a patient with full information and also in respect of what appears to be enhanced judicial willingness to scrutinise the provision of information to patients. Certainly if a therapeutic privilege exception does exist it needs to be exercised with extreme caution.

Informed consent

An alternative approach to the professional practice standard which has been adopted in a number of other countries such as Australia, Canada and the USA is that of 'informed consent' (e.g. *Rogers* v. *Whittaker* (1992), *Reibl* v. *Hughes* (1980)). Several states in the USA now require a standard of disclosure based upon the information which a 'prudent patient' would expect to receive. In *Sidaway* Lord Scarman who delivered a dissenting judgment supported this approach, saying that the patient should be given such information as a prudent patient would wish to know. While at that time the majority in the House of Lords rejected such an approach, today while the judiciary itself has still not explicitly imposed such a standard, in practice there has definitely been a movement towards the adoption of such an approach. Health care professionals are now being directed to give patients more information about certain types of treatment. There is a perceived need for enhanced frankness and openness by health care professionals. One of the issues emphasised in the debate around the unauthorised retention of human material including organs at Alder Hey and at a number of hospitals up and down the country has been the failure to obtain adequate consent from relatives for the retention of such material [58]. In clinical research following the controversy of the Griffiths inquiry the new research governance approach now emphasises the need for informed consent [59]. In the inquiry into the events at Bristol Royal Infirmary, Professor Ian Kennedy and his team have suggested a number of ways in which the provision of information could be improved [60]. The report emphasises in Chapter 23 the need for 'respect and honesty' in health care. An important message is the need for the health care professional–patient relationship to be seen as one of partnership. Consent is also to be seen as a process:

> 'Trust can be only sustained by openness. Secondly, openness means that information be given freely, honestly and regularly. Thirdly, it is of fundamental importance to be honest about the twin concerns of risk and uncertainty. Lastly informing patients and in the case of young children their parents must be regarded as a process and not as a one-off event.' [61]

The report recommends that: 'Patients must be given such information as enables them to participate in their care'. It suggests processes for improving the conveyance of information such as ensuring that information is evidence based, and that importantly 'information should be tailored to the needs, circumstances and wishes of the individual'. Such an approach if it becomes current in medical practice will surely represent a critical shift to a 'prudent patient' test. It is also reflected in recent GMC guidance 'Seeking Patient Consent: the ethical considerations', GMC London, 1999.

The courts, as indicated above, appear to be increasingly prepared to scrutinise the standard of disclosure proffered by health care professionals. It may also be the case that in the future should information be withheld from patients, claims will be brought under the Human Rights Act 1998. The trend is towards disclosure and this should be welcomed as part of the nurse's partnership in clinical practice with her patient. Co-operation rather than conflict will surely facilitate better patient care.

The questioning patient

The nurse may give the patient some explanation of the procedures and potential risks of their treatment but the patient may later approach the nurse and ask for further information. How should the nurse respond? In the House of Lords in *Sidaway* some of the members of the court indicated that there might be an obligation to provide a full reply if questions are asked. Lord Bridge said that:

> 'when questioned specifically by a patient of apparently sound mind about the risks involved in a particular procedure proposed, the doctor's duty must, in my opinion be to answer both truthfully and as fully as the questioner requires.' [62]

But these statements were obiter and not binding. Subsequently in *Blyth* v. *Bloomsbury AHA*, (1987), Lord Justice Kerr said that there was no obligation to disclose all information when a question was asked; it was sufficient if the information given was that which would be given by a responsible body of medical practitioners – the *Bolam* test. He stressed that the response of health care professionals to the patient's questions should depend on factors such as the circumstances, the nature of the information, its reliability and relevance and the condition of the patient. That case was however decided in 1987 and needs now surely to be placed in its historical context: recent judicial statements indicate a move towards willingness to recognise an obligation to answer questions (e.g. *Pearce* v. *United Bristol Healthcare NHS Trust* (1999)). The DoH have suggested that:

> 'If information is offered and declined, it is good practice to record this fact in the notes. However it is possible that patients' wishes may change over time and it is important to provide opportunities for them to express this.' [63]

The recommendation of Professor Ian Kennedy in the Bristol Infirmary Inquiry Final Report, emphasising that patients should be given the opportunity to ask questions and to seek clarification and more information, should be noted in this context. Following the Bristol Inquiry Report the Department of Health have issued a 'Reference Guide to Consent for Examination and Treatment' 2001 and new model consent forms. The Government in their response to the Bristol Inquiry Report have stated that they endorse this new guidance and confirm the principle that consent is a process and that the principle of consent is applicable to all clinical procedures – not simply to surgery. Moreover that 'patients should be given sufficient information about what is to take place, the risks, the uncertainties and possible negative consequences of the proposed treatment, about any alternatives and about the likely outcome, to enable them to make a choice as to how to proceed.' Learning from Bristol: The Department of Health's Response to the Report of the Public Inquiry into children's heart surgery at Bristol Royal Infirmary 1984–1995 Cm 5363 (2002) (pp. 139–140). Such an approach suggests that failure to answer patients' questions today is unlikely to be supported by a responsible body of professional practice. Today, it is submitted, a nurse should consider very carefully indeed before she decides to withhold information from a questioning patient, and any refusal will require very clear justification [64].

Causation

Even if a patient can establish that she should have been given more information, that by itself is not sufficient for an action in negligence to succeed (Chapter 6). She must go on to show that the failure to provide information caused the harm suffered by the patient. The present test used by the courts is subjective – would the patient have chosen differently had she been given more information? [65] The patient may find it very difficult to prove causation since in many cases the patient would have taken the decision to choose the treatment even if provided with more information.

7.3   Conflicts in disclosure

There has been considerable debate in nursing surrounding the concept of the nurse as patient advocate [66]. One part of the role of the nurse as advocate is in facilitating her patients to exercise their rights. The ability to make a free choice regarding one's treatment is perhaps one of the patient's most important rights. If the nurse is acting as a member of a health care team and she believes that the information given by a doctor in the team to a patient is insufficient, what should she do? Does the law require her to advocate for her patient? There is no express recognition in English law at present of the role of the nurse as patient advocate, but there may be situations in which she would be held liable for failure to disclose.

In their Guidelines for Professional Practice, the UKCC states that:

'Sometimes you may not be responsible for obtaining the patient's or client's consent as, although you are caring for the patient or client, you would not actually be carrying out the procedure. However, you are often best placed to know about the emotions, concerns and views of the patient or client and may be best able to judge what information is needed so that it is understood. With this in mind you should tell the other members of the health care team if you are concerned about the patient's or client's understanding of the procedure or treatment, for example, due to language difficulties.'

The nurse must ensure that sufficient information has been given in terms readily understandable to the patient so as to enable him to make a truly informed decision. It is for the nurse to state this opinion and to seek to have the situation remedied. The practitioner might decide not to cooperate with a procedure if convinced that the decision to agree to it being performed was not truly informed. [67]

But while the nurse may remonstrate with the doctor, what if the doctor ignores her views? The UKCC states that:

> 'There is potential for disagreement or even conflict between different professionals and relatives over giving information to a patient or client. When discussing these matters with colleagues or relatives, you must stress that your personal accountability is firstly to the patient and client. Any patient or client can feel relatively powerless when they do not have full knowledge about their care or treatment. Giving patients and clients information helps to empower them. For this reason, the importance of telling the truth cannot be over-estimated.' (p. 16)

The nurse may decide not to participate in a clinical procedure on the grounds that the patient has been inadequately informed, or she may decide to provide the patient with more information herself. But in taking either step she risks disciplinary proceedings and ultimate dismissal for disobeying orders [68].

In addition, in deciding to go ahead and disclose, the nurse runs the risk that her assessment of the amount of information the patient requires may be wrong. What if the patient is unable to cope with the information given and suffers a nervous breakdown? An action may be brought against the nurse claiming that she was negligent in disclosure. Whether such an action would succeed would depend on the test employed by the court. It is submitted that a court would assess whether she had acted negligently in disclosing, by reference to a professional body of nursing opinion.

A nurse may protest to a doctor that a patient has not been given sufficient information but on being told by the doctor to obey orders she may decide not to give the patient more information about treatment risks. But what if the treatment risk materialised and the patient suffered harm? Any negligence action for failure to provide adequate information would probably be brought against the doctor rather than the nurse [68]. If an action was brought against the nurse it might not succeed. In the past the courts have held that as long as a nurse is following doctors orders she will not be held liable (*Pickering* v. *Governors of United Leeds Hospitals* (1954)). But with the development of the role of the nurse as an autonomous practitioner and as advocate for her patient, this situation may change. If such an action was brought, a court would have to consider whether in remaining silent she had acted in accordance with a responsible body of professional nursing opinion [69].

It has been suggested that a nurse may be found liable if she undertakes a task under instructions which she believes to be 'manifestly wrong' [68], following comments made by the House of Lords in *Junor* v. *McNichol* (1959). It is possible that participation in treatment of a patient who has not been told of a very high risk of death or serious injury would come within this category. However, this would presumably only arise in the most exceptional case.

7.4   Conclusions

The nurse must confront the same difficult questions of disclosure as her medical counterpart when treating the patient as a sole practitioner. Her role is complicated however by the fact that she may feel that she has a role to play as advocate for her patient. The role of nurse as patient advocate has not yet been recognised in law and it remains to be seen to what extent this position will change in the future. At present, fear of placing her job in jeopardy and the risk of legal liability may constrain the nurse to do little more than simply protest. But the mere fact of disagreement may prompt reconsideration of what information should be given to the patient, a continued debate which must in the long term be to the patient's advantage. It is also important to note that both professional and legal developments are militating in favour of fuller, franker disclosure and enhanced respect for patient autonomy.

   If the Government go ahead, as they have indicated that they intend to in the document *Making Decisions*, and enact the Law Commission's proposals on mental incapacity, albeit in a truncated form, this will continue the task of clarifying the boundaries of capacity. The movement towards standardisation in clinical practice through the establishment of bodies such as the National Institute for Clinical Excellence, National Patient Safety Agency and the Commission for Health Improvement may facilitate the process of standardising approaches to disclosure. The recommendations of Professor Ian Kennedy in the Bristol Inquiry will also have an important part to play in defining the nature of consent to treatment in the future. The Human Rights Act 1998 is likely to lead to some of the questions surrounding consent to treatment being given further judicial consideration. But the legal process is simply the tip of the iceberg of clinical practice. Nurses have a vital role to play in the actualisation of the reality of respect for consent to treatment on the ward and in the community.

7.5   Notes and references

1. See generally on consent to treatment: Brazier, M. (1992) *Medicine, Patients and the Law*, Chapters 4 and 5, Penguin, London; Kennedy, I. & Grubb, A. (2000) *Medical Law*, Oxford, Chapter 5.
    University Press, Oxford, Mason, J.K. & McCall Smith, R.A. (1999) *Law and Medical Ethics*, 5th edn, Chapter 10, Butterworths, London; McHale, J. & Fox, M. (1981) *Health Care Law Text and Materials*, Sweet and Maxwell, London and also DoH (2001) *Reference Guide to Consent for Examination and Treatment*. Deparment of Health, London.
2. See for example Wicks, E. (2001) The right to refuse medical treatment under the European Convention on Human Rights 8 Med LR 17.
3. See for example, Chapters 9a, 10a and 12a in this book.
4. See for example, Kennedy, I. & Grubb, A. (2000) *Medical Law*. Oxford University Press, Oxford, Chapter 5.
5. See Mason, J.K. & McCall Smith, R.A. (1999) *Law and Medical Ethics*, 5th edn, p. 271.
6. Keown, J. (1989) The Ashes of AIDS and the Phoenix of Informed Consent 52 Med LR 790.

7. GMC (1997) *Serious Communicable Diseases.* General Medical Council, London.
8. See generally M. Gunn (1994) The meaning of incapacity. 2 Med LR 8.
9. Grubb (1994) 2 Med LR1.
10. *Mental Incapacity* (1995) Law Commission Report 231. The Stationery Office, London.
11. (1997) Cm 3803.
12. (1999) Cm 4465. McHale, J.V. (1998) Mental Incapacity: some proposals for legislative reform. *Journal of Medical Ethics*, 24, 322.
13. Delany, L. (1998) Responsibility and Capacity. *Health Care Risk Report*, 7, 70.
14. See *R* v. *Brown* [1993] 2 All ER 75.
15. Prohibition of Female Circumcision Act 1985 section 1.
16. See *Bravery* v. *Bravery* [1954] 1 WLR 1169.
17. This was suggested by Lord Edmund Davies in a statement made extra judicially – see (1969) *Proc. Roy. Soc. Med.*, 62, 633–4.
18. See Fox, M. & McHale, J. (1998) Xenotransplantation 6 Med LR 42.
19. Skegg, P.D.G. (1984) *Law, Ethics and Medicine*, p. 32. Clarendon Press, London.
20. See the comments of Mr Justice Bristow in *Chatterton* v. *Gerson* and M. Brazier (1987) Patient autonomy and consent to treatment: the role of the law. *Legal Studies*, 7, 169.
21. See discussion in Wicks, E. (2001) The right to refuse medical treatment under the European Convention on Human Rights. 8 Med LR 17.
22. See for example *Re L (medical treatment; Gillick competency)* [1998] 2 FLR 810.
23. See Grubb (1993) Commentary. 1 Med LR 92.
24. See further *C* v. *S* [1988] QB 135 and *Paton* v. *British Pregnancy Advisory Service* [1978] 2 All ER 987.
25. See further Kennedy, I. (1990) A woman and her unborn child; rights and responsibilities. In P. Byrne (ed) *Ethics and Law in Health Care and Research*. John Wiley, Chichester.
26. See discussion in Kennedy, I. & Grubb, A. (2000) *Medical Law*. Oxford University Press, Oxford.
27. In *AC* itself an enforced caesarean was rejected. The court did indicate that they may be used in suitable cases and mentioned a court decision very similar to *Re S*. However, they did not express an opinion on that case.
28. RCOG (1994) *A Consideration of the Law and Ethics in Relation to Court-Authorised Obstetric Interventions* and see also the revisions in (RCOG 1996) *Supplement to a Consideration of the Law and Ethics in Relation to Court-Authorised Obstetric Interventions.*
29. It was suggested that anaesthetic should be given through a mask, but when the risks of this procedure, namely that there was a possibility that a patient on whom this procedure is used may regurgitate and inhale the contents of the stomach, were explained to her, consent was refused.
30. Reference was made to the statement of Lord Justice Goff in *Collins* v. *Wilcock* [1984] 1 WLR 1172 as approved in *Re F* [1990] 1 AC 1, the judgment of Lord Templeman in *Sidaway* v. *Bethlem Hospital Governors* [1985] AC 871 at pp. 904–5 and Lord Donaldson in *Re T (an adult refusal to consent to medical treatment)* [1992] 4 All ER 649 CA.
31. [1997] FLR 426 at pp. 436–7.
32. [1997] FLR 437.
33. [1997] FLR 438.
34. Kennedy, I. (1990) A woman and her unborn child: rights and responsibilities. In P. Byrne (ed.) *Ethics and Law in Health Care and Research*. John Wiley, Chichester.
35. See *Bolam* v. *Friern Hospital Management Company* [1957] 2 All ER 118.
36. See for example Fennel, P. (1990) Inscribing Paternalism in Law: Consent to Treatment and Mental Disorder *Journal of Law and Society*, 29.
37. See for example Grubb, A. & Pearl, D. (1989) Sterilisation – courts and doctors as

decision makers. *CLJ* 380, and Law Commission (1995) *Mental Incapacity*. The Stationery Office, London. See also now *Re SL (Adult Patient Medical Treatment)* [2001] 2 FCR 452.

38. [1997] 2 FLR 439.
39. See, for example, *Airedale NHS Trust v. Bland* [1993] AC 879, *Re R* [1996] 2 FLR 99.
40. [1997] 2 FLR 441.
41. [1997] 2 FLR 439.
42. [1997] 2 FLR 445.
43. See, for example, Stern page 243.
44. *Consent to Treatment*. NHS EL (97) 32. See also *Good Practice in Consent*. NHS HSC 2001/023.
45. See also Grubb, A. (1996) Treatment without consent: pregnancy (adult). *Medical Law Review* 191.
46. See further discussion in Chapter 9A in this book.
47. Per Lord Elton Hansard (HL) 1982 cols 1064–5.
48. Reference was made to the judgment of Lord Mustill in *Airedale NHS Trust v. Bland* and to Lord Reid in *S v. Mc* [1972] AC 24.
49. [1998] 3 WLR 957.
50. See further Brazier, M. (1992) *Medicine, Patients and the Law*, p. 293. Penguin, London.
51. [1998] 3 WLR 953.
52. Bailey Harris, R. (1998) Pregnancy, Autonomy and Refusal of Medical Treatment. *Law Quarterly Review* 550, p. 554.
53. For example, *Re B* [1987] 2 All ER 206 and the discussion in the Law Commission Report *Mental Incapacity* as to the involvement of judicial scrutiny of such treatment decisions, e.g. Part VI of the Report.
54. See, for example, Kennedy, I. (1997) Consent: adult, refusal of consent, capacity *Medical Law Review*, 317, pp. 320–25.
55. See *Bolam v. Friern Hospital Management Committee* [1957] 2 All ER 118.
56. [1997] 3 WLR 1151.
57. See further the discussion of this issue by Grubb, A. (1997) 7 Med LR 61.
58. Report of the Inquiry into the Royal Liverpool Childrens Hospital (Alder Hey) (2001) http://www.rclinquiry.org.uk and Bristol Inquiry Interim Report *Removal and Retention of Human Material* (2000) http://www.bristol-inquiry.org.uk
59. Report of the Review into the Research Framework at North Staffordshire http://www.doh.gov.uk/wmro/northstaffs.htm and see Chapter 12A in this book.
60. Bristol Royal Infirmary Final Report (2001) Chapter 23.
61. Bristol Royal Infirmary Final Report, p. 286.
62. *Sidaway v. Bethlem Royal Hospital Governors* [1985] 2 WLR 503.
63. DoH (2001) *Reference Guide to Consent for Examination and Treatment*, para 5.6.
64. See for a similar approach GMC (1998) *Seeking Patients Consent: The ethical considerations*. General Medical Council, London.
65. See *Chatterton v. Gerson* [1981] QB 432.
66. See generally Winslow, G.R. (1984) From Loyalty to Advocacy A New Metaphor For Nursing. *Hastings Centre Report* 32. Bernal, E.W. (1992) The Nurse as Patient Advocate. *Hastings Centre Report*, 33.
67. UKCC (1996) *Guidelines for Professional Practice*, p. 18.
68. See further as to the extent of the obligation of a nurse to obey doctors' instructions, Montgomery, J. (1993) Doctors' handmaidens: the legal contribution. In McVeigh, S. & Wheelar, S. *Law and Medical Regulation*. Dartmouth, Aldershot.
69. See Brazier, M. (1991) Revised consent forms in the NHS. *Professional Negligence*, 148.

B   An Ethical Perspective – Consent and Patient Autonomy

Bobbie Farsides

Consent is a moral and legal cornerstone of contemporary health care. Interventions which proceed without the consent of the patient immediately require moral scrutiny, and even where it is claimed that consent has been given we want to ensure that this means much more than the mere fact that a form has been signed. It is important to show that far from being a protective mechanism for health care professionals, the primary role of consent is to protect patients, and particularly to protect their status as autonomous individuals who have an interest in remaining in control of their own lives.

In part A of this chapter, Jean McHale has given a very full account of consent in a legal context. However, she and other medical lawyers are quick to point out that the standards set by law are not necessarily those we would wish to reach through ethical argument. Nor indeed might the legally focused reasons for acquiring consent fully reveal why we consider it to be ethically important. In ethical terms consent is important because it demonstrates respect for autonomy, it protects the autonomous individual from certain harms, and through participating in a consent process the person's autonomy may be further enhanced [1].

Autonomy is both a prerequisite for consent and a product of it. It is also representative of a relationship between a patient and a health care professional which is contractual rather than hierarchical, egalitarian rather than paternalistic, and patient-centred rather than medically determined. Consent, when properly conceived, will look something like the concept defined by Raanon Gillon in his book *Philosophical Medical Ethics* [2]:

> '... a voluntary un-coerced decision made by a sufficiently autonomous person on the basis of adequate information to accept or reject some proposed course of action that will affect him or her.'

This definition offers what we might call a paradigm case or ideal type model, but Gillon is confident that it can be embraced by health care professionals and translated into practice. For this to happen, the health care professional must adopt a particular attitude to patients, and take seriously the duties implied by the definition.

7.6   Voluntariness, coercion and consent

Consent, Gillon tells us, is a 'voluntary and un-coerced decision'. By making this explicit he is not implying that health care professionals are in the business of directly coercing patients or forcing them into involuntary choices, but rather that the context within which decisions are made might not always enhance the voluntariness of the decision, and might sometimes be coercive. Furthermore the broader context within which the patient operates might have limiting effects of which the health care professional should be aware.

By definition patients have concerns about their health, and despite greater access to medical information the health care professional is still the expert upon whom they depend. Hospitals can be intimidating and alien environments within which people are stripped of many of their usual props, and where those aspects of their identity which give them confidence can be undermined. The sense of health care as a scarce resource might also have an impact, with individuals worrying about the consequences of their actions upon how and when they will be treated.

In broader terms patients do not shed their other social identities when they enter the hospital setting. For some individuals their ability to consent may be compromised by their position within their cultural group. For example, women within certain cultures might have the capacity to consent, but would not expect to have the right to determine what happens to them due to cultural norms and expectations. Individual women might therefore be unpractised in exercising choices of the type involved in consenting within a health care setting [3]. This could pose difficulties when they are faced with difficult choices such as whether to accept an offer of pre-natal screening for genetically inherited diseases common to their ethnic group [4].

It is of course important to avoid stereotypical assumptions and to determine in the particular case whether an individual is subject to such pressure. However, particularly in situations where consent is being discussed through an interpreter, it is important to explore whether a patient is being allowed to make a voluntary decision, or whether he/she is subject to coercive influences, be they overt or subtle.

7.7   Consent and autonomy

According to Gillon's definition, consent is the domain of 'sufficiently autonomous people'. This immediately affords us a class of patients unable to consent, but it also allows for less clear cut cases where a person's autonomy might be compromised or undeveloped, but the question remains about whether they are *sufficiently* autonomous to operate in the current situation. It also raises the profoundly important question of what to do in the absence of sufficient autonomy.

Autonomy is a fundamentally significant concept in Anglo-American bioethics, and the importance of respecting patient autonomy is clearly highlighted in the codes of ethics governing the main health care professions. There are many reasons why autonomy has become such a dominant concept, some historical, some cultural, and some to do with the success of particular models of analysis within bioethics.

In the latter part of the twentieth century an emphasis on individual autonomy sat happily with the prevailing political ethos which saw the breakdown of traditional socialism and communism, and a wide-scale shift towards market driven libertarianism. In a political climate which favoured individualism over collectivism and personal effort over state welfare it is hardly surprising that autonomy was what the advertising executives call a positive buzz word. The dominance of Northern European and American culture with its emphasis on such notions as privacy, individual initiative and consumerism led to the individual being appealed to and represented in most areas of their life as a potential exerciser of choice. To be autonomous was to fit into the picture of what it meant to be an effective and successful member of society [5].

In terms of professional culture within the health service the pendulum had swung against medical paternalism, and a general attack on the medical model of care led to a recharacterisation of the classic relationship between doctor and patient, and doctor and nurse. Instead of the all powerful doctor and his (sic) handmaid the nurse ministering to the sick patient, the relationship between carers and patient was now presented as a contractual model with each party having rights and duties. The patient became the client, and in some senses at least became indistinguishable from any other type of consumer. The nurse was encouraged to develop her own professional autonomy and where necessary act to promote that of the patients if it was under threat from the doctor [6].

Given its high profile within both academic and professional literature it is important to be clear about what one means by the term autonomy, and what one assumes is involved in paying it due respect. To quote Beauchamp and Childress [7], 'respect for the autonomous choices of other persons runs as deep in common morality as any principle, but little agreement exists about its nature and strength or about specific rights of autonomy'.

Here are just a few frequently quoted accounts of what it means to be autonomous, demonstrating the range of ideas theorists have seen in the concept:

'I am autonomous if I rule me and no one else rules I.' [8]
'A person is autonomous to the degree that what he thinks and does cannot be explained without reference to his own activity of mind.' [9]
'[A]cting autonomously is acting from principles that we would consent to as free and equal rational beings.' [10]
'I and I alone am ultimately responsible for the decisions I make and am in that sense autonomous.' [11]

The word autonomy is derived from the Greek *autos* and *nomia*, and means self rule. Most definitions remain true to this root, and include ideas of self governance, sovereignty, control and quite often independence. To be autonomous is to be in control of your life in a very particular way, referring as it does to rationality as opposed to mere freedom. Responsibility is quite appropriately seen as a closely related concept and the autonomous person may be free or unfree to act upon their autonomous choices, but in doing so must accept some responsibility for the consequences [12]. More extreme definitions sometimes appear to suggest that one can only enjoy full autonomy if the choices one makes are completely unaffected by others. However, this is not the only way to think about autonomy, and more recently theorists have attempted to offer definitions which do not commit them to the substantive independence seen as necessary by many of the philosophers quoted above.

Gerald Dworkin, who quotes all the preceding definitions in his own work, characterises autonomy as 'the capacity of a person critically to reflect upon, and then attempt to accept or change his or her preferences, desires, values and ideals.' [13]. To explain himself more fully he states:

> 'Putting the various pieces together, autonomy is conceived of as a second-order capacity of persons to reflect critically upon their first-order preferences, desires, wishes, and so forth and the capacity to accept or attempt to change these in the light of higher-order preferences and values. By exercising such a capacity, persons define their nature, give meaning to their lives and take responsibility for the kind of person they are.' (p. 20)

Despite the variety in these definitions it is possible to glean the essence of the concept, and it is obvious that valuing and respecting autonomy entails respecting the person's right to give or withhold their consent to interventions which will affect them. By participating in the consenting process the autonomous person has the opportunity to judge the choice within the larger context of their life, goals and projects and make a decision consistent with the values they hold and the path they wish to pursue.

7.7.1   Sufficient autonomy to consent

By making the criteria 'sufficiently autonomous' Gillon demands that we judge the capacity of an individual to act autonomously in a given situation, rather than label groups and individuals capable of giving consent or otherwise. This is consistent with the approach advocated in law. Instead of making stereotypical assumptions which might lead us to classify some types of people as non-autonomous, we have to judge the capacity of individuals to make particular decisions and choices. This is not to deny that some human beings fall outside the category of autonomous being, examples being the fetus, the neonate, and the person in persistent vegetative state [14].

However, groups such as children [15] and the cognitively impaired might benefit from closer attention and careful discrimination between individuals, and it would be incumbent upon those dealing with these groups to judge each individual in relation to the capacity required in a particular situation [16]. People with quite severe learning disabilities or mental health problems could be seen as autonomous in certain respects and circumstances, and therefore able to give or withhold their consent.

In some types of case there will be heated debate over the extent to which people can be autonomous and thereby capable of consenting. Examples differ in kind but might include people with eating disorders or people with non-mainstream religious views such as the Jehovah's Witness cited in part A of this chapter. In the first case there may be a real difficulty in ascertaining the extent to which the underlying illness affects a person's autonomy, but the fact that it is an illness rather than a chosen way of life will be seen to make a difference. Just as the substance abuser's or alcoholic's first-order desire for their drug impairs their autonomy, the person with an eating disorder is disproportionately determined by the relationship they have with food. Having said this, it is important to remember that even those who find aspects of their life dominated by illness or addiction might remain capable of making autonomous choices in other areas of their life.

One of the reasons that respect for autonomy and the prioritising of consent are seen as important in the context of health care delivery is because both are seen as a corrective for paternalistic attitudes. However, paternalism can be understood in a number of ways and it is at least possible that some forms of paternalism are morally acceptable in certain circumstances. Hard paternalism is defined as acting or choosing on another's behalf because you feel qualified to do so, and because you believe it to be in their best interest that you do so irrespective of their past or future consent, and irrespective of their belief that they are perfectly able to act on their own behalf. Such paternalism is difficult to justify, and by underlining the importance of acquiring consent even in difficult circumstances we protect against paternalistic practices of this type being widespread.

Soft paternalism on the other hand involves acting on another's behalf and in their best interest because you believe them to be temporarily unable to exercise their autonomy, which could translate into a temporary inability to participate in the consenting process. In such cases one might protect against the unacceptable excesses of paternalism by introducing another notion of consent often referred to as hypothetical consent. In such a case one might choose in the patient's best interest and with reference to ideas about what they might or might not consent to were they able to participate. Thus we intervene only because we consider them to be unable to consent for themselves, and in deciding for them we attempt to make a choice that they will ultimately accept.

7.7.2 Insufficient autonomy to consent

The question of how to proceed morally in the absence of consent is a difficult one. Various routes have been explored, for example the use of proxies, such as in the case of parents choosing for children [17]. However, proxy consent is not unproblematic, for example one has to decide *how* to decide for another. One could attempt to choose as they would have done had they been able to do so, or one could try instead to choose in their best interests. Neither route is easy.

Advance directives have been discussed frequently in recent years. Although their legal status remains ambiguous, the ethical principles behind such documents are clear, in that they attempt to allow an individual to give or withhold consent at a point at which their lack of capacity would usually exclude them. More usually they take the form of pre-stated treatment refusals, and as such their enforcement is dependent on the patient finding themselves in the clinical situations they have anticipated. In the case of organ donorship however, they take the form of a permission to act upon the person's body after death. In both cases problems might arise if the wishes of the person who signed the document conflict with those later responsible for their care.

7.7.3   Sufficient information

As clearly stated in Gillon's definition, the moral and legal requirement to acquire consent commits the health care professional to provide *sufficient* information to allow that consent to be given, therefore the room for negotiation is sometimes limited. In the conclusion to part A of this chapter Jean McHale points out that recent developments might contribute towards a standardisation of approaches to the disclosure of information [18]. However, there are contexts within which the autonomous patient must be allowed to determine the amount of information they are given. On the issue of prognosis, for example, a health care professional might have good reason to assume that it is in the interests of the patient to know their predicted future, but it would be difficult to justify imposing the information upon an autonomous individual who has clearly stated that they do not wish to know [19]. Thus the autonomy of the patient and the need to respect it might have to trump the health care professional's commitment to fuller disclosure and their own beliefs about what is in the patient's best interest. Just as Jean McHale requires the nurse to justify withholding information, the nurse must also have valid reasons for imparting information that the competent patient does not wish to receive [20].

The term 'adequate information' calls for judgement to be applied, and since at least the early 1990s there has been a great deal of debate around the issue of what counts as sufficient, with some commentators suggesting that the standards required in some contexts force doctors to be needlessly cruel in imposing information upon people [21]. One area of concern relates to clinical experimentation, where we have come to believe that the information sufficient for consent must be particularly detailed. As a research nurse will often be the person involved in the process of providing information and acquiring consent, she must contribute to the complex decisions about how much information is sufficient, and when more information is unnecessary and maybe even harmful [22].

7.8   Deliberation

The requirement that a patient should have the time and opportunity to deliberate before making a choice seems common sense. Health care choices often have far reaching effects, some of which will only become apparent upon reflection. Even in the most straightforward of decisions a patient will probably benefit from believing that they had been given time to decide rather than being rushed into a decision. Admittedly there will be emergency situations in which this will not be possible. For example, if an event occurs within childbirth which threatens the safety of the woman and the unborn child, a decision might have to be made with great haste. Furthermore, the practicalities of outpatient clinics might determine that certain choices need to be discussed and decided on in the course of one visit. However, generally speaking, time should be allowed for the patient to absorb the information given and think about the choice they might want to make. This could be particularly true, for example, when someone is faced with choices soon after receiving bad news. Many oncologists claim that once a patient has been given a cancer diagnosis little of what is said in the remainder of the consultation is heard let alone taken in. Therefore to ensure that consent can be given to any treatment proposed, it seems particularly important to handle carefully the transition between the initial information about disease status and later discussion about treatment choices.

7.9   The right to refuse or accept

It could be argued that many health care professionals perceive consent as relatively unproblematic for as long as people make the choices they expect them to make. However, it should be allowed that an autonomous patient might choose not to follow medical or nursing advice, hence Gillon's requirement that we acknowledge a right to accept *and* a right to refuse. Some refusals will be the product of misinformation, ignorance or cognitive impairment, but many will be as a result of a difference of opinion or belief between the patient or patient's guardian, and the health care professional.

The reasons for the difference could differ. Some people might attach themselves willingly and strongly to cultural or spiritual/religious beliefs which place them under particular moral obligations, which in turn means that they accept a certain loss of control over their choices without necessarily losing their autonomy. So, for example, a devout Catholic might refuse an offer of antenatal screening for Down's Syndrome because she knows that her beliefs exclude the possibility of terminating the pregnancy. Others might have very particular views about how they want their life to be shaped, and particularly how they want it to end, and they would make their choices consistent with these goals and standards, possibly even refusing life-saving treatments.

In the case of the person with religious views, the situation is complicated by the fact that we sometimes have a very narrow conception of the types of choices autonomous people make, and the types of belief that they can acceptably attach themselves to. We seem to have little difficulty in allowing some religions to determine the choices people make for themselves, yet in other cases we find the beliefs and consequent choices more difficult to accept. For example, a professional might allow that a devout Catholic would choose to risk a life-threatening tenth pregnancy rather than use contraceptives, whereas the same person might find it more difficult to accept a Jehovah's Witness rejection of a life-saving blood transfusion. It could be argued that the difference here is not between the choices being made, both of which could have devastating effects, but in our attitude to the two bodies of faith, one of which is considered mainstream and acceptable, the other less so [23].

In fact it could be argued that the perceived difference between these cases is the result of mere prejudice, given the equivalence of the consequences. Given this danger it is worth remembering that one obstacle to respecting the autonomy of others and their right to refuse might be the fact that we operate in an ideological context which is quick to define ideas outside the mainstream as inappropriate subjects of rational choice.

Hence the need to combine a commitment to respect for autonomy and the valuing of consent with a commitment to tolerance, that is a willingness to accept that people will make choices that we find unacceptable. For as long as these choices do not entail an unacceptable degree of harm to others we are obliged to accept what they choose and the reasons they give for doing so. The dilemmas we might face as a result of this are real, particularly when we see the demand that we should respect a patient's autonomy conflicting with the beneficently motivated duty of care we believe we have towards them.

7.10   The consent process: translating theory into practice

To translate a theoretical commitment to respect for autonomy into a practical reality requires that a nurse acquires certain skills and accepts a responsibility to practice them. Given the contact the nurse has with patients and the situations within which they meet and interact, the nurse will be required at different times to assess competence and voluntariness and autonomy, enhance it where it is lacking, respect it where it is present, and find ways of promoting the patients' interests and well-being where it is not present. The nurse will be a primary provider of information, and will often be best placed to judge the extent to which the patient has understood, digested and deliberated upon it. The nurse is often a key figure in the consenting process. Her involvement will require her to engage in a number of different types of activity and utilise a variety of skills.

Communication

One of the prerequisites to acquiring a morally and legally valid consent is to communicate effectively with the patient. Only by doing so will you understand them as an individual, and learn enough about the context from which they have come to the health care setting. One needs to establish how they are coping with being in the health care setting, and what they hope to gain from their contact with health care professionals. Such information also needs to be effectively and appropriately communicated within the multi-professional team caring for the patient. Relevant information needs to be appropriately staged and given in such a way as to inform without needlessly distressing.

Cultural literacy

Given the earlier claims about the extent to which a person's autonomy might be compromised or simply overlooked as a result of their cultural context, there are important reasons for nurses to understand the cultural context within which they operate and the beliefs and practices of the different groups that live alongside them. Cultural differences must be respected; however, tolerance and understanding does not commit one to permitting *all* choices because they are defended as culturally significant [24].

Clinical knowledge-base

Given the contemporary commitment to evidence based practice the nurse should be aware of what has been shown to be good practice in her field. The information which informs her own work should then be shared with patients in a manner which will assist in their decision making. However, there might be situations in which the nurse's understanding of the situation will differ from the view offered to the patient by others involved in his or her care. In such cases it is important that these differences are resolved between the professionals, so that the patient is not given conflicting or contradictory messages.

Support

The nurse has an important supportive role in helping those who are unable or unwilling to engage in the consenting process. This might entail acting as the patients' advocate, or it might often entail facilitating the patient in getting their own views heard, sometimes in situations where the patient is in conflict with both their family members and other professionals. To perform this role effectively the nurse may need to develop and enhance her professional autonomy, and thereby increase her power to represent the patient's view to her medical colleagues. She might also have to be non-judgemental and non-directive, acting simply as a rapporteur for the patient.

7.11   Conclusion

The nursing profession has a valuable contribution to make in ensuring that patients understand the significance of the consent they are asked for, and the obstacles that might lie in the way of their giving it. Individual nurses can help patients to exercise their autonomy, and provide them with the information they need to make choices consistent with their interests and goals. They can support their patients in what is often an alien and intimidating environment, and where necessary can act as their advocates. The nursing profession can challenge those aspects of the health care delivery system which work against the patient body being able to participate meaningfully in the decision making processes which affect their care.

7.12   Notes and references

1. Beauchamp, T. & Childress, J. (2001) *Principles of Biomedical Ethics, 5 edition*. Oxford University Press, Oxford.
2. Gillon, R. (1985, reprinted 1996) *Philosophical Medical Ethics*, p. 113. John Wiley and Sons, Chichester.
3. See Cullinan, T. Other societies have different concepts of autonomy. Letter to the BMJ republished in Len Doyal and Jeffrey S. Tobias (eds) (2001) *Informed Consent in Medical Research*. BMJ Books, London.
4. Rapp Rena, 'Testing Women Testing Fetuses', and Wolf, Susan. 'Erasing difference:

Race Ethnicity and Gender in Bioethics'. In Donchin, Anne & Purdy, Laura M. (1999) *Embodying Bioethics: Recent Feminist Advances.* Rowman and Littlefield, Maryland.

5. See Farsides, C. (1998) Autonomy and its implications for palliative care: a northern European perspective. *Palliative Medicine*, 12, pp. 147–51.
6. Farsides, C. Autonomy and Responsibility in Midwifery. In S. Budd & U. Sharma (eds) (1994) *The Healing Bond*, Routledge, London.
7. Beauchamp, T. & Childress, J. (2001) *Principles of Biomedical Ethics, 5th edition.* Oxford University Press, Oxford.
8. Feinberg, Joel (1972) The idea of a free man. In *Education and the Development of Reason* (ed. R.F. Dearden) p. 30. Routledge and Kegan Paul, London.
9. Dearden, R.F. (1972) Autonomy and Education. In *Education and the Development of Reason* (ed. R.F. Dearden) p. 453. Routledge and Kegan Paul, London.
10. Rawls, John (1971) *A Theory of Justice*, p. 516. Harvard University Press, Cambridge.
11. Lucas, J.L. (1966) *Principles of Politics*, p. 101. Oxford University Press, Oxford.
12. Farsides in Budd, S. & Sharma, U. (eds) *The Healing Bond.* Routledge, London.
13. Dworkin, G. (1989) *The Theory and Practice of Autonomy.* Cambridge University Press, Cambridge.
14. Harris, J. (1985) *The Value of Life.* Routledge, London.
15. Alderson, P. (1992) In the genes or in the stars? Children's competence to consent. *Journal of Medical Ethics*, 18, 119–24.
16. Buchanan, A.E. & Brock, D.W. (1989) *Deciding for others: the ethics of surrogate decision making.* Cambridge University Press, Cambridge.
17. See BMA Ethics Committee (2000) *Consent, Rights and Choices in Health Care for Children and Young People*, BMA, London, December.
18. See Chapter 7A and also Dimond, B. (2001) Legal Aspects of Consent 4: The duty to inform patients of risks. *British Journal of Nursing*, **10** (8) April/May, pp. 544–5.
19. Jackson, J. (2001) *Truth Trust and Medicine*, esp. Chapter 9, pp. 130–46. Routledge, London.
20. See Chapter 7A on omitting info.
21. Tobias, J. & Souhami, R. (1993) Fully informed consent can be needlessly cruel. *BMJ*, 307, 1199–201.
22. See Buckman, R. (1994) *How to Break Bad News*, esp. Chapter 4. Pan Books, London.
23. For an interesting discussion of this issue see Des Autels *et al.* (1999) *Praying for a Cure When Medical and Religious Practice Conflict.* Rowman and Littlefield Publishers Inc, Lanham, Maryland.
24. See Macklin, R. (1999) *Against Relativism: Cultural Diversity and the search for ethical universals in medicine*, Chapters 1–5 Oxford University Press, Oxford, also Heyd, David (ed.) (1996) *Toleration An Elusive Virtue*, Princeton, Bognor Regis.

Chapter 8

Responsibility, Liability and Scarce Resources

A   The Legal Perspective

Robert Lee

Arguments rage about the availability of resources for health care. In spite of government claims regarding additional resources and falling waiting times within the NHS, it is apparent that delivery of medical services takes place in a climate of resource constraint. The purpose of this section is to examine the legal problems which may arise for the nurse in attempting to provide patient care and maintain professional standards under such economic pressures. Among the issues considered are the possible allowances made by the courts if nurses are asked to perform duties which outstrip their competence or qualifications, and the options for the nurse faced with such a request. In order to consider this, it is necessary to explain the standard of care demanded by the law.

8.1   Standards of care

All nurses owe their patients a duty of care [1] Liability is likely to follow if that duty is breached [2]. This is an issue covered in detail in Chapter 6A, but it may be useful to reiterate some basic points here. A breach will consist of a failure to meet the requisite standard of care. Famously, that standard is determined by the *Bolam* test – 'the standard of the ordinary skilled man exercising and professing to have that special skill' [3]. This standard is objective. This is a well-established principle and was reiterated in the House of Lords in *Whitehouse* v. *Jordan* (1981) [4], on appeal from a judgment of Lord Denning in the Court of Appeal which seemed to propound 'the near infallibility of clinical judgement' [5]. Lord Edmund-Davies stressed that if a surgeon (as it was in that case) fails to meet the *Bolam* standard in any respect – even while within the exercise of clinical judgement – then the surgeon must be adjudged negligent. He cited with approval the *Bolam* test as applied in the decision of the Privy Council in *Chin Keow* v. *Government of Malaysia* (1967):

'[W]here you get a situation which involves the use of some special skill or competence, then the test as to whether there has been negligence or not is not the test of the man on the top of the Clapham omnibus, because he has not got this special skill. The test is the standard of the ordinary skilled man, exercising and professing to have that special skill.'

One possible criticism of the *Bolam* test is that it might allow a body of specialists within medicine to attest that a particular practice is followed within the profession even though it may be less than desirable. The real fear is that the experts called as witnesses may dictate to the court what amounts to beneficial practice rather than the court upholding objective standards. In the judgments of the House of Lords in *Bolitho* v. *City and Hackney Health Authority* (1996) it was emphasised that the body of opinion must be reasonable and must have a logical basis. Where this is in doubt it is open to the court to question the reasonable nature of the practice by taking into account whether the experts have addressed properly and adequately the risks and benefits to the patients of the practice before reaching a conclusion which is defensible. It should be said that it will be very rare indeed for the court to reach a conclusion that the views genuinely propounded by a medical expert were unreasonable.

The objectivity of the standard is crucial. The law will take no account of human failings in determining whether or not there has been a breach of the duty of care. Within any walk of life, people differ in their capacity to discharge a job. Some are more innovative or energetic; others are more thorough or painstaking. However, in imposing an external and objective standard, nurses are given some protection. Thus, there may be a reason why the nurse failed to meet the required standard – tiredness or inexperience for example. Nonetheless, negligence can and will be found. No-one need suggest that the nurse acted in bad faith. Decisions taken in good faith may lead to liability if the objective standard of skill and care is not met [6]. Equally, it will matter not that any failure is a single lapse in a long and trouble-free career. Liability may follow.

The point is well made in the judgment of Lord Justice Mustill in the case of *Wilsher* v. *Essex Area Health Authority* (1986) in which he speaks of the possible liability for injuries to a premature baby:

'If the unit had not been there, the plaintiff would probably have died. The doctors and nurses worked all kinds of hours to look after the baby ... For all we know, they far surpassed on numerous occasions the standard of reasonable care. Yet it is said that for one lapse they ... are to be found to have committed a breach of duty.'

It follows that medical personnel may be expected to perform at a standard which, in the circumstances, they would find difficult or impossible to meet. In the words of Brazier [7]:

'a doctor who carries on beyond the point when fatigue and overwork impair his judgement remains liable to an injured patient. The fact that the doctor was required by his employer to work such hours will not affect the patient.'

This raises a host of issues. In *Johnstone* v. *Bloomsbury Health Authority* (1991), the Court of Appeal held that the defendant health authority could require junior doctors, by an express term in their contract, to work an average of up to 48 hours per week overtime. However, in exercising its discretion to require that overtime working under the contract, the health authority could not load work onto the plaintiff to such a level that it was reasonably foreseeable that his health might be damaged. This, however, does not answer a second problem which is whether medical practitioners, who feel that the work structure is such that adequate care cannot be delivered to the patient, may then refuse to work further without incurring the risk that they would be held to be in breach of their contract of employment.

8.2   The problem of inexperience

One problem facing nurses is that much of their training is on-the-job. In the case of *Wilsher*, a junior and inexperienced doctor, wishing to monitor the oxygen in the bloodstream of a premature baby, mistakenly inserted a catheter into a vein rather than an artery. Sir Nicolas Browne-Wilkinson accepted in that case that, under ordinary principles of *Bolam,* it would be generally futile to plead inexperience as a reason for failure adequately to provide specialist or technical medical services, since fault would lie in embarking on the course of treatment in the first place. However, where, as in the instant case, a first year houseman is required to acquire the necessary skill and experience in order to qualify further, 'such doctors cannot be said to be at fault if, at the start of their time, they lack the very skills which they are seeking to acquire'.

This led Sir Nicolas Browne-Wilkinson to suggest that the standard should be fixed by reference to the post occupied by the person in question. Otherwise, 'the young houseman, or the doctor seeking to obtain specialist skill in a special unit would be held liable for shortcomings in treatment without any personal fault on his part at all'. He went on to argue that liability in English law rests upon personal fault so that liability should only follow if the acts or omissions of medical personnel fell short of their qualifications or experience.

This might give some consolation to nurses for it would mean that placed in situations in which their lack of experience exposed them to the threat of legal action, they could plead such inexperience and argue that they met the duty placed upon them personally. In fact as nurses become more specialist and as more responsibility is given to nurses in terms of nurse-led primary care, this notion of pleading 'inexperience' becomes more remote. But in any case, this judgment omits a vital part of the *Bolam* test and the majority of the Court of Appeal rejected it as a correct formulation of the law. The court stated that the standard of care must be set in accordance with the special skill which the person professes to have. The patient is generally in no position to enquire whether, for example, a nurse actually possesses such a skill, hence the objectivity of the standard. If nurses hold themselves out to the patient as competent to undertake a particular procedure, a duty of care will arise and will be breached if the procedure is negligently performed.

Sir Nicolas Browne-Wilkinson's suggestion of a requirement of personal fault has appeared in earlier cases on medical malpractice [8]. It is worth noting where it leads. It would introduce a subjective standard and in so doing might lead to the problem for nurses that a finding of liability would constitute a mark of personal failure. Whatever the perception of a medical negligence claim, fault is judged by an objective standard, and persons found liable may not actually be at fault. In moving the standard towards gross negligence Browne-Wilkinson's formulation would make it harder also for the patient to recover compensation for injury.

This, in part, may explain why the two other judges in the Court of Appeal preferred a more traditional pronouncement of the *Bolam* test. In the view of Lord Justice Mustill the duty ought not to be assessed in accordance with the actor performing the duty, rather with the act performed. The standard should be set according to the post occupied. In the words of the judge:

> 'the standard is not just that of the averagely competent and well informed junior houseman ... but of such a person who fills a post in a unit offering a highly specialised service.'

Lord Justice Glidewell substantially agrees with this, saying that:

> 'In my view, the law requires the trainee or learner to be judged by the same standard as his more experienced colleagues. If it did not, inexperience would frequently be urged as a defence to an action for professional negligence.'

The wording of both of these formulations is a little loose, but both are clearly intended to indicate that where a person holds out as possessing the requisite skill to provide a particular service, then the standard will be set in accordance with the reasonable skill of the average competent professional ordinarily providing that service. The case of *Djemal* v. *Bexley HA* (1995) followed the judgment in *Wilsher* in discounting the actual experience of a senior houseman in an A&E unit in setting the required standard of care.

8.3 Risk and precautions

Although the standard itself is 'objective and impersonal' (per Lord MacMillan in *Glasgow Corporation* v. *Muir* (1943)), the circumstances in which it is exercised will be highly relevant in determining breach. This is well illustrated by a Canadian authority (*Moore* v. *Large* (1932)). The case concerned the alleged negligence of a doctor who had failed to X-ray the shoulder of a patient following that patient's fall so that a dislocation of the shoulder was overlooked. The court could find no negligence:

> 'It has not surely come to this that if the cause of the trouble is not apparent to the eye of the surgeon or physician he must advise an X-ray or take the consequences to his reputation and to his pocket for not having done so. Is the X-ray to be the only arbitrator in such a case and are years of study and experience to be cast aside as negligible?' [9]

This would probably not be so today, but what has changed is not the availability of X-ray (it was available in 1932) but societal expectations of the use of this device in checking against the risk of a particular disorder. To take an X-ray in such circumstances would now be almost standard practice although interestingly, with the link with cancer, attitudes are changing again. Further, the acknowledgment of the risk and any negligence disregarding it are judged by the standards of the time of the incident and not when any case comes ultimately to court. As Lord Denning said in *Roe* v. *Ministry of Health* (1954), a case concerning contaminated anaesthetic:

> 'He did not know that there could be undetectable cracks, but it was not negligent for him not to know it at that time. We must not look at the 1947 accident with 1954 spectacles.'

This raises the question of how a breach of the standard of care may be determined.

Generally, it will require some balance between the good which the practitioner seeks to achieve by intervention and the risks run by a particular course of conduct in the light of the availability of precautions or safeguards. This may be illustrated by the case of *Mahon* v. *Osborne* (1939) in which there was seemingly obvious negligence in terminating an operation without removing a swab which was left under part of the liver and which caused a complication which eventually resulted in the death of the patient. Lord Justice Scott was prepared, however, to recognise circumstances 'where the patient has been taking the anaesthetic badly, and is suffering from shock' such that the doctor is anxious to terminate the operation and exercises discretion so that 'as soon as he has completed the removal of all swabs of which he is at that moment aware, he asks the sister for the count, and forthwith starts to close the wound'. In the judge's view, a finding of negligence would not be inevitable in such a situation. Here, the importance attached to preserving the life of a patient might outweigh the risk inherent in hastening the swab count.

It is possible to envisage a wide variety of situations within which risks, ordinarily intolerable in good medical practice, are run in situations of dire emergency. In the words of Lord Justice Mustill in *Wilsher*:

> 'full allowance must be made for the fact that certain aspects of treatment may have to be carried out in ... "battle conditions". An emergency may overburden the available resources, and, if an individual is forced by circumstances to do too many things at once, the fact that he does one of them incorrectly, should not likely be taken as negligence.'

Note that the absence of resources is not of itself a defence, but the fact of the emergency may change the circumstances in which nursing is conducted to the point that if an ordinarily competent nurse might reasonably have made a particular error under such pressure, then the court will not find negligence. This is well illustrated by a case from Manitoba, *Roydch* v. *Krasey* (1971) in which a doctor examined an intoxicated patient in a lorry at 1 AM with the aid of a torch. There was no negligence in his failure to diagnose injuries to the chest, ribs and lungs. One way of explaining this is to say that, under an objective standard, the difficulties in discharging the duty of care would have faced any practitioner working under such circumstances.

8.4   Staff shortages

This then raises the question of what will happen if, in the course of medical practice, a nurse is required to work under substandard conditions, or with an obvious shortfall in resources. Can such circumstances be taken into account in assessing breach of duty? In the following section, which considers shortages of nursing staff, the problem of inexperience will not be revisited; rather attention is directed here to problems created by overall shortages in the nursing resources required to discharge the needs of the patients.

There are a series of cases concerning the provision of nursing staff, many of which involved relatively straightforward issues of patient supervision. *Dryden* v. *Surrey County Council* (1936) is a case involving two elements of medical negligence. One involved the failure to remove a swab, leading to a finding of negligence against the surgeon. However, an action was also brought against the Council on the basis that the nurses, whom they employed, had failed adequately to supervise the plaintiff, so that the error went unnoticed. This element of the claim seems to have been rejected by the court on the basis that, as a matter of evidence, the plaintiff failed to exhibit symptoms which might have indicated a complication of this type. Nonetheless, the court did consider that element of the claim which argued that the responsibility of the Council lay in their failure to provide competent nursing staff as the ward was clearly understaffed. In fact, there were 54 beds in the ward and a nursing staff of one sister, one staff nurse and five probationers. This, as the judge admitted in a masterful piece of understatement, was not as good as 'the attention which a person will receive ... if ... he is fortunate enough to pay for the undivided attention of one nurse or ... two nurses'. However, in the view of the judge, neither the presence of such a large number of probationers, nor the fact that the matron had been seeking to gain an increase in staff, established 'negligence by under staffing'.

This, at first glance, may seem rather surprising. In fact, however, it may be saying little more than, whatever the level of staff, there will be no finding of negligence unless some injury can be attributed to the lack of nursing care. Where this is so, the court will be required to consider the level of nursing provision. This must be done for the particular ward in question, for once again the courts are dealing with risk of injury, and the nursing provision required in an intensive care facility may not be that of the ante-natal unit (*Knight* v. *Home Office* (1990)).

This point is brought home clearly by the case of *Robertson* v. *Nottingham HA* (1997) in which a series of errors of communication in the delivery of obstetric care resulted in the claimant (suing by her mother) bringing an action in negligence on the basis that her delivery at an earlier stage would have prevented the brain damage from which she now suffered. In fact the claimant both at trial and on appeal failed to prove that her brain damage resulted from the breakdown in communication. Nonetheless, the Court of Appeal emphasised that a health authority was under a duty to establish a proper system of care. That duty could not be delegated to others (see also *M* v. *Calderdale & Kirklees HA* (1998)) and the standard of care would be judged in accordance with what might reasonably be expected of a hospital of the size and type. In that case the standard expected was that ordinarily exercised in a large teaching centre hospital of excellence.

This point may be demonstrated also by cases in which known suicide risks have injured or killed themselves following admission to hospital. In *Thorne* v. *Northern Group Hospital Management Committee* (1964) the patient's husband had informed the nursing staff of his wife's threats of suicide, and the patient, who had been undergoing treatment on a medical ward of a general hospital, was due to be transferred from the ward to an outside neurosis unit for further assessment. She was left unsupervised when both the nurse and the sister left the ward together. The patient left the ward, returned home and committed suicide. The husband failed in his action against the Hospital Management Committee. In the view of Mr Justice Edmund Davies:

> 'The duty owed by hospital authorities and staff to a patient is that of reasonable care and skill in the given circumstances. Whether a breach of that duty has been established depends on the proven facts including what was known or should have been known about a particular patient and the fact that the defendants impliedly undertook to exhibit professional skill and administrative care of reasonable competence and adequacy towards their patient. They must take reasonable care to avoid acts or omissions which they can reasonably foresee would be likely to harm the patient entrusted to their charge; but they need not guard against merely possible (as distinct from reasonably probable) harm. On the other hand the degree of care which will be regarded as reasonable is proportionate both to the degree of risk involved and the magnitude of the mischief which may be occasioned to the particular patient in the absence of due care.'

This case may be contrasted with that of *Selfe* v. *Ilford and District Hospital Management Committee* (1970) in which the plaintiff, whose attempt at suicide by a drug overdose had failed, was admitted to a ward of 27 patients. The ground floor ward contained four known suicide risks, grouped at one end of the room. Selfe, a quiet and withdrawn man of 17, was left unattended on the ward when two of the three nurses on duty left the ward without informing the third. While that nurse was attending a patient elsewhere in the ward, Selfe climbed out of a window and made his way up to a roof from which he jumped. His attempt at suicide again failed, but he sued for his resultant injuries on the basis of negligent nursing supervision. Evidence indicated that, even with all of the nurses on the ward, an additional nurse was probably required. Mr Justice Hinchcliff found for the plaintiff, stressing that the high degree of risk on the ward required a commensurate increase in the care provided.

There are a number of cases which show, however, that where the staffing is adequate to meet the standard of care imposed upon the hospital or unit, a nurse will not be liable for every untoward incident on a ward. Examples of this principle include: *Gravestock* v. *Lewisham HMC* (1955) (injury following fall of nine year old running in ward while nurse bringing food through to the ward); *Cox* v. *Carshalton HMC* (1955) (inhaler slipped and scalded disabled minor as nurse away for matter of seconds); and *Size* v. *Shenley HMC* (1970) unreported (nurse failed to reach mentally unstable patient before he attacked the plaintiff).

8.5   Lack of resources

Once a finding of fact is made that provision is in some way inadequate, a related issue arises of whether it can ever be a defence to plead lack of resources. The answer is simply no. If nursing staff meet approved nursing practice to a *Bolam* standard, then this may refute a claim of negligence, but if they fall short of that standard, then, once again, it does not matter why, and lack of resources is no better an argument than that of tiredness or inexperience.

However, in spite of the objective nature of the standard, and the lack of any necessary element of personal fault in a finding of negligence, there is without question a move away from finding medical staff liable in situations in which lack of adequate resources makes it impossible to meet a required standard. This is clear from the judgment of Sir Nicolas Browne-Wilkinson in *Wilsher* in which he poses the following question:

> 'Should the authority be liable if it demonstrates that, due to the financial stringency under which it operates, it cannot afford to fill the posts with those possessing the necessary experience?'

He goes on to say:

> 'in my judgment, the law should not be distorted by making findings of personal fault against individual doctors who are, in truth, not at fault in order to avoid such questions.'

Similarly in *Robertson* v. *Nottingham HA* Lord Justice Brooke, in finding that the hospital system had been negligently run, expressed the following view:

> 'It would be unjust and unfair to hold that Dr X, after being let down ... by the negligence of others, was himself negligent...'

One can quibble with this. It is not the law which is being distorted; rather it is the law which is distorting the concept of blame. Nonetheless, this move away from the concept of individual liability on the part of a medical professional, in favour of asking questions about the organisation as a whole, is significant, and it is important to understand what it represents.

In broad terms, the courts have been very reluctant to interfere with resource decisions made in good faith within the NHS. Most famously, In *R* v. *Cambridge HA ex parte B (a minor)*(1995) the Court of Appeal refused to intervene when a health authority refused to fund treatment for a ten year old girl with leukaemia, even though at first instance Mr Justice Laws would have demanded that the health authority show that the priorities that it had established had taken account of all relevant factors. This was rejected by the Court of Appeal which stated that difficult resource decisions were not a matter for the courts. The courts would not be minded to intervene unless the decision made was manifestly such that no reasonable authority could have reached it – see *Associated Provincial Picture Houses* v. *Wednesbury Corporation* (1948) (*Wednesbury* unreasonableness).

This is a complex area which the writer has considered in much more depth elsewhere [10]. However, it is important to state that the first chinks in the judicial armour can be detected. To begin with, in a NHS which is subject in all sorts of ways to increasingly centralised control (e.g. through NICE and the development of clinical guidelines) there may be more room for the courts to insist that relevant guidelines and protocols are followed. Thus a decision not to pay for prescription costs of beta interferon to the alleged disadvantage of multiple sclerosis patients was said to be unlawful in failing to follow national policy as laid down by a government circular. However, the major development in this area must be the passage of the Human Rights Act 1998, giving the possibility of challenge by patients to treatment decisions. One can envisage potential claims under Article 2 (right to life) and Article 8 (right to family life) depending on the type of treatment and circumstances of the case. It may also be possible to invoke Article 6 claims (independent and impartial hearing) where significant decisions are taken without reference to the patient. But there is a more general point here. As described above it has been difficult to challenge treatment decisions except by reference to *Wednesbury* unreasonableness – a stern test indeed. Now, post the 1998 Act, there are signs of change. The House of Lords are beginning to speak of the need for public bodies to demonstrate that, where human rights may be at stake, decisions are proportionate (see for example the judgment of Lord Slynn in *R* v. *Secretary of State for the Environment, Transport and the Regions ex parte Alconbury and Others* (2001). This is in many ways what Mr Justice Laws would have demanded in *R* v. *Cambridge HA ex parte B* (1995), and it may allow courts to at least demand that the process of decision making by authorities is subject to scrutiny even though the courts will continue to disavow any wish to order the priorities for treatment.

8.6   From vicarious to direct liability

For many years, the view was taken that hospital authorities were not liable for actions of staff in discharging professional duties. This applied to nurses in the course of medical procedures under the guidance of the doctor whose control was thought to be 'supreme'. However, the hospital authority remained legally responsible to patients for 'purely ministerial or administrative duties' and these included 'attendance of nurses in the ward' (per Lord Justice Kennedy in *Hillyer* v. *St Bartholomew's Hospital* (1909)). This artificial division, and the concept of control which underpinned it, was difficult to maintain, and in *Gold* v *Essex County Council* (1942) Lord Greene expressed the view that:

> 'Nursing ... is just what the patient is entitled to expect from the institution, and the relationship of the nurses to the institution supports the inference that they are engaged to nurse the patients ... the idea that ... the only obligation which the hospital undertakes to perform by its nursing staff is not the essential work of nursing but only so called administrative work appears to me ... not merely unworkable in practice but contrary to the plain sense of the position.'

This case effectively established that a hospital authority would be vicariously liable for the negligence of an employee, such as a nurse. A mistake made by a nurse following the direct orders of a surgeon would probably not give rise to liability, but the surgeon no longer ruled 'supreme' even in the theatre. Following this case, a mistake by the nurse alone might mean that there would be no liability on the surgeon, but that vicarious liability might attach to the hospital authority.

It was established in cases such as *Cassidy* v. *Minister of Health* (1951) and *Roe* v. *Ministry of Health* (1954) that the test for vicarious liability was no longer one of control, but of whether the member of the medical staff was a permanent and integral part of the hospital staff. So fixed and well settled was this body of law, that from 1954 to 1990, under a governmental circular, health authorities defended claims in negligence on behalf of all staff. At date of judgment or settlement, damages would be apportioned, in accordance with the principles of vicarious liability, between the medical defence organisation and the health authority. Disputes as to the requisite shares of liability were rare.

In *Cassidy*, however, it had been suggested that certain liabilities might be direct, such that the duty of care could not be delegated 'no matter whether the delegation be to a servant under a contract of service or to an independent contractor'. For some years, this *dictum* of Lord Denning lay as an island of uncertainty in the stormy seas of medical malpractice litigation. In recent times, however, the concept of direct liability has received much greater attention. As Montgomery [11] points out:

> 'In a modern system of healthcare … the responsibilities of doctors overlap with those of nurses, midwives, managers and others. Direct liability on the part of the health and hospital authorities may represent an important tool to unravel the complexities of modem health provision.'

Direct liability may have advantages in overcoming problems of where to place responsibility amongst health care teams. Equally, it may assist the law in keeping track of standards, as pressure on resources sees the devolution of tasks to nurses which were previously performed by doctors.

All of this is a way of saying that direct liability may arise out of the failure of structures of health care delivery which have been put in place in order to discharge duties towards the patient. Thus, in *Bull* v. *Devon Area Health Authority* (1989) there was a gap of over an hour between the delivery of a first and a second twin. A significant passage of time prior to the case arriving before the court made it difficult for the defendant health authority to find evidence to dispute the claim of negligence, but Lord Justice Slade nonetheless stated that:

> 'It is possible to imagine hypothetical contingencies which would have accounted for a failure without any avoidable fault in the hospital's system, or any negligence in its working, to secure Mrs Bull's attendance by any obstetrician qualified to deliver the second twin between 7.35pm and 8.25pm. In my judgment, however, all the most likely explanations of this failure point strongly either to inefficiency in the system for summoning the assistance of the registrar or consultant, in operation of the hospital, or to negligence by some individuals in the working of that system.'

This point is supported also by Lord Justice Mustill, who speaks of a 'finding by the learned judge, amply supported by the evidence, that the system should have been such that the second twin would be delivered as soon as practicable after the first'. In considering the submission that the hospital 'could not be expected to do more than their best, allocating their limited resources as favourably as possible', Lord Justice Mustill makes the following response:

'I have some reservations about this contention, which are not allayed by the submission that hospital medicine is a public service. So it is, but there are other public services in respect of which it is not necessarily an answer to allegations of unsafety that there were insufficient resources to enable the administrators to do everything they would like to do. I do not for a moment suggest that public medicine is precisely analogous to other public services, but there is perhaps a danger in assuming that it is completely *sui generis*, and that it is necessarily a complete answer to say that even if the system in a hospital was unsatisfactory, it was no more unsatisfactory than those in force elsewhere.'

Cases like *Bull* and *Wilsher* demonstrate that there are an increasing number of instances in which there seems to be an organisational failure in the delivery of health care. If a health authority is at fault in the performance of its functions, this may be described as negligence, notwithstanding the difficulty in locating particular employees who might be said to be negligent. Arguably, this is the basis of the decision in the case of *Lindsey County Council* v. *Marshall* (1936), and also other earlier cases such as *Collins* v. *Hertfordshire County Council* (1947), which found negligence 'in the management and control of the hospital'. A number of Commonwealth authorities [12] have also found negligence in the organisation of the hospital itself.

This distinction between direct and vicarious liability was described by Lord Justice Brooke in *Robertson* when he stated that:

'If effective systems had been in place ... then the Health Authority would be vicariously liable for any negligence of those of its servants or agents who did not take proper care to ensure, so far as it is reasonably practicable, that the ... systems worked efficiently. If on the other hand, no effective systems were in place at all ... then the authority would be directly liable in negligence...'

In either event, this should allow a patient suffering a medical accident to recover, but as we move towards more systems-based approaches (through clinical protocols and the like) this type of analysis may become more common.

Finally, it may be worth noting cases involving the administration of drugs and blood products. In the Court of Appeal decision in *Blyth* v. *Bloomsbury Health Authority* (1987) [13], the defendant health authority appealed against a judgment of Mr Justice Leonard, in which he found that the health authority was negligent in failing to follow a system put in place to monitor the use of the drug Depo Provera. The appeal succeeded, the Court of Appeal finding that the judge had reached the decision, not supported by the evidence, that there had been divergence from a system put in place within the hospital. Nonetheless, the Court of Appeal seemed to have accepted that the tests used by Mr Justice Leonard in looking at whether 'on a normal day an effective system existed by which patients could get advice on contraception from those who were equipped with the necessary information to enable them to give it fully', and whether 'exceptionally something went wrong' were acceptable tests within themselves. Implicit in the Court of Appeal's judgment is the necessity for a health authority to ensure that patients within the hospital are sufficiently well counselled in relation to drugs administered.

In *Re HIV Haemophiliac Litigation* (1996), an application by the plaintiff to the court for an order requiring the Department of Health and Social Security (DHSS) to produce departmental documents relating to its policies for the importation of blood products was resisted by the DHSS, on the basis that the plaintiffs did not have a good cause of action either by breach of statutory duty or in negligence. The Court of Appeal gave judgment on the preliminary issue of whether or not the DHSS might be in breach of statutory duty under section 3 of the National Health Service Act 1977, or otherwise negligent in the design of a system to secure the physical health of the people, and the prevention, diagnosis and treatment of illness within England and Wales. This was said to result from its failure to ensure a self-sufficiency in blood, as a result of which haemophiliacs were treated with Factor VIII blood products contaminated with the HIV virus, imported from the USA. The Court of Appeal found that the relevant sections of the 1977 Act did not found an action for breach of statutory duty as it was not clear that Parliament had intended to allow individual enforcement and recovery (and see also *Danns* v. *Department of Health* (1995)). However in relation to negligence the Court of Appeal found an arguable case. In their words:

> 'It is obvious that it would be rare for a case on negligence to be proved having regard to the nature of the duties under the 1977 Act, and the fact that, in the law of negligence, it is difficult to prove a negligent breach of duty when the party charged with negligence is required to exercise discretion and to form judgments upon the allocation of public resources. That, however, is not sufficient ... to make it clear for the purposes of these proceedings that there can in law be no claim in negligence.'

It seems, therefore, that hospitals may increasingly have to face direct liability for their failure to organise adequate systems of health care delivery. Thus, in an era of resource constraint, if the delivery of health care is inadequate, it may become easier rather than more difficult for the patient to find a remedy. This is not least because the courts have traditionally been very protective of doctors (in particular) and that when negligence alleged is that of the organisation, rather than the medical professional, certain obstacles to medical negligence litigation may be removed.

8.7   Case study

The principles considered above can be illustrated by the use of a case study.

N is a sister on night duty and is in charge of a small rural hospital which some time ago closed its accident and emergency facility. Shortly before midnight on a snowy winter's evening, two people arrive by car at the hospital. R says that he has found, on the roadside very near to the hospital, an injured person, V, who accompanies him. V has been the victim of a hit-and-run incident. V is fully conscious, but appears to have been hit in his upper body and may have broken a number of bones. He is also bleeding badly from the head. The nearest accident and emergency facility is ten miles away. There is no doctor currently on duty at the rural hospital which has a sign at the gate advising that there is no accident and emergency unit within the hospital, and that persons wishing for emergency treatment should report to their nearest accident and emergency hospital.

One interesting issue here is whether N must offer treatment to the patient. In *Barnett* v. *Chelsea and Kensington Hospital Management Committee* (1968) three nightwatchmen had vomited continually since drinking tea in the early hours of the morning of New Year's Day. On finishing their shift they presented themselves to an accident and emergency department of a London hospital. They reported to a nurse who telephoned the casualty officer. Without examining the men, he told the nurse to send them home with instructions to call their own doctors in the morning. Five hours later, one of the men died from arsenic poisoning. Although the subsequent claim failed on the lack of proof of causation, it was said that where a person with obvious symptoms of illness presents himself to an accident and emergency department, a duty of care arises so that skill and care should be employed in the diagnosis of any injury.

This is so even though there will be no prior relationship with the patient. However, the general view taken by English law is that 'if a person undertakes to perform a voluntary act he is liable if he performs improperly, but not if he neglects to perform it'. It is for this reason that certain jurisdictions have enacted 'good samaritan' statutes which either place a positive duty on doctors to stop at the scene of an accident, or offer immunity to medical staff who choose to render assistance.

Although there is a statutory duty to provide sufficient accident and emergency services to meet reasonable requirements within a locality, in practice this duty will prove very difficult to enforce before the courts. There is now a significant body of case law which demonstrates that the courts will rarely intervene to review a decision on resource allocation or enforce a claim to be admitted to treatment. Nonetheless, if a non-accident and emergency hospital chooses to admit a patient to treatment, then a duty of care will arise. It follows that, in purely legal terms, N would be free to refuse treatment to V and urge R and V to present themselves to the nearest accident and emergency department. Nonetheless, once N opts to render care and assistance to V, then a duty of care arises and the question then relates to the applicable standard of care. It is clear that liability may result from negligent treatment or advice rendered by N or any failure of communication in providing V with emergency treatment.

However, given that the unit is not an accident and emergency unit, then in accordance with the case of *Roydch* v. *Krasey* (1971) (section 8.3) the circumstances in which treatment is rendered will be taken into account in determining the requisite standard of care. In *Knight* v. *Home Office* (1990), it was said that a prison hospital owes a duty of care to a mentally ill patient which is of a lower standard than that of a specialist psychiatric hospital. In that case, it was said that:

'In making the decision as to the standard to be demanded the court must bear in mind as one factor that resources available for public services are limited and that the allocation of resources is a matter for Parliament … the facilities available to deal with an emergency in a general practitioner's surgery cannot be expected to be as ample as those available in the casualty department of a general hospital.'

In *Phelps* v. *Hillingdon LBC* (1998) it was said that the only duty of a 'medical rescuer' was not to 'negligently create further danger or make the ... situation worse'. What will prove of importance is that N adequately communicates, to anyone else rendering treatment to V, the steps which she has taken and that she arranges for the necessary specialist care as expeditiously as possible.

8.8   Scarce resources and professional responsibility

Questions relating to the relevant standard of care are also significant for nurses in another context. As stated above, the law demands no more than a reasonable standard of care rather than standards of treatment which are at the cutting edge of medical science. But what should nurses do if they become convinced that patients are facing unacceptable levels of risk because the regime of treatment regularly falls short of reasonable standards? Two problems may arise for the nurse who decides to seek publicity to draw to the attention of the public the inadequacy of the care offered. The first is that the identification of a particular patient may breach principles of medical confidentiality. In addition, any public disclosure might amount to a breach of the contract of employment.

The UKCC's Guidelines for Professional Practice (1996) do not suggest an absolute duty of professional confidence. Although clause 10 of the Code of Professional Conduct instructs the nurse to protect all confidential information concerning patients and clients ... and make disclosures only with consent...' the Guidelines allow for 'exceptional circumstances' in which confidentiality must give way to disclosure upon a court order or where this is necessary in the public interest.

This is in accordance with the general law, although following the Human Rights Act 1998 English law will have to conform with Article 8 of the European Convention on Human Rights and the right to respect for private and family life. In *Attorney General* v. *Guardian Newspaper (No. 2)* (1990) Lord Goff stated that 'although the basis of the law's protection of confidence is that there is a public interest that confidence should be preserved and protected by law, nevertheless, that public interest may be outweighed by some of the countervailing public interest which favours disclosure'. However, in *X Health Authority* v. *Y* (1988) 2 All ER 648 any public interest in the disclosure of the fact that two practising doctors were being treated as AIDS patients was outweighed by the general public interest in retaining the confidentiality of AIDS related information on a patient's file. The High Court in this case intervened to restrain the publication of the disclosure when leaked by employees.

However, in the case of *W* v. *Egdell and Others* (1990) a consultant psychiatrist was employed by a patient's solicitor to prepare a report on the patient for use in the consideration of the patient's release or transfer from a secure hospital. When no use was made of that report (which highlighted the long-standing nature, not previously drawn to the authorities' attention, of W's interest in home-made bombs) the psychiatrist himself disclosed the report to the medical director of the secure unit. In turn the hospital forwarded the report to the Secretary of State. The Court of Appeal stated that whilst mental patients should be free to seek advice and assistance from independent doctors, nonetheless given the wider public interest in public safety, this form of disclosure by the psychiatrist was thought not to be in breach of any duty of confidentiality. (See also the interesting case of *Woolgar* v. *Chief Constable of Sussex Police* (1999) in which the Court allowed that the police could pass information about a nurse to the UKCC where public safety so required.)

Thus, although it might be possible to argue that disclosure of patient related information serves wider public interest in highlighting the decline in the standard of care, this is by no means obvious. Where possible, particular patients should not be identified, or if this is inevitable, then the nurse should seek the permission of that patient to refer to the particular case. Note that the public interest in ensuring that patients are not inhibited from seeking treatment may mean that confidentiality can attach even to non-identifying information concerning medical treatment (see *R* v. *Department of Health ex parte Source Informatics Ltd* (1999).

Nurses may also be troubled that voicing opinions on the regime of care may lead to disciplinary action by the employer. Indeed the fear of such disclosures led to the introduction into contracts of employment of express requirements prohibiting disclosure to the media of matters relating to the working responsibilities of employer and employee. In certain instances, it could be argued that, even in the absence of an express clause, implied duties of fidelity might dictate that any public disclosure would amount to a breach of the employment contract. Prior to 1999 there were well documented incidents in which health service employees have faced disciplinary proceedings or dismissal, apparently as a result of complaints concerning shortfalls in the standard of care. Where this led to the dismissal of an employee, that employee could consider redress by an industrial tribunal. However this was unlikely to lead to reinstatement, even where the tribunal found in favour of the dismissed nurse.

This situation changed radically in 1999 following the passage of the Public Interest Disclosure Act 1998. This allows employees to make 'protected disclosures' without victimisation or dismissal. All NHS employees are protected by these provisions, and there is no ceiling on the compensation that may be awarded if victimisation is proven. Among the categories of protected disclosure are the failure to comply with legal obligations, and the endangering of the health and safety of any individual. This may cover past as well as ongoing malpractice. However the Act also governs the manner of disclosure, encouraging initial internal disclosure if the 'whistleblower' is to receive the protection of the Act. Here a nurse may have a number of options if wishing in good faith to make a disclosure. It may be possible/appropriate for the nurse to speak directly to the persons retaining responsibility for the malpractice in question, or to his/her employer, to the Department of Health or some other relevant government department (if working in the NHS), or to an appropriate (prescribed) regulatory body – such as the Health and Safety Executive.

Disclosure outside these categories will only gain the protection of the Act in limited circumstances. For example, disclosure for personal gain (e.g. a payment from the media) will not be protected. Moreover, the nurse would have to show that internal disclosure would have been ineffective as leading to the concealment or destruction of evidence, or victimisation, or because previous, similar disclosures had been ignored. Where there is public disclosure, a court or tribunal can take into account a number of factors relating to the seriousness of the incident, issues of patient confidentiality, the workings of internal proceedings, etc. in deciding whether the disclosure is protected by the Act.

In the case of exceptionally serious disclosures it is possible to make public disclosure immediately, without the need to show fear of victimisation, likely cover-up or previous inaction. However it would be rare indeed for a nurse to be justified in going immediately to the media, when other options, such as a Member of Parliament or a professional association are available. Unfortunately there is nothing in the Act to require internal procedures to deal with complaints by nurses concerning the inadequacy of patient care. This may mean that disclosure is no easy matter for a nurse as he or she informs immediate supervisors, then the employer, only to witness prevarication or inaction. This may drag the nurse into the uncomfortable territory of increasingly public disclosure, where the nurse is already unpopular and may fear more subtle forms of prejudice – such as the failure to gain promotion.

Nonetheless, increasingly, there are professional demands made upon nurses. The UKCC Code of Conduct suggests that the nurse must report circumstances which could jeopardise standards of practice and must also report circumstances in which an appropriate standard of care cannot be provided. Such reporting should be to 'an appropriate person or authority'. Again, the UKCC Code suggests that nurses should 'decline any duties or responsibilities unless able to perform them in a safe and skilled manner'. Increasingly it seems that nurses cannot merely stand by and ignore declining standards of patient care. It is the nurse who is seen as occupying the role as patient advocate, and arguably nurses find themselves under a more direct professional duty to take action in relation to resource shortfalls than do the doctors.

8.9   Case study

W is a night duty charge nurse on a ward for acutely ill patients. She believes that the standard of care for those patients has dropped dramatically due to two events: the withdrawal of one night nurse, on a permanent basis, from ward duty, and the replacement over time of a number of more experienced nurses by junior staff. Matters come to a head when a patient dies in distressing circumstances, in a situation which W believes was largely a consequence of lack of adequate supervision on the ward.

Under the UKCC's Code of Conduct, W here should 'report to an appropriate person or authority, having regard to the physical psychological and social effects on patients and clients, any circumstances in the environment of care which would jeopardise standards of practice'. Similarly it is said that she should 'report to an appropriate person or authority any circumstances in which safe and appropriate care for patients and clients cannot be provided'. W clearly finds herself in this situation, and if the hospital in which she works operates a complaints procedure, then she would be advised to follow that procedure and voice her concerns accordingly. If no response is forthcoming, or if such complaints are swept aside, then W may wish to raise the matter with persons further up the management ladder even through to the chair of the health authority or Trust where that appears to be appropriate. Alternatively, at some point W may wish to report to the Royal College of Nursing (RCN).

On a strict interpretation of confidentiality rules it could be argued that the passage of information even between those in the health care system should take place only to serve the treatment of the patient. However, if this principle was to be followed rigorously, investigations into medical accident might be inhibited. The General Medical Council allows that doctors must judge whether it is appropriate to pass on patient information to others within the health care system so that they can perform their duties. Here the permission of the patient cannot be obtained, and public disclosure might cause distress to relatives. Arguably, however, disclosure within the health care system ought to be permissible. However, further problems may arise, where, instead of effecting any remedy, the disclosure by W leads to further problems at work. If W finds herself the subject of formal disciplinary proceedings, or indeed victimised in some way by line managers as a result of the complaint, how should W react? Prior to the 1998 Act there were few available remedies here. Section 27B of the Employment Rights Act 1996 (as amended by the Public Interest Disclosure Act 1998) allows that W should suffer no detriment as a result of her actions. If W can show any element of detriment as a result of her actions she will be able to bring a claim for compensation.

This course of action may also invite press comment, whether or not W actually instigates this. At this point, W will have to take care to avoid breaching professional confidentiality rules in any statements to the press. However, insofar as W and those giving evidence on behalf of W need to give evidence as to the particular events which led to the complaint, the disclosure will generally be permissible under professional conduct rules. Under the UKCC Code, disclosure is allowed 'where required by the order of a court'. This does not exactly cover the situation of a tribunal which will not generally proceed by witness summons or the sub-poena of witnesses. Nonetheless, it is difficult to see that a health authority or Trust would have much success in seeking to restrain by court action the disclosure of information, where that information is being legitimately used to pursue a remedy in an industrial tribunal. Indeed one in-built advantage of the 1998 Act is that it is in the long-term interests of employers to ensure that internal complaints are dealt with in a speedy and responsible manner.

8.10   Conclusion

The continual pressures to meet targets and to cap spending have had a dramatic and radical impact not only on the methods of service delivery but also on the demands and expectations placed on various health care professionals and the allocation of resources. The development of responsibility on all levels, financial, administrative and professional, down the line from the hospital administrator to the individual nurse implies that issues surrounding professional accountability and autonomy require closer examination.

This change in the underlying philosophy of the delivery of health care in some ways is running in tandem with the growth of legal problems which may arise for the nurse. Problems arise in attempting to provide patient care and maintain the professional standards expected of the 'ordinarily skilled' practitioner. The changes have had, and continue to have, resources implications. The reduction of resources may increase the instances in which nurses are placed in situations which require them to perform duties which it could be argued are beyond their level of competence or qualification. The development of professional skill and qualification is directly dependent on the training received 'on-the-job'.

If resources are stretched the qualified nursing staff will be fully utilised in the delivery of patient care, with time for training limited. Unrealistic demands may be placed on the student or newly qualified nurse, yet, in the eyes of the law, the standards required will remain objective. The spectre of liability demands that attention be given to demonstrable training for, and the maintenance of standards of, the professional nurse. It will be up to individual nurses to show that their qualifications and training are sufficient to the role and task in each and every situation.

Of necessity, the changes in the NHS will not only have personal and professional implications for the nurse but also implications of a systemic nature. The role of the nurse in relation to the patient as well as to the nurse managers will be tested. The nurse has been seen to be the advocate on behalf of the patient and also accountable to a manager. However, the nurse could possibly be placed in a situation where there is a conflict of interest. The UKCC Code deals with the obligatory reporting by nurses when witnessing poor standards of patient care. The 1998 Act offers some protection where the nurse chooses to act in the patients' interests. Yet at the heart of the matter is the relationship between cost, quality and quantity of treatment which it is not open to the individual nurse to resolve.

8.11   Notes and references

1. See *Barnett* v. *Chelsea and Kensington HMC* [1968] 1 All ER 1068; *Gold* v. *Essex CC* [1942] 2 All ER 237; *Urbanski* v. *Patel* [1978] 84 DLR (3d) 650; Lee, R. (1979) Hospital admissions – duty of care. *New Law Journal* p. 567.
2. Liability will not inevitably follow for a number of reasons. There may be no resulting damage, or the medical error may not be the causative factor or later injury, or the damage may be too remote.
3. Note the incorporation of this principle into statute: Congenital Disabilities (Civil Liability) Act 1976, section 1(5).
4. See also Deutsch, R.L. (1983) Medical Negligence Reviewed. *American Law Journal*, 87, p. 674.
5. Brazier, M. (1987) Patient Autonomy and Consent to Treatment: The Role of the law, *Legal Studies*, p. 170. For a wider review of Lord Denning's approach to standards of care see McLean, S. (1981) Negligence – a dagger at the doctor's back?. In Robson, P. & Watchman, P. (1981) *Justice, Lord Denning and the Constitution*. Gower, Aldershot. 1981.

6. See *Whitehouse* v. *Jordan* [1981] 1 All ER 267 and in the USA, *Demmer* v. *Patt* 788 F2d 1387 (8 Cir 1986).

7. Brazier, M. (1992) *Medicine, Patients and the Law*, 2nd edn. Penguin, Harmondsworth.

8. Most famously by Lord Denning in *Whitehouse* v. *Jordan* (1980) 1 All ER 650.

9. Quoted by Picard, E. (1984) *Legal Liability of Doctors and Hospitals in Canada*. Carswell, Toronto.

10. See Lee, R.G. (1998) Judicial review and access to health care, in *Judicial Review and Social Welfare* (Buck, T.) Carswell, Toronto.

11. Montgomery, J. (1987) Suing hospitals direct: what tort? *New Law Journal*, 137, p. 703, in reply to Bettle, J. Suing hospitals direct: whose tort is it anyhow? *New Law Journal*, 137, p. 573.

12. See *Commonwealth* v. *Introvigne* (1982) AWR 749, *Kandis* v. *State Transport Authority* [1984] 154 CLR 672 (both Australian HC) and *Albrighton* v. *Royal Price Albert Hospital* [1980] 2 NSWLR 542 CC.A), *Yepremian* v. *Scarborough General Hospital* [1980] 110 DLR (3d) 513 which seems to accept this possibility; also Dugdale, A. & Stanton, K. (1989) *Professional Negligence*, 2nd edn, para 22.22, Butterworths, London, who, speaking of duties to provide treatment under the National Health Services Act 1977, state that 'it is undoubtedly the case that the effect of basing this duty on statute is to ensure that it is non-delegable in its nature'.

13. *The Times* 11 February 1987 (Court of Appeal). Quotes which follow are taken from the report at [1993] 4 Med LR 151, 156.

B An Ethical Perspective – How to Do the Right Thing

David Seedhouse

8.12 Introduction

Health care resources are scarce. This is an unfortunate fact of life. In those cases where there are not enough to go around difficult choices must be made. Sometimes nurses must make these choices. This may mean that they cannot help everyone they would like to. It may mean that they will not be able to offer as much to each patient as they would ideally wish to, but this is not a perfect world. In order not to waste resources, and in order to be as fair as possible across the health service, all nurses must be aware that rationing is sometimes necessary. Nurses must recognise these facts; nurses must do the right thing.

This, at least, is the official position: it is held (and fostered) by governments preoccupied by the need to keep health care costs in check [1], by several health economists [2], some of whom devote considerable energy to the production of technical 'rationing formulae'; and it is increasingly (though often grudgingly) accepted by many nurses. Slowly but surely the 'official line' has also come to be believed by many of the general public, who listen to the various experts and – not unreasonably – conclude that if those in the know see the need to ration, then there must indeed be such a need.

But is the official position true? Certainly not everyone accepts it. For instance, it has been argued that the basic duty of any government must be to defend its people against threats to life and safety, and that since in normal circumstances health care does this much better than any other sort of public provision (and is infinitely more useful than an idle army), governments must – as a matter of obligation to their subjects – switch military funding to health services [3]. It is also claimed that in the USA, where spending on health care consistently consumes around 14% of the gross domestic product, there are already more than enough health services to go round; the problem is that not everyone who needs them can get access (millions of Americans do not have health insurance and cannot afford to pay privately to get the help they need) [4].

It is further argued, against the official view, that the belief that the development of new medicines and technologies must fuel growing patient demand *ad infinitum* is based on a myth [5]. It is argued that just as a doubling of public toilets or public bus services would not automatically double the desire (or need) of the public to make use of them, so too there is a finite amount of kidney disease, a limit to the number of people who can benefit from coronary by-pass surgery, and so on. Perhaps if more buses were supplied very cheaply, or even at no cost to the user at all, their use would increase, but even so there will always be a natural limit on the number of people who would like to travel from A to B at one time.

It is not easy to judge which one of these positions – the 'official line' or that of the 'rebel camp' – is correct. Clearly, both are at least partly true. For instance, where there are more potential recipients than donated organs there is an undeniable scarcity of this particular resource. On the other hand, it is equally incontrovertible that if money were to be taken from some expensive 'high-tech' or over-provided medical services, and spent instead on the provision of better and more comprehensive 'preventive services', many 'health needs' now not met because of scarcity could be provided for.

What is clearest of all, however, is that there are considerable philosophical and practical uncertainties underlying the 'resources debate', most of which are unlikely to be resolved in the foreseeable future. The nature of 'health care cost' and 'health care benefit' is not agreed in theory [6]. Nor is it yet physically possible to collate even the simple financial costs of many modern health services [7]. And even if credible classifications and calculations were to be developed, even if someone were to invent a comprehensive 'health service slide rule', the accuracy and appropriateness of these taxonomies and methods of calculating would inevitably be challenged. It would, for instance, remain the case that different individuals would value even identical services (and identical results) in different ways. For one person a few more days of life, even in great pain, might be of immense value – while for another there would be no point at all.

8.13 Nursing in scarcity

What can nurses do when faced with such intangibles? These days almost all nurses work in environments where managers, and others, are openly concerned about efficiency, avoiding waste, and reducing cost wherever possible.

What is the nurse, concerned about how best to use scarce resources, to do? How can she be fair? How can she deal with perceived injustice? How can she make any difference at all?

Whether or not any individual can make a difference within massive, complex systems depends on two factors. Firstly, and obviously, what she can do depends on whether or not she is in a position of any power and influence. Secondly, and less obviously, what she can do depends upon the clarity with which she has formulated her goals. Philosophy (or clear thinking) can do nothing about the first factor, but it can help (albeit only a little) with the second. With practice a nurse can improve her understanding of both general situations and her own circumstances, she can learn to define the meaning of key terms (such as 'resource', 'rationing' and 'fairness'), and she can become better able to identify her role (and the limits of her role).

It is not possible in this chapter to provide a philosophical education. In order to learn philosophy there is no substitute for a carefully formulated programme of study undertaken over several years. However, it is possible to show how a philosophically informed nurse might at least begin to react to resource allocation problems, and in so doing to offer insight into one method of coping with seemingly impossible situations.

8.14   A number – or a free person?

Nursing is a hierarchical and often authoritarian profession. All groups of nurses have 'pecking-orders', and those nurses who do not toe the line can, in some circumstances, suffer severe reprimand. This is a deep-seated aspect of nursing culture. It is an equally long-established tradition that most nurses are of a lower rank to doctors. These circumstances are changing somewhat nowadays, with the advent of nurse managers and as nursing is increasingly thought of as a profession. However, for very many nurses it remains the case that they are able to exert only a very limited influence on health service policy.

So, when it comes to 'doing the *right* thing', most nurses apparently have very little choice; the 'right thing' is defined by 'the system' in which they are a 'cog' or a 'number' and their only option is to implement it. The 'right thing', in other words, is handed down to them (this might be called 'doing the right thing 1'). Of course, there is an alternative form of 'doing the right thing', which can be defined as a nurse taking that course of action which she has, after careful deliberation, deemed to be the best – whether or not this is the action recommended by the system. The 'right thing', in this form, is a matter of conscience and intelligent reflection (and might be called 'doing the right thing 2').

How might the nurse 'do the right thing' in the two case studies offered by Robert Lee in part A of this chapter?

8.14.1   Case one

Consider again the first case study of the nurse (N) on night duty in charge of a small hospital where R brings V, the victim of a hit-and-run accident, despite the sign at the gate advising that there is no accident and emergency unit there (section 8.7).

As far as 'doing the right thing 1' is concerned, Robert Lee has already given part of a possible answer that 'in purely legal terms, N would be free to refuse treatment to V and urge R and V to present themselves at the nearest accident and emergency department'. Officially the hospital does not provide accident and emergency services, so there is no legal obligation on the nurse to do anything. Furthermore, if this hospital is cost-conscious, and if the management have made it clear that emergency cases are not to be treated, then to 'do the right thing 1' the nurse must turn the potential patient away – and must do so whatever her feelings about it, and whatever help she might have been able to give. Since she would have 'done the right thing' there would be no sanction 'the authorities' could take against the nurse.

However, in this case (as in all cases) the nurse might instead consider 'doing the right thing 2' – that is, she might not simply follow the regulation course, but first take the trouble to analyse the situation for herself, and then act according to the result of her own reasoning. Of course, if she decides that she must advise V and R that she cannot help them, and that they must attend the nearest accident and emergency hospital, then the practical outcome will be the same. However the nurse herself will have thought more thoroughly than if she had merely obeyed the rules, and may well feel more confident (and more in charge) as a result.

But how is she to carry out this analysis? How might she structure her thinking if she decides to 'do the right thing 2'? N does have the option to help the injured person, but if she does so she might well place herself at greater personal risk than if she were simply to turn V and R away. As stated in section 8.7, 'once N opts to render care and assistance to V, then a duty of care arises and the question then relates to the applicable standard of care. It is clear that liability may result from negligent treatment or advice rendered by N or any failure of communication in providing V with emergency treatment.' So what should N do?

Certainly, 'doing the right thing 2' is the more complicated – and potentially more fraught – option. What factors should the nurse take into account? How might she begin to think clearly about this case? If she does decide to deliberate on the situation she must do so quickly, and under considerable emotional pressure – neither of which are conducive to clear reasoning. Given this, the nurse might find it helpful to organise her thinking under three distinct headings: context, outcomes and obligations.

Context

Firstly, N must assess the risk. 'Risk', of course, is a general term which might be interpreted in several ways. The nurse might, for instance, think about:

- the risk to the injured party (if he is not instantly helped how will he be affected?);
- the risk to her conscience (what if she begins to help and the patient dies – or what if she does not help and the patient dies?);
- the risk to her future career, and so on.

She must also, prior to any further deliberation, decide whether any intervention she could make would do any good. If it would not, and if it is clearly better that V attends a working clinic, then obviously that is where he should go. If, on the other hand, she decides she could give some help, she must also work out how *effective* she would be and how *certain she is of her judgement* about her effectiveness. Also, if there are other patients whom she might be helping instead of V, she must consider whether she should assist them before she turns her attention to V.

The context, in this case as in most cases which nurses have to deal with, is one of uncertainty. N simply does not know for sure what the outcome of any of her options will be. Because of this it is very important that she reflects, in the abstract, on her *priorities*.

Outcomes

● Is she, for example, most concerned with the reputation of the hospital?
● Is she concerned for the safety of her other patients, who may be endangered if she devotes herself solely to the care of V?
● Or is her priority the injured person directly in front of her?

She may not, in a short space of time, be able to think through all the ramifications, but it will help her considerably if she feels she understands which of these possible goals are, in principle, the most important.

Obligations

Does she have any obligations or duties which override the *context*? Must she, for instance, as a 'caring professional' do all she can to help V, who is clearly suffering? This is for her to decide. However, as she thinks about this she must be aware that not only must she justify her decision to herself, but she may also have to justify it to others. So, if she decides she is obliged to intervene wherever she sees suffering, she must also be able to say whether this is a *general obligation* and is always incumbent on her, or whether there are factors (such as *context* and *outcome*) that may sometimes cancel out such a duty.

8.14.2   Case two

Consider now the second case study (set out in section 8.9) of W, the night duty charge nurse believing that the standard of care had dropped prior to a patient dying in distressing circumstances. In this case, even more than the first, there are evidently two distinct 'right things to do'. 'To do the right thing 1' in this case is either to do nothing because the context is so overwhelming (the nurse may know that similar staffing difficulties are being experienced across the country – how can her situation be made an exception?), or to pursue the matter through the 'official channels', as explained in section 8.9. However, since all the 'official channels' are themselves part of the system which allows (or is forced to allow) such a situation to arise, it is extremely unlikely that this course of action will bring about an improvement in the situation on the nurse's ward. 'To do the right thing 1' would almost certainly mean that little would change.

   However, if the nurse 'does the right thing 2' it may be a different matter. Although she might in the end reach the same conclusions as generated by 'doing the right thing 1', the nurse must first try to think as an individual uninfluenced by the system. What, she might ask, *ought* to be done in these circumstances? The questions she must address are similar to those considered by N in Case one, and again might usefully be divided into the three categories.

   What are the risks in this *context*? Will 'whistle-blowing' be effective? How important is the nurse's career? (There are well-known examples of nurses destroying their careers in the pursuit of causes they believe to be just.) Are the nurse's *obligations* to her patients paramount, or does she have wider duties (to her colleagues or to those future patients she might not be able to care for if she is suspended from work or sacked)? In principle, what *outcomes* does she value most highly? Is her own happiness paramount? Or is it crucial that the patients on her ward get the best possible service? If the latter, does it matter that if she succeeds in getting what she wants for her ward, resources may be moved from other hard-pressed parts of the hospital – so decreasing the quality of service to other patients? If she finally decides that the *context* is simply unacceptable, and that something must be done to improve it, then 'doing the right thing 1' may very well cease to be an option.

8.15   Principled solutions?

Some nurses may find it helpful to try to apply 'ethical principles' to resource allocation dilemmas. This approach has been widely recommended in recent years, and most texts on 'nursing ethics' contain sizeable sections on 'basic', 'ethical' or 'philosophical' principles [8]. A quartet of principles are regularly advocated, and it is likely that most nurses will at least have heard of them. They are: 'non-maleficence' (do no harm), 'beneficence' (do good), 'respect autonomy' (respect the patient's choice), and 'justice' [9]. (See Chapter 2.) The attraction of this group of principles is that they seem to offer an uncomplicated structure within which to organise one's thoughts. Moreover, it seems possible to seize on just one of these principles in order to 'solve' a dilemma. If, for instance, a nurse feels that a doctor is not taking the wishes of a patient seriously she might describe this as 'unethical' behaviour purely because the doctor is not 'respecting auton-omy' (so ignoring or overriding any alternative justifications the medic might have). Most nurses will have personal experience of cases in which this has hap-pened – and might well consider it fair criticism – but it is very important not to confuse the assertion of single principles (however justifiable) with 'ethical ana-lysis'. The latter is a much more complicated procedure which – if it is to be done at all properly – must involve reflection upon a range of 'ethical principles' together with the other considerations (*context, outcomes, obligations*) already mentioned in this section.

This is not to say that the use of the principles is unhelpful. The point is that any thoughtful ethical analysis is bound to place considerable intellectual demands on the health care analyst. In Case two it might appear that the hub of the matter is a straightforward clash between the ideal of 'efficiency' and the principles of 'justice'. It might, in other words, seem to nurse W that her patients are being unjustly treated, and that their interests are regarded as secondary to those of the hospital as a whole (which must be run as 'efficiently' as possible). However, if W is seriously to argue this case then it is not enough for her merely to cry 'unjust!' since 'justice' can be understood in more than one way, and can even be interpreted in ways which contradict each other.

For example, there are those who think that the key to understanding 'justice' is to treat people first and foremost *in accord with what they deserve*; others disagree, arguing that the basic criterion of justice is *need*; and there is a further group who believe that justice can come about only when people's *rights* are upheld [10]. What is more, sophisticated analysts tend to blend and adapt these different understandings in subtle ways, depending on the matter under scrutiny. Any contemplative analysis of the merits (or justice) of the management of the acutely ill patient must consider and explain what justice means in this case (whether the patients have the same *right* to treatment as other patients in the hospital, and so no special priority; whether they have *needs* of such gravity that they are entitled to treatment before those with lesser needs; whether this set of patients merits privileged attention and so *deserves* priority treatment for some reason).

Philosophers are used to such discussions, and often spend much time trying to disentangle the various issues, only to see them knot together again the moment they move their attention elsewhere. Such detailed reflection requires a fair amount of expertise − and countless hours − neither of which are usually available to the nurse. And this can place the nurse who sees that these are complex matters, and who recognises that they can be properly dealt with only by careful analysis, at a considerable disadvantage. If she tries to protest in an intelligent way it is very easy to defeat her. Her opponent can say: 'We don't have the time for this sort of reflection'; or, 'What you are suggesting requires an analysis of *everything* we do, and this is not a practical proposition' (which of course means that everything can continue unchanged − inertia is not only a natural tendency but also a powerful weapon in the hands of those who are happy with the status quo). Her opponent might also ask: 'What do you mean by justice?', knowing full well that any credible answer must take more time and effort than almost any nurse can give (and knowing that even if the nurse does attempt an answer it will be very easy to say later: 'please spell out your interpretation of need/rights/equity' or whatever other terms she has not fully explained).

In such circumstances the nurse has three strategies open to her. She might spend many hours developing her case (she might even enlist the help of a trained philosopher); she might take a simpler course and analyse her work problems using the 'context, outcomes and obligations' framework (in the knowledge that this is by no means all there is to ethical analysis); or she might take her opponent on, on his own terms. Whenever he says, 'Could you expand on that?' or 'What do you mean?', then the nurse might ask in turn 'What do you mean by efficiency?', 'How do you justify removing resources from this ward and increasing them on that?' or 'What are your principles for resource allocation within this hospital, and on what grounds do you justify these?'.

8.16   Conclusion

This part of the chapter has raised questions, but only sketched out answers to them. The rest is for the individual nurse to decide, and there are many books and papers available to which she might turn for more detailed guidance. What is most important is that each nurse realises the complexity of any resource problem she is facing, and, if she so decides, is able to tackle it in a systematic manner. If she genuinely tries to do this, and if she feels she has arrived at a defensible decision, then there is probably little more she can do. She cannot change the world, and whatever she does she is hardly likely to unsettle governments focused so intently on financial balance sheets.

Nevertheless, there will always − if only occasionally − be times when the nurse can do something to change things for the better. If, for example, she decides not only to treat V (in Case one) but to publicise the fact in local newspapers (so both promoting the hospital as a compassionate organisation and letting it be known that were funds available an accident and emergency service could be provided or reinstated) then she might have an impact. Moreover, if the nurse were to contact the relatives of the patient who died 'in distressing circumstances' (in Case two) and enlist their support she might campaign intelligently and effectively for more resources. On both strategies she would face very significant risks – indeed she could expect censure from the system were her involvement to become known – but she would at least stand a chance of making a desirable difference. She would, in other words, be working for justice as a combination of meeting needs, deserts and upholding rights – through positively discriminating in favour of those patients closest to her.

In general, a great deal rests on the following question, and how it is answered in the coming years: whether nurses in general continue mostly or only 'to do the right thing 1' or whether the profession increasingly aims 'to do the right thing 2' (and commits its own resources to ensuring this). If the former, then it is hard to see how nurses will be able to justify their claim to professional status, but if the latter, and the majority of nurses become able and willing to think through the question 'How best might I act in this situation?' (rather than ask 'What am I *supposed* to do here?') then nurses, as a group, might perform an enormous service: they might open up the health service to internal debate, to genuine conversation (without fear of sanction and reprisal) about how best to deliver public health services – not least when there are not enough of them to go round. And it is certain that it is only by continually considering whether 'to do the right thing 1' or 'to do the right thing 2' that nurses will exercise their 'moral muscles' sufficiently to effect resource allocation injustices for the better, since never to consider 'doing the right thing 2' eventually and inevitably destroys the capacity for moral reasoning [11] [12].

8.17   Notes and references

1. See *Health Care Analysis* 1993; **1**(1) *passim*.
2. Williams, A. (1992) Cost-effectiveness analysis: is it ethical? *Journal of Medical Ethics*, 18, pp. 7–11.
3. Harris, J. (1991) Unprincipled QALYs: a response to Cubbon. *Journal of Medical Ethics*, 17, pp. 185–8.
4. Hackler, C. (1993) Health Care Reform in the United States. *Health Care Analysis*, **1**(1), 5–13.
5. Smith, A. (1987) Qualms about QALYs. *The Lancet*, 1X34–36.
6. Seedhouse, D.F. (1994) *Fortress NHS: A Philosophical Review of the National Health Service*. John Wiley and Sons, Chichester.
7. Culyer, A. (1992) The morality of efficiency in health care – some uncomfortable implications. *Health Economics*, **1**(1) p. 7–18.
8. Thompson, I., Melia, K.M. & Boyd, K.M. (1988) *Nursing Ethics*, Churchill Livingstone, Edinburgh.
9. Gillon, R.P. (1985) *Philosophical Medical Ethics*. John Wiley and Sons, Chichester.

10. Miller, D. (1976) *Social Justice*. Oxford University Press, Oxford.
11. Seedhouse, D.F. (2000) *Practical Nursing Philosophy: The Universal Ethical Code*. John Wiley and Sons, Chichester.
12. Seedhouse, D.F. (2001) *Health: The Foundations for Achievement*, 2nd edn. John Wiley and Sons, Chichester.

Chapter 9

Mental Health Nursing

A   The Legal Perspective

Michael Gunn and M.E. Rodgers

Whilst there are many issues which face nurses working with people with mental illness or a learning difficulty, this chapter will consider what are perhaps the more commonly encountered problems, in addition to looking at some of the future developments for this area of practice. The chapter will therefore deal with: treatment under the Mental Health Act 1983 (MHA) [1]; treatment falling outside that Act; the use of the nurse's holding powers under section 5(4) of the MHA; the care and management of violent or aggressive patients; the debate on compulsory detention of individuals with personality disorders; and treatment in the community. Readers should be aware that a comprehensive review of the MHA is in progress, however legislation is unlikely to be forthcoming until 2002 at the earliest [2].

9.1   Treatment under the Mental Health Act 1983

Treatment for mental disorder may lawfully be given under the MHA provided the patient is detained under the Act by means of a non-emergency section. It is important to stress that treatment for physical problems is not under consideration here.

   If nurses are to be involved in the treatment of a patient, they must first be able to satisfy themselves whether the patient is detained under a relevant section. The Fifth Biennial Report of the Mental Health Act Commission [3] stressed the importance of the nurses' role, and it is the nurses' legal and ethical input to this area of law which will be covered in this chapter.

9.1.1   First stage: is the patient a detained patient?

A nurse must be able to make sure that the appropriate detention documentation for a non-emergency section is present in the patient's ward file. The nurse is, therefore, looking for documentation which indicates that the patient is detained under any of the following:

- section 2 (for assessment including medical treatment);
- section 3 (for treatment);

- section 36 (remand of accused person to hospital for treatment);
- section 37 (hospital order, with or without a restriction order under section 41);
- section 38 (an interim hospital order);
- section 46 (an order relating to a member of the armed forces);
- section 47 (a transfer of a prisoner, with or without restrictions under section 49);
- section 48 (transfer of a civil or remand prisoner, with or without restrictions under section 49).

It is not necessary for the nurse to be sure that the patient is lawfully detained. The function of ascertaining the legality and appropriateness of detention is for the hospital managers, a function which is normally delegated to the medical records department. In any case, section 6(3) of the MHA ensures that it is appropriate to rely on the forms since it provides:

'Any application for the admission of a patient under this Part of this Act which appears to be duly made and to be founded on the necessary medical recommendations may be acted upon without further proof of the signature or qualification of the person by whom the application or any such medical recommendation is made or given or of any matter of fact or opinion stated in it.' [4]

What is usually required, therefore, is that the nurse files and then is able to find in the notes, the relevant forms indicating that the patient has been admitted under one of the sections to which reference has already been made. If the patient has been admitted under section 2, the nurse is looking for:

(1)   the application form which must be either Form 2 (where the nearest relative [5] was the applicant) or Form 3 (where an approved social worker [6] was the applicant);
(2)   a form for the medical recommendation (either one copy of Form 4 where the recommendation was done jointly or two copies of Form 5 where the recommendations were done separately); *and also*
(3)   Form 15 which indicates that the patient has been accepted by the hospital as a detained patient.

If the patient has been admitted under section 3, the nurse is similarly looking for:

(1)   the relevant application form (Form 8 where the applicant is the nearest relative and Form 9 where the applicant is an approved social worker);
(2)   the relevant form stating the medical recommendations (one copy of Form 10 where there is a joint medical recommendation and two copies of Form 11 where there are separate recommendations); *and*
(3)   a copy of Form 15.

If the patient is detained under section 36, section 37, section 38 or section 46, there must be documentation from a court indicating the imposition of the section. If the patient is detained under section 47 or section 48, there must be a warrant from the Home Secretary directing the transfer of the patient to the hospital.

9.1.2   Second stage: does the treatment fall within the MHA?

Nurses must be able to satisfy themselves that the treatment proposed is treatment that may lawfully be carried out under the MHA. Medical treatment is widely defined by the Act in section 145(1):

> ' "[M]edical treatment" includes nursing, and also includes care, habilitation and rehabilitation under medical supervision. . .'

For the purposes of assessing the legality of the particular activity in question, treatment is classified into three different groups covered by sections 57, 58 and 63. The following discussion will deal with these sections in reverse order since section 63 is, in most cases, the first that would be considered to permit treatment of a detained individual. Sections 58 and 57 deal respectively with what can be suggested to be more invasive treatments or treatments that are recognised as giving rise to greater concern. For these treatments to be given either the procedure stated in section 57 or 58 must be followed or the urgent treatment provisions in section 62 must be applied.

Treatment without consent

Treatment provided under the remit of section 63 is treatment for mental disorder given by or under the supervision of the patient's responsible medical officer (rmo), and does not require the patient's consent. Treatment will generally be by means of drug therapy, although the definition of treatment in the MHA is a wide one, as has been seen above.

   Patients, therefore, can be provided with any form of medical treatment which is for their mental disorder without their consent. This proposition does not apply to the special forms of treatment that fall under sections 57 and 58 (that is psychosurgery, surgical implantation of hormones to reduce male sexual drive, electroconvulsive therapy and medication continued after the first three months of administration); for these the special procedures outlined below *must* be followed.

   Patients can be given medication for their mental disorder, under section 63, for three months before the special procedure under section 58 has to be followed, in relation to medication. The three month period commences when medication was first given, which will not necessarily be the same time as when the patient was first detained. As the Mental Health Act Code of Practice states:

> '16.12 The 3 month period starts on the occasion when medication for mental disorder was first administered by any means during a period of continuing detention ... The medication does not necessarily have to be administered continuously throughout the three months.'

For the nurse participating in the administration of medication, it will be necessary to establish first, that the patient is detained; secondly, that the medication is being given for the patient's mental disorder; and, thirdly, that the treatment is being given less than three months since it started. It will not be possible to check the notes for a form, since none is required under section 63; this requirement only applies to treatment excluded from this section. Thus clearly recording the first

administration of medicine is vital, as is ensuring that the legally relevant information and documentation is readily available for inspection.

In recent years, it has become apparent that one particular issue on the
application of section 63 can cause difficulty. This is in determining whether a
particular treatment is, indeed, *for* the patient's mental disorder as opposed to a
physical disorder or condition. Two situations can be highlighted where the
boundary between treatment for physical conditions or for a mental disorder has
resulted in legal discussion. The first concerns the treatment of anorexia nervosa,
particularly where the patient is an adult (where the patient is a child the treatment
might be given without recourse to the MHA in some circumstances). The Mental
Health Act Commission, in its Fourth Biennial Report, stated that in its view 'severe
anorexia nervosa falls within the definition of mental disorder.' [7] If this is the
case, then an individual may be admitted to hospital, provided all other criteria are
satisfied, under section 2 MHA for assessment (which may be followed by treatment), or alternatively section 3 MHA for treatment, where an assessment has
already been carried out and reflects the current situation [8]. It is also the view of
the Mental Health Act Commission that 'treatment of anorexia nervosa necessary
for the health or safety of the patient, including involuntary feeding and maintenance of hydration, is permissible in patients whose anorexia is causing serious
concern' [9].

The only basis on which this opinion may be predicated is that these forms of
activity fall within the definition of treatment within the Act and that section 63 is
the relevant section authorising treatment. No-one, it is submitted, can dispute
that, given the wide definition of medical treatment in the Act, involuntary feeding
does fall within 'treatment'. Anorexia nervosa is a mental disorder. But the
essential question, as required by the wording of section 63, is whether the
treatment is *for* the mental disorder from which the patient is suffering. The courts
have held that, if treatment is capable of being ancillary to core treatment – i.e. it is
nursing care 'concurrent with the core treatment or as a necessary prerequisite to
such treatment or to prevent the patient from causing harm to himself or to alleviate the consequences of the disorder,' – it will be upheld as lawful under section
63 [10].

The second area of discussion is in relation to compulsory caesarean sections. A
series of cases has been presented to the courts where the question of whether
treatment is for a physical problem or for a mental disorder has been the issue [11].
While different outcomes have resulted from these cases, there appears to be an
adherence to the principles put forward in *B* v. *Croydon Health Authority* (1994) in
that the treatment for the physical condition must be ancillary to the treatment for
the mental disorder for it to be regarded as treatment *for* the patient's mental
disorder and thus the treatment can be given under section 63 (to a detained
patient) without her consent. Hence in *Tameside and Glossop Acute Services Trust* v.
CH (1996), the caesarean was sanctioned on the basis that:

'... an ancillary reason for the induction and, if necessary, the birth by caesarean
section is to prevent a deterioration in the [patient's] mental state. Secondly,
there is the clear evidence ... that in order for the treatment of her schizophrenia
to be effective, it is necessary for her to give birth to a live baby. Thirdly, the

overall structure of her treatment requires her to receive strong anti-psychotic medication. The administration of that treatment has been necessarily interrupted by her pregnancy and cannot be resumed until her child is born. It is not, therefore, I think stretching language unduly to say that achievement of a successful outcome of her pregnancy is a necessary part of the overall treatment of her mental disorder.' [12]

By contrast in *R* v. *Collins, Pathfinder Health Services Trust, St George's NHS Trust ex parte S* (1998) [13], despite the patient being detained under the provisions of section 2 of the MHA, the court refused to accept that the caesarean section was lawful:

'Section 63 of the [MHA] may apply to the treatment of any condition which is integral to the mental disorder . . . provided the treatment is given by, or under the direction of, the responsible medical officer. The treatment administered to S was not so ordered; she was neither offered nor did she refuse treatment for mental disorder. . . . In the final analysis, a woman detained under the Act for mental disorder cannot be forced into medical procedures unconnected with her mental condition.' [14]

With respect, this appears to be much the more appropriate approach. It is difficult to imagine that, when Parliament passed section 63, it expected that its interpretation would be so wide as to include caesarean sections. If there is an inability to treat under the MHA owing to lack of nexus between the disorder and the treatment required, that will necessitate an understanding of the common law provisions affecting patients who lack capacity to consent. These will be considered later in this chapter and have also been dealt with in Chapter 7.

Treatment under section 58

The second group of treatments for mental disorder consists of electro-convulsive therapy (ECT) and the continuation of the administration of medication, by any means, for mental disorder three months after the person was first administered that medication when a detained patient. As can be seen, this latter situation follows on from the treatment that can lawfully be given under section 63. The treatments covered by section 58 are very common [15] with continuation of medication being the most frequently used. For nurses, it is essential that they ensure their involvement is lawful, whether the nurse is involved in the distribution of medicine for self-administration or is actually undertaking the administration of the medication.

Once the nurse has identified that the patient is detained, the nurse must then establish if the administration of medication requires a form in the patient's notes. Having ascertained that the section 63, three month time frame has expired, a formal record must exist before further medication can lawfully be provided. Two alternatives exist for the legality of administration to be established. First, the patient must have consented to it. For that consent to be valid under section 58, it must be verified by either the patient's own doctor (the rmo) or a Second Opinion Approved Doctor (a SOAD, who will be appointed as such by the Secretary of State for Health, but whose day-to-day involvement is monitored by the Mental Health Act Commission). To verify the consent, they will have 'certified in writing that the patient is capable of understanding [the] nature, purpose and likely effect [of the treatment] and has consented to it' (section 58 (3)(a)).

Alternatively, if the patient cannot, or will not, consent, the medication may continue, but only if a SOAD has 'certified in writing that the patient is not capable of understanding the nature, purpose and likely effects of that treatment or has not consented to it but that, having regard to the likelihood of its alleviating or preventing a deterioration of [the patient's] condition, the treatment should be given' (section 58 (3)(b)). The simplest means of ensuring that one of these alternatives exists is for the nurse to check which form, if any, is in the patient's file. If the patient is consenting to treatment, it must be covered by a Form 38; if the patient is not consenting, a Form 39 must be present. The question for the nurse, initially, is not whether the patient is consenting, but whether there is a form apparently proper on its face which entitles the nurse to be involved in the treatment of the detained patient.

In most hospitals, where thought has been given to the issue, a copy of the relevant form is kept with the medicine card, so that the legal authorisation for the treatment of the patient may be checked every time a drug is administered. This is a simple procedure which enables an easy check to be made. It is surprising, however, how frequently the relevant form is not kept with the treatment card and how frequently the nurse does not realise the significance of the form, and the importance of checking that it covers the treatment in question.

In addition to the issue of checking the lawfulness of treatment, the nurse may be involved in other matters relating to treatment of the detained patient. Treatment covered by Form 38, where the patient consents, does not give rise to a statutory review of the need for treatment [16]. The MHA Code of Practice, however, at paragraph 16.35 requires that, as a matter of good practice, 'all treatments … should be regularly reviewed and the patient's treatment plan should include details of when this will take place'. The Code of Practice, while not specifying intervals for review, suggests that a new Form 38 should be completed when:

(1)   there is a change in the treatment plan from that recorded;
(2)   consent is re-established after being withdrawn;
(3)   there is a break in the patient's detention;
(4)   there is a permanent change of rmo;
(5)   the patient's detention is renewed (or annually, whichever is earlier);
(6)   there is change in the hospital where the patient is detained. [17]

As well as being good practice, reviewing treatment regimes will enable regular consideration to be given to the question of the patient's continued consent. A patient retains the right to withdraw consent to treatment at any time (section 61), and nurses should be aware of the need to assess continuing consent whenever delivering medication. In the event that consent is withdrawn the nurse should request the attendance of the rmo who may be able to encourage the patient to accept the treatment. By so doing, the nurse will ensure compliance with their own professional code of practice, and will also act in accordance with the MHA Code of Practice which states:

'Where a patient withdraws consent he or she should receive a clear explanation, which should be recorded in the patient's records:

. . .

(7)   of the likely consequences of not receiving the treatment;

(8)   that a second medical opinion … may or will be sought, if applicable, in order to authorise treatment in the continuing absence of the patient's consent;

(9)   of the doctor's power to begin or continue urgent treatment under [the emergency provisions] until a second medical opinion has been obtained, if applicable.' [18]

The need to check Form 38 is not only relevant to continued consent, but assists in highlighting those cases where the drug or its dosage listed has changed since the form was originally signed. In this situation the treatment may be unlawful. While the MHA itself does not require specific drugs to be named, or specific dosages, the Code of Practice does suggest that medication should be listed by name. However, the Code of Practice goes on to state that the rmo should '[ensure] that the number of drugs authorised in each class is indicated, by the classes described in the British National Formulary (BNF). The maximum dosage and route of administration should be clearly indicated for each drug or category of drug.' [19] Where specific drugs are named, no further drug may be administered unless a new Form 38 is completed. To avoid this problem most SOADs when signing Form 39 do not list specific drugs, but categories according to the BNF, and do not specify the dosage unless it will exceed the recommended BNF upper limit.

Little mention has been made of ECT, and it is true that ECT is in a minority of section 58 treatments insofar as SOAD activity is concerned. The Mental Health Act Commission's Eighth Biennial Report also highlights a striking difference in the usage of ECT between the genders with 15.4% of requests for men compared to 42.7% for women [20]. When second opinions are requested, it is unusual for them not to be provided regardless of whether ECT or medication is at issue. Whether this implies improper collusion or an acceptable recommendation for treatment at the outset is not clear. For ECT, clear indicators for its use are documented. The Code of Practice now requires patients who are being treated with ECT to have been 'given a leaflet which helps them to understand and remember, both during and after the course of ECT, the advice about its nature, purpose and likely effects' [21]. The requirement of the Code of Practice for the maximum number of proposed ECT applications to be included within the patient's treatment plan should be seen to be both good practice and consistent with a participative approach to patient care. However, it is worth noting that Fennell queries whether there are 'appropriate and effective safeguards' [22] so far as ECT is concerned.

The nurse may not play a major role in the administration of ECT but will clearly have a role in the assessment of whether the treatment should take place. As with administration of medicine, the patient may consent to ECT. If so, and the nurse were concerned about the patient's capacity to consent, the first step would seem to be to raise it with the rmo. If this has no effect, the suggestion of seeking the involvement of a SOAD would seem sensible. If, however, this is not done, recording dissent may be the only step left that the nurse feels able to take. This dissent would be identified by the Mental Health Act Commission and potentially investigated. A more recently introduced alternative may be to utilise the Public Interest Disclosure Act 1998 [23], although how willing a nurse may be to take this route is uncertain.

Treatment under section 57

The treatments covered by section 57 are psychosurgery and the surgical implantation of hormones to reduce male sexual drive (the two procedures are deemed neurosurgery by the Mental Health Act Commission). In order for them to be performed, the patient must consent and this must be verified by a SOAD and two members of the Mental Health Act Commission (from an internal panel appointed for this purpose). These three must 'have certified in writing that the patient is capable of understanding the nature, purpose and likely effects of the treatment in question and has consented to it' (section 57(2)(a)). Also, the SOAD must certify that, 'having regard to the likelihood of the treatment alleviating or preventing a deterioration of the patient's condition, the treatment should be given' (section 57(2)(b)). These requirements are certified as being satisfied by the completion of a Form 37. If there is no Form 37, the treatment cannot go ahead. The presence of a Form 37 will also be required if the treatment is planned for an informal patient, being a patient who is not detained under the MHA by virtue of a section. These two forms of treatment, which raise considerable ethical and legal issues, are carried out relatively rarely on detained patients [24]. Owing to this limited use, more attention has been spent on the preceding treatments authorised by sections 58 and 63.

Emergency treatment under section 62

Before moving on to consider treatment outside the MHA, it is worth noting that the requirements in the Act relating to sections 57 and 58 may be sidestepped in an emergency by virtue of section 62. In these cases it is important for nurses to ensure that they are satisfied that the criteria of section 62 are met, since reliance upon another person's view (i.e. the doctor's) may not be sufficient to protect the nurse from action where the treatment turns out to be unlawful. At the very least, it is necessary for the nurse to ensure that there is documentation that the section has been satisfied. This may be done via a local form (as suggested by the Code of Practice in paragraph 16.41) or some other recording system.

It may be necessary for the nurse to assess whether the treatment actually satisfies section 62, as part of the nurse's duty to account to the patient. The section provides:

'(1)Sections 57 and 58 above shall not apply to any treatment –

(a) which is immediately necessary to save the patient's life, or
(b) which (not being irreversible) is immediately necessary to prevent a serious deterioration of his condition; or
(c) which (not being irreversible or hazardous) is immediately necessary and

represents the minimum interference necessary to prevent the patient from behaving violently or being a danger to himself or others.

(3) For the purposes of this section treatment is irreversible if it has unfavourable physical or psychological consequences and hazardous if it entails significant hazard.'

Frequently, this section has caused debate. However, it should very rarely be used. It can only apply where the patient is detained and where one of the four forms of treatment is proposed: that is, psychosurgery, the surgical implantation of hormones to reduce male sexual drive, the administration of medicines after the first three months, and ECT. The provisions of section 62 apply to no other form of treatment. It would appear difficult to see how neurosurgery is likely to be necessary in an emergency, especially in the light of the few cases that are considered for section 57 treatments. Additionally, it is difficult to see how the requirements to the section can ever be satisfied in relation to the administration of medicines. Even if a patient has only once been administered a medicine for mental disorder, the three month rule operates at which point an assessment of that patient's needs for medication, including prn (as required) medication should be made and, depending on the outcome, a Form 38 or 39 brought into being. It is, therefore, the case that section 62 may only be of any real use with regard to the provision of ECT in an emergency, where, for example, a patient is in a catatonic stupor and might otherwise die. Despite the stringent conditions for using section 62, and the requirement in the Code of Practice to monitor why and for how long section 62 treatment is continued, the Mental Health Act Commission has often commented on the inappropriate use made of this section [25].

9.2   Treatment outside the Mental Health Act 1983

For the nurse, the questions are often fairly straightforward when the person is a detained patient and the treatment falls within the MHA. However, the position is not so clear cut where the treatment falls outside the remit of the Act. The nurse may be involved in the care of a person who is an informal patient, or who is detained under an emergency section of the MHA, or who is a patient for whom treatment is proposed for a physical disorder. In these situations, the MHA treatment provisions will be of no assistance.

9.2.1   First stage: Is the patient competent?

If treatment is to be provided in these circumstances, it must be ascertained whether the person is competent to consent to treatment. It must always be assumed that the patient is competent, regardless of their medical history or any 'label' that may be attached to them. It is only if it is shown that the patient is not competent that anything other than the consent of the patient may be relied upon. Despite the clear importance of this requirement, the matter did not receive judicial attention until the 1990s. The issue of competence was considered peripherally in *Gillick* v. *West Norfolk and Wisbech AHA and the DHSS* (1985) where the House of Lords discussed the ability of young adults consenting to medical treatment. In the Lords' opinions, the question of competence was linked to the individual's ability to understand and be of sufficient maturity to make decisions on treatment. In *Re T (adult: refusal of medical treatment)* (1992) the courts did not investigate the meaning of capacity in any great depth stating that '[w]hat is required is that the patient knew in broad terms the nature and effect of the procedure to which consent (or refusal) was given' [26]. The court went on to state that the medical practitioner had a duty to give the patient appropriately full information as to the nature of the treatment and the likely risks of treatment which does, to a limited degree, expand upon the concept of 'broad terms'. Subsequently, in the case of *Re C (adult: refusal of treatment)* (1994) the court adopted a test requiring that the patient must 'sufficiently understand the nature, purpose and likely effects of the proffered' treatment. In so doing, the judge adopted a proposal by an expert witness that the decision making process should be divided into three stages: 'first, comprehending and retaining treatment information, second, believing it and third, weighing it in the balance to arrive at choice'.

This test for capacity has been adopted by the Code of Practice, but with a little more by way of explanation:

'15.10 An individual is presumed to have the capacity to make a treatment decision unless he or she:

- is unable to take in and retain the information material to the decision especially as to the likely consequences of having or not having the treatment; or
- is unable to believe the information; or
- is unable to weigh the information in the balance as part of a process of arriving at the decision.'

The Code of Practice also makes it clear that capacity can be variable, and so should be assessed at the time the treatment is proposed [27]. It is also important to remember:

'Mental disorder does not necessarily make a patient incapable of giving or refusing consent. Capacity to consent is variable in people with mental disorder and should be assessed in relation to the particular patient, at the particular time, as regards the particular treatment proposed.' [28]

The nurse's involvement may either be to assist in an assessment of a person's competence to make a treatment decision or to decide whether there is sufficiently clear guidance available to act on the basis that the person is not competent. In the first scenario, nurses are being asked to proffer independent views from the professional perspective on the matters raised by the definition of competence quoted. In the second, nurses need to be sure that there is an indication that the person is incompetent so that the treatment in which they are to engage is justified without the patient's consent. Nurses may not always be involved in assisting in an assessment of competency (and certainly it will not include all nurses working with a particular patient). All nurses must, however, be able to check the records to see whether the patient is regarded at the time of the treatment as being not competent to consent to the particular treatment in question. To be involved in these various activities, therefore, a nurse needs to be professionally qualified and skilled to assist in determining capacity and to be capable of identifying the warning signs that the patient may not be competent to consent. The nurse also needs to be sufficiently aware to consider the legal situation prior to being included in the treatment of the patient.

9.2.2   Second stage: Where the patient is competent

It is quite clear that, where patients are competent, their decisions must be followed. This is so even where the patient is dying and it is life-saving treatment which is refused, and this is a principle propounded in numerous cases, for example, *Re MB (medical treatment)* (1997) and *R v. Collins, Pathfinder Health Services Trust, St George's NHS Trust, ex parte S* (1998) [29]. In the event of a dispute or uncertainty surrounding capacity, the courts have indicated that they should be involved in deciding the issues, and this should be done as soon as possible. However, the fact that a decision by a patient is deemed 'irrational' or 'contrary to what is to be expected of the majority of adults' [30] should not automatically give cause to doubt as to the patient's competence. The nurse clearly has a role to play in identifying potential problems of this nature and in so doing will be complying with their professional code of ethics which requires the nurse to act as advocate for their patient.

9.2.3   Third stage: Where the patient is not competent

If a patient is not competent, treatment may be given provided it is in their best interests. By 'best interests' in this context is meant that the treatment provides some form of therapeutic benefit and a responsible body of other similar treatment providers would also give the same treatment [31]. In certain situations a reference to the court to confirm the validity of treatment may be required, for example where a mentally incapable patient is to be sterilised, or a patient in a persistent vegetative state is to have any life maintaining equipment disconnected or treatment stopped [32].

   Where reference to the court is not required, the treatment provider must ascertain whether, according to the standards of their profession, the treatment which is proposed would be carried out by a responsible body of that profession. The question which may arise is whether the nurse is required to comply with the doctor's request that treatment be provided. This places the nurse in a difficult position if he or she is not satisfied that the treatment being proposed is indeed in the best interests of the patient according to proper nursing standards. In a case such as this (and considered more fully elsewhere in this book) it is submitted that the nurse should be wary of simply following the doctor's instructions without at least raising and recording any doubts there may be about the proposed course of action.

   A best interests approach is not a surprising one where the patient is not, and has not been, capable of expressing any treatment wishes. But defining a person's best interests may be problematical. It may fail adequately to achieve the proper balance, as Fennell points out, between the obligation to show respect for persons (that is concern for the person's welfare and the sanctity of life) and the obligation to respect the wishes of the person – that is the balance between paternalism and autonomy [33]. It should be noted that the current best interests test does not solve the 'ethical differences which may occur within care teams concerned with the treatment of incapable patients' [34].

Not all treatment of incapable patients will fall to be considered by reference to the best interests test. It is widely accepted by the courts that a competent patient can make a valid statement as to treatment in advance of the treatment situation arising. Such 'Advance Directives' are subject to restrictive interpretation [35]:

- the patient must have had capacity at the time of making the statement;
- only clear refusals of specified treatment will be upheld;
- if there is any doubt as to validity, a declaration may be obtained or treatment given in line with the best interests test;
- basic care cannot be refused (there is uncertainty as to what constitutes basic care);
- requests for specified types of treatment cannot be binding;
- refusal of treatment which would fall within the remit of the MHA treatment provisions cannot be refused by way of an advance directive.

Some form of investigation should therefore be carried out to ascertain if an advance directive exists, although the lengths to which medical professionals should go to comply with this have not been the subject of judicial consideration.

It should be noted that an incompetent patient who may be compliant in the sense of remaining in hospital does not need to be detained formally in order that treatment is provided. The provisions of section 131 prevail, in that detention should only occur where it is needed in accordance with the relevant criteria of the detention section. Any treatment provided will need to comply with the concept of best interests under the common law [36].

9.3   Looking to the future: *Who Decides? Making decisions on behalf of incapacitated adults* and *Making Decisions*

As the above has shown, clarity and precision are somewhat lacking in the current legal framework where treatment is being considered for a person who cannot consent. The Law Commission has produced consultation documents in the past on this matter, without any proposals being taken forward for legislation. In 1997 the Government produced a Green Paper, *Who Decides? Making decisions on behalf of mentally incapacitated adults* [37] which covered a range of legal issues relating to individuals who lacked capacity and this paper substantially reflects the preceding Law Commission Report on Mental Incapacity. In so doing, *Who Decides?* promotes the ideal, already mentioned, that there should be a presumption against lack of capacity. If capacity is in doubt, a new statutory definition of incapacity has been suggested thus (para. 1.4):

'A person should be regarded as without capacity if at the material time he is:

- unable by reason of a mental disability to make a decision on the matter in question; or
- unable to communicate a decision on that matter because he or she is unconscious or for any other reason.'

The expectation of the Green Paper is that a functional approach will be used in assessing capacity – in other words considering capacity at the time the decision needs to be made, in line with existing case law. The approach of the courts to the nature of the information to be understood for capacity to exist is also favoured:

'The Law Commission recommended that a person should not be regarded as unable to understand the information relevant to a decision if he or she is able to undertand an explanation of that information in broad terms and simple language including other languages if appropriate or other forms of communication such as audio tapes. They also recommended that a person should not be regarded as incapable of communicating their decisions unless "all practicable steps to enable him or her to do so have been taken without success".' [39]

Where an individual is deemed incapable, the best interests test for treatment will be retained, but with modifications [40]:

'In determining a patient's best interests regard should be given to –

- the ascertainable past and present wishes and feelings of the person concerned and the factors the person would consider if able to do so;
- the need to permit and encourage the person to participate as fully as possible in anything done for, and any decision affecting, him or her;
- the views of other people whom it is appropriate and practical to consult about the person's wishes and feelings and what would be in his or her best interests; and
- whether the purpose for which any action or decision is required can be as effectively achieved in a manner less restrictive of the person's freedom of action.'

This approach to assessing best interests is not without its own drawbacks, as has been covered in Chapter 7; however it does merit consideration simply for the fact that if enshrined in statute, the medical profession will be able to adopt a consistent approach to all patients without the loss of the subjectivity of each individual case.

That the proposals will be incorporated into legislation is now clear with the publication of *Making Decisions* [41]. The Government has accepted that a new statutory definition of incapacity is needed and agrees the presumption against incapacity will stand. The proposals of the Law Commission in relation to 'best interests' and determining 'best interests' were also accepted. The proposals by the Government do however include additions to this latter test, and hence in establishing what is in a patient's best interests the following will have to be considered [42]:

- whether there is a reasonable expectation of the person recovering capacity to make the decision in the reasonably foreseeable future
- the need to be satisfied that the wishes of the person without capacity were not the result of undue influence.'

What has been left uncertain with respect to *Making Decisions* is the timing for implementation, which will have to be by means of an Act of Parliament. The Lord Chancellor's Department stated in the report itself [43]:

'Clearly, legislative changes can only be made when Parliamentary time allows.'

9.4   The nurse's holding power – section 5(4) of the Mental Health Act 1983

The MHA has provided nurses with a specific power to detain patients for a short time [44] although this power may only be exercised within the limits of the section. Section 5(4) provides:

'If, in the case of a patient who is receiving treatment for mental disorder as an in-patient in a hospital, it appears to a nurse of the prescribed class [45]

(a)   that the patient is suffering from mental disorder to such a degree that it is necessary for him to be immediately restrained from leaving the hospital; and

(b)   that it is not practicable to secure the immediate attendance of a [doctor] for the purpose of furnishing a report under [section 5(2)],

the nurse may record that fact in writing; and in that event the patient may be detained in the hospital for a period of six hours from the time when that fact is so recorded or until the earlier arrival at the place where the patient is detained of a [doctor] having power to furnish a report under [section 5(2)].'

This power presents a nurse who has the appropriate training/qualification with an important professional responsibility. The power is to be exercised by the nurse making a professional judgement as to whether the power should be utilised – as stated by the Code of Practice: '[i]t is the personal decision of the nurse who cannot be instructed to exercise this power by anyone else' [46]. If, following an assessment by the nurse, the power is not exercised and the patient either comes to harm, or harms someone else, it does not follow that the nurse is necessarily liable to any legal action *Palmer* v. *Tees Health Authority* (1999). What will be assessed is whether the decision not to exercise the power was taken reasonably. If it was a reasonable decision, that is, it was a decision which a group of responsible qualified nurses would have made in the same situation, no liability will follow. It is a power in which there is an element of risk-taking and following guidance will reduce, although not eliminate, the risks

Hence, it is wise for nurses to be familiar with the guidance in the Code of Practice, paragraph 9.2 which states:

'Before using the power the nurse should assess:

(a) the likely arrival time of the doctor as against the likely intention of the patient to leave. Most patients who express a wish to leave hospital can be persuaded to wait until a doctor arrives to discuss it further. Where this is not possible the nurse must try to predict the impact of any delay upon the patient;

(b) the consequences of a patient leaving hospital immediately – the harm that might occur to the patient or others – taking into account:

- the patient's expressed intentions including the likelihood of the patient committing self-harm or suicide;
- any evidence of disordered thinking;
- the patient's current behaviour and in particular any changes in usual behaviour;
- the likelihood of the patient behaving in a violent manner;
- any recently received messages from relatives or friends;
- any recent disturbances on the ward;
- any relevant involvement of other patients;

(c) the patient's known unpredictability and any other relevant information from other members of the multi-disciplinary team.'

As section 5(4) is written, it appears that the holding power can only be invoked after the completion of the written record (on Form 13) and hence restraint would not be permitted until after the making of the record. However, this in some cases would be wholly impractical, for example, where the patient unexpectedly leaps out of bed and runs out of the ward. In these situations, it can be argued that the common law will permit restraint for one of a number of reasons, for example, to prevent crime, to safeguard the well-being of others, or to fulfil the duty owed to the patient. The filling out of Form 13 would therefore take place as soon as possible after the restraint being used. The Code of Practice is somewhat ambiguous on this point. In paragraph 9.6, it seems to suggest that the power may be invoked without completion of Form 13, but paragraph 9.4 indicates that to use the power the Form must be completed. The case law on the subject is also unclear and unhelpful. In *Black* v. *Forsey* (1988) the House of Lords decided, in the context of Scottish Mental Health Act provisions, that a common law power to 'arrest the insane' [47] could not be used because of the specific statutory limitation. In addition, in *R* v. *Bournewood NHS Trust ex parte L* (1998) [48] the Court of Appeal suggested that de facto detention was unlawful where Mental Health Act powers to detain were available. The fact that the House of Lords overruled the Court of Appeal would suggest that it will still be permissible to detain a patient whilst invoking section 5(4) with completion of the documentation afterwards.

In addition, it is clear that section 5(4) is a power which assumes an appropriate level of staffing. Indeed, paragraph 9.9 of the Code of Practice states that '[a] suitably qualified, experienced and competent nurse should be on all wards where there is a possibility of section 5(4) being invoked'. Hence appropriate staffing will be an essential prerequisite for the use of the power, but, also, adequate staffing may lessen the likelihood of the power being used. Failure to staff the ward adequately will mean the section cannot be exercised at all, or only with great difficulty. The MHA, therefore, implicitly requires wards to be staffed with at least one nurse who is appropriately qualified, and it may be the case that many hospitals/wards will fail to reach this standard. Whether the nurse has knowledge of the particular patient or is trained in the specific area of mental disorder, before being able to use section 5(4), is a matter of good practice only. The legislation requires only qualification and adherence to the process.

The use of the holding powers available under the MHA has been a source of concern for many years. The Mental Health Act Commission has commented both in its Seventh Biennial Report and its Eighth on the high, and increasing, use made of the powers. The fact there is '[h]igh usage does not necessarily imply misuses,' [49] but raises the question whether more patients should be detained under sections 2 or 3 of the MHA. If the usage is lowered, it may be that more dubious methods are being used to prevent patients leaving hospital care:

> 'For example, Commissioners are aware of instances where patients have been warned that they would be detained under section 5(2) if they tried to leave. Such a threat, or implied threat, of the use of compulsory powers amounts to de facto detention. It also raises serious questions about the distinction between voluntary and compulsory admission and whether the safeguards of the Act are being denied to those patients coerced into informal admission.' [50]

9.5   Detention by informal methods

One of the major controversies concerning detention is the use of methods, for example confusion locks, which mean that informal patients cannot leave the hospital but there is no statutory authority to detain. As mentioned earlier, it has now been decided, by the House of Lords in *R* v. *Bournewood NHS Trust, ex parte L* (1998), that an incompetent, but compliant, patient does not require formal detention to validate their presence and treatment in hospital. This is despite the argument that the individual's rights, and hence protection, will be greater if formally sectioned. The protection for health professionals may also be argued to be greater where they are dealing with a detained patient. However, where that incompetent but otherwise compliant patient has a tendency to wander and thus be a danger to themselves or others, sectioning may be seen as an option, but a very drastic one. The Code of Practice suggests that locking doors *may* be permitted but should be seen as a last option and should be part of a patient's care plan:

> 'The safety of informal patients who would be at risk of harm if they wandered out of a ward or mental nursing home at will, should be ensured by adequate staffing and good supervision. Combination locks and double handed doors should be used only in units where there is a regular and significant risk of patients wandering off accidentally and being at risk of harm. There should be clear policies on the use of locks and other devices and a mechanism for reviewing decisions. Every patient should have an individual care plan which states explicitly when he or she will be prevented from leaving the ward. Patients

who are not deliberately trying to leave the ward, but who may wander out accidentally, may legitimately be deterred from leaving the ward by those devices. In the case of a patient who persistently and/or purposely attempts to leave a ward or mental nursing home, whether or not they understand the risk involved, considerations must be given to assessing whether they would more appropriately be formally detained...' [51]

The extent to which this advice can completely represent the legal situation is a matter of debate, which has not been simplified by the *Bournewood* decision. Restricting a person's freedom is false imprisonment, but certain restrictions are permissible. Since the patients in these situations are owed a duty of care by the staff, it may be appropriate to determine that there is no false imprisonment where the patient is unthinkingly trying to leave, but that where the patient is making a purposeful desire to leave the ward, prevention without statutory authority may not be lawful. Needless to say, compliance with the Code of Practice would be best practice and would at least provide a nurse with a possible defence to any legal action.

9.6   The management of violent or aggressive patients

For some considerable time patients who present violently or aggressively have been a matter of concern for the staff most closely involved with their care and treatment. As long ago as 1977, the Confederation of Health Service Employees in its report, *The Management of Violent and Potentially Violent Patients* [52], attempted to address this thorny issue. More recently it has come to the fore in relation to handling a group of patients perceived to be particularly problematic, that is patients suffering from personality disorder. These issues are covered in the proposed reforms to the MHA and are discussed below.

9.6.1   The informal or detained patient

Common law justifications

It is submitted that reliance on the common law indicating that people may defend themselves or others is the proper basis upon which to authorise activity to deal with a violent or aggressive patient, whether that be by way of physical force, seclusion or medication. Where some sort of physical response is necessary, the least force necessary safely to contain the problem which the patient presents, should be used. In many cases this may be holding the patient, or properly trained staff using control and restraint techniques. Where such force is unlikely to be sufficient or where its use may be harmful to the patient, staff and/or other patients, seclusion may be necessary. In some cases an appropriate alternative may be medication (possibly by way of sedation).

These activities have not been justified on the basis that they are 'medical treatment' within the MHA (where the patient is detained) or part of a treatment programme to which the patient has consented. Where the person is detained, it is submitted that regarding these activities as 'treatment' even in the light of the very wide definition of treatment permitted by the MHA is not correct. Treatment, regardless of the definition, should always be intended to have some curative or ameliorative purpose or expectation, which will not be the case with the techniques mentioned. As regards an informal patient, the same is true, but as the patient may consent to treatment, it may be tempting to use the patient's consent as justification for restraint. While this is not impossible, it is suggested that it is difficult and also poor practice.

Seclusion

It is assumed that seclusion, albeit controversial, is lawful and will continue to be used even if only rarely. 'Seclusion is the supervised confinement of a patient in a room, which may be locked to protect others from significant harm' [53].There is nothing inherent in seclusion which makes it unlawful, but it is subject to abuse by using it for too long, or as a means of punishment, and then it becomes an unlawful interference with a patient's freedom of movement or bodily integrity. Hence, the Code of Practice emphasises in paragraph 9.16, that seclusion should be seen 'as a last resort' and be 'for the shortest possible time'. In addition, seclusion should not be used:

'● as a punishment or threat;
● as part of a treatment programme;
● because of shortage of staff;
● where there is any risk of suicide or self-harm.'

If seclusion is imposed on informal patients, it should be a trigger to consider the formal detention of the patient.

The Code of Practice also offers guidance as to the need for each hospital to have a policy on seclusion and for the procedure to be applied. Paragraph 19.18 provides that the decision to use seclusion may be made by the nurse in charge of the ward. If seclusion is initiated without the involvement of the patient's rmo, they must be notified at once in order that they may attend. Having placed a patient into seclusion, the duty of care owed to the patient demands that account be taken of the change in circumstances, and thus the Code of Practice further provides:

'19.19 A nurse should be readily available within sight and sound of the seclusion room at all times throughout the period of the patient's seclusion, and present at all times with a patient who has been sedated.

19.20 The aim of observation is to monitor the condition and behaviour of the patient and to identify the time at which seclusion can be terminated ... the patient should be observed continuously. A documented report must be made at least every 15 minutes.

19.21 The need to continue seclusion should be reviewed every 2 hours by 2 nurses (1 of whom was not involved in the decision to seclude) and, every 4 hours by a doctor. A multidisciplinary review should be completed by a consultant or other senior doctor, nurses and other professionals, who were not involved in the incident which led to seclusion if the seclusion continues for more than 8 hours consecutively; or 12 hours intermittently over a period of 48 hours.'

Regarding where the seclusion takes place, the Code of Practice provides:

'19.22 The room used for seclusion should:

- provide privacy from other patients;
- enable staff to observe the patient at all times;
- be safe and secure;
- not contain anything which could cause harm to the patient or others;
- be adequately furnished, heated, lit and ventilated;
- be quiet but not soundproofed and with some means of calling for attention; the means of operation should be explained to the patient.

Staff may decide what a patient may take into the seclusion room, but the patient should always be clothed.'

The Mental Health Act Commission collates information on the usage made of seclusion and this has been an area that merited 'particular attention'. Their Eighth Biennial Report indicated that nearly 5000 episodes of seclusion were used in 1997/8 in relation to just under 2000 patients. In addition, and perhaps of more concern, is the statement that 'there is a considerable number of units where policies are either inadequate or out of date and the guidance in the Code is not followed' [54].

9.7   Patients or individuals with personality disorders

As highlighted above, there has recently been an increase in concern, on the part of the Government, in relation to individuals deemed to have a dangerous severe personality disorder where their condition is not amenable to treatment. As such this minority of personality disorder sufferers cannot be legally detained under the MHA (other than, possibly, for a very short time under section 2 or section 4). This is because, in the detention section provisions, personality disorder is classed within the category of 'psychopathic disorder', and can only justify detention if the treatment is 'likely to alleviate or prevent deterioration' of the disorder [55]. The result is that these individuals who are classed as having a dangerous and serious personality disorder will be left in the community where they 'pose a risk of serious offending' [56]. Whilst the proposals are couched in terms of ensuring that these individuals receive the help they need, it is not surprising that this is set in the context of protecting the rest of society. As such, the nature of the proposals may be questioned as being potentially Draconian in their application, and at odds with the concept of innocent until proven guilty.

The basic thrust of the proposal is for the following [57]:

'• legislative powers for the detention of dangerous severely personality disordered people for as long as they present a risk to the public, and powers of supervision and recall following release from detention;

- arrangements for identification of dangerous severely personality disordered people and assessment of risk based on agreed national protocols;
- a case management system for those who have been assessed;
- conditions for managing people in detention that protect the public and are safe for staff and those who are subject to detention; programmes for the management of dangerous severely personality disordered people, in detention and following discharge from detention, based on best practice including risk assessment...'

While it is true to say that these provisions will affect a very small minority of individuals – assessed at around 2000 in the discussion document since it is necessary for the individual not only to have a personality disorder but for it to be both dangerous and serious – the impact is certainly wider. The ability to detain to prevent offending, and where offending need never have occurred in the past, is harsh, albeit for the aims of protection of the public and is the area that is likely to cause the greatest moral and ethical debate. Detention in this situation would be via the civil law, and would result in the dangerous person being kept in facilities run by the health service 'whether or not they were likely to benefit from treatment in hospital' [58], with an expectation that the facilities would be separate from other mental health units. If the individual has offended, the criminal courts would have the power to give a variety of different disposals, which all look towards assessment of risk and detention in specialist units, albeit that the specialist units may be jointly run by the health and prison services.

The method of implementation of any or all of these proposals will be either by minor modifications to the existing legal regime, or by introducing new powers for the civil and criminal courts. Regardless of the means to introduce the powers, unless accompanied by rigorous assessment procedures, they represent a possible retrograde step in the way in which society sees the mentally disordered person.

9.8   Treatment in the community

The context of the above discussion has been on treatment and care of the mentally disordered patient within the hospital or nursing home. However, many mentally ill people are perfectly able to live in the community and receive treatment with only out-patient visits or short in-patient stays. For these individuals, treatment will be with their consent since the treatment provisions in the MHA only permit compulsory treatment when the patient is in hospital or when they are on leave of absence under section 17 MHA. While on leave of absence the patient may be recalled at any time if necessary in their interests or the interests of others. In addition, if the detention section is to be renewed, the patient must be recalled to hospital, with the intention that the patient then remains in hospital.

Hence, there has been a long running debate on the need for community treatment orders, and incidents involving mentally ill people in the community, such as Ben Silcock, have served to continue the discussion. Following the Silcock incident, where Silcock, who suffered from schizophrenia, was mauled by a lion at London Zoo after entering its enclosure, the Department of Health examined the issue of community treatment and produced an internal review report [59]. In addition the Royal College of Psychiatrists recommended a new supervision order, which would enable compulsory treatment to be given in the community [60]. However, despite the calls for compulsory treatment orders, these provisions were not introduced. Instead, a form of supervision order was enacted giving certain powers to the supervisor. Crucially however, the supervisor's powers fall short of compulsory treatment and arguably the supervision order is less effective for this omission.

The Mental Health (Patients in the Community) Act 1995 amends the MHA by introducing a series of new sections whereby 'after care under supervision' can be sought by the patient's rmo before the patient leaves hospital. The application is made under section 25A and is designed to secure the appointment of a supervisor and with a view to securing the provision of after care services by virtue of section 117 MHA. Only patients who have been detained under section 3 are liable for a supervision application, and equally only section 3 patients will qualify for after care under section 117. The making of a supervision order will not guarantee that any after care services are in fact provided and given that after care responsibilities are normally shared between the health and social services, resource implications cannot be ignored. What is clear is that any mentally disordered patient who is discharged and receives section 117 services, will not be liable to assessment to contribute towards the cost of those services (*R v. Richmond London Borough Council ex parte Watson and Others* (1999)).

In addition to having to provide those services that the service provider assesses as being needed under section 117, section 25D sets out further requirements which may be imposed upon the individual. These are:

'(a) that the patient reside at a specified place;
(b) that the patient attend at specified places and times for the purpose of medical treatment, occupation, education or training; and
(c) that access to the patient be given, at any place where the patient is residing, to the supervisor, any registered medical practitioner or any approved social worker or to any other person authorised by the supervisor.'

These requirements differ only slightly from the powers of guardians appointed under section 7 MHA, the difference being that the supervisor can require the patient to attend at specified places for medical treatment. This may in all possibility be an out-patients clinic or the community psychiatric nurse's clinic. If the patient does not attend, the supervisor may take or convey the patient to the place for medical treatment – a form of community arrest perhaps? However, having got the patient to the medical practitioner, there is no method prescribed in the amended MHA to force the patient to comply with the treatment. Instead of a compulsory community treatment order, what has been produced is a watching power which merely enables the supervisor, in reality, to consider whether re-admission to hospital is warranted in the event of failure to comply with treatment.

For the community nurse the after care under supervision presents very little change in the way patients must be treated, since ongoing consent must be checked and refusal complied with where the patient is capable. When a patient refuses treatment, and is subject to supervision, the only additional duty will be to inform the supervisor in order that they may consider the options. However, how this will fit with duty of confidentiality is a further ethical dilemma, but one which would generally fall in favour of disclosure in the public interest.

9.9   Reforms

As mentioned at the start of this chapter, the Government has carried out a consultation exercise into reforming mental health law and treatment of individuals with mental disorders. The result of this consultation was the publication of a White Paper on 20 December 2000 [61], although it is clear that no new legislation will be enacted as a matter of urgency since the White Paper states 'When Parliamentary time allows, we will introduce a new Bill...' [62]. While the White Paper contemplates a radical shake-up in mental health legislation, and does contain many changes, it is suggested that many of the practicalities and ethical aspects of caring for mentally ill patients will not alter in any fundamental way. In terms of general themes for the legislation, the expectation will be that 'people with mental illness or other mental disorders should ... be treated in the same way as people with other illness or medical conditions' [63], which is no different to the MHA. However there will be increasing emphasis on the need to protect the public from harm where patients refuse treatment or do not realise they are in need of care and attention; hence the legislation will seek to ensure that high risk patients are dealt with as highlighted earlier in this chapter [64]. The provision of care and treatment will be expected to follow a clear 'Care Programme' which should be designed to meet the needs of the individual patient in the least restrictive manner wherever possible, taking into account the best interests of the patient and having discussed it with the patient's relatives or another person [65]. In terms of ethics, this may mean dealing with breaches of patient confidentiality and consent, although this is not discussed in the White Paper in any way.

One of the major changes introduced is that in detaining patients all powers will be subject to consideration by a new, full time Mental Health Act Tribunal [66]. The Tribunal will be required to authorise all use of compulsory powers of detention after the initial stages of assessment of the patient, a change that will clearly bring the legislation within the European Convention on Human Rights.

The means to detain patients, in the context of the procedure to be followed, will also be a major departure from the current system, although the need to comply with formalities and the consequences ethically for the nurse practitioner will remain the same. Detention using formal powers under the new regime, if enacted, will be a three stage process [67] and will be related to a different, and broader, definition of mental disorder. This definition will cover 'any disability or disorder of mind or brain, whether permanent or temporary, which results in an impairment or disturbance of mental functioning' [68]. The stages of detention will 'have to be followed consecutively in every case' [69]; however it is not expected that the time taken on each stage will be the same, subject to any maximum time frame specified.

The first stage will be the decision to begin assessment and initial treatment of a patient, this decision being made by two doctors and a social worker or other qualified mental health professional. In establishing whether or not to use compulsory powers, the professionals must be certain that the patient has a mental disorder that warrants further assessment/treatment and whether without this the patient or others will be placed in a situation of harm.

The second stage will be one of formal assessment and initial treatment, rather than the decision to do so. The patient will be detained for up to 28 days and it is expected that a care plan is produced within 3 days of this detention commencing. To continue detention after this 3 day period, the clinical supervisor will have to believe the criteria for longer term detention are met. These criteria are covered in the third and final stage, where patients will only be detained after their case has been examined by the Tribunal. In addition to the existence of a mental disorder, the Tribunal must be satisfied it warrants care and treatment to protect the interests of the patient or others and that there is a care plan which addresses the therapeutic benefits to the patient, or if the patient is a risk to others, that deals with managing the patient's behaviour. The Tribunal will only be able to authorise detention for a maximum of 6 months initially, but can on review extend the period.

As can be seen, this new regime has clear links to the existing legislative structure, but is now one of much more legal formality. The powers of the Tribunal will not only be in relation to detention of patients, but will also extend to the treatment of the patient in the community. However, the White Paper does not go so far as to suggest that treatment will be forcibly given to patients in the community except in a clinical setting [70] – the fact that the White Paper does not define clinical setting being of some concern.

In addition to the detention provisions, there are also changes to the safeguards suggested [71]. These include the appointment of a nominated person who will ensure that the patient and their best interests are represented, the setting up of a patient advocacy service and the requirement for specified treatments to be administered to the patient only after approval from a doctor on the expert panel to the Tribunal or where the patient has consented. Safeguards will also be introduced for those patients deemed incapable but compliant, as in the *Bournewood* case referred to earlier [72]. In these situations the patient will have to be fully assessed, a care plan produced, and the patient seen by a doctor on the Tribunal experts panel who confirms or changes the care plan. The patient's records will include this finalised care plan. Disagreements as to the nature of the care plan raised by relatives or carers are expected to be dealt with informally without recourse to the Tribunal.

While the need for reform of the MHA is perhaps overdue in today's NHS structure, it must be a reform that in reality addresses all the concerns arising from the MHA's shortcomings. The question of whether the reforms expounded in the White Paper can achieve this will be debated long after the passing of a new Mental Health Act.

9.10   Notes and references

1. See generally, Hoggett, B.M. (1996) *Mental Health Law*, 4th Edn, Sweet & Maxwell, London; Gostin, L.O. *Mental Health Services: Law & Practice*, Looseleaf, Shaw & Sons, London; and Jones, R.M. (1999) *Mental Health Act Manual*, 6th edn, Sweet & Maxwell,

London and Bartlett, P. & Sandland, R. (2000) *Mental Health Law Policy and Practice*, Blackstone Press, London.

2. Reforming The Mental Health Act, December 2000, Cm 5016, The Stationery Office, London.
3. Mental Health Act Commission (1993) *Fifth Biennial Report 1991–1993*, at para. 7.15. The Stationery Office, London.
4. See *R* v. *South Western Hospital Managers, ex parte M* [1994] 1 All ER 161.
5. The definition of a patient's nearest relative can be found in section 26 MHA.
6. Note the MHA requires each local authority to appoint sufficient approved social workers and also that the Mental Health Act Code of Practice, Department of Health, London, March 1999 suggests at para. 2.35. that an approved social worker should be the preferred applicant.
7. Mental Health Act Commission (1991) *Fourth Biennial Report 1989–1991*, at para. 6.18. The Stationery Office, London. A Guidance Note (No. 3) was subsequently issued by the Commission in August 1997.
8. See further the discussion by Jones, R.M. (1999) *Mental Health Act Manual*, 6th edn, p. 21, Sweet & Maxwell, London, on the ability to use section 2 where a patient is already well-known to the health care professionals and approved social workers.
9. Mental Health Act Commission, *Fifth Biennial Report* 1991–1993, at para 7.0 and see the Mental Health Act Code of Practice, 1999, at para. 16.5
10. *B* v. *Croydon Health Authority* [1995] 2 WLR 294, per Lord Justice Hoffman, at p. 298.
11. For example, *Re S* [1994] 4 All ER 671, *Tameside & Glossop Acute Services Trust* v. *CH* [1996] 1 FLR 762, *Re MB (Medical Treatment)* [1997] 2 FLR 426 and and *R* v. *Collins, Pathfinder Health Services Trust, St. George's Healthcare NHS Trust ex parte S* [1998] 3 WLR 936. It should be noted that not all of these were decisions under the MHA, but came under the common law provisions of 'best interests'.
12. per Mr Justice Wall at p. 773.
13. See note 11.
14. per Lord Justice Judge at p. 958.
15. This is indicated by the fact that in the period 1997–1999 14 475 requests for second opinions were completed by the Mental Health Act Commission, with 72.9% being in respect of medicine only and 28.2% for ECT only. This represented an increase in requests of over 25% from the previous reporting period although this may in part be due to the effect of *R* v. *Bournewood Community and Mental Health Care Trust, ex parte L* [1998] 3 All ER 289. Mental Health Act Commission, *Eighth Biennial Report 1997–1999*, The Stationery Office, London, at Table 8 and para. 6.36.
16. This is in contrast to treatment provided under section 57 and section 58(3)(b) where section 61 places a duty on the responsible medical officer to review the necessity of treatment.
17. Mental Health Act Code of Practice 1999 at para. 16.35, Department of Health, London.
18. Mental Health Act Code of Practice 1999 at para. 16.19, Department of Health, London.
19. Mental Health Act Code of Practice 1999 at para. 16.14, Department of Health, London.
20. Mental Health Act Commission, *Eighth Biennial Report*, 1997–1999, at Table 8, The Stationery Office, London.
21. Mental Health Act Code of Practice, 1999, para. 16.10, Department of Health, London.
22. Fennell, P.W.H. (1990) Inscribing paternalism in the law: consent to treatment and mental disorder. *Journal of Law and Society*, **17** (29) 40.
23. This Act seeks to protect individuals disclosing information in the public interest and to enable the individual to claim legal redress in the event of victimisation following disclosure. It is important to note that the Act only covers certain types of information disclosed and specifies how the disclosure should be carried out. For example, if a

nurse were to make disclosures to the local media this would not be within the terms of the Act and no protection from victimisation would be granted.

24. Over the two year period 1997–1999 covered by the latest Mental Health Commission Biennial Report only 17 referrals for neurosurgery were made – a figure which is considerably lower than for any previous period.
25. For example see the *Eighth Biennial Report 1997–1999*, at para. 6.22, The Stationery Office, London.
26. Per Lord Donaldson at p. 798.
27. Mental Health Act Code of Practice, 1999, at para. 15.11, Department of Health, London.
28. Mental Health Act Manual, 6th edn, para. 15.12, Sweet & Maxwell, London. See also Gunn *et al.* (1999) Decision making capacity, *Medical Law Review*, 7, p. 269, available electronically at www.oup.co.uk/medlaw/.
29. See note 11.
30. Per Lord Donaldson in *Re T* [1992] at p. 796.
31. See for example *Re F (mental patient: sterilisation)* [1990] 2 AC 1 and *Airedale NHS Trust v. Bland* [1993] AC 789.
32. These issues will be covered generally by Practice Directions – for example *Official Solicitor's Practice Note* [1996] 2 FLR 111 and *Practice Note (persistent vegetative state: withdrawal of treatment)* [1996] 4 All ER 766.
33. Fennell, P.W.H. (1990) Inscribing paternalisation in the law: consent to treatment and mental disorder. *Journal of Law and Society*, **17** (29) 29.
34. Fennell, *ibid* at page 43.
35. See further Mental Health Act Code of Practice, para. 15.11 and the BMA (1995) *Code of Practice on Advance Statements about Medical Treatment*, BMA, London.
36. *R v. Bournewood* [1998] see note 15.
37. Cm 3808, 1997 Lord Chancellor's Department, The Stationery Office, London.
38. The Law Commission, *Mental Incapacity*, Report No 231 (Summary) London 1995.
39. *Who Decides? Making decisions of behalf of mentally incapacitated adults*, Cm 3808, para 3.18. Lord Chancellor's Department, The Stationery Office, London.
40. Law Commission Report No. 231 (Summary), (1995), at para 1.5. *Mental Incapacity.*
41. *Making Decisions. The Government's proposals for making decisions on behalf of mentally incapacitated adults.* October 1999 Cm.4465. Lord Chancellor's Department, The Stationery Office, London.
42. *Making Decisions* at Chapter 1 para 1.12. See also Rodgers, M.E. (2000) Making decisions for the mentally incapacitated, *Health Care Risk Report*, **6** (3) 10.
43. Introduction para 7.
44. See Dimond, B. (1989) 'The Right of the Nurse to Detain Informal Patients in Psychiatric Hospitals in England and Wales'. *Medical Law* pp. 535–47.
45. *The Mental Health (Nurses) Order 1998 (SI 1998 No 2625)* defines who will be a nurse of prescribed class of a 'nurse registered in any part of the register maintained under section 7 of the Nurses, Midwives and Health Visitors Act 1997 which is mentioned in paragraph (2)'. Paragraph 2 refers to nurses in Part 3 (first level nurses trained in the nursing of persons suffering from mental illness), Part 4 (second level nurses trained in the nursing of persons suffering from mental illness (England & Wales)), Part 5 (first level nurses trained in the nursing of persons suffering from learning disabilities), Part 6 (second level nurses trained in the nursing of persons suffering from learning disabilities (England & Wales)), Part 13 (nurses qualified following a course of preparation in mental health nursing) and finally Part 14 (nurses qualified following a course of preparation in learning disabilities nursing).
46. Mental Health Act Code of Practice, 1999, at para 9.1. Department of Health, London.

47. As it was described by David Lanham in an article of that title in *Criminal Law Review* (1974) p. 515.
48. See note 15.
49. *Eighth Biennial Report 1997–1999*, para 4.26 and see also Table 4. The Stationery Office, London.
50. Eighth Biennial Report 1997–1999, para 4.28, The Stationery Office, London.
51. Mental Health Act Code of Practice, 1999, para 19.27. Department of Health, London.
52. Confederation of Health Service Employees (1977) *The Management of Violent and Potentially Violent Patients.*
53. Mental Health Act Code of Practice, 1999, para 19.16. Department of Health, London.
54. Mental Health Act Commission, *Eighth Biennial Report* 1997–1999, para 10.18. The Stationery Office, London.
55. See further sections 1 and 3 of the Mental Health Act 1983. Also see Barlett, P. & Sandland, R. (2000) *Mental Health Law Policy and Practice*, Blackstone Press, London, for a discussion on the relevant case law.
56. *Managing Dangerous People with Severe Personality Disorder: Proposals for policy development*. Home Office, July 1999, Executive Summary. The Stationery Office, London.
57. Chapter 3, para 5, and also see further note.
58. *Managing Dangerous People with Severe Personality Disorder: Proposals for policy development*. Home Office July 1999, Executive Summary. The Stationery Office, London. Chapter 3, para 20.
59. *Department of Health Legal Powers on the Care of Mentally Ill People in the Community* (1993) Department of Health, London.
60. Royal College of Psychiatrists Community Supervision Orders (1993) Royal College of Psychiatrists, London.
61. *Reforming The Mental Health Act*, December 2000, Cm 5016, The Stationery Office London. It should be noted that the paper is in two parts.
62. Para 8.3 Part 1.
63. Para 2.2 Part 1.
64. High Risk patients are covered in Part 2 of the White Paper.
65. Para 2.21 and Chapter 5, Part 1 of the White Paper.
66. Para 2.28, Chapters 3 and 4, Part 1 of the White Paper.
67. Chapter 3, Part 1 of the White Paper.
68. Para 3.3, Part 1 of the White Paper.
69. Para 3.9, Part 1 of the White Paper.
70. Para 13, Part 1 of the White Paper.
71. Safeguards for detained patients in terms of representation and consent to treatment being covered in Chapter 5, Part 1.
72. Safeguards for patients treated in the absence of compulsory powers being dealt with in Chapter 6, Part 1.

B   An Ethical Perspective – Compulsion and Autonomy

Harry Lesser

In mental health nursing the same issue dominates both legal and ethical discussions. This is the issue of the use of compulsion, whether in the form of compulsory treatment or compulsory restraint: when, if ever, it should be used, and what methods of compulsion should be employed. The crucial difference ethically between mental and physical illnesses is that it is commonly held that compulsory treatment can be justified only if a person's mental judgement is impaired to such a degree that they lack the competence to decide for themselves how they should be treated. This can arise in various ways – with children, people who are unconscious, people under the influence of drink or drugs – but it can arise from the illness itself only if the illness is a 'mental illness' or has damaging mental effects. Hence both legally and ethically, and with regard both to general guidelines and to the treatment of individual people, decisions have to be made as to when it is right to treat someone without their permission and/or against their will. (These are different: an unconscious patient may be unable to give consent but on recovering consciousness be very glad to have received treatment and not feel they would have opposed it if they had been able to.)

These issues arise ethically at three points: there are ethical problems of how to carry out the law as it stands, of assessing the law as it stands, and of assessing proposed changes in the law as they arise. The first of these is perhaps the most important in practice, but professional groups, such as nurses, can influence the law; and in any case it is always important to consider the law from an ethical standpoint, even if one has for the time being to accept it as being the law. Accordingly, I will consider all three in turn.

9.11   The ethical use of compulsion

In considering all three, I shall assume that the shift in the way compulsion is viewed morally, in theory if not always in practice, is a shift in the right direction. It is nowadays widely agreed that in dealing with adults, even mentally disturbed adults, the presumption should be that compulsion is to be avoided, and that it is the use of compulsion that requires a justification. There are two reasons for this: that individual autonomy is a value to be preserved whenever possible, unless it thwarts other important values (some would say, even then), and that people are normally the best judges of their own interests, even if they are not perfect judges. Both in technical philosophy and in practical life there is a dispute as to whether both reasons are valid, and if only one, which one, and also as to exactly how strong our commitment to autonomy should be. But that our presumption should be in favour of autonomy is widely, and I think rightly, agreed.

There are also two main grounds for overriding individual autonomy, but here it is the two in combination rather than as alternatives that are needed. The patient or client must be unable to make a rational decision about treatment, and they must be likely to injure themselves or others if nothing is done. We shall consider later whether one of these could be ethically sufficient, but for the moment we may take it that when both are believed to be present compulsion is regarded as necessary, whether in the form of compulsory hospitalisation, compulsory medication or other treatment, or compulsory seclusion or restraint.

Some of these decisions, especially the decision to detain a person in hospital, will be taken by people other than nurses. Chapter 9A explains very carefully and clearly the legal position of the nurse once this has happened. This may involve only making sure that the proposed treatment is lawful under the Mental Health Act, or it may involve decisions as to whether the patient is competent and whether they are dangerous to themselves or others. It is in these cases that there is an obligation on the nurse to carry out the law ethically.

To carry out the law ethically means, in this context as in many others, to take its provisions seriously, and not to take action for other reasons or on other criteria. The question whether a patient is competent – which can be a very difficult one – must be decided with regard to the individual patient, and not on the basis that a certain type of person, or a person with a certain type of disorder, or a person making a certain sort of decision, is necessarily incompetent; Chapter 9A points out that the law intends all this to be excluded. Similarly, the judgement whether seclusion is necessary needs to be made with regard to the individual, without a presumption that all members of some particular group are inclined towards violence.

Secondly, as well as being imposed on the right criteria, restraint and compulsory treatment must always be imposed for the right reasons. The main 'wrong reason' is as a punishment, but it is very important for nurses to remember that one can be punitive informally and even unconsciously. The best policy may be for nurses to acknowledge their (often justified) anger with certain patients and then to exercise professional self-control, rather than failing to admit the hostility, which may then influence their actions while remaining unnoticed.

The other 'wrong reason' is administrative convenience. To use seclusion when a patient is likely to be violent or seriously disruptive is obviously right and necessary; but, despite the temptation, to use it when they are only a nuisance is not. There are practical worries regarding this, that in some hospitals the use of seclusion is too frequent and the correct legal guidelines are not only not properly followed but also not properly explained during training. The result is that a culture of the use of seclusion (or of other forms of restraint or compulsory treatment) for, in effect, punitive or administrative reasons, has developed. The problem here is that it can be very difficult to determine in this area the reasons or criteria for making any particular decision. But the ethical requirement is clear: it is to avoid the temptation to abuse one's power and use criteria not allowed by the law, and to follow the law strictly in making decisions.

9.12   Ethics and the current law: Szasz's view

But one still has to ask whether the law as it stands is in fact ethically ideal, or even right. Here the most radical attack comes from those such as Thomas Szasz [1] who believe that compulsory medical treatment, even for the 'mentally ill', is never justified. Even restraint, they hold, is justified only as a punishment for a crime already committed, or to prevent imminent violence, and never because a person 'may be dangerous' or 'may injure themselves or others'. Szasz's ground for this is that all those who injure themselves or others, however bizarre the circumstances, still act out of free choice and not because their mental judgement is impaired. Hence the supposed 'mentally ill' (who in Szasz's view are not mentally ill, but either physically ill or not ill at all) may, like other criminals, be punished for harming other people and they may be forcibly prevented from committing a crime; but what they do to themselves, if they are adults, is their own business, and they may not be restrained in advance, any more than anyone else who has committed no crime.

Szasz has been prepared to admit that there are a few people, such as those with advanced Alzheimer's disease, who are so incapable of making any decision that one has to act on their behalf, as one must when a patient is unconscious. But he maintains that the vast majority of people, including those with a brain disease or illness (the existence of which Szasz admits) are not so mentally impaired that they are incompetent to make decisions or are not responsible for their actions. Although there is no obvious way of conclusively disproving this position, there is a great deal of empirical evidence against it.

This evidence comes partly from the behaviour of the 'mentally ill' and partly from what they say, either at the time of the illness or subsequently. This evidence shows, or strongly suggests, first, that there are people who suffer such distortions of perception, whether visual, auditory (e.g. hearing voices) or tactile, that they become unable to determine what is real and what is not. Secondly, there are people whose emotional state makes them unable to make any kind of serious considered judgement; this can happen, for example, in manic states which make it impossible to keep one's attention focused for more than a few seconds, or states of clinical depression in which the ability to take even a trivial decision or the sense that a decision is possible, or that it matters, can disappear. Thirdly, there are people who develop radically irrational beliefs, based on no evidence – for example that a family member is really an imposter or an alien – and who as a result reach radically false and irrational conclusions about what they ought to do.

This is very much a layman's account, and by no means exhaustive. But I hope it serves to make the following point. Among the 'mentally ill' are people whose capacity to make rational judgements, even about their own condition and treatment, is impaired; the cause of this is clearly sometimes physical, but it is a matter of dispute whether it is always physical. Sometimes (not always) this is so serious as to amount to a really radical impairment. If this is the case, although the impairment may sometimes be harmless in practice and leave the person with bizarre ideas but no problems in living, it may also happen that the impaired judgement is likely to lead to self-neglect, self-harm or violence to others. And when this happens, considerations of the welfare of either the person themselves or of others require that there be intervention, with or without consent. Autonomy is not violated by this, since the interference with mental functioning makes the person already non-autonomous.

So one may object to Szasz that, given a serious look at the empirical evidence from words and behaviour, there are people who lack the competence to decide whether or not they should receive medical treatment and who in the absence of treatment are likely to do either themselves or others harm, whether by neglect or by active violence. However, by no means all the 'mentally ill' are in this category, and perhaps only a small minority. Not all mental illnesses, as normally defined, affect a person's judgement (some, for example, only make them unhappy), and even those that do may not affect it in any radical way. So there will always be a problem of deciding whether the use of compulsion is right in any particular instance; and it is important to remember that in the past compulsion at all levels – hospitalisation, treatment and restraint – has been very much misused and over-used, and great harm has sometimes resulted. Nevertheless, great harm also sometimes resulted from failures to intervene when necessary. The decision to use compulsion thus has to be made as best one can; and as Chapter 9A shows, sometimes it falls on the nurse.

The nurse has to decide the facts: whether the patient is competent and whether they are potentially dangerous. Ethically, as much as legally, the crucial things are, first, to make the decision on these criteria and not on any others (such as administrative convenience or a wish to punish), and secondly to decide the 'facts' using the considerations laid down by the law as appropriate, avoiding general-izations that even if true may not apply to the individuals.

9.13   Ethics and forms of treatment

One problem remains. The law sets no limit on what treatments may be used, provided there is a reasonable chance of success; ethically, too, a treatment unlikely to succeed and unpleasant or invasive in nature is obviously to be avoided. But ethical objections have been raised to various treatments of mental illness even if they succeed, partially or entirely. Physical treatments, behaviourist techniques and some forms of psychotherapy have all been objected to. Is there any basis for these objections?

We begin with the physical treatments – psychosurgery, ECT and drugs. Psychosurgery is now little used, if at all, and ECT, once used fairly indiscriminately, seems to be largely confined in its use to patients with conditions such as serious endogenous depression, where it can be of help and even perhaps prevent suicide. The use of drugs has, on the other hand, greatly increased, and with growing success; but success is by no means invariable. There is thus a growing, but far from complete, understanding of when these treatments work. It is presumably not in dispute that they should not be used for conditions for which there is no evidence of success, or persisted with for a patient for whom a treatment has now been tried and has failed. But what general objection to their use might there be?

Two have been put forward: that they only tackle the symptoms and not the underlying problem, and that they are inherently invasive and manipulatory and hence degrading. But neither of these seems to work as an overall objection. The first may be true, but can be met by pointing out that to ease the symptoms is to do at least some good, sometimes a great deal, and that the symptoms may need to be relieved before the patient can begin to tackle the underlying problem. A clinically depressed person may have excellent reasons for being depressed and much to be depressed about, but the depression may need to be lifted by medication or even ECT before they are able to do anything about the social or personal causes of their depression.

The second argument, that it is inherently wrong to try to alter a person's mental state by these physical means rather than by rational argument, has more force. But it may be met by pointing out that the proper use of physical treatments (it is not disputed that these can be misused) is to remove obstacles to rational thinking which are themselves often – though perhaps not always – either physical in origin or made worse by the current state of the brain or nervous system. To use drugs to end the hearing of voices or the experience of hallucinations or of sudden frightening changes in perception is to restore the opportunity to be rational, not to take it away. Similar considerations apply to behaviourist treatments, in places where they are still used; if they are working, and if the aim is to free a person from behaviour patterns and habits that interfere with rational choice – such as alcoholism or compulsive gambling – it is hard to see what objection there can be to their use.

The ethics of psychotherapy are more complicated. As far as I know, no objections have been raised to psychotherapy in general, but objections have certainly been raised to particular forms of psychotherapy and particular ways of carrying it out. The basic objection is to covert manipulation; there may be lip-service to the idea that the therapist is being non-directive and non-judgemental but nevertheless there can be considerable concealed pressure from the therapist, or, in group therapy, from the whole group, to adopt certain views and ideas. The extreme case of this concerns the retrieval of buried memories; there is still an unsolved problem, regarding supposed memories of child abuse, as to when a genuine trauma has been recalled and when false ideas have been planted in the client's mind.

The existence of these various problems has the following consequences. There seems to be no form of treatment, of those currently used, that is in principle ethically unacceptable. But equally any form of treatment can be used in an un-ethical way, which in the context of mental illness typically means a manipulative way. Also, any form of treatment may be wrong for a particular patient, always or at a particular time. This creates two obligations for the nurse. First, to administer treatment, in any form, not only with sensitivity and humanity, as is always required in nursing, but also with the special obligation to be honest and non-manipulative. In this case, the obligation is clear, though carrying it out is not always easy.

More difficult is the problem of dealing with the, hopefully rare, situation in which the nurse is convinced that the wrong treatment is being used. Sections 11 and 12 of the UKCC Code of Conduct impose a clear duty to report this, if the nurse is convinced that standards of practice are being jeopardised, or safe and appropriate care is not being provided. There are good reasons, both moral and prudential, for the nurse to need to be very sure before taking action, but such situations do arise. The final decision must rest with the individual; once again, the problem is not unique to mental health nursing.

We may therefore conclude that in mental health nursing the law as it stands presents no ethical problems; indeed in this area the main difficulty for the nurse is perhaps the temptation, sometimes very much encouraged by the general hospital ethos, to comply with the law superficially but actually to act on rather different principles. On the other hand, although I have argued that the criticisms of the law as it stands, and of the general way in which mental illness is handled, do not in fact stand up, they do nevertheless point to certain dangers. There is a permanent need to be on the alert, and to try to ensure that compulsion is not being used inappropriately or excessively and that treatments are effective and non-manipulative.

9.14   Proposed changes in the law

All this relates to the law as it is. But the law is probably going to change before too long. The exact details are not settled but a White Paper *Reforming the Mental Health Act* has been published. The proposals in this White Paper raise in particular three ethical issues. The first concerns the provisions for compulsory treatment or detention. The intention is that compulsion should be a last resort, that the patient's rights should be safeguarded and that the combination of the two criteria of 'impairment or disturbance of mental functioning' and the risk of harm to the patient themselves or to others ('the need for specialist care in the patient's best interests *or* a significant risk of serious harm to others') should remain necessary to justify any compulsion. But there is a question whether in practice the new legislation will make it easier to justify compulsion, and the exact wording of the Act may well be crucial. At the moment, this is only a possible issue.

More important are the two new developments that are proposed. The first is the use of Community Treatment Orders (CTOs). These have been discussed as a possibility for some years, and they have been used in parts of the USA and Australia. The grounds for their introduction are as follows. There are people who can cope with life in the community and are no danger to themselves or others, provided they remain on medication. It is argued that it is unnecessary and undesirable for them to remain in hospital, but it is still necessary to ensure that they take their medication. This could be done in two ways: by an order which authorises the forcible administration of the medication if they do not take it voluntarily, or by an order for them to be compulsorily returned to hospital if they fail to remain on their medication. It is most likely that orders of the second type, which are less objectionable, will be proposed, but this is not certain – see part A of this chapter.

Three objections have been made to CTOs: that they are impracticable to operate, that they would damage the relationship between the client and the nurse or social worker, because the latter would have to take on a policing role, and that they would be an infringement of personal freedom. The first two objections might well apply to orders of the first type, but do not seem to apply to orders of the second type, in which the 'policing' role of the nurse would be limited to reporting the failure of the client to take their medication, and in which there would be no physically forced treatment, although the client would be compulsorily hospitalised if they refused treatment.

Would this violate a person's autonomy? When it was applied to people who would otherwise be detained compulsorily in hospital, it surely would not, since, though it would restrict them to some degree, they would be left much more free than would otherwise be the case. There is also a clear logic to this policy, when applied to the appropriate people; they require detention only if they do not take medication and therefore will not be detained as long as they do take medication. But there is one danger, that precisely because it is a mild and popularly acceptable limitation on freedom, it will be used too widely, and will be used not only to keep people out of hospital but also to restrict the freedom of people who otherwise would be left alone or would be allowed to leave hospital without further restrictions. (There is some evidence that this has happened in Australia.) This, though, does not invalidate the use of CTOs; rather it demonstrates that, like most uses of compulsion, it is open to abuse and needs proper monitoring. In principle, though, there seems to be no valid objection on the ground of freedom or autonomy.

The other proposed innovation is the provision of authority to detain people with 'Dangerous Severe Personality Disorders' (DSPDs) in hospital. The problem has been, as is well known, that some of the people in this category have a mental impairment which makes them very dangerous to other people, but because it is one for which there is at the moment no treatment they cannot be compulsorily admitted to a hospital. The Mental Health Act has, as part of the grounds for compulsory admission, the requirement that it is appropriate for the patient 'to receive medical treatment in a hospital' and the treatment 'is likely to alleviate or prevent a deterioration of his condition'. This is something that so far we have not dealt with in either the legal or ethical parts of this chapter, because we have been concerned with the role of the nurse which begins after the hospitalisation. But at this point it becomes important.

There are very few people in this category, but they are very dangerous and some of them have committed serious assaults or even murder when out of hospital. So the motivation to 'plug the loophole' is very clear. Is it, though, a violation of freedom to force into institutions people who have committed no crime and whom the institutions cannot help? The answer, once again, would seem to be 'no', provided the people who are 'dangerous' have been correctly identified. If they have, the protection of others is an adequate ground for detaining them in hospital until they are no longer dangerous: indeed it would seem to be a positive duty to do so.

Once again, there seems to be no objection in principle, but some danger of abuse in practice: can the people who are really dangerous be identified, how likely is it that some people who are no risk to others will be compulsorily detained, and, apart from this risk of mistakes, might there be pressure to detain people who are not dangerous but are a great nuisance? There is also a particular issue of competence, discussed in an article by Giordano [2]. Normally, it is taken that if a person is compulsorily admitted to hospital they may also be compulsorily treated for their mental disorder (see part A of this chapter). But here either no treatment is available, so that they will be given only care, or (perhaps this is more likely) various treatments will be tried with only a low expectation of success. Moreover, even if these people are mentally disturbed and dangerous, and therefore are rightly detained, they may still be competent to evaluate the proposed care and treatment, and might quite rationally decide to reject a form of treatment on the ground that it was very unlikely to alleviate their condition. Ethically, do they have the right to refuse treatment, and if they do should this right be legally protected? I leave this question for the reader to consider.

9.15   Consequences for nurses

What difference will all this make to the nurse's duties and responsibilities, if it passes into legislation? The obligation to give treatment sensitively and honestly will apply equally to treatment under a CTO. There would also be the legal requirement to report failure to receive treatment. And there would be an ethical obligation, if not a legal one, to report if anyone, in the nurse's informal opinion, was wrongly on a CTO, if either their condition was so improved that no compulsory medication was necessary or so much worse that there was a need for them to be returned to hospital before they harmed themselves or others.

Similarly with those suffering from a DSPD, the obligation to give care or treatment (if any) would be the usual one. Again, there would be an obligation to report the fact if the nurse became strongly convinced that someone was being wrongly detained. There might also be the special feature that there would be a group of compulsorily admitted mental patients entitled, like patients with a physical illness or voluntary mental patients, to take their own decisions about treatment. But overall the situation would be similar. Essentially, mental health nursing, under current conditions, does not involve any fundamental conflicts between law and ethics. The ethical obligations of the nurse are rather to administer care and treatment under the law with sensitivity, humanity and honesty, and to check that the law is not mistakenly applied or, either deliberately or unconsciously, abused. For it would seem that as long as compulsion is applied only when justified legally, it will also be justified ethically. In this area of nursing, strict adherence to law and to ethics seem to coincide.

9.16   Acknowledgements

I am very grateful to the Philosophy and Ethics of Mental Health unit at Warwick University for the seminar on *Reforming the Mental Health Act* at SOAS on 5 April

2001. I have made use of the papers of Professor Fulford (Warwick), with reference to the importance of studying the exact words used in legislation; Ms Humphrey (Department of Health), with reference to her exposition of the White Paper proposals; Dr Szmukler (Institute of Psychiatry), on the difficulty of predicting who is dangerous; Professor Richardson (Queen Mary Westfield) on CTOs in Australia; and Mr Parsons (solicitor), on DSPD and the law.

9.17   Notes and references

1. Szasz, T. (1962) *The Myth of Mental Illness*. Secker & Warburg, London.

Chapter 10
The Critically Ill Patient
A   The Legal Perspective

Linda Delany

This chapter examines the legal aspects of the dilemmas inherent in nursing critically ill patients. Caring for patients whose life hangs in the balance or whose prognosis is very uncertain, generates challenging problems which the law has sought to address. In recent years, a number of court rulings have provided new guidance in this sphere by refining the basic negligence and consent principles which apply in health care. Thanks to the Human Rights Act 1998, the European Convention for the Protection of Human Rights and Fundamental Freedoms has also begun to make its influence felt. Other legislation has been sparse, but, by contrast, there has been no shortage of authoritative guidelines emanating from government departments, the Royal Colleges, the UKCC and the professional associations. Nurses, midwives and health visitors cannot afford to neglect any of these developments.

To reflect the law's own approach to treatment decisions in critical illness cases, patients will, in this chapter, be divided into the following broad categories: babies and young children, teenagers, adults able to make their own decisions and adults unable to do so. The legal rules relating to each category will be examined separately, but some general points can be made at the outset.

Firstly, nurses treating very ill patients should be clear about the criminal implications of knowingly causing their death. Providing pain relief with drugs which, as a side-effect, may shorten life, can be acceptable but acts aimed primarily at hastening death are forbidden. Withdrawing treatment, in the knowledge that death will result, can be legitimate, and is discussed in more detail in sections 10.1.2, 10.4.4 and 10.4.5.

Secondly, English law has traditionally extended a large measure of professional freedom to doctors. The courts have felt unable to dictate to doctors and have refused to let patients do so. Coercive remedies against doctors have simply not been made available, on the grounds that doctors should not have to choose between their professional judgement and a court order (*Re J (a minor) (wardship: medical treatment)* (1990). This is apt to cause conflict particularly in cases involving children, whose parents oppose the medical decision to withhold treatment. Even in such situations, however, the courts have remained steadfast in their approach. Nurses may have to absorb the tensions which obviously arise on such occasions. On a more positive note, they may be able to mediate between the patients, their families and the doctors, when disagreements about treatment options arise. They should not hesitate to draw on and share their own insights into a patient's requirements.

The third and final point concerns the limits to the courts' powers over the allocation of health care resources. While courts are allowed to vet how decisions are made, they must confine themselves to procedural points, and ignore the benefits which patients might derive from receiving the resources they request. The cases have shown that no exception is made even for critically ill patients whose survival depends on treatment being funded [1].

The courts' reluctance, highlighted above, to secure health care services for patients, may prove to be incompatible with the requirements of the European Convention, which, because of section 6 of the Human Rights Act 1998, must be complied with whenever possible by our judges. As under Article 2(1) of the Convention, 'Everyone's right to life shall be protected by law', our courts should surely now be prepared to scrutinise the merits of at least those decisions which deny a patient potentially life-saving treatment.

At local level, scarcity of resources should be monitored by nursing staff. Nurses have been reminded by the UKCC that they infringe their Code of Professional Conduct if they fail to report their concerns about inadequate resources to an appropriate line manager [2]. The duty to report arises whenever patient care or welfare is at risk.

10.1   Babies and young children

10.1.1   The significance of parental responsibility

The importance attached by the law to a patient's ability to consent to medical procedures produces an obvious problem in the case of children. As children lack the legal capacity to give a valid consent, nurses who treat them are exposed to the risk of being sued for 'battery', the unauthorised physical contact with another person. To overcome this difficulty, the law allows consent to be given by proxy. In an extreme emergency, anyone looking after a child can offer or authorise medical treatment [3]. For example, if the condition of a child in hospital deteriorated suddenly then no consent to intervene on his or her behalf would be needed. If time permits, however, the consent of a person with parental responsibility for the child must be sought *Gillick* v. *West Norfolk and Wisbech Area Health Authority* (1985).

Mothers acquire parental responsibility automatically. So do fathers if they are married to the mother of their child at the time of the birth. Unmarried fathers have the option of applying for parental responsibility through the courts, or entering into a parental responsibility agreement with the mother [4]. The form of such an agreement is prescribed by law, and to be valid, the agreement must be recorded at the High Court. These legal hoops that unmarried fathers must jump through are under review at the time of writing, the Lord Chancellor's Department having proposed that signing the birth register should entitle a father to parental responsibility [5]. At present, though, an unmarried father's capacity to act as proxy for his children should be investigated before his instructions are complied with. If this seems officious or embarrassing, it may help to remember that schools too have to explore this issue before accepting a father's authority over a pupil.

10.1.2   Acting in the best interests of children

The proxy powers conferred by parental responsibility must by law be exercised in the best interests of the child. What is in the best interests of critically ill children was explored by the Royal College of Paediatrics and Child Health in 1997. Their report, *Withholding or withdrawing life saving treatment in children. A framework for practice* [6], identified the following five situations in which palliation rather than a continuation of life-saving treatment 'might be considered':

(1)   where brain-stem death has been diagnosed;
(2)   where the child has developed permanent vegetative state;
(3)   where the child has 'such severe disease that life sustaining treatment simply delays death without significant alleviation of suffering';
(4)   where survival with treatment is possible but will be accompanied by an intolerable degree of physical or mental impairment;
(5)   where 'in the face of progressive and irreversible illness, further treatment is more than can be borne'.

Typical of the last category would be a child with cancer whose initial treatment has failed. The first and second categories are self-explanatory. The third category is exemplified by the 1999 case of *Re C (a minor)(medical treatment)* (1997) (in which, incidentally, the court explicitly approved the report's approach to this type of case). C was a severely disabled and terminally ill little girl, aged 16 months at the time that her case went to court. She suffered from spinal muscular atrophy, type 1, weighed only 5.4 kg, and her condition was deteriorating. She nevertheless seemed to interact with her parents, appearing to recognise them and smiling at them. In the view of C's medical team, her interests demanded the withdrawal of ventilator support, non-resuscitation in the event of respiratory arrest, and palliative care till she died. C's parents, who were orthodox Jews, wanted her to be kept alive as long as possible. In view of the disagreement, the health authority applied to the High Court, which authorised the doctors to ease C's suffering, and to permit her life to end peacefully and with dignity.

The situations which trouble all concerned most, are undoubtedly those which make up category 4 above and involve children who with medical intervention will survive indefinitely, but whose survival entails pain and distress. Several such cases have come before the courts. One of the earliest and most controversial was that of *Re J (a minor)(wardship: medical treatment)* (1990). J had been born at 27 weeks gestation, with very severe and permanent brain damage. The medical evidence, some four months after J's birth, suggested that he was probably blind and deaf, had epilepsy, would probably develop serious spastic quadriplegia, and was unlikely to develop speech. J was however judged to feel pain to the same extent as other babies. He had been oxygen dependent for significant periods in his young life and suffered sudden collapses resulting in the need for artificial ventilation. The medical team proposed that they should not reventilate J the next time his breathing stopped. In assessing where J's best interests lay, the Court of Appeal considered the distress and hazardous nature of reventilation, the risk of further deterioration if J was subjected to it, and his extremely unfavourable general prognosis. Because J's disabilities seemed to make his life intolerable the court was prepared to spare him further invasive medical intervention.

The judgment, and others like it, can be criticised for the importance which was attached to the medical opinions about the baby. Psychologists, physiotherapists, teachers and respite centre staff are among the professionals who could, better than doctors, illuminate whether a disabled child might learn to interact with others, or at least to derive some satisfaction from his or her life. But unless such professionals are already involved with the young patient, they are unlikely to have the opportunity to give evidence to the court. Potentially valuable insights are thus neglected, and an incomplete assessment becomes the basis for the court's decision.

The judges in *Re J* ruled that there is no need to involve the courts where family and professionals agree that treatment should be withheld from a child. However, in the more recent case of *Re C (a baby)* (1996), the High Court suggested that the issue of referral to court should be decided in the context of each specific situation. Such a selective approach may fail to meet the requirements imposed by Article 2 of the European Convention on Human Rights. As was explained at the start of this chapter, our domestic law is now expected emphatically and transparently to protect life. This surely must entail that the decision to let a child die rather than 'inflict' treatment should go to court for an assessment of where the child's best interests lie. Furthermore, explicit criteria will need to be devised to guide decision making where a child's life is at stake.

10.1.3   Family disputes about treatment

Where adults share parental responsibility for a child, does the consent of just one of them, acting independently, protect the team treating the child? The answer provided by the Children Act 1989 in section 2(7) is affirmative. Nevertheless, in 1999 the Court of Appeal ruled that there were some decisions which should not be acted upon unless everyone with parental responsibility agreed [7]. Examples given were sterilisation and circumcision, rather than any treatments likely to apply in the case of critically ill children. Unfortunately, the judgment did not spell out in exactly which other circumstances one consent only would be inadequate. Caution suggests that for irreversible procedures, particularly controversial ones, the consent of all who share parental responsibility should be obtained.

Proceeding on the basis of just one consent where there is conflict may anyway seem so invidious that going to court becomes preferable. It is at least an option available to 'piggy-in-the-middle' professionals seeking to respect the position of the dissenting adult. The latter, under Article 8 of the European Convention, in any case has the right to participate in the decision [8]. Because medical treatment disputes are regarded as complex, they must be referred to the High Court (*Re R (a minor) (blood transfusion)* (1993)) rather than the Family Proceedings or County Court.

10.1.4   Disagreement between the family and the professional carers

Where there is serious disagreement about the best course of action, either the family or the health care team (backed by the relevant health authority) may ask the High Court to intervene. Alternatively, social services may invoke the court's jurisdiction. The court will take account of the views of all involved in caring for the child and of the child's legal representatives, before reaching its own independent assessment of the balance of advantages or disadvantages of the particular medical step under consideration (*Re T (a minor) (wardship: medical treatment* (1996)). The views of the nursing team can and should be very influential (*Re C (a minor) (wardship: medical treatment* (1989)).

Although the courts' intrusion into family life could amount to unjustified state interference under article 8(2) of the European Convention, it is usually deemed necessary 'for the protection of health or morals, or for the protection of the rights and freedom of others'. The aim of safeguarding a child's physical, psychological or emotional welfare is thus considered to be a legitimate basis for court intervention.

Understandably, treatment decisions concerning critically ill children have frequently reached the courts. In *Re D (wardship: medical treatment)* (2000) the applicant NHS Trust cared for a 19 month old boy suffering from severe, worsening, irreversible lung disease, coupled with heart failure, hepatic dysfunction, renal disjunction and learning difficulties. The Trust wished to spare him artificial ventilation in the event of respiratory or cardiac failure but his parents disagreed strongly with this approach. The High Court sided with the Trust in this case, finding that the benefits of a probably short extension to life-span were outweighed by the distress intensive mechanical treatment would inflict. Similarly, in the 1999 case of baby C, discussed in section 10.1.2 above, the High Court, despite the opposition of the parents, agreed with the health authority that ventilator support should be withdrawn from a terminally ill little girl.

By contrast, in *Re T (a minor)(wardship: medical treatment)* (1996), it was the parents who objected to medical intervention. T at the time of the hearing was 17 months old. He suffered from the life-threatening liver defect biliary atresia, and the medical recommendation was a liver transplant. He had had an operation already, and his pain and distress at that time had persuaded his parents that he should not undergo major surgery. Of the three transplant teams consulted, one was prepared to respect the views of the parents, but one was determined that a transplant should go ahead. The parents, who were themselves trained health professionals experienced in the care of young, sick children, found that their opposition to the transplant was referred to social services, and from there to the High Court.

Although the High Court judge ruled that a transplant was in T's best interests, the Court of Appeal disagreed. The judges were not convinced that a short but happy life, ending in peaceful death, was a worse option than 'a lifetime of drugs and the possibility of further invasive surgery'. Instead, they looked beyond T's purely medical interests to the 'broader considerations' which applied and concluded that the views of the parents could be allowed to determine T's future treatment. Although in *Re T*, the 'broader considerations' were put forward by the parents, it will often fall to a child patient's nurses to alert others to relevant issues and concerns.

No doubt the most controversial case to feature conflict between parents and health care professionals, was that involving the conjoined twins born in Manchester on 8 August 2000 (*Re A (children) (2000)*). The weaker twin only lived because her circulation was sustained by her stronger sister. Unless a separation was performed, the heart of the stronger twin would fail and both would die. The health authority sought permission to separate the twins, which would allow the stronger one to survive but kill the weaker one immediately. The parents refused to sanction the death of one daughter, but they were overruled by the Court of Appeal. Although the judges stressed that their decision 'was authority for the unique circumstances of the case' only, they did in effect sanction the active killing of the weaker twin, albeit out of concern for the best interests of her stronger sister. The ruling is difficult to reconcile with the protection for respect to life demanded from the state by Article 2 of the European Convention.

10.1.5   Neglecting the child's medical needs

Where the medical needs of children are neglected by those with parental responsibility, the latter forfeit their right to make treatment decisions. If time permits, the case should be referred to the High Court. If there is no time for this, the health care team should proceed to do what it thinks best for the child. This is the basis on which the children of Jehovah's Witnesses are given blood products against their parents' wishes. Nurses should be prepared for the difficulties inherent in these painful situations. They should, before any emergency arises, familiarise themselves with their employer's guidance on how to deal with the parents in such circumstances.

10.1.6   Case study [9]

Adam, aged 5, has been out playing with his friends, and is discovered, completely immersed, in a shallow pool. Despite attempts to resuscitate him, scans reveal global brain damage. Four days later he starts to suffer whole body decorticate extensor spasms, which, judging by his facial expressions and cries, cause him great pain and distress. Anti-spasmodic drugs seem to help initially, but then Adam develops a tolerance to them. Hypertension, tachycardia and difficulty with the control of respiratory secretions, set in. Adam's deteriorating physical condition, and his suffering, persuade Adam's father to ask the health care team to discontinue artificial nutrition and hydration.

Adam's health care team should primarily liaise with the people who have parental responsibility for Adam. This may exclude Adam's father, if he was never married to Adam's mother and took no steps to acquire parental responsibility. Even if the father does have parental responsibility, Adam's mother's wishes should be ascertained. If both parents have parental responsibility, but they disagree over Adam's treatment, the safest course of action is to refer the case to court. If Adam's mother shares the father's viewpoint, the health carers should consider whether they too think that withdrawal of artificial nutrition and hydration is in Adam's best interests. Factors which favour the proposal are the little boy's gradual decline, the very poor prognosis and the intense pain and suffering he must endure. To be weighed against these are the general concern with preserving life and the interaction Adam still has with his environment. The team should be satisfied that Adam's pain cannot be controlled. The guidance from the Royal College of Paediatrics and Child Health should be considered. Adam's condition overlaps categories 3, 4 and 5 of the guidance (see section 10.1.2). Adam's nurses will play a significant part in interpreting the responses of their young patient and gauging his distress and pain levels. They will also be able to ensure that his parents' views are adequately communicated to the rest of the health care team.

If cessation of treatment seems to serve Adam's best interests, the agreement of the parents does not preclude an application to the court by the health authority. Indeed, referring the case to court seems appropriate given the protection of the right to life conferred by the European Convention on Human Rights. The court will usurp the decision-making power of the person(s) with parental responsibility for Adam. The judge would reach his or her decision in the light of the medical evidence and after considering the wishes of the parents. The presumption in favour of preserving life would be balanced against the need to limit suffering which could not generate commensurate benefits. If the court authorised cessation of treatment, it would expect such medical and nursing care as would comfort Adam until he died, to be administered.

10.2   Teenagers

10.2.1   Capacity to consent

The provisions of section 8 of the Family Law Reform Act 1969, ensure that by the age of 16 at the latest, teenagers can give their own consent to medical treatment. Many will reach sufficient maturity to authorise specific procedures at an earlier point. Assessing that maturity is something which the professional treating the teenager must do in the light of the guidance offered in the case of *Gillick* v. *West Norfolk and Wisbech Area Health Authority* (1985): capacity to understand all the issues surrounding the proposed treatment is the vital criterion.

The above rules do not prevent health authorities and social services, or even a relative, from referring a medical dilemma to court, using the wardship or inherent jurisdiction. Once this has been done, the decision of the court can overrule that of any young person, however competent, who has not yet reached the age of 18 (*Re W (a minor) (medical treatment)* (1992)).

Teenage consent to medical treatment has not proved controversial in the sphere of critical illness. Where medical advice is accepted and followed, no conflict arises for the health care team involved. The situation is however very different where a young person refuses vital treatment. This problem is considered in the next section.

10.2.2   Capacity to refuse treatment

Although the principle of 'Gillick competence' was clearly meant to apply to all medical treatment decisions, rather than just to consent, the law will not allow teenagers to refuse essential treatment. The case of *Re W (a minor)(medical treatment: court's jurisdiction)* (1992) confirmed that children, whatever their age or maturity, lack power to override the consent which a person with parental responsibility gives in their best interests. Sixteen year old W's severe anorexia meant that she was close to death at the time of the legal proceedings. The local authority which had parental responsibility for her, wished her to receive treatment at a clinic which W refused to attend. The Court of Appeal overruled her refusal, holding that neither section 8 of the Family Law Reform Act 1969 nor the concept of 'Gillick competence' applied to refusal of treatment. The judges, alive to the family conflicts which might ensue when teenagers and their parents disagree about treatment, did however suggest that health professionals should, as a matter of ethics, refer difficult cases to court. They also emphasised that the views of teenage patients must be explored and given due weight in accordance with their age and maturity.

The guidance given by the Court of Appeal in *Re W* was adopted in the recent case of *Re M (child: refusal of medical treatment)* (1999). M was a 15 year old girl who suffered the sudden onset of heart failure. It became clear that her survival depended on her undergoing a heart transplant. Although M herself opposed the procedure, her parents agreed with her health care team that the transplant was in her best interests. There was thus sufficient legal consent for the proposed transplant to go ahead, but in view of what had been said in *Re W*, the health authority decided to refer the case to court. The urgency of the situation meant that a duty judge had to be contacted, and the decision made overnight. M's views were conveyed to the judge via her solicitor, and although they were overridden, the judge prepared a careful record of his reasoning for M's benefit.

Decisions like *Re W* and *Re M* would have little effect if they could not be implemented. The courts have recognised that force may be needed if essential treatment is to be delivered to an unwilling young patient. Although orders authorising a minimum degree of force or restraint are issued sparingly and cautiously they are available on application to the court [10]. The Royal College of Nursing has issued guidance on the problems related to forcing young people to undergo treatment [11].

10.2.3   Participating in decision making

To nursing staff caring for teenage patients, the law may not seem sensitive enough to the principle of respect for autonomy. However, the rather limited scope which teenagers in the past had to affect treatment decisions, acquired new potential for growth under the European Convention on Human Rights. Its emphasis on the significance of human life (Article 2), of due process (Article 6) and family privacy (Article 8), is likely to result in new respect for a young person's point of view and right to participate in the decision-making process.

Attention should also be paid to the provisions of the Convention on Human

Rights and Biomedicine 1997. A supplement to the European Convention on Human Rights, this second Convention resolves 'to take such measures as are necessary to safeguard human dignity and the fundamental rights and freedoms of the individual with regard to the application of biology and medicine' [12]. Article 6(2) insists that 'the opinion of a minor shall be taken into consideration as an increasing determining factor in proportion to his or her age and degree of maturity'. A violation of this Article, while not actionable by itself, could be challenged in proceedings brought to enforce a European Convention on Human Rights provision.

10.2.4   Case study

Three years ago, Bushra, then aged 12, underwent chemotherapy and a bone marrow transplant to treat her leukaemia. Although her condition improved temporarily, it has now deteriorated again and a second bone marrow transplant has been proposed. Bushra refuses to consent to the operation because she does not believe that it will be successful and because she dreads the isolation and the side effects of the chemotherapy. She understands that she will die without the transplant. Bushra's mother consents to the intervention.

Strictly speaking, the health care team can proceed on the basis of Bushra's mother's consent. The team is, however, reluctant to do so in view of Bushra's age, the strength of her objections, and her understanding of the situation based on her earlier experience of treatment. The decision is taken to contact the High Court, which in turn arranges legal representation for Bushra. Her views are conveyed to the High Court judge dealing with the case. After weighing them up carefully, and balancing them against the evidence as to the chances of Bushra's health improving, he decides to override her wishes and authorises the bone marrow transplant. He provides a full record of his reasons so that Bushra will be able to read and follow his thinking for herself. Before and after the transplant, Bushra's nurses will need to help her come to terms with what has happened.

10.3   Adults able to make their own decisions

10.3.1   Refusal of treatment

Where adult patients are critically ill, the temptation to intervene on their behalf regardless of their wishes may be hard to resist. But even life-threatening conditions do not validate non-consensual treatment. The UKCC warns registered practitioners against assuming 'that only they know what is best for the patient'. Instead, patients who reject proposed treatment should be encouraged 'to realise that they are capable of deciding what is in their own best interests' [13]. A summary of the discussions and decisions should be kept with the patient's records [14].

The courts have repeatedly asserted the right of patients to reject medical procedures in any circumstances. However, faced with a refusal to consent to life-saving treatment, nurses, in common with other health care professionals, should give 'very careful and detailed consideration to the patient's capacity to decide' (*Re T (adult: refusal of treatment)* (1992)). The more serious the decision, the greater the capacity needed to make it.

Authoritative guidance on how patients should be approached was made available by the Court of Appeal in the case of *Re MB (medical treatment)* (1997). Medical teams should start from the presumption that patients have the capacity to reach their own decisions. Patients are entitled to make irrational or foolish choices. Scope for overriding their wishes arises only when there is evidence of impaired mental functioning. Pain, shock, medication, fatigue and drugs may induce temporary loss of competence. So may fear, if it destroys the ability to make decisions.

Where there are genuine reasons to doubt a patient's capacity, the safe course is to determine a treatment plan which is in the patient's best interests, and to invite the court to declare it lawful. Procedural safeguards to protect the patient in such a case were put in place by *Re MB* and must be strictly complied with.

10.3.2   Maternal-fetal conflict

Where a pregnant woman wants her baby to be born alive and healthy, its safe birth will normally be in her best interests. But where the wishes of a competent mother rule out a safe birth then, according to *Re MB*, they must nevertheless be complied with because they override her own best interests and those of the fetus. The issues raised in such a situation are more fully discussed in Chapter 7 on consent.

10.3.3   Denying treatment to patients

When critically ill patients are referred for intensive treatment but fail to respond, the decision to cease treatment must be considered. Whenever possible, patients should participate in the decision process. Their wish to continue treatment should not easily be countermanded but the final decision lies with the health care team. In relation to cardiopulmonary resuscitation policy, the Royal College of Nursing has jointly with the British Medical Association and the Resuscitation Council (UK) produced guidance on the applicable legal and ethical standards [15]. Patients at foreseeable risk of cardiopulmonary arrest can expect to be fully consulted on plans to attempt resuscitation or to withhold it. If patients oppose the making of a 'Do Not Attempt Resuscitation Order', no order should be issued. Discussions and decisions are to be fully documented, signed and dated, in patients' records. The views of all on both the medical and nursing team should be obtained.

10.3.4   Case study

Carla, aged 30, has been admitted to hospital following a car accident. She has suffered an open fracture of the left femur, laceration of the left femoral artery and a closed fracture of the right femur. She is conscious, and despite repeatedly being told that she will die unless treated with blood products, she refuses transfusion on the ground that it is against her religious beliefs.

The health care team should presume that Carla is able to make her decision, unless there is clear evidence to the contrary. Her refusal of a transfusion should be carefully recorded. Although her beliefs are unconventional, she is entitled to base her refusal on them. It is possible that the trauma of the accident and pain which she suffers impair her capacity to consider treatment, but this conclusion should only be drawn if she appears unable to absorb or process the information she is given. A transfusion should not be administered in this case without a court declaration that it is lawful. Such a declaration is not likely to be forthcoming. Aggressive resuscitation, and, if necessary, intensive care should be offered, if the resources for this are available. Patients like Carla have survived in similar circumstances but this may not make their choices easier to accept.

10.4   Adults unable to make their own decisions

10.4.1   General principles

Adults who lack the legal capacity to make treatment decisions cannot give a valid consent to medical interventions, nor can anyone else do so on their behalf (*Re F (mental patient: sterilisation)* (1989)). It is, however, lawful to treat them provided that treatment is in accordance with the appropriate professional standard and is in the best interests of the patient concerned (*Re A* (1999)). Nurses have a key role to play in the process of determining what is in a patient's best interests. As a matter of good practice, the patient's family should be consulted, but the final say rests with the health care team. The courts can be asked to issue declarations indicating whether or not a proposed intervention is lawful. Once a referral has been made it falls to the court to assess where the patient's best interests lie (*Re SL (adult patient) medical treatment* (2000)).

The law in this area is under review. Recommendations for law reform by the Law Commission [16] and the Lord Chancellor's Department [17] have been incorporated into the report *Making Decisions* [18], presented to Parliament by the Lord Chancellor in October 1999. Several of the proposals in the report are in line with the provisions of the 1997 Convention on Human Rights and Biomedicine which supplements the European Convention on Human Rights. However, *Making Decisions* does not insist on quite the same level of protective representation for patients. Its specific recommendations will be referred to at relevant points in the text which follows, even though no timetable has yet been drawn up for implementing them.

10.4.2   Advance directives

Patients increasingly prepare for the onset of their own mental incapacity by producing a set of instructions as to the treatment they would seek, or seek to avoid at that point. Known as 'advance statements', such instructions may take a variety of forms, ranging from signed, witnessed documents to a spoken wish.

Statements requesting specific treatment options should normally be respected, but cannot override professional judgements, as in law no-one can dictate how health care teams should proceed. By contrast, the cases of *Re T (adult: refusal of treatment)* (1992), *Airedale NHS Trust* v. *Bland* (1993) and *Re C (adult: refusal of treatment)* (1994) confirmed that statements which take the form of an advance refusal of treatment have full effect in law, provided that they are clearly drafted, with full understanding of their implications, and cover the circumstances which subsequently occur. It follows that the flouting of an advance refusal allows a patient to claim compensation in respect of the unauthorised physical contact.

The case of *Re T*, mentioned in the last paragraph, illustrates some of the problems linked with advance refusals. T was a young pregnant woman admitted to hospital after a road traffic accident. A decision was made to deliver her baby by caesarean section, and the issue of administering blood was raised in this context. T, whose mother was a fervent Jehovah's Witness, asked whether there was a substitute treatment and was told that there was. She then signed a form of refusal of consent to blood transfusions. The form was not read out or explained to her, nor was she advised of the risk to her own health and life which her refusal entailed. Following the caesarean section (the baby was stillborn), T's condition deteriorated and she was transferred to intensive care. After she became unconscious, her father and boyfriend sought a declaration from the court that it would be lawful for the hospital to administer blood, despite T's prior refusal.

The Court of Appeal emphatically endorsed the right of adults to reject medical advice and treatment, if their decision is reached while they have the capacity to make it. The judges then explored T's capacity at the point at which she refused the transfusion. They found that her capacity had been undermined by the influence of her mother, by the pain and confusion T was in and by the failure to fully advise her of the potentially serious consequences of her decision. In the light of this finding, the proposed blood transfusion was declared lawful.

The decision shows that advance refusals must be approached with some caution, and with attention to the circumstances in which they were made, if these are known. Additional guidance on their implementation can be found in the 1995 Code of Practice, *Advance Statements about Medical Treatment* [19], prepared by the BMA for health professionals. The Code recommends that:

> 'all staff involved ... should have an opportunity of presenting their views. From a patient's viewpoint, nurses are often the most accessible professionals.... nurses may have had closer contact than others with the patient, and those close to the patient. Nurses are often adept in translating technical medical language and discussing practical outcomes of treatment and care. They may gain particular insight into whether patients were consistent and coherent in their views.'

Although for several years the Law Commission has recommended that there should be legislation in this sphere, *Making Decisions* confirms that the Government prefers the law to develop case by case [20]. Nurses must accordingly strive to monitor new court decisions which are relevant to advance statements.

At European Convention level, advance refusals are only weakly recognised [21]. The European Convention on Human Rights contains no direct reference to them.

Article 9 of the Convention on Human Rights and Biomedicine requires them merely 'to be taken into account': thus they need not always be complied with. The Convention's *Explanatory Report* advises practitioners to check that their patients' wishes continue to apply 'and are still valid, taking account in particular of technical progress in medicine' [22].

10.4.3   Decisions by proxy

According to *Making Decisions*, the Government proposes to enact legislation conferring on people with mental capacity the power to appoint a proxy to take medical decisions for them, after the onset of incapacity. The person appointed would not be able to authorise the withdrawal of artificial nutrition or hydration unless explicitly invested with that power [23].

10.4.4   Patients in, or close to, permanent vegetative state

It could be argued that patients in, or close to, permanent vegetative state (PVS) are not critically ill. Provided that their nutrition and hydration are maintained, such patients may survive for many years. It should, however, be recognised that the perceived futility of life in PVS presents dilemmas akin to some of those associated with critical illness. Furthermore, the emergencies which arise during the nursing of PVS patients are often life-threatening.

In *Airedale NHS Trust* v. *Bland* (1993), the House of Lords upheld a declaration that the doctors' proposal to withdraw food and water from their patient was lawful. In the judgement of the medical team (and the family), keeping Anthony Bland alive had become futile, because there was no hope that he would ever recover from the carefully diagnosed PVS he was in. The court accepted that this judgement was one which a respectable body of medical opinion shared, and agreed that the continuation of artificial nutrition and hydration was not in the best interests of the patient. The Law Lords did request that the moral, social and legal issues raised by the case should be reviewed by Parliament and, as an interim safeguard for patients, insisted that life-sustaining treatment should be withdrawn from adults in PVS only with the backing of a court declaration.

Since the decision in *Bland*, the clinical description of PVS has received much attention. In 1994 the House of Lords' Select Committee on Medical Ethics recommended the setting up of a working group to produce guidance on the diagnosis and management of PVS. A Working Party of the Royal College of Physicians responded to the challenge in 1996 with the publication of *The Permanent Vegetative State* [24], which set out guidelines subsequently endorsed by both the BMA and the Official Solicitor. According to the guidelines, the diagnosis of PVS is not absolute but based on probabilities. A diagnosis should not be made until the patient has been in a continuing vegetative state for more than 12 months following head injury, or more than 6 months following other causes of brain damage. As soon as the patient's condition has stabilised, rehabilitative measures such as coma arousal programmes should be instituted. Reports based on clinical and other observations of the patient over a period of time, will often be needed.

Nevertheless, diagnosis of PVS remains difficult, and ever since the decision in

Bland, courts have struggled to fit the clinical aspects of cases into the guidelines' framework. In *Frenchay NHS Trust* v. *S* (1994), the Court of Appeal heard arguments questioning the PVS diagnosis of the 24 year old male patient, who had suffered acute and extreme brain damage after taking a drug overdose. The nurses on the health care team were convinced that S seemed to suffer, and medical reports recorded what appeared to be voluntary and volitional behaviour. Attempts at rehabilitation had been made for two years, which called into question the confidence with which PVS had been diagnosed in the first place. Although there was no doubt among the judges that the decision to allow S to die promoted his best interests, it is clear from this case that PVS guidelines need not always be strictly adhered to. It is worth noting that the trigger for referring the case to court was the dislodging of S's feeding tube.

More recently, in the case of *Re D (medical treatment)* (1997), a hospital trust applied for a declaration that artificial nutrition and hydration could be withdrawn from a patient who did not exhibit all the diagnostic criteria normally associated with PVS. A year before the High Court hearing, D had been diagnosed as being in vegetative state with remote prospect of recovery. A PVS diagnosis followed in December 1996. However, D's condition did not fit that paragraph of *The Permanent Vegetative State* which requires that there should be no nystagmus in response to ice water caloric testing and that the patient should not be able to track moving objects with the eyes or show a 'menace' response. Some limited pathways between the cerebral hemispheres and the brain stem had apparently continued to function and it was argued on D's behalf that this gave her an interest in being kept alive. The judge, however, could find 'no evidence of any meaningful life whatsoever', the medical evidence having established that D had no feelings, no hearing and could not see. As it was not in the patient's best interests to be kept alive, he granted the declaration sought by the NHS Trust.

It is now clear that the withholding of treatment from PVS patients is not deemed to infringe Article 2 of the European Convention on Human Rights which protects people's right to life. In the cases of *NHS Trust A* v. *M* (2000) and *NHS Trust B* v. *H* (2000), decided in October 2000, the High Court ruled that treatment may cease where, as in PVS cases, there is no positive obligation to prolong life. The court issued declarations that artificial nutrition and hydration could lawfully be withdrawn from two female patients in PVS.

10.4.5 Borderline cases

Where there is evidence of a real possibility that meaningful life continues for the patient, cessation of treatment (which according to *Bland*, includes artificial nutrition and hydration) would obviously be harder to justify than it is in the PVS cases. Health care teams and the courts would have to balance factors similar to those taken account of in children cases at present (see section 10.1.2 earlier in this chapter).

Some insight is provided by the case of *Re R (adult: medical treatment)* (1996). R, at 23, was described as operating cognitively and neurologically at the level of a newborn infant. He also suffered poor physical health, including recurrent chest infections and ulceration of the oesophagus. The High Court decided that treatment could be withheld from R at the point where his life became 'so afflicted as to be intolerable'. Proposed interventions would have to be assessed in the light of the benefits they could confer on the patient.

Where there is doubt as to how to proceed, treatment can be initiated with a view to assessing its effects on the patient. Although it may be emotionally easier to withhold treatment than to withdraw it, such a policy has no legal justification. Of course, if treatment is withdrawn, basic care should always be provided, and oral nutrition and hydration should be offered.

New guidelines [25] issued by the British Medical Association recommend that the decision to cease treatment should be taken by the clinician in overall charge of the patient's care, in the light of the best available clinical evidence and the views of the rest of the health care team. Withholding or withdrawing artificial nutrition or hydration should additionally require authorisation by a senior clinician outside the team. It should, however, not be necessary to go to court in each case.

10.4.6   Case study [26]

Declan, aged 88, suffered a massive stroke 15 days ago. He is completely paralysed on one side of his body and almost completely on the other. His condition has steadily deteriorated and he is now unable to chew or swallow food. He no longer appears to recognise, or respond to, his only child, Siobhan, or to the nurses. The medical team are unsure whether to commence artificial nutrition. Siobhan claims that her father would not wish his life to be prolonged in this way.

As Declan cannot comprehend or process the factors involved, he has lost the capacity to make his own decision about artificial nutrition. As his daughter has alerted the health care team to what her father's wishes were likely to be, she should be asked whether Declan prepared an advance refusal. If there is evidence that a refusal was drawn up, attempts should be made to obtain the latter or some record of it (perhaps in the medical notes kept by Declan's GP). If such a refusal was issued with understanding of its implications and deals with the situation which has now arisen, it is binding on the health care team.

In the absence of an advance refusal, the health care team must consider whether the provision of artificial nutrition would benefit Declan. It can be withheld if this serves Declan's best interests. Declan's prospects of recovery and the likely quality of his life then, should be assessed. If the decision is to withhold treatment, it should, in compliance with the 1999 BMA guidelines, be vetted by a neurologist outside the team. A cautious team might seek a court declaration.

10.5   Conclusion

Legal problems commonly associated with the delivery of health care tend to present themselves in acute form during the management of critical illness. Assessing the patient's capacity to make treatment decisions and working out where a patient's best interests lie become more difficult than usual. The need for limits to the duty to maintain life, and for court intervention at key points of uncertainty, is highlighted. As this chapter has shown, the law's response has been twofold. The basic framework of principles within which nurses are expected to work has been augmented to cope with new dilemmas. At the same time, health care professionals have been encouraged to refer problem cases to court. The resulting decisions and regulations have added to the complexity of the law within which nurses must operate. Attention to legal developments and a sound understanding of legal requirements have become vital components of a professional approach to nursing critically ill patients.

10.6   Notes and references

1. See, for example, *R* v. *Central Birmingham Health Authority ex parte Walker* [1987] BMLR 32; *R* v. *Cambridge Health Authority ex parte B* [1995] 2 All ER 12 (CA).
2. UKCC (1996) *Guidelines for Professional Practice*, p. 15, para. 38. United Kingdom Central Council for Nursing Midwifery and Health Visiting, London.
3. Children Act 1989 section 3(5).
4. Children Act 1989 section 4.
5. Lord Chancellor's Department (1998) Press Notice 201/98: Parental responsibility to be conferred on unmarried fathers.
6. Royal College of Paediatrics and Child Health (1997) *Withholding or withdrawing life saving treatment in children. A framework for practice*. Royal College of Paediatrics and Child Health. London.
7. *Re J (specific issue orders: child's religious upbringing and circumcision)* [2000] 1 FLR 571 at 577 (d).
8. *W* v. *United Kingdom*, July 8, 1987. Series A, No 121; 10 EHRR 29.
9. Based on the case of *Re: Representation Attorney-General* (1995) 3 Med LR 316.
10. See *Re S (a minor) (consent to medical treatment)* [1994] 2 FLR 1065, and *Re C (detention: medical treatment)* [1997] 2 FLR 180.
11. The Royal College of Nursing (1999) *Restraining, holding still and containing children: guidance for good practice*. Royal College of Nursing. London.
12. Preamble to the Convention on Human Rights and Biomedicine. 4 April 1997.
13. UKCC (1996) *Guidelines for Professional Practice*, p. 10, para. 19. United Kingdom Central Council for Nursing Midwifery and Health Visiting, London.
14. P. 13, para. 30.
15. British Medical Association, Resuscitation Council (UK) and Royal College of Nursing (2001) *Decisions relating to cardiopulmonary resuscitation*. BMA, London.
16. Law Commission (1995) *Mental incapacity* (Law Com No 231). The Stationery, London.
17. Lord Chancellor's Department (1997) *Who decides? Making decisions on behalf of mentally incapacitated adults*. Cm 3803. The Stationery Office, London.
18. Lord Chancellor's Department (1999) *Making Decisions*. Cm 4465. http://www.open.gov.uk/lcd/family/mdecisions/indbod.htm. Accessed on 03/11/99.
19. British Medical Association (1995) *Advance Statements about Medical Treatment*. BMA. London.
20. Introduction, para. 20.
21. Nys, H. (1999) Physician involvement in a patient's death: a continental European perspective. *Medical Law Review*, 7, 208–246, at 211.
22. Para. 62.
23. Para. 2.6.

24. Royal College of Physicians (1996) The permanent vegetative state. *J. Roy. Coll. Physicians*, 30, 119–121.
25. British Medical Association (1999) *Withholding and withdrawing life-prolonging medical treatment*. BMJ Books, London.
26. Based on the facts of *In the Matter of Tavel* (1995) 661 A.2d 1061.

B   An Ethical Perspective – Declining and Withdrawing Treatment

Robert Campbell

What does it mean for a patient to be critically ill? The *Oxford English Dictionary* defines 'crisis' as:

> '(*path.*) The point in the progress of a disease when an important development or change takes place which is decisive of recovery or death.'

'Critically ill' is not a synonym for 'dying'. We should remember that critically ill patients may recover. The *OED* also defines 'critical' as (among other things):

> 'involving suspense or grave fear as to the issue, attended with uncertainty or risk.'

The prognosis for critically ill patients is often very uncertain. We should always remember that a critically ill patient may die or may recover. We cannot know for certain which will happen.

However, patients with a strong chance of recovery and a clearly indicated and effective treatment present few ethical dilemmas for those who care for them. The truly challenging situations are those where treatments are contested, of uncertain value or unavailable, or where the probability is high that no treatment will be beneficial and the likeliest prognosis is poor.

10.7   Consent

Often such situations are ethically challenging because of the issue of consent. In law to touch someone against their wish is battery, and medical treatment, especially in critical situations, usually involves procedures far more invasive than merely touching. For everyday treatments like having a tooth filled or an eye examination, consent is both presumed and implicit in the patient's simply being there. For more complex, unusual or potentially dangerous interventions, more formal procedures are needed to establish consent. This is because both the law and morality assume that consent involves more than simple acquiescence. To consent in any real sense one must know what one is consenting to, and one's consent must be genuine, i.e. unforced. I ask you to give me your autograph and you sign the bottom of a blank sheet of paper. I subsequently type a deed of gift on the paper transferring all your worldly wealth to me. No one would suppose that this constituted a genuine agreement. You did not realise that you were agreeing to anything, let alone that you were agreeing to be pauperised. Likewise, a patient must understand the nature of the treatment proposed if any verbal or written declarations are to count as genuine consent. What counts as 'understanding the nature of the treatment' is more complicated, but courts have held, quite reasonably, that it involves more than simply being told what will be done. In particular, it also involves having some understanding of the likely consequences – both good and bad – and of how likely they are.

Consent to treatment is problematic for critically ill patients for two reasons. First, because their condition may make it hard for them to express consent, or it may mean that they are unable to give consent at all (because they are unconscious, or no longer capable of full consent – see section 10.8.1); or secondly, because the difficulty of deciding on an appropriate course of treatment may not be wholly a matter of medical science. For example, it can happen that a particular procedure becomes less and less effective each time it is performed and the benefit to the patient declines correspondingly. This can be especially true of palliative or symptomatic care which does nothing to arrest an underlying condition. At some stage a judgement must be made that the benefits are now too negligible or too heavily outweighed by the discomfort of the treatment or its possible side effects. Equally, a treatment may be uncertain and, although the degree of uncertainty may be a matter of medical science, the question of whether the risk is worth taking is not. For a patient with advanced cancer there can be a difficult decision of whether an outside chance of aggressive chemotherapy securing a remission is worth the severe discomfort the treatment will certainly cause. Some might think that, when it is a matter of life or death, any chance, however remote, is worth taking. Others, who might be more temperamentally risk-averse, could see it as a gamble not worth taking.

10.7.1   Why does consent matter?

The job of the therapeutic team is to do their best for the patient, given the resources at their disposal. Indeed, this is more than their job; it is their legal and moral duty once the patient has been accepted as a patient. And it is hard to see how the patient, unless in some way deranged, can object to this. After all, is it not one of our informal tests for how sensible and rational someone is that they should want the best for themselves? Why should we also need their consent? There are four major reasons why we do.

The first is related to the issue raised at the end of the previous section and has to do with expertise and the authority that goes with it. Most would agree that, unusual exceptions notwithstanding, medically trained staff are more likely to know what the likely prognosis is of a given intervention or treatment. That knowledge gives them an authority which may be unfashionable but is nonetheless real for that. However, judgements to do with how much risk is worth taking or how much pain or discomfort may be discounted against future benefit, lie outside that area of expertise. The expertise in these matters, and hence the authority, lies with the person who has to take the decision. (See also the fourth reason below.)

The second reason is located in the idea of a *person*. Most human beings are persons and most persons are human beings, but the terms do not have the same meaning [1]. A human being is a member of the biological species *homo sapiens sapiens*; a person is a moral agent who has plans and purposes and the capacity for free choice. From the point of view of personhood, all persons are morally equal in as much as there is no inherent reason for preferring one person's plans and purposes to another's. It is not always possible, of course, for all persons to pursue all their purposes. These may well conflict and there may be a need for mediation, compromise, negotiation and accommodation. But such procedures do not ignore a person's moral agency. On the contrary, they only make sense when they are addressed to an agent as an agent.

Disregarding a patient's right to consent to or to refuse treatment ignores the fact that the patient is an agent and assumes that your plan to treat a patient in a particular way is the only plan that matters. It is, in Kantian terminology, to treat the patient as a means to an end and not as an end-in-herself [2]. It, therefore, fails to accord that patient the respect and dignity due to a person whose moral importance is as great as your own. And if you believe that your plans and choices are important, then you must acknowledge that those of other persons are just as important. To fail to do so is a failure of logic as well as a failure of morality.

The third reason why consent matters concerns human psychology rather than logic or morality. A patient whose agreement to treatment has been sought and obtained will feel empowered in a number of ways. Firstly they will *own* the treatment as an equal member of the team which has decided on it. They will be acting, rather than acted on. Secondly, they will be less apprehensive about what will happen since, if the agreement is real and not just stage-managed, they will understand what is involved and its implications. And thirdly, they will have retained control over their situation and, in situations where people are profoundly vulnerable and probably distressed, this is clearly, and in some cases literally, vital. They will feel, and be, *autonomous*. And since that term means no more than being a free moral agent, a person, this second point connects us back to the first. It is also important to see that this process of empowerment will go on whether the patient agrees with the proposed course of treatment or whether they refuse it.

The fourth reason why consent matters concerns what might be called fallibilism. People can be wrong and, in particular, they can be wrong about what is good for another person. The medical team is composed of experts in various fields, but the only person who is an expert on what is good for me is me. The concept of fallibilism applies here too, admittedly. I can be wrong about what is in my own best interests; we all know that can happen. But I am less likely to be wrong about it than someone else is and, in any case, if I am wrong I bear the consequences. If someone else is wrong about what is good for me, I still bear the consequences. So I have an incentive to get it right that they lack [3]. It is, therefore, vitally important when decisions need to be taken about what will be good for me, that I take them, even though I may need expert advice from others. What this means, in practice, is that I must have the opportunity to decide whether to accept the treatment offered even though others may feel that I am wrong in the decision I come to.

10.8   Refusing treatment

It is clear that, in English and American law, I do seem to have the opportunity to refuse treatment. Treatment carried out without my consent is usually actionable. What is less clear is how far I have the right to decline treatment when such treatment is, or is likely to be, life-saving. For though the corollary of the necessity for consent might seem to be that, without my consent, treatment cannot be carried out, in practice the refusal of life-saving treatment is often regarded as prima facie evidence of an inability to give or withhold consent on a rational basis [4].

There is a troubling lack of symmetry between consenting to treatment, on the one hand, and declining life-saving treatment, on the other. For if the moral importance of consent is to be located in the idea of autonomy, i.e. self-determination, then choosing a course of action which you know is highly likely to result in your death seems inconsistent with this. Self-determination disappears when there is no self left to determine. Perhaps we can merely pass over this as a puzzling oddity since there are many other examples of it which we accept quite readily: people who risk their lives, and lose them, in the attempt to help others; people who choose death rather than the violation of some principle or value which seems to them more important than their own lives; and people who rationally choose to commit suicide. Counselling this latter category does, however, raise some practical difficulties also thrown up in dealing with those who refuse life-saving treatment. For the general principle that people should make their own decisions and learn from their own mistakes cuts a little too deeply here. If choosing suicide or refusing treatment turns out to have been a mistake, then it is, in the nature of things, too late to learn anything from that. Just as consent can only be genuine if the patient fully understands what she is consenting to so, equally the decision to refuse life-saving treatment should only be respected if it is clear that the patient understands the consequences of the refusal and also that the refusal is exactly what it seems to be.

10.8.1   *Capacity*

This last point is related to both knowledge and understanding. Clearly I cannot be said to have consented to something if I am kept in ignorance of, misled about or simply fail to understand, its nature. Doctors, like any other group with specialist knowledge, are capable of explaining something in such a way that no non-specialist could hope to understand it. This is much rarer than it used to be and many doctors are now trained in communication skills. Nonetheless it is not always easy to explain a complicated matter in terms which are both clear to the lay-person and, at the same time, accurate and complete. Nor are patients always very good at admitting that they have not understood a word and would like it explained again. It is always possible, in other words, for anyone to give apparent consent which is undermined by lack of knowledge or genuine understanding. There are, however, classes of people for whom consent is problematic, not in specific cases but in general. These are people who, in legal terminology, lack the *capacity* to give consent, not because they *don't* understand but because they *can't* and can't be brought to understand. Small children are an obvious example. It isn't that they cannot make choices, but that they do not understand the world well enough to realise what their choices might imply. Their developing knowledge means that they are gradually better able to understand and, therefore, more and more able to give consent which is real and informed. Capacity is, in other words, not something which either exists or does not. It is a gradual thing. Children can be in a position to be told or consulted about what may happen without being ready to take the final decision for themselves. Or else they may be ready to take decisions in some areas but not in others (see section 10.2.1 in part A of this chapter). In practice, the law's willingness to allow young people under 18 to make treatment decisions will rest on the seriousness of those decisions (see section 10.2.2). Equally with adults it can be true that capacity can be diminished or partial.

For example, there is the case of *Re T* (see section 10.4.2 in part A of this chapter), where the court decided that a refusal of treatment was made under the undue influence of the patient's mother and that there was reason to believe that the patient did not fully understand its implications. There might be enormous difficulty in determining this kind of issue. In the American case of Mary C. Northern [5], she was described by the guardian appointed for her by the court as '... 72 years of age ... [and] ... in possession of a good memory and recall, responds accurately to questions asked her, is coherent and intelligent in her conversation and is of sound mind'. She was suffering from gangrene in both feet consequent upon frostbite and burns, but refused to have the feet amputated, as her surgeons were urging her to. Though otherwise apparently entirely rational, it emerged in conversation that she very much wanted to live *and* very much wanted to save her feet. She did not seem able to grasp that there was only a one in ten chance that both things could happen and resolutely refused to consider, except as abstract hypotheses, that she would have to choose between them. The court decided to authorise surgery, apparently accepting the view that an otherwise apparently competent adult might, nonetheless, be incompetent in the matter of one specific decision. In the light of the transcripts, which are too lengthy to quote here, this would seem to have been the right decision. Mary Northern seems to have combined a general rational competence with a pathological block with regard to the condition of her feet, which she believed had got better and about which her physicians were lying or mistaken.

How are we to distinguish such cases from the case study about *Carla* in section 10.3.4? May we characterise Carla as an otherwise rational patient with a pathological block about blood transfusions? We might wish to argue that she is not irrational, she simply has beliefs which the rest of us do not share but cannot disprove. But Mary Northern's irrationality, in the end, came down to her refusal to give up a belief about the condition of her feet which no one was able to prove to her was false. There is no easy answer to the question of what makes belief irrational. It may help resolve the problem of distinguishing non-standard religious beliefs from those of people like Mary Northern that Mary Northern's came from nowhere, that they were ungrounded by anything apart from what seems to be a desperate attempt to wish the circumstances other than they actually were. Most religious beliefs do form a system, they are shared by large numbers of people and they are culturally transmitted – they have rational validation even if not by those who do not share them. This is hardly conclusive, but it is persuasive.

10.8.2   Balancing rights and duties

There is another factor, however, in section 10.3.2 which is disquieting. What if the mother's refusal of treatment did not just involve herself, but also her unborn baby. The case of *Re S* (1992) cannot be considered a precedent in English law, but it raises the issue of how far a person's refusal of treatment can be allowed to impact on a third party. For it is clear that the judgement arrived at in that case (where a full term fetus in a transverse lie threatened the life of both fetus and mother) turned on consideration of the welfare of the fetus as well as the rationality of the mother's decision. Whatever the legal position, this cannot be ducked. The fetus was at term. The law may not recognise the rights of an unborn child, but morally it would be curious to assert that a fetus at term is in any significant way different from a newborn baby. What might be arguable is whether its life may be saved at the cost of what has been called 'a massive intrusion into a person's body' [6], i.e. a caesarean section.

In a parallel American case, that of Angela Carder, the original decision to permit the caesarean section was overturned on appeal and Angela Carder's parents won undisclosed damages from the hospital in a separate action for medical malpractice, wrongful death and violation of civil rights. In that case neither the mother nor the child survived the operation. Though the mother was suffering widespread and irreversible cancer of the bone and lungs, the death certificate listed the caesarean as a contributing factor [7].

A caesarean section is a major surgical intervention, with all the risks and dangers that that involves. It would seem unreasonable to *require* someone to take those risks in order to benefit someone else. In an American case, the courts ruled that someone cannot be forced to donate bone marrow (a procedure considerably less risky than a caesarean section) even where failure to do so would result in the death of a third party (because only one person could be found who was tissue-type compatible) [8]. But it does not follow that that person had no *moral* obligation to be a bone-marrow donor, and that we may not think badly of him for ducking it. Nor is there an exact carry-over from that case to *Re S*. Those who willingly become pregnant have, in doing so, already accepted a degree of responsibility for the welfare of the child they carry. And a caesarean section is not so dangerous or unusual an intervention that it is obvious that no one could be expected to risk it. Nor are the declared grounds for refusal as coherent as they may seem. The couple in *Re S* were reported as believing that a caesarean was against their principles as born-again Christians. According to *The Guardian*, most evangelical Christians would not share the view that a caesarean section was impermissible and would, indeed, advocate one if the child's life was at risk, and Jehovah's Witnesses do not object to caesareans as long as they do not involve blood transfusions [9].

Here there is clearly a balance to be struck between anyone's right to refuse life-saving treatment and the rights of the unborn child (which must have some moral force even if not normally recognised in English law). There must also be a question mark, though perhaps no more than that, over the coherence of the reasons given. These considerations ought to affect what happens when treatment is refused, or indications given that it will be. For a refusal in the circumstances of section 10.3.4 or *Re S* will not be accepted at face value. Efforts will and should be made to explain the consequences of the refusal and to persuade the patient to reconsider. It would be desirable, in such a case, to ask for the patient's spiritual adviser to offer counselling. If the patient is simply mistaken about what his/her religious beliefs require, then the situation could be resolved at this stage without resort to law.

Such a reaction to a refusal of treatment can only be properly understood in terms of our moral disquiet about the decision taken and/or the reasons for it. But though there are good moral reasons for wishing to oppose such a decision, it may well be that there are equally good policy reasons for not giving that opposition legal force. We may, in other words, disagree, perhaps profoundly, with the decision without thinking that it would be right to enforce another course of action on the patient. And, clearly, there are excellent reasons for thinking that a general policy of enforcing caesarean sections on unwilling women would be an extremely bad thing.

10.9   Advance directives

As mentioned above, it can happen that patients are no longer capable of consenting to treatment. This may be because of mental or physical deterioration or both. In such cases treatment becomes a matter of what the health care team consider to be in the patient's best interests (see section 10.4.1). Ordinarily it might be thought that such a situation would be eased if there exists what has come to be called an 'advance directive'. This could take the form of anything from a simple statement ('If it comes to it, I don't want to be kept alive as a vegetable') to the much more formal 'living will' which is becoming common in the USA. There, a living will can be of two kinds. There is the simpler formal declaration of the circumstances in which you would no longer wish further treatment, for example. There is also a durable power of health care attorney which, effectively, nominates a proxy to take decisions on your behalf should you no longer be able to do so yourself [10].

The first of these is recognised under UK law, but the second is not. This is a shame, because in many ways the first is problematic. First of all, it is invariably hypothetical ('this is what I want *if* the following circumstances apply ...') and also general rather than specific. This is inevitable since, in writing a living will, we are trying to anticipate what might happen rather than dealing with an actual situation. What it means, however, is that it may still be difficult to determine how the will was meant to apply since the circumstances will not necessarily be precisely those envisaged. This is especially true if the will maker is not – and most of us are not – medically qualified or knowledgeable. There is also a problem of timescale, for two reasons. The first is perhaps the most obvious: that treatments may change in the interval between drawing up the will and it coming into operation. Someone who anticipates that they would rather be allowed to die than undergo a particular kind of treatment might well have opted differently had they known the extent to which that treatment had improved. The second reason concerns change in personal identity over time. To what extent is it reasonable for a younger version of me to legislate on what will be in the best interests of an older me? I might, by the time it is necessary, come to have taken an entirely different attitude to risk-taking, for example. Or I might have become an entirely different person.

Dworkin [11] cites the case of Margo, someone with Alzheimer's dementia who 'despite her illness, or maybe somehow because of it, ... is undeniably one of the happiest people I have known. There is something graceful about the degeneration her mind is undergoing, leaving her carefree, always cheerful' [12]. This is an unusual consequence of Alzheimer's disease which, more often, leaves people anxious, confused and profoundly disoriented. But that is the point. Had Margo considered the prospect of dementia and executed an advance directive, she might well have decided that she would not wish to receive treatment for any other life-threatening illness once she was suffering from Alzheimer's. Had she done so, and the relevant situation had arisen, would it be better to respect the autonomy of the person Margo had once been and comply with the wishes set out in the advance directive? Or would it be better to address the best interests of the person Margo now is, and treat her for any adventitious, life-threatening illnesses unless and until the Alzheimer's deteriorated much further? [13]

10.10   Withdrawing treatment

Consent to or refusal of treatment is not the only problem in this area. There can be patients from whom treatment can be withdrawn, on the grounds that they are, in fact, dying and it would be considered neither proper nor humane simply to prolong the dying process. Both the American and British Medical Associations endorse this view, as do the Catholic and Anglican Churches:

> 'The cessation of the employment of extraordinary means to prolong the life of the body when there is irrefutable evidence that biological death is imminent is the decision of the patient and/or his immediate family.' [14]

> 'In its narrow current sense, euthanasia implies killing, and it is misleading to extend it to cover decisions not to preserve life by artificial means when it would be better for the patient to be allowed to die. Such decisions coupled with a determination to give the patient as good a death as possible, may be quite legitimate' [15]

> '... normally one is held to use only ordinary means ... that is to say, means that do not involve any grave burden for oneself or another ... Consequently, if it appears that the attempt at resuscitation constitutes such a burden for the family that one cannot in all conscience impose it upon them, they can lawfully insist that the doctor should discontinue those attempts and the doctor can lawfully comply.' [16]

'The distinction between deliberate killing and the administration of painkilling drugs or the withdrawal of treatment such as to have the effect of shortening life, though sometimes a very fine one in practice, must remain a guiding principle.' [17]

It is widely believed that this position involves drawing a moral distinction between active and passive euthanasia. Many people seem to think, if they think that euthanasia can be justified at all, that it can be more readily justified if it is passive rather than active. Many people also seem to think that, whereas English law strictly forbids active euthanasia, it does, sometimes, allow that passive euthanasia may be permissible. Both doctors and lawyers talk as if they believe that this is so. For example:

'A Down's syndrome child is born with an intestinal obstruction. If the obstruction is not removed, the child will die. Here . . . the surgeon might say 'As this child is a mongol . . . I do not propose to operate; I shall allow nature to take its course'. No one could say that the surgeon was committing an act of murder by declining to take a course which would save the child.

A severely handicapped child, who is not otherwise going to die, is given a drug in such amounts that the drug itself will cause death. If the doctor acts intentionally then it would be open to the jury to say: yes, he was killing, he was murdering that child.

There is an important difference between allowing a child to die and taking action to kill it.' [18]

'No paediatrician takes life; but we accept that allowing babies to die – and I know the distinction is narrow, but we all feel it tremendously profoundly – it is in the baby's interests at times. [19]

This is potentially most misleading, and should not be taken at face value. I am not a legal specialist, and the law in this area is complicated, but it is perfectly clear that being passively responsible for someone's death is, *in itself*, no defence in law to a charge of either murder or manslaughter. In *R* v. *Bonnyman* (1942) Bonnyman was a doctor who realised that his wife was exhibiting all the symptoms of diabetes, and he refrained from telling her. Thinking that she merely had a particularly bad bout of influenza, she did not seek treatment and died. Dr Bonnyman was found guilty of manslaughter by criminal negligence. There are many other such cases. In *R* v. *Pitwood* (1902) Pitwood was a level crossing keeper who failed to close the gate when a train was approaching and was held to be responsible for the deaths that ensued; in *R* v. *Gibbins and Proctor* (1918) Gibbins and Proctor were found criminally responsible for the death of their child whom they had failed to feed; in *R* v. *Stone and Dobinson* (1977) Stone and Dobinson were convicted of manslaughter for the neglect of a dependent relative who died in their care.

English law holds that murder and manslaughter, specifically, are crimes which can be committed either by act or omission. Of course, where a death is caused by someone's action, it is usually relatively easy to identify the responsible agent. He or she is the one who performed the action in question. But who is responsible when someone dies as a result of a failure to act? The responsible agent here is anyone who failed to act *when they had a legal duty to act*. According to one authority [20], this duty can arise either through a contract, a special relationship (such as parent and child or doctor and patient) or where a person has voluntarily undertaken the care of another. But in a famous case – *Donoghue* v. *Stevenson* (1932) – Lord Atkin held that I owe a duty of care to:

'... persons who are so closely and directly affected by my act that I ought reasonably to have them in contemplation as being so affected when I am directing my mind to the acts or omissions which are called in question.'

This definition of the duty of care is so much more comprehensive that it is perhaps fortunate that it is only applicable in civil – tort – cases. Either way, it is clear that health care teams owe a duty of care to their patients and that wanton or reckless neglect of that duty which results in death can result in a criminal prosecution for murder or manslaughter. Why, then, did the House of Lords, in the case of *Airedale NHS Trust* v. *Bland* (1992) authorise the non-treatment of the patient when it was known that it would lead to his death?

Tony Bland was a victim of the Hillsborough football disaster. As a result of his injuries he was comatose and remained in what is known as a persistent vegetative state until 1993 when his parents applied through the courts for permission for artificial nutrition and hydration to be withdrawn. The courts held that artificial nutrition and hydration was a form of treatment. They also held that, in view of the extreme unlikelihood of Mr Bland's ever regaining consciousness, the treatment was of no benefit to him and withdrawing it would take the form of a legal omission rather than commission, i.e. the medical team had no duty to continue to treat Mr Bland. The arguments were:

(1) A doctor is under no duty to continue to treat a patient where such treatment confers no benefit on the patient.
(2) Being in a persistent vegetative state with no prospect of recovery was regarded by informed medical opinion as not being a benefit to a patient.
(3) The principle of the sanctity of life was not absolute, for example
     – where a patient expressly refuses treatment, even though death may well be a consequence of that refusal,
     – where a prisoner on hunger strike refuses food and may not be forcibly fed,
     – where a patient is terminally ill, death is imminent and treatment will only prolong suffering.
(4) Artificial hydration and nutrition required medical intervention for its application and was widely regarded by the medical profession as medical treatment.

The governing principle here was not that it was permissible to let a patient die so long as he/she was not actually *killed*. It was rather that *caring* for a patient (in cases where cure was not possible and recovery was extremely unlikely) did not require medical interventions which were of no benefit to the patient. But it is also clear that the treatment in question was not a *disbenefit* to Bland. If it did him no good, it also did him no harm. If doctors were under no duty to continue to treat Bland, they were also under no duty not to. But there was a benefit – to Bland's relatives and friends, especially his parents, who were to be spared the grief of continuing to see their son in this exceptionally distressing condition and would, finally, be able to mourn the loss they had suffered two years before. That is not a negligible benefit, by any means, and if, whatever happened, nothing more could be done to harm or benefit Bland himself, it seems right to let the choice of outcome be decided by what would most benefit those closest to him.

But it is interesting to compare the case of Tony Bland with that of *R v. Cox* (1992). Dr Nigel Cox was found guilty of attempted murder in 1992 for administering a lethal dose of potassium chloride to a patient, Lilian Boyes who, dying and in acute pain, had pleaded with him to help her die. It is indeed, hard to see how, on the face of it, this case is to be distinguished from that of *Bland*, without invoking the distinction between active and passive euthanasia. The remarks of Lord Justice Butler-Sloss in the Court of Appeal hearing of *Bland* would seem to do just that:

> 'The position of Dr Nigel Cox, who injected a lethal dose designed to cause death, was different since it was an external and intrusive act and was not in accordance with his duty of care as a doctor. The distinction between Mr Bland's doctors and Dr Cox was between an act or omission which allowed causes already present in the body to operate and the introduction of an external agency of death.' [21]

The Guardian's leader writer called that position a 'philosophical nonsense' (20 November 1992) and maybe it is, if taken at face value. What is not true is that there is no other morally relevant distinction to be drawn between the two cases. What follows should not be seen as implying any criticism of Dr Cox who, it would seem, was placed in an extremely difficult situation and, in all good faith, was probably doing what he believed was the only thing he could do to help Ms Boyes. But whether Cox's decision was the right one in the circumstances, the explanation for its rightness must be different from the explanation of the rightness of withdrawing treatment from Tony Bland.

The source of this distinction is an old notion, thought by many to be now discredited, called 'the principle of double effect'. It should, I think, be seen not as a rule for resolving moral problems but as a guide which can clarify what is at issue in particular cases. It relies on a distinction between what one intends and what one merely foresees as a result of one's actions. The principle suggests that, whereas one is fully responsible for what one intends to do, one is not responsible for foreseen but intended effects of one's actions, provided that:

(1) what is done must be, at the least, morally permissible;
(2) what is intended must include only the good and not the bad effects of what is done;
(3) the bad effects must not be the *means* whereby the good is brought about;
(4) there must be *proportionality* between the good and bad effects of what is done.

Whereas Dr Cox must have intended Lilian Boyes' death as the only way, as he saw it, of sparing her further pain and suffering, the medical team treating Tony Bland intended to spare him further suffering (or at least to spare his relatives, given that Tony Bland himself may have been aware of nothing at all) whilst foreseeing that this would probably lead to his death. This distinction may have no practical consequences in those two actual cases, given that both led to the death of the patients concerned. It matters, nonetheless, insofar as they are treated as precedents for action in future cases which may look superficially similar.

It is not because it is merely a matter of allowing a patient to die rather than acting in order to bring about their death, that passive euthanasia is permissible. In cases where the patient's death is imminent or where treatment is painful and offers only a very remote chance of success, then it is justifiable, if the patient and/ or his or her relatives consent, to cease to continue treatment.

Moral responsibility for an event is not determined by whether it came about because one acted or failed to act; it is determined by one's intentions and duties. If there is no duty to treat, and also persuasive reasons for not doing so, it must normally be entirely permissible to withdraw treatment, even if to do so results in the death of the patient.

So what about Dr Cox? Clearly he cannot be excused on these grounds, for they do not apply to his case. What can be said is that it is possible to imagine circumstances where the suffering of the patient is so great and the possibility of immediate remedy so small that killing the patient is the only available means of preventing the pain. In national disasters or wars such circumstances may arise, or in parts of the world where medical resources are extremely limited. In those circumstances it is possible that acting so as to bring about the death of the patient as easily and quickly as might be would not be wrong [22]. It may be that those were the circumstances in which Nigel Cox found himself. Without being a part of the situation it is impossible to say. It must be a matter of judgement and one which I hope I never have to exercise. For that reason it cannot be said conclusively that what Cox did was wrong, but, also for that reason, it is also a matter which the law, on policy grounds, can never permit.

10.11   Notes and references

1. For example, it has been doubted whether babies, fetuses, or those who, whilst still biologically alive, lack any response to the world around them are persons in the strict sense of the term. (See Robert F. Weir (1989) *Abating Treatment with Critically Ill Patients*, Oxford University Press, New York, pp. 70–71 and 405–12.) It can also be argued that higher apes and cetaceans (dolphins, porpoises and whales) might conceivably be persons in the required sense. (See Peter Singer (1979) *Practical Ethics*, Cambridge University Press, *passim*.) A useful source on the whole debate is H. Kuhse & P. Singer (eds) (1999), *Bioethics*, Part IV. Blackwell, Oxford.
2. But see E. Matthews (2000) Autonomy and the Psychiatric Patient, in *Journal of Applied Philosophy*, **17** (1). He sees this as a misinterpretation of Kant and would prefer to ground the point on Mill's argument. (See note 3.)
3. For a more complete, and classic, exposition of this view, see John Stuart Mill, *On Liberty*. (There are many editions of this, but a good one which includes critical essays is edited by John Gray and G.W. Smith (1991) *J.S. Mill On Liberty In Focus*, Routledge, London.)
4. See Margaret Brazier (1992) *Medicine, Patients and the Law*, 3rd edn, pp. 449–50. Penguin, Harmondsworth.

5. *State of Tennessee Dept of Human Services* v. *Mary C. Northern, C.A. Tennessee, Middle Section*, 7 Feb. 1978; cited in John Arras and Nancy Rhoden (eds) (1989) *Ethical Issues in Modern Medicine*, 3rd edn, pp. 72–9.
6. Judge John Terry, in the case of Angela Carder (district of Columbia Court of Appeals, 1990), the American case cited in evidence in *Re S* (*The Guardian*, 20/10/92).
7. See *The Guardian*, 20/10/92, p. 23.
8. See The *Montreal Gazette*, 27/7/78; the case is discussed in R. Campbell, D. Collinson (1988) *Ending Lives*, pp. 174–5. Blackwell, Oxford.
9. See *The Guardian*, 14/10/92, p. 3.
10. See Margaret Brazier (1992) *Medicine, Patients and the Law*, 3rd edn, pp. 457–8. Penguin, Harmondsworth.
11. R. Dworkin (1994) *Life's Dominion: An Argument about Abortion, Euthanasia, and Individual Freedom*, pp. 218–9. Vintage Books, New York.
12. A.D. Firlik (1991) Margo's Logo, *Journal of the American Medical Association*, 265, 201. Quoted by Dworkin (1994) (see note 11).
13. See also R. Dresser (1995) Dworkin on Dementia: Elegant Theory, Questionable Policy, *Hastings Center Report*, 25, 6, and D. Degrazia (1999) Advance Directives, Dementia, and 'The Someone Else Problem', *Bioethics*, 13, 5, pp. 373–91.
14. *Journal of the American Medical Association* (1974) 227. See also the British Medical Association (1981) *The Handbook of Medical Ethics*, BMA, London.
15. Church of England National Assembly (Board for Social Responsibility) (1975) *On Dying Well*, p. 10, Church Information Office, and *The Guardian* 20/11/92, (leading article).
16. Pope Pius XII, *The Pope Speaks*, 4 (4) 396.
17. Principles endorsed by the House of Bishops of the Church of England in October 1992, as cited by David Sheppard in a letter to *The Guardian*, 27/10/92.
18. *Obiter dicta* in the case of *Arthur* (1981) taken from trial transcripts cited by H. Kuhse, A Modern Myth ..., *Journal of Applied Philosophy*, 1, 1.
19. Expert testimony from consultant paediatricians in the case of *Arthur* (1981) cited in D. and M. Braham, The Arthur Case, *Journal of Medical Ethics*, vol. 9, pp. 12–15.
20. Smith and Hogan (1996) *Criminal Law*, 8th edn, p. 51. Butterworths, London.
21. Court of Appeal: *Airedale NHS Trust* v. *Bland*, 9 December 1992.
22. See Church of England National Assembly (Board for Social Responsibility) (1975) *On Dying Well*, Church Information Office.

Chapter 11

Clinical Governance

A   The Legal Perspective

Jo Wilson

The main purpose of health care delivery is to secure, through the resources available, the greatest possible improvement in the physical and mental health of the population. Achieving clinical quality and effective risk management is the aim of every clinician so it may seem surprising that there is apparently so much variation in practice between hospitals, departments and even individuals, all trying to deliver the same service. Some local customisation is of course desirable, but the variations in both quality of care and quality of delivery of care would suggest that many of the principles which should underpin any quality service are not always addressed. The reasons for this are complex, but may relate to a historic narrowness in the training of health care professionals; an inability to implement change; fears of failure and threats to clinical autonomy and clinical freedom due to lack of evidence based practice; and a poor record in effective team working. The concept of clinical governance ensures that quality of care is central to the delivery of care for all professional groups. It aims to ensure clear systems are in place to promote and check that health care professionals are working towards quality standards.

Clinical governance within health care organisation therefore provides a clear framework for the achievement of quality improvement. Quality in this context means clinical care as well as customer care and getting things right first time and every time. Risk management is about avoiding the potential for unwanted outcomes and getting things right every time. Clinical governance encompasses all the processes needed to achieve the highest quality clinical practice possible, within available resources. Clinical governance represents a major opportunity for health professionals as it gives the professionals the authority they need to make the health service work more effectively.

Since the early 1990s there has been strong support to develop the clinical effectiveness agenda through robust arrangements for quality improvements, clinical audit and clinical guidelines. In the 1997 UK Government White Paper [1] *The New NHS Modern Dependable*, the systems of clinical governance mark a fundamental and significant shift towards involving clinicians in the assurances of both quality, security and accountability in health care delivery. The paper states:

'The Government will require every NHS Trust to embrace the concept of clinical governance, so that quality is at the core, both of their responsibilities as organisations, and of each of their staff as individual professionals.'

In order to achieve this the Government has legislated a new duty for the quality of care and working in partnership. Under these arrangements chief executives now carry ultimate responsibility for assuring the quality of the services provided by their NHS Trust, just as they are already accountable for the proper use of resources. In *A First Class Service Quality in the NHS* [2], clinical governance is 'defined as a framework through which the NHS organisations are accountable for continuously improving the quality of their services and safeguarding high standards of care by creating an environment in which excellence in clinical care will flourish'. The principles of clinical governance apply to all those who provide or manage patient care services in the NHS. It requires staff to work in partnership providing integrated care [3] within health and social care teams, between practitioners and managers and between the NHS, patients and the public.

11.1   Principles of clinical governance

Clinical governance incorporates a number of processes, including:

- clinical audit;
- evidence based practice in daily use supported within the infrastructure;
- clinical effectiveness;
- clinical risk management with adverse events being detected, openly investigated and lessons learned;
- lessons for improving practice are learned from complaints;
- outcomes of care;
- good quality clinical data to monitor clinical care with problems of poor clinical practice being recognised early and dealt with;
- good practice systematically disseminated within and outside the organisation and clinical risk reduction programmes of a high standard being in place.

There is an expectation for all clinicians to fully participate in audit programmes, including speciality and subspeciality national external audit programmes and the four confidential enquiries endorsed by the Commission for Health Improvement. Clinical governance has placed a duty of responsibility on all health care professionals to ensure that care is satisfactory, consistent and responsive; each individual will be responsible for the quality of their clinical practice as part of professional self-regulation. The aim will be to strengthen the current systems of quality assurance based on evaluation of clinical standards, better utilisation of evidence based practice and learning the lessons from poor performance. The clinical governance framework builds upon professional self-regulation and performance review; it takes account of existing systems of quality control and includes all activity and information for quality improvements. It is based on partnership and driven by performance based on efficiency, effectiveness and excellence.

Any framework for clinical quality must be amenable to monitoring and assurance of compliance with the policies of the health care organisation. An excellent way to achieve this is through Multidisciplinary Pathways of Care© [4] (MPCs©) which have utilised clinical guidelines, standards, outcomes and variance analysis. MPCs can incorporate components of effective care, including evidence based practice, clinical audit, change management, multidisciplinary working and performance management. Multidisciplinary means that all members of the team should have an equal say and, although teams require a leader, there is little doubt that effective teams allow individuals to take leadership for particular objectives or responsibilities of that team's performance. Effective teams who are self-managed, self-directed and accountable will identify problems with variations from their targets and will have responsibility for correcting those problems for quality of care improvements.

11.2   Clinical governance processes

The main issues that health care organisations are addressing, and are producing evidence about, are that these systems of clinical governance are in place and are producing the right outcomes. These include the following:

- clinical quality improvements integrated with the overall organisational continuous quality improvement programmes to identify and build on good practice;
- good practice systematically disseminated;
- clinical risk reduction programmes in place;
- professional self-regulation/assessment including the development of clinical leadership skills;
- evidence based practice systems in place;
- adverse events, near misses and incidents detected, openly investigated and lessons learned;
- complaints to be dealt with positively and the information used to improve the organisation and care delivery;
- high quality and performance measurement data collected to monitor clinical care and support professionals in delivering quality care;
- poor clinical performance dealt with appropriately to minimise harm to patients and other staff;
- staff should be supported in their duty to report concerns about colleagues' professional conduct and performance, and procedures developed for early action to support the individual to remedy the situation;
- continuing professional development through lifelong learning aligned with clinical governance principles.

11.3   Dimensions of clinical governance

There are three dimensions to clinical governance which are:

(1)   Corporate accountability for clinical performance with the chief executive/ chair of the governing body with overall responsibility 'accountable officer'

role. There may be a board sub-committee led by a clinical professional such as the medical director or chief nurse and the expectation of monthly reports to the board, and arrangements in the annual report. There will be clear lines of responsibility and accountability for the overall quality of clinical care. NHS Trusts were required to produce their first clinical governance external reports by April 2000 and then on an annual basis.

(2) Internal mechanisms for improving clinical performance including individual accountability, self and professional regulation. Professional self-regulation was aimed at giving health professionals the ability to set their own standards of professional practice, conduct and discipline. The emphasis will be on lifetime learning through continuing professional development programmes as an integral part of quality improvement. With total involvement of staff in shaping the health care delivery system and planning change through open communication, collaboration and improving patient care.

(3) External mechanisms for improving clinical performance, e.g. Commission for Health Improvement (CHI), the watchdog with a smile and sharp teeth [5]. The Commission for Health Improvement is a statutory body responsible for reviewing the NHS to support those who are developing and monitoring local systems and multidisciplinary standards for clinical quality. CHI provides national leadership to develop and disseminate clinical governance principles. CHI independently scutinises local clinical governance arrangements to guarantee that local systems to monitor, assure and improve clinical quality are in place, through a rolling programme of local reviews of service providers. It has the capacity to offer specific support on request when local organisations face particular clinical problems. It also investigates and identifies the sources of problems and work by troubleshooting with organisations on lasting remedies to improve quality and standards of patient care. CHI assesses NHS progress in achieving the standards set in the National Service Frameworks and the uptake of the National Institute of Clinical Excellence (NICE) guidance on the clinical and cost effectiveness of different treatment options, and oversees critical incident enquiries to ensure the best outcomes for patients and the service. CHI also identifies problems and barriers to progress and makes recommendations to help overcome them.

These three dimensions are to ensure that there are proper processes in place for continually monitoring and improving clinical quality. Every health care organisation has a clinical professional to take charge of quality issues, and the legal duty of quality is imposed on every organisation. CHI works with and helps organisations to develop quality criteria, monitoring, measurement and evaluation as well as policing the adoption and operation of clinical governance. It helps the NHS to identify and tackle serious or persistent clinical problems with the capacity for rapid investigation and intervention to put these right. The core functions of CHI will be discussed later in the chapter.

11.4 Elements of clinical governance

Clinical governance provides a framework or mechanism through which clinicians and managers recognise their individual and collective responsibilities and accountabilities in respect of quality of care, and by which the health care organisation fulfils its statutory duty for the quality of care. It is a framework to co-ordinate quality improvement and quality assurance efforts with a full range of activities which aim to promote, maintain and improve the standards of patient care. Figure 11.1 demonstrates the range of activities through patient-centred care with a focus on accountability along a range of mechanisms to ensure implementation.

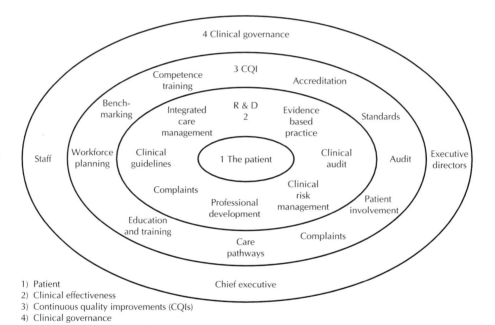

1) Patient
2) Clinical effectiveness
3) Continuous quality improvements (CQIs)
4) Clinical governance

Fig. 11.1 The elements required for clinical governance.

Most of the elements of clinical governance are not new to good clinicians and managers, but the framework brings them together under one umbrella providing a protective mechanism for both public and staff knowing that their local health care organisations are actively developing structures to improve quality and standards of patient care. It is about having efficient and effective systems of communication with staff and patients where robust infrastructures are established to proactively develop evidence based quality health care.

11.5   Risk management

Risk management is the lynch-pin which pulls together all the different elements of clinical governance. It also pulls together the accountability frameworks and clear reporting mechanisms to meet the corporate governance and controls assurance requirements. The clinical governance framework encompasses all the aspects of high quality provision such as quality assurance strategies, continuous quality improvements, clinical effectiveness, clinical audit, risk management and organisational and staff development. Good risk management awareness and practice at all levels is a critical success factor for any organisation. Risk is inherent in everything that an organisation does: treating patients, determining service priorities, managing a project, purchasing new medical equipment, taking decisions about future strategies, or even deciding not to take any action at all.

Risk management provides the best service for patients through obtaining a synergy between risk management, quality and the law. It also allows for the establishment of multidisciplinary standards of care and best practice guidelines to enhance professional development of nursing and medicine. The changes in health care delivery, with much higher expectations from patients, greater clarity of roles and responsibilities of clinicians and the emphasis on devolving decision making as close to the patient as possible, are meant to affect the entire performance of health care delivery. For most senior managers, nurses and doctors, the environment in which they operate has grown increasingly turbulent and complex with increasing demands on resources and increases in workload. They must contend with the more universal issues of monitoring patient activity, quality and evaluation through clinical audit, cost control, providing accessible and equitable services with relevance to the local population health care needs and social acceptability, as well as efficiency and effectiveness – all while ensuring their organisations' survival.

The commissioners of health care, on behalf of their clients, look for the best and most efficient health care delivery systems giving the best value for money by improving access, equity and quality of care without increasing the cost of services. To improve value, providers must understand and maximise the linkages between its two basic components – cost and quality. Both the cost and quality of care are components in determining the value of the health care delivered, and both are elements of health care risk. To begin to manage these elements of risk, the process of health care risk modification can be applied. The focus of health care risk modification is intensely on the systems and practices that affect patient care in order proactively to manage overall cost and appropriateness of care delivered. All aspects of the system – physical works, equipment, security, training, management, nursing, medicine, allied health professionals, etc. – have a role in increasing or modifying health care risk.

11.6   Risk

Risk in its simplest form is the potential for unwanted outcome. This is a very broad definition which ranges from patient dissatisfaction with having to wait too long or not being communicated with, to the patient having the wrong operation or suffering permanent disability or wrongful death. This can be further applied to health care settings where risk takes several forms, including:

- Patient injury while in the health care organisation's care resulting in extensive resource utilisation to correct the injury
- Decreased productivity resulting from time and resources spent in clinical negligence litigation
- Tarnished reputation of health care providers resulting from patient injury
- Clinical liability awards to injured parties and legal costs related to the litigation process
- Patient unhappiness and dissatisfaction, often due to lack of information and ineffective communication
- Hidden cost to the people in terms of pain and injury, locum cover costs, stress suffered by the individual involved and reduction in the quality of care delivery. The resource costs of replacement, facility downtime and improvements and the reputation of the professionals, the facilities and the public relations to improve local and public perceptions.

In each of these we can see elements of financial costs and decreased quality, which can place providers at a distinct disadvantage within the health care system.

11.7   Risk modification

Modification is the changing of circumstances, the environment and behaviour ultimately to lower the potential for and amount of health care risk. The risk management tools help to identify areas where health care continuous quality improvements can be made. The result is improved outcomes, patient satisfaction and the documentation of care delivery. Poor communication between professionals and with patients is the commonest reason for patients/relatives to make complaints or even take out litigation in order to acquire the necessary explanation and information. The Medical Protection Society estimates that in 90% of cases presented to it over a three year period, failure to communicate featured as a major component of the case. In addition, Action for Victims of Medical Accidents (AVMA) estimates that more than 50% of the complaints it receives are due to communication problems. In order to modify clinical risk and manage it appropriately our two best forms of risk prevention are effective communication and excellent documentation.

Risk management is designing and directing activities that establish the conditions for organisation success within the context of service delivery. Management should evaluate the effectiveness of clinical practice, patient satisfaction and outcomes and examine the frequency/severity and defensibility of claims. This does not mean practising defensive medicine but having the best defensibility in place if and when things do go wrong. Taken together, these definitions create a broader interpretation of risk management and begin to present risk solutions – through the implementation of risk modification for providers of health care.

Risk management is the system identification, assessment and reduction of risks to patients and staff:

- through providing appropriate, effective and efficient levels of patient care
- prevention and avoidance of untoward incidents and events
- learning the lessons and changing behaviour/practices as a result of near misses, incidents and adverse outcomes
- communication and documentation of care in a comprehensive, objective, consistent and accurate way.

11.8   Controls assurance

Controls assurance [6] is a system of management which is fundamental to governance in the NHS. It exists to inform NHS boards about significant risks within the organisation for which they are responsible. It is intended to assist NHS staff, including chief executives and board members, to identify risks, to help them determine unacceptable levels of risk, and to then decide on where best to direct limited resources to eliminate or reduce those risks. One of the fundamental assumptions of controls assurance is that all statutory and mandatory requirements with which NHS organisations need to comply represent a risk of some sort. That is, these requirements exist because they are designed to control a risk that could threaten the organisation, the people, or the environment. Similarly, best practice or good practice guidance exists to advise on accepted, although not always 'evidence based', options for dealing with potential risks. Thus 'non-compliance' with standards and 'risk' are synonymous in the context of controls assurance.

Controls assurance has a large part to play in meeting the governance and risk management agendas and is being implemented using the Australian and New Zealand risk standards, through a self-assessment process to allow Trusts to prioritise and assess the severity of their own risk exposure. Controls assurance is a holistic concept based on best governance practice which conforms with the Combined Code of Practice on Corporate Governance. It is a process designed to provide evidence that NHS organisations are doing their 'reasonable best' to manage themselves so as to meet their objectives and protect patients, staff, the public and other stakeholders against risks of all kinds.

Fundamental to the process is the effective involvement of people and functions within the organisation through the application of the self-assessment techniques to ensure objectives are met and risks are properly controlled. Risk management and internal control are firmly linked with the ability of an organisation to fulfil clear objectives.

11.9   Developing best clinical practice

In order to establish best clinical, and in time, evidence based practice, health care practitioners should identify areas in the practice from which clear clinical questions can be formulated. This will be supported by identifying the best-related evidence available from the literature, critically appraising the evidence for validity and clinical usefulness and then implementing and incorporating findings into practice. The loop must then be complete in terms of having ongoing measurement of performance against expected outcomes or against peer review.

Figure 11.2 outlines a way in which these measurements can be formulated for best results. In undertaking research and a literature review the most up-to-date evidence based practice is obtained and this can be aplied within Integrated Care Management (ICM), Multidisciplinary Pathways of Care© (MPCs) and Clinical Guidelines. This is one of the best ways of testing compliance and applicability of the best practice and localising this to the organisation to ensure it is clinically effective and produces the best clinical outcomes. The real test comes from the audit and re-audit to ensure practice and behaviour changes in applying best practice, are maintained and improved with clinical effectiveness and efficiency with improved clinical outcomes.

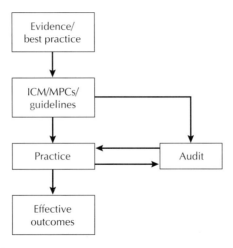

Fig. 11.2   Audit to find best clinical practice [7]. J.H. Wilson, 1999.

11.9.1   National Institute of Clinical Excellence (NICE)

The National Institute of Clinical Excellence has a single focus to promote clinical and cost effectiveness through clinical guidelines, best practice and audit. The functions of NICE centre around providing a single focus for work to promote clinical and cost effectiveness, producing guidance on new and existing health interventions such as therapies and drug treatments, and the production of ongoing audit methodologies. Following a period of review, new treatments and technologies could be proclaimed as a national standard and could therefore be included within a National Service Framework. NICE is also responsible for the dissemination of clinical guidelines, best practice and audit through education and training of professionals and the production of appropriate patient information.

11.9.2   The Commission for Health Improvement (CHI)

This is a statutory body which provides independent scrutiny of local efforts to improve quality and to help address any serious problems. CHI is conducting a rolling programme of external review over every four years to ensure that effective systems to continuously improve patient care are in place. If a problem is identified regionally with a particular organisation prior to the planned programme, CHI will make an immediate visit to assess the situation.

The core functions of CHI are to:

- support, develop and disseminate clinical governance principles;
- independently scrutinise local governance arrangements to support, promote and deliver high quality services;
- advise on local clinical governance arrangements;
- review the implementation of National Service Frameworks and guidelines produced by the National Institute of Clinical Excellence;
- identify serious or persistent clinical problems;
- concentrate on clinical issues; however, they will become involved in management issues where these are contributing to clinical problems;
- increasingly take on responsibility for overseeing and assisting with external NHS incident inquiries in England and Wales as appropriate.

The CHI review report will be communicated in writing and through a presentation and discussion with health care providers involved. Once the report has been agreed and an action plan formulated with the health care provider, a summary report will be made public by publication and being available on the internet. CHI will not only highlight areas for improvement but will also identify and share examples of good practice.

11.9.3   The National Service Framework

The National Service Framework has set national standards and defined service models for specific service or care groups. It has put in place programmes to support implementation and established performance measures against which progress is measured. National Service Frameworks have:

- set national standards and defined service models for a specific service or care group;
- put in place programmes to support implementation;
- established performance measures against which progress within an agreed time-scale can be measured.

Frameworks have been developed for cancer, mental health, older people and cardiology services. The National Priorities Guidance 2000/01–2002/03 covers the following areas:

- reduction of waiting lists and times;
- prompt and effective emergency care;
- maintaining financial stability;

- restoring working balances;
- prevention and control of communicable disease especially:
  - hospital acquired infection
  - reduction in anti-microbial resistance
  - meeting immunisation targets.

11.9.4   The National Framework for Assessing Performance

In line with the service framework a consultation document on the use of clinical indicators in the NHS was issued in July 1997. The indicators attempt to make the best possible use of existing data and focus on six areas: health improvement, fair access to services, effective delivery of appropriate health care, efficiency, patient and care experiences and health outcomes of NHS care. Mature and responsible use of the information could support clinical governance, leading to improvements in quality of care where local investigation highlights any shortcomings.

The performance assessment framework [7] results will be published annually. As a first step the UK Department of Health plan to publish a range of clinical indicators on a named hospital basis at least annually. NHS Trusts are expected to develop effective performance management approaches to meet local and national health care targets, financial and quality controls, implementation of service frameworks and systems for tackling serious or persistent clinical problems. Criteria will be set nationally with assessments by the regional offices. CHI will carry out independent verification of the assessments. Many of these processes are included within service and financial frameworks, annual agreements, business plans and performance reviews. These performance management reviews need to include having the right people in the right place, at the right time, with the right skills and competencies to deal with effective patient care delivery. Each Trust board within the organisation should be asking the following questions:

- Are there robust standards of the registration and up-to-date practices of all health care providers?
- Are there clear standards of good practice, usage of clinical indicators and outcome measurements?
- Does the organisation have a framework with demonstrable fitness to practice for all health care providers?
- Are there effective, supportive and fair procedures to remove unfit health care providers while further training, skills analysis and competency reviews are undertaken?
- Is there a corporate approach with managers and clinicians working together to provide safe risk management, high quality and effective systems to meet the organisational needs and targets?

NHS organisations will be publicly classified as 'green', 'yellow' or 'red' organisations:

'Red organisations will be those who are failing to meet a number of core national targets. Green organisations will be meeting all core national targets and will score in the top 25% of organisations on the Performance Assessment

Framework, taking account of "value added". Yellow organisations will be meeting all or most national core standards, but will not be in the top 25% of Performance Assessment Framework performance.'

Green light organisations will be rewarded with greater autonomy and national recognition and they could even have the ability to take over persistent failure red light organisations.

These NHS organisations will need to be supported by good human resource management to produce a quality workforce with ongoing education, training, individual job plans, competency and skills analysis and lifelong learning.

11.9.5   NHS Plan [8]

The ambitious and far-reaching reform in the guise of the NHS Plan proposes to deal with issues such as:

- investment in NHS facilities and staff;
- changes for patients, including greater choice and protection;
- cutting patient waiting times, improving health and reducing inequality;
- changes for NHS doctors, including new consultant contracts and new quality based contracts for GPs;
- new responsibilities and changes for NHS nurses, midwives, therapists and other NHS staff;
- changed NHS systems.

There are proposed structural changes with some new organisational bodies which will include:

- NHS Modernisation Agency
- National Independent Reconfiguration Panel
- National Performance Fund
- The NHS Leadership Centre
- NHS Appointments Commission
- National Clinical Assessment Authority
- NHSplus: National Agency
- Patient Advocacy and Liaison Service (Pals)
- UK Council of Health Regulators
- Patients' Forums
- Citizens Council (NICE)

Some of these new organisations and groups will inevitably make an impact on clinical risk and health litigation management policies and procedures. A new and more effective complaints system looks likely to be introduced making it more independent and responsive to patients. Patients will have a firmer and an official platform from which to voice opinions and concerns. The initiatives should give patients more of a say in what happens, locally and nationally. Patients will have direct responsibility on every NHS Trust board, elected by the patients' forum. The forum will be supported by Pals and will have the right to visit and inspect any aspect of the Trust's care at any time. Pals' staff and forum members will also have access to the new NHS Leadership Centre's programmes.

11.9.6   Lifelong learning

Delivering quality standards will very much depend on three elements, which are the setting up of proper clinical governance, the establishment and maintenance of lifelong learning and ongoing professional self-regulation. Lifelong learning is an investment in quality that underpins clinical governance, is important to the recruitment and retention of well-trained professionals and has to meet the needs of both health professionals and the NHS. The NHS Human Resources Strategy has addressed suggestions of how this will be achieved in order to provide the appropriately trained staff to give the best services and quality of care to patients. A specially earmarked modernisation fund will be used to provide the training and development that staff need to renew and enhance their skills for the future. The NHS will be aiming to recruit and retain a quality workforce which has the capacity, skills, diversity and flexibility to meet the needs of the service.

11.9.7   Professional self-regulation

Health and social care professionals currently set standards for professional practice but usually on a uniprofessional basis. This needs to move towards sharing best practice and working on a multidisciplinary basis through integrated care. This would provide a mechanism for ensuring the essential element of professional self-regulation in the delivery of quality patient services, with professions being openly accountable for the standards and their enforcement. This would certainly start to address the challenge of the aims of the White Paper in terms of trying to strengthen and modernise, and to restore public confidence in health and social care. Clinical audit has an important role in professional self-regulation. It enables clinicians to hold a mirror to their everyday work and through discussion with peers and guidance from their professional bodies, make any relevant changes.

For this reason the various professional bodies are increasingly requiring that clinical audit is a key component of all specialist training and are encouraging their members to continue such practice beyond their training. Health commissioners and NHS Trusts also need to encourage and support clinicians to include audit in their professional self-regulation and continuing educational development programmes. This includes ensuring that adequate resources, including protected time and support, are available. It also includes sharing the information and implications of clinical audit studies, which should become integrated into the clinical risk and clinical governance strategies in ensuring that changes do occur and lessons are learned and shared throughout the health care system.

11.9.8   Clinical audit

Clinical audit is a crucial tool for ensuring improvements in the quality of patient care. One of the key components of clinical governance is for all clinicians to participate in internal and external clinical audit systems. Clinical audit will provide a comprehensive framework for quality improvement activity and processes for monitoring clinical care using effective information and clinical record systems. It provides a formal approach to questioning clinical practice and to developing new practices and to ensuring they meet continuous quality improvements and clinical outcomes. It considers the effectiveness, efficiency and humanity of care and can be used to enhance education and develop clinical excellence in dealing with the structure, process and outcomes of health care.

An effective clinical audit programme helps to give necessary reassurance to patients, clinicians and managers that an agreed quality of service is being provided within available resources. It is performed to improve standards of care, to raise awareness of costs, to eliminate waste and inefficiency, and as a valuable educational tool for peers, juniors and other professionals. It is an educational process for clinicians, identifying inappropriate and inefficient clinical practices and inadequate support. It can lead to increased consumer awareness and choices about health care, as information becomes more readily available about clinical activity, quality of services and health outcomes. Clinical audit has an important role in risk management in revealing where care is ineffective or below acceptable standards and in encouraging its replacement with effective care and improved clinical outcomes.

Clinical audit (see Fig. 11.3) through the monitoring of standards and best practice can assist clinicians in having robust processes for the identification of effectiveness, efficiency and appropriateness of the clinical care provided. The clinical governance involvement occurs when standards are not met or best practice is not being applied and it is all about having interventions to fix the problem through internal scrutiny. This will also be supplemented by open and external review and participation in national audit programmes including speciality and subspeciality national external audit programmes endorsed by the Commission for Health Improvement. Clinical governance places a duty of responsibility on all health care professionals to ensure that care is satisfactory, consistent and responsive; each individual will be responsible for the quality of their clinical practice as part of professional self-regulation. It will strengthen the

Fig. 11.3 Clinical audit: monitoring standards and best practice. J.H. Wilson, 1999.

current systems of quality assurance and clinical audit based on evaluation of clinical standards, better utilisation of evidence based practice and learning the lessons from poor performance. The clinical governance framework builds on professional self-regulation and performance review; it takes account of existing systems of quality control and includes all activity and information for quality improvements.

11.9.9   Clinical and cost effectiveness

Clinical audit should be an activity that aims to produce change where change is necessary and share lessons to be learnt, as well as working towards the delivery of services of the highest possible standard to individual patients and to populations. However, the debate about clinical versus cost effectiveness and affordability is part of the same spectrum of activity and must be considered. The criteria for doing this are outlined in Fig. 11.2 which shows the areas which need to be considered and balanced in order to provide the most appropriate care. The balance needs to be struck between effectiveness, appropriateness and acceptability which inevitably, when dealing with health care, cannot be audited as perfect when judged against all these different criteria, and a judgement will be required about what is reasonable. Resources will always be limited, and clinical audit should play a leading part in ensuring optimal use of resources.

11.10   Conclusions

In order to obtain both organisational and professional governance all of the clinical professions must have structures and systems of clinical governance to maintain professional accountability. These must be integrated and reconciled with NHS accountability systems and structures at all levels. The key to successful implementation of clinical governance is to be able to demonstrate the development of an accountability structure which ensures that monitored changes in clinical practice as a result of identification of failures in quality are judged against the defined standards and their outcomes. Health care organisations now have to show clear lines of accountability, reporting mechanisms, risk management and ongoing quality measures to meet the governance agenda.

Clinical audit focuses on the patient and his or her use of resources, the care given and the outcomes achieved. Quality improvements cover three main areas: more flexible access to services; greater sensitivity to individual treatment needs; and improvement in technical competence. Audit provides the systematic reviews of treatments, and lessons learned will improve standards, reduce clinical risk exposure and raise the quality of care. This is exactly what clinical governance needs to achieve in enhancing lifelong learning through education and developing clinical excellence through processes, systems and outcomes of healthcare delivery. However, it must be remembered that clinical audit is a continuous process and a means to an end and not an end in itself. In order to be effective the audit loop must be closed and there must be ongoing re-evaluation for assurance of best and up-to-date practices.

Clinical governance will have an important part to play in restoring public confidence in health care delivery through demonstrating quality assurance and control mechanisms. Patients and their families place trust in health care professionals and they need to be assured that their treatment is up to date and clinically and cost effectively applied by staff whose skills have kept pace with evidence based practice and new techniques. The emphasis must be on processes that are simple to use and able to demonstrate the production of effective results. It must be seen as going hand in glove with clinical risk management in terms of modifying the healthcare providers' behaviour to provide safe, effective and high quality patient care. Quality and risk are two sides of the same coin and must work in synergy to provide better patient care. Effective clinical governance and risk management will make it clear that quality is everybody's business. Clinical governance, however, must not be seen as an end in itself; the aim is to end unacceptable variation in practice, but it is more important that clinicians are accountable and responsible for differences in practice, not simply seeking to homogenise care.

11.11   Notes and references

1. Department of Health (1997) *The New NHS Modern Dependable*, Cmnd 3807. The Stationery Office, London.
2. Department of Health (1998) *A First Class Service Quality in the new NHS*. The Stationery Office, London.
3. Wilson, J.H. (1996) *Integrated Care Management: The Path to Success*. Butterworth and Heinemann, Oxford.
4. Wilson, J.H. (1992) An Introduction to Multidisciplinary Pathways of Care. Northern Regional Health Authority, Newcastle Upon Tyne.
5. Walshe, K. (1998) Cutting to the heart of quality. *Health Management* May, pp. 20–21.
6. NHS Executive (1999) *Guidelines for Implementing Controls Assurance in the NHS*. Controls Assurance Team, Quarry House, Leeds.
7. Wilson, J.H. (1999) The route to clinical governance. *Healthcare Risk Report*, **5**(4) March.
8. *The NHS Plan: A plan for reform*. Command Paper 4818. Stationery Office, London.

B   An Ethical Perspective – Quality and Judgement

Lucy Frith

Clinical governance is the latest 'big idea' for the NHS [1]. The main aim of clinical governance is to improve the quality of care provided by the NHS. At first sight this seems a common sense message – we should aim to provide the best health care that we can and always be seeking to improve the quality of that care. Surely, this is what health providers have always done? The main new facet of clinical governance is that it makes health organisations legally responsible for the quality of the health care they deliver, creating a statutory duty to improve the quality of health care. With this legal responsibility comes accountability. The chief executive of every Trust is responsible for the quality of care and individual practitioners are held to be more accountable.

Clinical governance can be defined as:

'A framework through which NHS organisations are accountable for continuously improving the quality of their services and safeguarding high standards of clinical care by creating an environment in which clinical care will flourish.' [2]

There are three main components of clinical governance:

(1) *Setting standards:* Bodies such as the National Institute for Clinical Excellence and the National Service Frameworks will set standards and aim to ensure equality of access and standardisation of health provision throughout the NHS.
(2) *Putting these standards into practice:* Measures such as care-pathways and clinical guidelines will implement these standards and recommendations for care. Clinical governance aims to create a more open environment where professionals will share good practice and participate in lifelong professional learning.
(3) *Monitoring these measures:* Bodies such as the Commission for Health Improvement, set up in September 1999, will publish information on the performance of Trusts in terms of three dimensions of quality: effectiveness

(health outcomes), equity (access to their services), and humanity (patients' and carers' views).

With these three elements of clinical governance as a broad framework I want to consider the ethical aspects of this new policy. Clinical governance can be seen as a move towards a more ethical health care policy. Stressing the importance of the quality of health care and ensuring that someone is legally responsible for clinical performance will, hopefully, result in a better service for patients. Further, patients' and carers' views will be given more prominence in, for example, the national patient and user surveys and this is a welcome development.

However, although quality of health care provision is something we all want, the term 'quality' is very hard to define. As Professor Campbell notes:

> 'to measure quality we need to know the values to which we all aspire and, in reality, the worlds of patients, clinicians, managers and educators are often far removed from one another.' [3]

The term 'quality' is a value judgement; it is an expression that the intervention provides us with certain outcomes that we think are desirable. Quality is not a scientific term, it is our opinion of the outcomes data. It is our judgement of whether the intervention is appropriate or helpful for the condition we want to treat and is an expression of how we compare it to other treatments. So, rather than assuming that by employing the term 'quality' we can answer the questions of what we should be doing with certainty, we need to remember that there could be disagreement over the definition of quality and there will not be one 'right' way of defining or interpreting the term. Hence, questions of what we should be doing will require us to make important value judgements and these should be made explicit so that they can be subject to justification.

11.12   Setting standards

Various bodies have been established to set standards and policies for the NHS. The National Institute for Clinical Excellence (NICE), established on 1 April 1999, produces evidence based clinical guidelines and information on good practice. A key function is the systematic appraisal of medical interventions. An example of this is the appraisal of the flu vaccination Relenza. In October 1999 NICE stated that there was not enough evidence that Relenza benefits those who are most at risk of flu and recommended that it should not be prescribed. The National Service Frameworks have the overall aim of ensuring equity of access and standardisation of care for all patients in the NHS and link related policies to formulate an integrated national policy. For example, the Tobacco White Paper and the National Priorities Guidance are brought together to create an integrated policy for coronary heart disease. These frameworks bring together the best evidence of clinical and cost effectiveness, with the views of users, to determine the best ways of providing a particular service.

However, before it is possible to speak of how to improve the quality of health care practice we need to have some notion of what we mean by quality in this context. The aim of setting standards in clinical governance is to determine the 'best' treatment or approach to a condition and implement these findings across the whole of the NHS. These standards will be set by considering the medical evidence and by employing a rigorous methodology to determine the best treatment scientifically. There is an implicit assumption that by establishing the quality of a treatment in this way it can be done without recourse to values or personal opinion. I want to consider this view that this method will tell us which treatments are 'better' scientifically and argue that although medical science can make an important contribution to treatment decisions, value judgements still come into quality assessments and these should be explicitly recognised.

It could be argued that by using such a scientific methodology to set standards, values can be eradicated completely from this whole process. There is an implicit strand running through the literature that by using such tools in setting standards, decisions will be made on a more objective basis. Book titles such as *The Scientific Basis of the Health Service* conjure up images of a value free utopia. It is easy to suppose that as the evidence of effectiveness is improving, we are increasing our knowledge base and thus decreasing the need for values. Medicine in both clinical practice and research is concerned with establishing the facts of the matter, and scientific method is often thought to be defined by impartiality and objectivity.

'It is the objective nature by which the evidence based medicine paradigm approaches the question of "what are we doing" and "how can we do better" that causes health care providers and funding agencies to increasingly adopt this paradigm as a primary principle.' [4]

Underlying this position, that by employing the tools of evidence based medicine (EBM), values can be eradicated from the standard setting process, are two assumptions: the improvement in medical evidence gives us a more accurate picture of which treatments work, and the use of systematic reviews can provide us with mechanisms that enable us to gain accurate knowledge of these findings. These findings are then implemented in clinical practice; because the findings are thought to be objective it is inferred the decision is objective too – values have no role to play. Given this understanding, by using high quality evidence standard setting decisions can be made on a 'scientific' basis and therefore are supposedly open to less interpretation. As Klein *et al.* note, this appears to allow decision-makers, 'the prospect of less pain, [and] less responsibility for taking difficult decisions' [5].

So, by the application of the methodology of EBM, can bodies aiming to set national standards of service provision decide what is the best treatment without recourse to any value judgements? I will argue that this is not possible for two reasons. First, the very term effectiveness is a subjective one in that it incorporates important value judgements. Second, even if what is the best treatment could be proven scientifically and objectively, we would still need to use value judgements to help tell us how to use that information. I will deal with these points in turn.

11.12.1   Effectiveness and value judgements

To say a treatment is effective, and hence of better quality, incorporates non-objective value-judgements, namely a judgement of what is a good outcome. It is generally argued that clinical trials are designed to find out certain effects of a drug, for example the lowering of plasma cholesterol levels; these effects are capable of being measured by a piece of laboratory equipment. The findings that this equipment produces will be independent of the experimenters' perceptions and hence can be said to be objective. This point is accepted. However, in what follows I argue that the significance given to the effect and whether that effect is to be termed a good outcome, are not factors inherent in the data but the values we impose on the data.

Randomised control trials (RCTs) are designed to produce data on the effectiveness of a treatment. These trials can be organised in two ways. First, by comparing the new treatment with a placebo and second by comparing it with an existing treatment. The clinical trial, that seeks to provide information on the comparison between a new treatment and/or a placebo and an existing treatment, is a practical technique to enable clinicians to make working comparisons between different treatments. These trials are often called intention-to-treat trials as they are designed to establish the clinical effect of the drug or treatment.

The purpose of intention-to-treat trials is to assess whether a drug works not how it works. They provide information on what treatment is *better* than another or more *effective* than a placebo. It is in this assessment of what makes a treatment better than another that trials incorporate evaluative elements. The researcher makes a value judgement as to whether a particular effect is good or bad and hence whether the treatment is effective. Effectiveness, good outcomes, quality, a 'better' treatment are not pre-existing facts waiting to be discovered by medical science: they are value-laden assessments of the weight given to a particular effect of the treatment. Thus, to say a treatment is effective is summing up one's opinion on the data.

For example, a clinical trial may produce data that say that treatment X has a 48% success rate in treating a given condition. Such data do not automatically tell us whether this treatment is an effective treatment for our given condition and whether we should recommend it to our patients. Our assessment of how good the 48% success rate is cannot be objectively determined, but is dependent on a number of factors. First, the severity of the condition being treated. If a condition is life threatening a 48% chance of success would be very good and the treatment would be judged to be very effective. Second, the acceptable level of side-effects of this treatment will depend on the type of condition that is treated. If the condition is life threatening we will bear very bad side-effects to achieve this 48% success rate (i.e. the side-effects of chemotherapy are very severe but held to be acceptable). However, for a minor complaint we would not see such side-effects as acceptable and would not class the treatment as an effective one. Third, the existence of other treatments and how the new treatment compares will influence how effective we judge our treatment to be. If there is another treatment Y with a 60% success rate and comparable side-effects our treatment will not be seen as effective. If treatment Y has much worse side-effects than our treatment X, determining which treatment is most effective will be a matter of individual clinical judgement and will depend on the goals and preferences of the standard setting authority.

It could be said that it is not important that the results produced by clinical trials incorporate a particular view of what defines a good outcome. If we can formulate a general consensus over what constitutes a good outcome then this can provide an adequate foundation for non-subjective agreement over outcomes. I would respond to this argument by raising two points: in the first place, it is very hard to gain consensus over what constitutes a good outcome. Even basic imperatives like preserving life can be contentious in certain situations. For instance, patients in persistent vegetative states, if correctly diagnosed, will never recover from the coma and it has been argued that simply preserving their life is unwarranted. Secondly, even if a consensus can be reached it is still important to recognise that this is a particular view of a good outcome and it is possible that in different times (or places) a different view of a good outcome could prevail.

11.12.2   How we employ the data in practice

To turn to the second argument: if we agree that clinical trials produce generally accepted factual data about the interaction of particular drugs or therapies, how can these facts establish which course of action should follow from them? 'The evidence itself will not automatically dictate patient care but will provide the factual basis on which decisions can be made' [6]. No matter how good one's evidence is, it will not automatically determine which course of treatment should be recommended. The evidence of effectiveness may form the basis of a very good reason for pursuing a particular course of action, but value judgements are needed to tell us whether we *should* take that course of action.

EBM claims that by using evidence that is of a higher quality, more scientific and more objective, it can make clinical decision making more objective. This is, to my mind, a confusion between two different things, the quality of evidence and the decision. While a decision that is made on the basis of good evidence will be of a higher quality, it will not be more objective in the sense that it is independent of value judgements or our perceptions and priorities. The evidence may be more objective but the decision is not, as it necessarily incorporates the values of those making the decision. This confusion leads to the belief that the evidence will indicate the course of action to be taken and that it is possible to locate the *best* treatment for a condition. As Muir Gray says in *Evidence Based Health Care*: 'Decisions about groups of patients or populations are made by combining three factors: 1. evidence; 2. values; 3. resources.' [7].

A central area where values shape how we should use the data and scientific evidence is that of priority setting. When bodies such as NICE decide on which care-pathways or which drugs to recommend they have to balance two possible competing claims: do we promote the interests of individual patients as paramount and focus on the effectiveness of the treatment? Or should this individual ethic make way for concerns over the collective good, a population based ethic, and focus on the cost effectiveness of the treatment? I think this is one of the key value judgements that has to be made by all health care systems and it is not a dilemma that can be solved by appealing to scientific evidence; it is a dilemma that can only be solved by deciding what kind of values we wish to see drive health care.

Alan Maynard, Professor of Health Economics at York, argues that EBM focuses on finding out which treatments are most effective and is therefore grounded in the individual ethic [8]. EBM is concerned with finding out what is the most effective treatment for a particular patient. However, the treatment that is the most effective might not also be the most cost effective. A physician who adopted the population based ethic would be more concerned with recommending a treatment that was cost effective and in the interests of society as a whole rather than just the interests of the individual patient. Maynard illustrates this tension between the individual and population-health ethic with an example.

A purchaser is choosing between two treatments, A and B. Therapy A produces 5 health years (HY) and therapy B produces 10 HY; leaving aside the problem of how to define health years, we can say treatment B is the more effective treatment and should be purchased. This would be purchasing according to the individual ethic, to do the best for the individual patient and provide the most effective treatment.

However, therapy A produces a HY for £300 and therapy B produces a HY for £700; given a fixed budget of £70 000 therapy A will produce over 130 more HY than therapy B. So, if one adopted the population ethic and was concerned with maximising the number of health years gained with a specific budget, then therapy A should be purchased. Hence, when making decisions as to what care-pathways to recommend, a value judgement has to be made as to whether the relevant evidence is that of effectiveness or that of cost effectiveness. As Maynard's example indicates, with different value judgements different treatments will be purchased.

A clear example of such a deliberation by NICE is the consideration of the drug beta interferon used in the treatment of multiple sclerosis. Sufferers of the disease argue that the drug is the only medication that prevents relapses, giving them relief from the symptoms of multiple sclerosis. Sir Michael Rawlins, the chairman of NICE, issued a press statement in June 2000 saying that other than people who are already being prescribed the drug it should not be made available on the NHS. The reasons for this decision were, 'on the basis of very careful consideration of the evidence, [beta interferon's] modest clinical benefit appears to be outweighed by its very high cost' [9]. This example illustrates two important points. First, patients and patient groups, in this case the MS Society, could have different definitions of an effective treatment from those the standard setting agency holds. The MS Society do not agree with NICE's assessment that beta interferon has only 'modest clinical benefit'. Second, cost is a factor in weighing up what treatments should be recommended and in this case it was claimed that the outlay to the NHS was not justified by the benefit it produces for the recipients. In such a deliberation there is no scientific way of answering the question of what this treatment is worth. It is a matter for society to decide what values and priorities are important.

11.13   Putting clinical governance into practice

One of the main ways in which quality will be managed under clinical governance is through the employment of care-pathways and clinical guidelines. In this section I argue that such guidelines could adversely affect the interests of the individual patient. I first give a brief outline of the rationale behind the introduction of clinical guidelines and then consider how these guidelines can affect patient care.

Part of the process of clinical governance is to assess systematically current practice and formulate clinical guidelines that represent best practice. Since April 1994 all Trusts have had to show that they have started to develop clinical guidelines. The NHS Executive stated that, 'on the advice of the Clinical Outcomes Group, [they have] begun to commend a selected number of high quality guidelines' [10]. The rationale behind guidelines is an attempt both to increase the quality of care and to reduce the inequalities in access to health care. The regional variations in service delivery and health outcomes have been seen as a central problem for the NHS. For example, the number of hip replacements in people over 65 years varies from 10 to 51 per 10 000 of the population. In Manchester the death rate from coronary heart disease in people aged under 65 years is nearly three times higher than in West Surrey [11].

There can be ethical dilemmas raised by implementing guidelines in practice. Treatments which produce the desired effect can differ from person to person. Even patients with identical manifestations of a particular disease could give different weight to various outcomes depending on personal taste, social and family situations, life priorities and so on. When used to promote greater quality of health care, guidelines can incorporate an assessment of quality that is held to be the same for all patients. This could come into conflict with an individual's particular conception of desirable benefit and their own personal quality assessment.

Many authors have drawn attention to the importance of recognising that good outcomes must be seen as relative to the patient. Hopkins and Solomon [12] illustrate this point with the example of the management of stroke patients. They say that the course of the treatment and the outcomes of rehabilitation cannot be predetermined, because each person's disability is unique. Hence the therapist has to concentrate on the goals and needs of the particular patient. This illustrates that effectiveness is usually seen as a relative concept, relative to the individual who receives the treatment. This is an implicit recognition of the role that values play in the definition of effectiveness.

However, supporters of clinical guidelines might argue against this view of the treatment process. They might argue that there are enough similarities between patients suffering from the same condition to see them as being members of the same patient group (in statistical language forming part of the same reference class of patient). Therefore, all that needs to be established is which group the patient belongs to and then the appropriate clinical guideline can be followed. Patrick Suppes, for example, has argued that a decision regarding the individual patient can be extrapolated from other cases: [13]

> 'Even though patients may vary in many respects (age, wealth, etc.), the direct medical consequences and the direct financial cost of a given method of treatment are the most important consequences, and these can be evaluated by summing across the patients and ignoring more individual features.' (p. 151)

Suppes is right in one respect. It may be possible to construct broad generalisations about patients' preferences for certain medical consequences. However, these would have to remain at a very broad level as many of the individual factors affecting these consequences are ignored. For example, financial cost may not be an issue for someone very wealthy, whereas for others even the cost of a simple prescription could be prohibitive. Others may value their life in so far as they are able to look after their children. Although it might be possible to ascertain the types of consequences that are, on the whole, most important, it is impossible to predetermine their respective value objectively.

Guidelines rely on patient homogeneity, that is patients being very similar. In stroke rehabilitation, where patient variation is high, it is difficult to write a precisely defined clinical guideline. There are, on the other hand, areas of health care where patient variation is much lower, the removal of wisdom teeth for example. When this is the case guidelines can be useful.

'In conditions such as day case surgery, a single patient record is easy to introduce. In an intensive care setting, where variations are more common, a pathway together with freehand documentation may be more suitable.' [14]

There may be areas where guidelines are more applicable; however, this should not be extended to areas of health care provision where guidelines may be inappropriate. Even when patients are suffering from the same condition guidelines should not be applied unthinkingly. Room should be made for the needs and wants of the patient to be accommodated. It could be argued that due to the individual nature of many treatment decisions, it could be difficult to produce guidelines that reflected each patient's treatment preferences.

However, guidelines can be used in a positive way and could increase patients' autonomy by involving them in the very formulation of guidelines and setting of standards. Patients often have very different perspectives from the health care professionals and soliciting their views on their health care provision could be invaluable. The National Service Frameworks are charged with bringing together the views of service users to determine the best way to provide particular services [2] and as part of the monitoring process there will be a national patient and user survey to determine these perspectives. An example of involving patients is the commissioning of The College of Health, an organisation dedicated to patient-centred care, by the Royal College of Physicians to produce patient-centred guidelines on conditions such as rheumatoid arthritis and rehabilitation after stroke.

Guidelines can also be distributed to patients to enable them to be better informed. When patients enter hospital they can be given a copy of the clinical guidelines and this can indicate what should be happening during the course of their treatment. It will give them an informed basis on which to question and challenge their treatment provision. This model has been adopted by a Liverpool hospital. The guideline is explained to the patient and they usually have access to it during their stay in hospital [14]. The patients therefore have a document that they can refer back to at any stage and so do not have to take in all the information at the beginning of their treatment. Used in this way guidelines can be a useful aid to communication between patient and health carer. This will ensure that the consent the patient gives is based on a full understanding of what the treatment involves. Clinical risk management (CRM) schemes are designed to eliminate complaints and by giving the patient a greater understanding and hence control over the treatment, complaints and dissatisfaction could be reduced.

11.14   Monitoring

I shall now consider how the implementation of clinical governance schemes is to be monitored. The Commission of Health Improvement, set up in September 1999, aims to support organisations and will conduct rolling reviews of all Trusts and primary care trusts. One of the main ways that the provision of health care is monitored in practice is through the adoption of clinical risk management programmes (CRM) [2]. It is the responsibility of the health care professional to promote the welfare of individual patients and ensure that they receive the best care. In this section I examine how such schemes can be used to create an environment which makes it easier for professionals to carry out their ethical duties in practice, looking at the issues of near-miss reporting and professional competence.

11.14.1   Near-miss reporting: an ethical environment

One aspect of CRM that can be used as an important measure for preventing harm to patients is near-miss reporting and notifying of adverse events. For example, every year 28 000 written complaints are made about aspects of hospital treatment; £400 m has been paid out in settlement of clinical negligence claims; and 15% of hospital infections may be avoidable and cost the NHS nearly £1 billion [16]. To rectify such problems:

> 'The NHS needs to develop: a unified mechanism for reporting and analysis when things go wrong [and] a more open culture, in which errors or service failures can be reported and discussed.' [16]

This could be used to create a working environment which helps the professional to practise ethically. The hospital appoints a risk manager to compile information on accidents or possible accidents and this forms the basis of changes designed to protect the patient from further incidents. This mechanism can improve patient care and is a means by which CRM can promote ethical practice. As Professor Jones says, 'It cannot be ethical to continue with a method of providing health care that exposes patients to unacceptable risks of having an adverse outcome' [17]. This move by the medical profession to examine why medical accidents have occurred is a very positive trend.

The professional codes of conduct for doctors and nurses all state the ethical duties of the professional in terms of the duties to the individual patient. The UKCC Professional Code of Conduct (1992) [18] states, 'act, at all times, in such a manner as to safeguard the interests of individual patients'. Doctors are bound by similar dictates to consider the welfare of the individual patient as paramount: 'The safety of the patients must come first at all times' [19].

Clearly any reduction in processes leading to patient harm, incidents of staff incompetence and general bad practice are to be applauded. However, there could be a potential difficulty with this approach when one considers the context in which it operates. Janet Lyon [20] has argued that, in order for an adequate system of near-miss reporting to operate, the staff must be able to trust their employer to use the information responsibly. Various cases demonstrate that this might not be the case. Dr Stephen Bolsin, a consultant anaesthetist at Bristol Royal Infirmary, spent five years trying to draw attention to the problems with the paediatric cardiac surgery delivery. In light of such concerns the 1998 Public Interest Disclosure Act was passed to enable employees to raise concerns about dangerous or poor practice without endangering their careers, protecting whistle-blowers from sacking or victimisation.

Even with legal safeguards in place staff members could feel threatened by having to report mistakes and accidents to the risk manager [21]. The NHS Executive has stated that 'the results of the risk management process should not be used for punitive or disciplinary purposes' [22]. It also states that the information given should be kept confidential and that the informant should remain anonymous. Such confidentiality could ensure that the near-miss reporting scheme could effectively carry out the stated aims. This would be beneficial to both staff and patients and would ensure that the ethical aims of CRM schemes could be realised. As long as the possible fears of the staff are borne in mind by employers, a culture of trust could be fostered and non-punitive mechanisms developed for addressing the concerns of employees.

11.14.2   The bad doctor

A specific problem clearly arises when a health carer is reporting a colleague who is allegedly incompetent. This issue has been brought to the fore of public debate by the events at the Bristol Royal Infirmary and the consequent inquiry. The GMC's longest running disciplinary hearing recorded verdicts of professional misconduct against three senior doctors. The press reporting of these cases was emotive and largely hostile and exemplified the reduced public confidence in the ability of the medical profession to police itself [23].

The General Medical Council stipulates that it is a doctor's duty to inform the appropriate authority about a colleague whose performance is questionable:

> 'You must protect patients when you believe that a colleague's conduct, performance or health is a threat to them ... if necessary you must tell someone from the employing authority or from a regulatory body.' [19]

The Tavistock Group's statement on 'Shared ethical principles for everyone in health care' says that all health carers have a responsibility for improving the quality of health care [24]. The UKCC also has requirements in their code of conduct that nurses should, 'report to an appropriate person or authority any circumstances in which safe and appropriate care for patients cannot be provided'.

The appropriate response to an allegation of incompetence clearly depends on the type of accident or incompetence that is reported. Serious misconduct or wilfully disregarding the welfare of the patient should merit disciplinary action. The issue that is of more concern here is a genuine accident or mistake that the practitioner did not wilfully cause. Whether the accident was caused by a lack of skill or an inadequate process, these factors should be able to be addressed without the practitioner facing any form of disciplinary procedure.

One mechanism introduced by clinical governance schemes to improve and monitor health care professionals' performance is professional self-regulation.

'This process gives health professionals the opportunity to set their own standards of professional practice, conduct and discipline. To justify this freedom and maintain the trust of patients and their families, the professions are required to be accountable in an open manner for the standards they set and the way in which these are enforced.' [25]

Continuing professional development and lifelong learning is seen in the White Paper *A First Class Service* to be an essential component of clinical governance and a way of setting and monitoring standards. These could be positive moves in giving the professions clear standards and the appropriate training to meet them.

11.15   Conclusion

Clinical governance can be seen as a positive move by the Government to ensure that both Trusts and individual practitioners are more accountable and are held to be responsible for the quality of the care they deliver. However, although quality of health care provision is something we all want, the term 'quality' is very hard to define. Once it is recognised that questions of what we should be doing have important ethical dimensions, then these ethical and value judgements can be debated. Where possible value judgements can be formulated by general agreement, and at the same time these debates can allow those who use the service to have a say in what kind of NHS they wish to see.

11.16   Notes and references

1. Goodman, N. (1998) Clinical governance. *BMJ*, 317, 1725–7.
2. Secretary of State for Health (1998) *A first class service, quality in the new NHS*. NHS Executive, Leeds.
3. Campbell, A. (1999) Clinical governance: the ethical challenge to medical education, *Medical Education*, 33, 870–71.
4. Cooper *et al.* (1996) Pulmonary artery catheters in the critically ill: An overview of using the methodology of EBM. *Critical Care Clinician*, 12(4), 777–94.
5. Klein, R., Day, P. & Redmayne, S. (1996) *Managing Scarcity: Priority setting and rationing in the NHS*. Open University Press, Buckingham.
6. Rosenberg & Donald (1995) Evidence based medicine: an approach to clinical problem solving. *BMJ*, 310, 1122–6.
7. Muir Gray, J. (1997) *Evidence-based Health Care: how to make health policy and management decisions*. Churchill Livingstone, London.
8. Maynard, A. (1997) Evidence-based medicine: an incomplete method for informing treatment choices. *The Lancet*, 349, 126–8.
9. NICE (2000) Appraisal of Beta Interferon and Glatiramer for the treatment of Multiple Sclerosis. Press Release, issued 21 June 08:30, ref. NICE 2000/020.
10. NHS Executive (1996) *Promoting clinical effectiveness*. The Stationery Office, London.
11. Secretary of State for Health (1997) *The new NHS, modern, dependable*. The Stationery Office, London.
12. Hopkins & Solomon (1996) Can contacts drive clinical care? *BMJ*, 313, 477–8.
13. Suppes, P. (1979) The logic of clinical judgement: Bayesian and other approaches. In

Clinical Judgment: A Critical Appraisal, (ed. Engelhardt *et al.*) D. Reidel Publishing Company, Dordrecht, Holland.

14. Kitchiner, D. & Bundred, P. (1996) Integrated care pathways. *Archives in Disease in Childhood*, 75, 166–8.

15. Rigge, M. (1999) Patient expectations of clinical governance. In *Clinical governance: making it happen* (eds M. Lugon & J. Secker-Walker). The Royal Society of Medicine Press, London.

16. DoH (2000) *An organisation with a memory: report of an expert group on learning from adverse events in the NHS*. Department of Health, London.

17. Jones, M. (1997) *Clinical Risk Management*. Institute of Law Medicine and Bioethics, Liverpool.

18. UKCC (1992) *Professional Code of Conduct*. UKCC, London.

19. GMC (1995) *Duties of a doctor*. The General Medical Council, London.

20. Lyon, J. (1996) *The Trojan Horse: Problems of CRM*. MSc Dissertation, University of Liverpool.

21. See Wu, A. (2000) Medical error: the second victim, *BMJ*, 320, 726–7, for a discussion of the practicalities of talking about mistakes.

22. NHS Executive (1994) *Risk Management in the NHS*. The Stationery Office, London.

23. Davies, H. & Shields, A. (1999) Public trust and accountability for clinical performance: lessons from the national press reportage of the Bristol hearing. *Journal of Evaluation in Clinical Practice*, 5(3), 335–42.

24. Smith, R. *et al.* (1999) Shared ethical principles for everybody in health care: a working draft from the Tavistock Group. *BMJ*, 318, 248–51.

25. Swage, T. (2000) *Clinical Governance in Health Care Practice*, Butterworth Heinemann, Oxford.

Chapter 12
Clinical Research and Patients

A   The Legal Perspective

Marie Fox

The issue of clinical research on human patients poses complex bioethical and legal dilemmas for nurses who may be involved in research. Throughout the 1990s nurses have been assuming a greater role in conducting clinical research, in part because involvement in research may help to validate their professional status, and also due to the increasing emphasis on evidence based medicine. Nevertheless, it has been argued that there are still too few nurse researchers and that most nurses in practice are not sufficiently research aware [1]. In an attempt to remedy this, the most recent national strategy for nursing, midwifery and health visiting is committed to developing 'a strategy to influence the research and development agenda, to strengthen the capacity to undertake nursing, midwifery and health visiting research, and to use research to support nursing, midwifery and health visiting practice' [2]. Such initiatives make it imperative for nurses to have a clear understanding of the ethical and legal implications of engaging in clinical research.

The fundamental ethical and legal issue raised by research involves a balancing exercise, between the interests of the health professional carrying out research and of medical science itself on the one hand, and on the other, the welfare of those human patients who are the subject of medical research [3]. Against that backdrop, the aim of this chapter is to explore the legal framework within which clinical research may be conducted. It is worth noting that there is a relative absence of specific legal rules regulating research. Thus, although the Animals (Scientific Procedures) Act 1986 regulates research which may lawfully be carried out on animals [4], and the Human Fertilisation and Embryology Act 1990 imposes constraints on experiments on human embryos, there is no comparable statutory regime which licenses research on human patients. Equally, the common law in this area is marked by the absence of case law pertaining specifically to medical research. The only exception to this is in the case of drug trials. The upshot is that the legal framework governing research largely draws on the principles laid down in relation to consent to conventional medical treatment.

Given this absence of detailed domestic legal regulation, guidance for health professionals derives mainly from principles enshrined in international declarations and codes of practice promulgated by professional bodies. However, in the future this is likely to change given the introduction of a new framework for clinical governance and the increased involvement of the European Union, discussed below.

12.1　Definition of clinical research

Clinical research is traditionally classified in a number of ways. It is first distinguished from conventional treatment, which uses approved methods and techniques for therapeutic purposes. It is then sub-divided into two broad classes of research. The first consists of those which do not involve any direct interference with the subject, for example, those involving psychological observation [5], and the use of personal medical records or tissue samples [6]. Once again it can be difficult to draw distinctions between this and the second category – invasive research – which gives rise to much greater concern, as it involves direct physical or psychological interference with the subject. My focus in this chapter will primarily be on the issue of invasive research on human beings, but in the light of recent concerns, the issue of research using personal information and tissue samples is discussed below. Invasive research on subjects is conventionally further divided into two types:

(1)　therapeutic research is performed on a patient, and the use of new methods and techniques carries prospects of direct benefit to the patient;
(2)　non-therapeutic research involves the use of new procedures or drugs for purely or mainly scientific purposes which are unlikely to benefit the individual participant. While it may herald some collective benefit, the aim of the trial is the acquisition of scientific knowledge [7].

It is worth noting that this therapeutic/non-therapeutic dichotomy, which has generated much bioethical scholarship, has recently been subject to attack. Commentators have suggested that it is a problematic distinction for the following reasons. First, it is often difficult to distinguish between research and innovative therapy. For instance, it is unclear whether a new surgical technique, such as keyhole surgery, should be subject to special regulation, as the introduction of a new drug procedure would be [8]. Secondly, in response to the lobbying of well organised health pressure groups, such as AIDs patients, high quality clinical care and responsible research have come to be recognised as a continuum rather than a dichotomy [9].

　　Notwithstanding the validity of these points however, there may be good reason to retain the distinction between therapeutic and non-therapeutic research, given that advances attributed to non-therapeutic research have been obtained at the cost of many blighted lives. In this regard, it is significant that these costs have been disproportionately borne by members of oppressed groups in society [10]. A major advantage of the distinction is that it enables commentators to argue that there should be a greater obligation to disclose risks in the context of non-therapeutic research. Consequently, considerable controversy has been generated by the recent revision of the Declaration of Helsinki – the most prominent international agreement governing research – which in 2001 abandoned the distinction between therapeutic and non-therapeutic research.

12.2   Regulation of clinical research

12.2.1   International declarations

The Declaration of Helsinki was promulgated largely as a result of the involvement of health professionals in medical experimentation amounting to torture on stigmatised social and ethnic groups in Nazi Germany. Indeed many ethico-legal concerns raised by clinical research have their roots in the Nazi era. The aftermath of the Nuremberg trials of Nazi war criminals witnessed the promulgation of the Nuremberg Code, which in 1964 was revised and expanded by the World Health Organisation's Declaration of Helsinki. This has subsequently been amended in 1975, 1983, 1989, 1996 and 2001 [11].

   While the Nazi-era experiments remain some of the most appalling abuses of research, numerous subsequent examples highlight the continuing need for international regulation [12]. One of the major preoccupations is conducting medical research on subjects in non-Western low income countries, where standards may be lower and subjects less likely to benefit from expensive drugs marketed in the 'developed' world. Trials of AIDs drugs and vaccines in particular have prompted controversy [13]. Domestically, all nursing research carried out in the UK should comply with the fundamental principles enshrined in this declaration.

   These stress that the first responsibility of the health professional is to his or her patient, and that considerations related to the well-being of the human subject should take precedence over the interests of science and society (para. 5). Risks to the patient should be carefully evaluated and researchers should be confident that they can be satisfactorily managed, and that subjects are fully informed of them (para. 17). Furthermore, biomedical research must conform to generally accepted scientific procedures, be approved by an appropriate ethical review committee, carried out by those who are scientifically qualified and supervised by a clinically competent medical professional (paras 13–15). The 1975 revision of the Helsinki declaration recommended codes of practice for researchers, and has resulted in guidelines promulgated by national bodies, of which the most prominent are those produced by the Royal College of Physicians [14], and the Royal College of Nursing [15], as well as the guidelines which the Department of Health has issued for Local Research Ethics Committees [16]. These are underpinned by similar principles to those contained in the Helsinki declaration. More recently, the Council of Europe's Convention on Human Rights and Biomedicine (1997) reaffirmed these principles. It also stressed that the interests and welfare of the human being shall prevail over the sole interest of society or science and that any intervention in the health field, including research, must be carried out in accordance with relevant professional standards and obligations [17].

   Although such guidelines are useful in stipulating patient rights and stressing the ethical obligations of researchers, they are not directly enforceable in law, and indeed the UK has yet to sign the Convention on Human Rights and Biomedicine. Moreover, inevitably guidance is framed in terms which leave considerable discretion to the researcher, particularly in assessing physical, psychological and emotional harm.

12.2.2   The criminal law

Notwithstanding the considerable discretion thus entrusted to the scientific researcher, it should be noted that all activities by health professionals, as is the case with all citizens, are circumscribed by the criminal law. English criminal law provides that undue harm may not be inflicted on an individual even if they are prepared to consent to the infliction of such harm (*R v. Brown* (1993)). In a consultation paper, *Consent in the Criminal Law*, the Law Commission (the body which deals with law reform issues in England and Wales) addressed the subject of what harm a person may legitimately consent to. It provisionally suggested that:

> 'a person should not be guilty of an offence if she causes injury to another, of whatever degree of seriousness, if such injury is caused during the course of properly approved medical research (i.e. approved by a Local Research Ethics Committee) and with the consent of the other person'. [18]

This is consistent with the Law Commission's general stance regarding medical treatment, which is that legitimate clinical procedures may be undertaken regardless of the degree of harm which may result. However, the Commission did not consider the issue of how acceptable risk may be defined. This leaves open the question whether a high risk trial may be undertaken if the patient is prepared to accept that risk – a matter considered below in the context of xenotransplantation. Certainly, failure to obtain the consent of an individual before they are included in a clinical trial may give rise to a criminal prosecution for battery. There is a remote possibility that a prosecution could be brought for manslaughter if a research subject died while participating in a high risk trial.

12.2.3   The civil law

As well as potentially constituting a criminal offence, battery/trespass to the person is also a civil wrong entitling the patient to sue for compensation. Thus, where any research involves examining, operating on or injecting the patient, consent must be obtained in advance for it to be carried out lawfully; unauthorised contact entitles the patient to damages. Consequently, obtaining adequate consent to participation is the key legal requirement in relation to nursing research since, in the absence of statutory regulation, authority to carry out research on an adult human subject derives from that person's consent [19]. Effectively, English law imposes responsibility on the individual research subject to protect themself from abuse by giving or withholding consent [20]. The upshot, as Berg has argued, is that virtually all documented cases of abuses of medical experimentation have been those which failed to employ satisfactory informed consent procedures [21]. Given this, it is not surprising that the key principle enshrined in the Helsinki declaration is that:

> 'each potential subject must be adequately informed of the aims, methods, sources of funding, any possible conflicts of interest, institutional affiliations of the researcher, the anticipated benefits and potential risks of the study and the discomfort it may entail. The subject should be informed of the right to abstain

from participation in the study or to withdraw consent to participate at any time without reprisal. After ensuring that the subject has understood the information, the physician should then obtain the subject's freely-given consent, preferably in writing. If the consent cannot be obtained in writing, the non-written consent must be formally documented and witnessed' (para. 22).

Similarly, in a nursing context, the UKCC's Guidelines for Professional Practice provide, *inter alia*, that arrangements for obtaining consent must be clearly understood by all those involved; patients must not be exposed to unacceptable risks; and they should be included in the development of proposed projects where appropriate [22].

The major issue in relation to consent to nursing research is how to ensure that the consent is 'freely-given' and 'informed'. As we saw in Chapter 7, in relation to medical treatment, the courts have stated that so long as a patient gives a very general consent to an operation being undertaken, the health professional will not be liable in the tort of battery (*Chatterton* v. *Gerson* (1981)). In *Sidaway* v. *Bethlem* (1985) the House of Lords rejected the view that the doctrine of informed consent forms part of English law in the context of medical treatment [23]. Nevertheless, although there have been no decided English cases on the duty of disclosure pertaining to medical research, it is generally accepted by legal commentators that the law as set out in *Sidaway* and subsequent cases does not apply in the context of research [24]. Thus, someone who volunteers for research is entitled to a fuller explanation of the nature of the trial and risks it carries than would be the case in relation to medical treatment. It is highly probable that English law would follow Canadian law [25], in adopting an objective test requiring a researcher to disclose all relevant facts which a reasonable subject would wish to know, and to provide the opportunity for questions, to which full and honest answers would be given [26]. This means that if inadequate information is given to a research subject the researcher could be liable in negligence proceedings.

However, given that researchers themselves may lack adequate information about the risks of a proposed new drug or course of treatment, some commentators question whether informed consent is truly possible in the context of clinical research [27]. Certainly it is questionable whether the intended experimental subject can validly consent to procedures the results of which are uncertain, of dubious benefit or clearly harmful – issues which are canvassed below in relation to xenotransplantation [28]. It is thus not surprising that in those few court cases in which judges have explored the issue of consent, they have tended to limit their role to ensuring that fully informed, voluntary consent has been given. Yet, as Tobias has pointed out, notwithstanding the legal emphasis on informed consent 'neither lawyers, ethicists, nor medical scientists have so far agreed precisely what this term actually means' [29]. Furthermore, McNeil has contended that the emphasis which courts have traditionally placed on consent is inadequate to regulate experimentation on human subjects. In his view, the focus on consent fails to fully address issues such as the weighting of the risks and benefits of experimentation for subject and society, and enables courts to avoid issues like whether they should endorse guidelines for researchers [30].

Legislative guidelines do exist in relation to trials of new pharmaceuticals.

Under the Medicines Act 1968 and the Medicines for Human Use (Authorisation Etc.) Regulations 1994, before drugs are used in clinical trials, a clinical trial certificate (CTC) must generally be obtained from the licensing authority, unless a clinical trial exemption has been granted [31]. CTCs will only be granted where prior research indicates that harm to humans will be unlikely. A complex reporting system has been established under this legislation to monitor the impact of the drug in question, whereby unexpected outcomes during treatment with the drug must be reported to the Committee on Safety of Medicines. However, in 2001 queries were raised about the effectiveness of these procedures [32]. Earlier that year a European Directive was issued on the approximation of the laws regulating clinical trials of medicinal products, which aims to ensure that good clinical practice is observed in the design, conduct, recording and reporting of clinical trials on human subjects [33].

12.2.4   *The relationship between the investigator and research subject*

Further concerns stem from the problematic nature of the relationship of the research subject with the health care professional engaged in research. As McNeil argues, the history of human experimentation is one of imbalance in favour of the interests of the researcher [34]. It has been extensively documented how in the research context the role of the health care professional has changed from that of a physician (or more recently a nurse) to a scientific investigator, to become, in Jay Katz's term, a 'physician-investigator' (or 'nurse-investigator'). Not only does this entail a potential conflict of loyalties to patients, employers and research aims, owing to the multiple priorities as teacher, researcher, health professional and administrator [35], it also means that the researcher is likely to be seen in a more ambivalent light by the subject. Kennedy has suggested that a health professional's primary duty to care for their patient is inevitably compromised by their duty to carry out clinical trials with due scientific rigour [36]. The researcher's commitment to such rigour leaves the patient in an even more disempowered position than is normally the case in engagement with health professionals, since requirements of scientific ideology generally require the researcher to view the subject with dispassion and detachment [37]. As Katz points out [38], it follows that:

> '. . . the commitment to objectivity invites the investigator's thought processes to become objectified and, in turn, to transform the human beings who are the subjects of research into data points to be plotted on a chart that will prove or disprove a research hypothesis'.

Such power imbalances are especially likely to arise where the research subject is differentiated from the investigator by factors such as gender, class, race and ethnicity, which may make communicating more difficult. Given these power imbalances, researchers need to bear in mind Morehouse's claim that '[t]here are many ways of introducing a research project to a patient which fall short of pressurising the patients, but certainly do not conform to total objectivity' [39]. This may be particularly true in the case of vulnerable groups of patients, discussed below. The Declaration of Helsinki provides that:

'When obtaining informed consent for the research project the physician should be particularly cautious if the subject is in a dependent relationship with the physician or may consent under duress. In that case the informed consent should be obtained by a well-informed physician who is not engaged in the investigation and who is completely independent of this relationship' (para. 23).

In common with many legal documents, the Helsinki declaration focuses on the role of doctors. However, the tension between scientific dispassion and concern for the patient is likely to be particularly disconcerting for nurses. Not only is it arguable that nursing is more firmly grounded in notions of care and nurturance than other health professions [40], but in practice nurses tend to have closer relationships with their patients than do doctors. It may follow that nurses are viewed as better placed to explain the consequences of enrolment in a trial to a patient and to obtain their consent. Certainly, if a nurse finds herself in the position of seeking consent, guidelines promulgated by bodies such as the Medical Research Council (MRC) and General Medical Council (GMC) stress the need for explanations to be given in clear and easily comprehensible language. Any special communication or language needs of the participants should be taken into account.

As pointed out by the Griffiths Review into the conduct of research trials involving children at North Staffordshire Hospital during the 1990s [41], it is important to appreciate the difficulty of understanding and giving a valid consent at a time of severe physical, psychological or emotional stress (para. 14.3.6). Potential subjects should also be given written information and time to reflect on it. Draft guidance, on which the GMC is currently consulting, stresses that patients or volunteers are entitled to an explanation as to why they have been asked to participate, which should include an accurate description of the patient's clinical condition [42]. The MRC suggests that it is useful, as well as good practice, to seek advice from consumers or lay persons in drafting information for potential subjects [43]. As noted above, participants should also be clearly informed of their right to withdraw from participation at any time without reprisal [44]. Additionally, they must be given an explanation of how personal information will be stored, transmitted and published.

12.2.5   Consent to randomised controlled trials

Particular problems arise in the context of consent to randomised controlled trials (RCTs). In recent years RCTs, which aim to compare treatments or approaches in two or more groups of subjects who are allocated randomly to those groups [45], have been promoted as the most scientifically valid method of evaluating procedures [46]. Those who endorse randomisation (which aims to rule out a purely psychological reaction to new drugs) argue that if drugs are not investigated using randomisation and blinding of both researchers and patients to the process, then there is a strong possibility that bias will enter the study and affect the results. However, others have argued that RCTs may adversely affect the health professional–patient relationship by harming the bond of trust and mutual respect which is the ideal of medical practice [47]. Oakley suggests that RCTs are ethically problematic since chance allocation may be antithetical to good ethical practice [48]. In particular, she expresses concern at how:

'the tension between the scientific aims of research and the humane treatment of individuals ... is expressed in the very strategy of designing an experiment so as to restrict people's freedom to discuss with one another the commonality of the process in which they are engaged'. (p. 188)

What is certain is that the weighing up of risks and how they are presented to potential participants is crucial with RCTs. Fletcher *et al.* suggest that the fundamental issue is the purpose for which the research is being carried out, and that generally a trial should only proceed 'if the likely benefits to the individual taking part in the research and/or to society as a whole far outweigh the risks of participation' [49]. Furthermore, the Declaration of Helsinki provides that '[p]hysicians should cease any investigation if the risks are found to outweigh the potential benefits or if there is conclusive proof of positive and beneficial results' (para. 17).

Given the uncertainties until such a point is reached, RCTs pose considerable problems for the law on informed consent, since the technique of randomisation makes it more difficult for the researcher to fully explain the risks to an individual patient. Certainly, the crucial issue in obtaining consent will be how the risks and benefits of the proposed research are presented to the patient. Tobias has pointed to the practical difficulties of gaining informed consent in such trials, especially given the potential for misconception and anxiety if the consequences of randomisation are fully explained to the patient. He argues that instead we should trust health professionals to engage in randomisation without explicit consent [50]. However, the consensus among legal commentators endorses Kennedy's view that with RCTs it is particularly important that the materiality of risk should be defined according to what the particular patient would want to know [51].

Numerous problems with the process for obtaining such consent were highlighted by the Griffiths Review into events at North Staffordshire, in which nurses were centrally involved (para 9.3.5) [52]. The review panel found that the nursing sister assigned to a project focusing on the treatment of respiratory problems in the premature new-born baby did not appear to have been provided with a protocol or system of documentation which made sure that everything was complete for all patients. It found that in general the nursing staff lacked adequate research experience, yet were not offered any training, for the tasks that they were being asked to do. Inadequate supervision by the researchers, coupled with a lack of support from the Trust nursing management, contributed to problems in documenting whether consent forms had been completed [53]. There were particular concerns about the adequacy of information given to parents who were asked to enter their children in a trial in which a new technique – continuous negative extrathoracic pressure (CNEP) – was compared with the conventional treatment of positive pressure ventilation, given that some of the children subsequently suffered brain damage or died. Hopefully the introduction of more detailed guidance on clinical governance (detailed below) will obviate these problems, but nurses who are concerned by the conduct of trials should be prepared to 'blow the whistle' [54].

Another contested feature is the extent to which placebos should form part of RCTs. At the time of writing, under UK law patients may be given new treatments, established treatments or placebos, depending on the group to which they are allocated. However, a further controversial amendment to the Declaration of Helsinki now states that the use of so-called placebo controlled trials is only acceptable if there is no standard proven treatment of the disease being investigated (para. 29) [55]. Guideline 7 of the revised version of the CIOMS guidelines [56] provides that any decision to use placebos in place of the best current method 'requires a sound scientific and ethical reason', and the commentary on this guideline adds that a placebo-control group need not be untreated, since the treatment to be tested and a placebo may each be added to the standard treatment.

12.2.6   *Research using personal information or human tissue*

Many significant medical advances have resulted not from research trials involving human subjects, but from the use of personal health information or human tissues samples retained following post mortem examinations. For instance, such research has improved understanding of suspected health hazards, facilitated recognition of the epidemiology of new diseases (such as new variant CJD and its relation to the BSE epidemic) and led to ways of reducing cot deaths. For many years such research was seen as less ethically problematic than research on human subjects, especially as well co-ordinated use of such material can reduce the research demands on patients and the need for animal research. Yet more recently such research has become hugely contentious. In particular, public outcry over unauthorised retention of children's organs at both Bristol Royal Infirmary and Alder Hey Hospital in Liverpool has led to subsequent public inquiries and recommendations for legislation [57].

In the meantime new guidelines have been issued by a number of professional organisations [58]. Interim guidance promulgated by the BMA highlights the importance of recognising the emotional implications for grieving relatives of a request to retain tissue [59]. Given the findings of the Bristol and Alder Hey inquiries, it stresses that parents and relatives should have the opportunity to receive as much detail as possible about the post mortem examination and subsequent use of tissues, although any request to receive only limited information should be respected (Guideline 2). The document also recommends viewing consent-giving as a process rather than a single event, so that relatives should be given the opportunity to speak to various health professionals at different stages before making a final decision about long-term use and retention of tissue (Guideline 4). However, whilst recognising this, the BMA also takes the view that where possible, it should be the responsibility of the 'responsible clinician' (normally the consultant) to obtain consent, unless relatives have built up a particular rapport with another member of the team with whom they would prefer to discuss the matter (Guideline 5). Relatives should be made aware that they may consent to certain pieces of tissue being used and not others, and that they may authorise some uses of tissue but not others (Guideline 9).

New MRC guidelines similarly focus on consent [60]. They recommend a two-part consent process, the donor first being asked to consent to the specific experiments that are already planned and then to give broader consent for storage and future use for certain types of research. These guidelines also highlight the importance of written consent and the need for information to potential participants to be presented in a form they can understand.

Similarly the use of personal information in medical research has proven contentious. The MRC has issued guidance stating that researchers should ensure that they have each person's explicit consent to obtain, hold and use personal information where this is practicable [61].

12.3   Ethical review

12.3.1   Research ethics committees

To a certain extent the regulatory focus has now shifted from an emphasis on obtaining consent to ensuring compliance with codes of research practice, following the introduction of ethical review. Since 1968 official NHS policy has been that local research ethics committees (LRECs) should be established to oversee clinical research within the NHS. LRECs are governed by Department of Health guidelines (1991) in which their function is defined as advising on whether a research proposal is ethically acceptable. The Department of Health is currently engaged in a consultation exercise on draft new governance arrangements for NHS research ethics committees [62]. Ethics committees are envisaged as independent bodies, comprising both health care professionals and lay persons, who are charged with the responsibility of protecting the rights and well-being of human subjects involved in a trial. The DoH guidelines recommend that the first question to be asked by each research ethics committee is whether the scientific merit of the proposal has been correctly assessed by the researcher. The committee must take into account any discomfort or distress which the project may cause the research subject, any hazards which may arise during the project and precautions which should be introduced to deal with them. It must then carefully assess the extent to which the health of the research subject will be affected by involvement in a trial. Para. 7.3 of the present guidelines states that:

> 'Benefit may be weighed against risk in two different ways. First and most obviously the patient may benefit. This is typified in a therapeutic trial where at least one of the treatments offered may be beneficial to the patient. Benefits may be considerable, for example, in cancer treatment and may counter balance even high risk to the individual. Second, society rather than the individual may benefit. In such situations however large the benefit, to expose a participant to anything more than a minimal risk needs very careful consideration and would rarely be ethical.'

12.3.2   The limitations of research ethics committees

Although the existence of ethics committees is clearly desirable, there are considerable limitations to their effectiveness as a mechanism for scrutinising and monitoring clinical research. First, there is no requirement for trials undertaken outside the NHS to receive ethics committee approval, although some private organisations have established their own ethics committees. Therefore, a researcher contravenes no law in carrying out research without ethics committee approval. However, failure to obtain such approval will lead to difficulties in publishing research.

Moreover, there is considerable dispute over variations in the practices of ethics committees, especially since trials are scrutinised on a local rather than national basis. In 1996 the Department of Health recommended that regional bodies – multi-centre research ethics committees (MRECs) – should be established to scrutinise multi-centre research protocols where it is proposed to undertake a number of trials at different locations throughout the country. While this certainly reduces variation in local rates of approval, since LRECs are required to state reasons if they reject a protocol approved by an MREC, a cynical view is that they are a convenient way of enabling researchers and drug companies to gain approval for projects notwithstanding objections at a local level. It is also worth noting that with the growth of new areas of biotechnology, such as reproductive technologies, gene therapy and xenotransplantation, a proliferating number of committees have been established to oversee research, with consequent problems concerning the overlapping roles and functions of these various bodies [63]. However, the research governance framework (see end of this section) promulgated in 2001 aims to eliminate such variations in practice.

The limitations of research ethics committees became strikingly apparent during the investigation into research on children at North Staffordshire Hospital. The Griffiths Inquiry found that, although the North Staffordshire LREC generally operated in accordance with Department of Health Guidelines, the level of detail in their minutes compared unsatisfactorily with minutes provided by a selection of other LRECs to the review. Additionally, the computer-held register of research projects failed to include all the details required by the guidelines. The inquiry also noted a lack of clarity in respect of how and when variations to a research project were to be reported [64]. Moreover the LREC was criticised for doing little to ascertain whether its opinion was well informed or bore any relation to what other ethical review committees did or might have done in similar circumstances – something which is increasingly regarded as good practice (para. 9.2.2). These criticisms indicate the increasingly onerous duties which are entailed by membership of such committees.

A further concern about the role of research ethics committees is that they have inadequate resources to monitor research, once the initial approval is granted [65]. McNeil contends that research ethics committees are typical of self-regulating groups in their failure to deal adequately with non-compliance [66], especially if the researcher is not seeking overseas grants or publication in international journals [67]. Although the Declaration of Helsinki stresses the obligation on researchers to provide monitoring information to the ethical review committee and in particular to report adverse events (para. 13), there is generally no sanction for failure to do so. In an effort to tackle this, the Medical Research Council requires that applicants for funding include with their research protocol their plans to ensure independent supervision of the clinical trial. They recommend that this involve the establishment of a trial steering committee which should include at least one of the principal investigators conducting the research, and at least three independent members, one of whom would chair the committee. It would meet to approve the final protocol before the start of the trial and thereafter at least annually to monitor the progress of the trial and to maximise the chances of completing it within the agreed time scale [68]. In similar vein, the consultation paper on draft governance arrangements for RECs encourages RECs to follow up their initial grant of approval by seeking progress reports. Nevertheless, until the implementation of the Clinical Trials Directive (see p. 257), the absence of any legal provision for monitoring remains a concern, since in practice most committees approve over 90% of research proposals after asking the researchers to consider minor modifications [69].

In the USA similar criticisms led to the establishment of a National Bioethics Advisory Commission to provide advice and recommendations on the appropriateness of certain government policies and practices in bioethics, including principles for the ethical conduct of research [70]. Some commentators have called for a similar commission to be set up in the UK [71]. Such developments are now being superseded at European level by the adoption of the EU Directive on trials of medicinal products, which, as noted above, aims to ensure conformity among EU member states. The Directive stresses the importance of monitoring clinical trials. Before commencing any clinical trial of medical products, the sponsor will be required to submit a valid request for authorisation to the competent authority of the relevant member state. If a member state has objective grounds for considering that the conditions in the request for authorisation are no longer met, or has doubts about the safety or scientific validity of the clinical trial, it will have powers to suspend or prohibit the clinical trial, or inform those responsible for conducting the trial how to remedy the situation (Article 12). Member states will be required to appoint investigators to inspect the sites on which clinical trials are conducted (Article 15) and they must report all serious adverse events (Article 16).

In addition to general doubts about the operation of research ethics committees, their composition is a matter of some concern. In its advice to nurse researchers, the UKCC recommends that they have regard to the make-up of the LREC, and whether there are registered practitioners on it [72]. However, a more pertinent problem is the under-representation of lay people and the fact that one British study found that women and ethnic minority groups are poorly represented [73]. A further issue relates to the lack of training for members. Thus, the North Staffordshire Inquiry found that many members of the ethics committee had never been offered training. This is a central plank of the new clinical governance framework and the proposed new Department of Health guidance on research ethics committees. The North Staffordshire Inquiry also stresses that appointment of members should be an open process, compatible with Nolan standards and requiring public advertisement in the media as well as professional networks and the submission of CVs. It proposes that out of the recommended 12–18 members there should be a balanced age and gender distribution, while efforts should be made to recruit ethnic minorities and those with disabilities.

12.3.3   Research fraud and deception

A further obstacle to ensuring accountability of researchers is that cases of deception and fraud have been reported with increasing frequency throughout the 1990s [74]. Since scarce funding leads to pressure to demonstrate results for money invested and to publish widely for career advancement, there is considerable temptation to falsify results. Recently numerous prestigious journals have acknowledged the extent of research fraud [75]. Although the Royal College of Physicians have stressed the necessity of following good practice and indicated in 1991 the need to establish a body to investigate allegations of fraud, no action has yet been taken on this proposal [76]. In the meantime it remains the case that it is the threat of litigation that holds researchers accountable. A more general problem with publishing research is that articles are much more likely to secure publication if the conclusions are positive, with the result that published research provides only a very incomplete picture of research projects actually undertaken [77].

12.4   Vulnerable groups of research subjects

Researchers need to be sensitive to the fact that some groups of potential subjects may be particularly vulnerable to pressure to participate in medical research, either because of doubts regarding their competence to participate or because of their situation where vulnerability is exacerbated by institutional and attitudinal factors. Particular concerns have been raised regarding research on children or mentally incompetent adults, and it is widely recognised that these groups should be accorded special protection. A specific failing identified by the Griffiths Review at North Staffordshire was the lack of specific guidance to researchers on how valid consent is to be obtained in vulnerable groups. Too often it was simply assumed that researchers were aware of the useful guidance contained in the Royal College of Physicians' guidelines. Once again this highlights the need for researchers to be fully informed of their legal obligations and current professional guidance.

12.4.1   Children

While most research may be undertaken on competent adults, the different developmental, physiological and psychological differences in children, which make age- and development-related research important for their benefit, may necessitate the use of child subjects [78]. As we saw in Chapter 10, the law permits a child to consent to medical treatment if she is over 16 or is *Gillick*-competent [79]. The Department of Health Guidelines provide that these principles apply to therapeutic research, but stress that 'research proposals should only involve children where it is absolutely essential to do so and the information cannot be obtained using adult subjects' [80] In the case of non-therapeutic research, the guidelines suggest that 'the child must be subject to no more than minimal risk as a result of his/her participation' [81]. Once again, no guidance is provided on the nature of minimal risk, although the British Paediatric Association has stressed the special need for caution in weighing up risks and benefits where research on children is proposed [82]. Guideline 14 of the draft CIOMS guidance [83], *Research Involving Children*, provides that prior to undertaking research involving children the researcher must ensure that:

'– children will not be involved in research that might equally well be carried out with adults;
– the purpose of the research is to obtain knowledge relevant to the health needs of children;
– a parent or legal guardian of each child has given permission;
– the consent of each child has been obtained to the extent of the child's capabilities;
– the child's refusal to participate in research must always be respected unless, according to the research protocol, the child would receive therapy for which there is no medically acceptable alternative;
– the risks of participation are justified, and should not be greater than the risk attached to routine medical or psychological examination, unless an ethical review committee is persuaded that slight or minor increases above such risk are permitted because the object of the research is sufficiently important.'

Researchers should note that it is important to take account of the different capabilities of children. Thus, older children who are capable of giving informed consent should be selected ahead of younger children, unless there are significant age-related scientific reasons to include younger children [84]. The CIOMS guidance suggests that it may be assumed that children over the age of 13 will normally be competent to give consent. However it adds that their consent should be complemented by that of a parent or guardian, although it is not strictly necessary in law. The recent European Directive also stresses that minors should receive, from staff with experience with minors, information pertaining to the trial and its risks and benefits (article 4(b)). Where a child or young person lacks the requisite maturity to consent herself, the researcher should obtain proxy consent from the person with parental power. However, it is highly questionable whether a child may be compelled to be involved in a clinical trial, even if the proxy decision-maker consents [85].

12.4.2 The mentally incapacitated adult

Although incompetent adults differ from children in many ways, similar issues are raised by proposals to carry out research on these groups. Once again the competence of the incapacitated person will have to be carefully assessed in relation to the particular procedure. As discussed in Chapter 7, a patient may be competent to consent to one form of treatment but not to another. This applies equally in the research context. The DoH Guidelines provide in para 4.7 that:

'Research on mentally disordered people requires particular care and sensitivity bearing in mind that they are vulnerable and some may not be able to give consent. There is a need to weigh the rights of an individual to consent or to refuse to take part in research and the particular status of those unable to consent against the need for research to advance the knowledge and treatment of mental disorders.'

The Convention on Human Rights and Biomedicine provides that non-therapeutic research on the incapacitated may *exceptionally* be carried out, provided that it entails only minimal risks and burdens for the individual concerned and has the aim of contributing:

> 'through significant improvement in the scientific understanding of the individual's condition, disease or disorder to the ultimate attainment of results capable of conferring benefit on the person concerned or other persons in the same age category or afflicted with the same disease or disorder or having the same condition (Article 17).'

The revisions to the CIOMS guidance [86] suggest that in cases where prospective subjects lack capacity to consent, permission should be obtained from a legally appointed guardian or responsible relative (Guideline 15). However, under English law, in contrast to the situation with children, there is no available proxy consent-giver for the incompetent adult [87]. As we saw in Chapter 7A, medical treatment may be provided if it is in the patient's best interests [88]. Recent cases on consent (see Chapter 7A) have paid greater attention to human rights concerns in assessing best interests and there are compelling arguments that the *Bolam* test is a wholly inappropriate basis on which to determine whether an incompetent adult may be enrolled in a research project. It is thus suggested that undertaking non-therapeutic research on a mentally incompetent adult is prima facie unlawful [89].

These concerns over the legal uncertainty and the vulnerability of the mentally incompetent adult led the Law Commission to propose that non-therapeutic research may be undertaken in certain situations but subject to additional safeguards. In particular, it suggested that any such proposal should be referred to a new mental incapacity research committee. This proposed new body would have to be satisfied that it was desirable to have knowledge of the participant's incapacitating condition, that any trial would not expose the participant to more than negligible risk, and that this information could not be obtained by research on those who were competent to consent [90]. Subsequently, a Government Green Paper on mental incapacity has questioned whether it is desirable to establish yet another body to scrutinise clinical trials [91], so that it seems unlikely that this proposal will be enacted. However, as one commentator has pointed out, there are advantages in referring this type of complex decision to a body which has built up specialist knowledge, rather than leaving it to be determined at a local level [92].

12.4.3 Other vulnerable groups

Researchers should be conscious of the fact that other potential subject groups may feel under particular pressure to participate in research, not through doubts about their competence, but because their circumstances render them vulnerable. Nurses will typically carry out research on patients, and patients may feel compelled to participate out of a sense of obligation to the health professionals treating them. Other groups who may feel a similar obligation are medical and nursing students. Great care needs to be taken to explain rights to refuse or withdraw consent when research is proposed for these groups. Particular care may also be necessary with pregnant women, or women of child-bearing age, in view of the possible effects on the fetus should the research subject be or become pregnant [93]. However, it is controversial to label them as 'vulnerable' and it is important that such women should not be excluded from research protocols, as discussed in section 12.4.5.

12.4.4   Inducements and conflicts of interest

When recruiting members of vulnerable groups for clinical research, it is particularly important that LRECs examine the extent to which the patient may be influenced by financial inducements. The DoH Guidelines for LRECs provide that any payment to volunteers in trials should be limited to payment for expense, time and inconvenience reasonably incurred [94].

Aside from inducements for subjects to enter trials, health care professionals also need to be sure that inducements or perks from drug companies sponsoring trials do not influence how they present benefits to potential participants. In 2000 it was reported that the outgoing editor of the prestigious *Journal of the American Medical Association* had called for restrictions on stock ownership and other financial incentives for researchers, claiming that growing conflicts of interests were tainting scientific research [95]. That this has come to be regarded as a pressing ethical concern is reflected in the revised Declaration of Helsinki, which hitherto had been silent on the need for transparency about economic incentives in research. It now provides that all possible conflicts of interest should be disclosed (para. 22, see section 12.2.3). In its recent guidance, the Medical Research Council has pointed to the potential for conflicts of interest, where a researcher's scientific judgement could be unduly influenced by a secondary interest, such as financial gain or personal, academic or political advancement. It suggests that researchers should automatically ask themselves, 'Would I feel comfortable if others learn about my secondary interest in this matter or perceived that I had one?'. If the answer is negative, that signals that the interest must be disclosed and addressed according to the appropriate policies established by employers, peer review bodies or journals [96].

12.4.5   The pool of available research subjects

Given the historical emphasis on protecting research subjects from the impact of research, the exclusion of potential subjects from consideration for clinical protocols has only been identified as a significant bioethical issue since the 1980s. This follows a paradigm shift in how enrolment in clinical trials is viewed [97]. While research on human subjects was initially perceived as a necessary aspect of public health, and then as a transgression of individual rights tantamount to torture, it has since the 1980s increasingly come to be regarded as an avenue of access to better medical care. This shift was largely prompted by the thalidomide and DES drug disasters, which led to criticisms of the policy of excluding pregnant women from trials, given the catastrophic impact of these drugs on children born to women who took them during pregnancy [98]. As noted above, pregnant women have historically been categorised as a vulnerable group of patients, and as a result, guidance issued to researchers often explicitly excluded certain women from biomedical research, particularly if they were pregnant or of child-bearing age.

While explicit exclusions are now less common, in the UK the DoH Guidelines state that if it is intended to use women as research subjects, the possibility of their being or *becoming pregnant* should always be considered, and the researcher should always justify the recruitment of women of child-bearing age [99]. This provision raises important questions concerning the autonomy of both pregnant women [100] and women of child-bearing age. While the justifications for such explicit exclusions are generally couched in the rhetoric of protecting women and their unborn children, it is more likely to be due to fears of liability for any teratogenic impact on the unborn child. However, Merton has convincingly argued that such fears are more apparent than real, since no successful claim has been brought and a proper warning of known and unknown risks would in all probability extinguish the strict liability claims of both subjects and their children for either pre-natal or preconceptual harm [101]. Furthermore, excluding women from research may ultimately be a more dangerous legal stance; pharmaceutical researchers in particular leave themselves open to law suits by excluding women, given that their products are then aggressively marketed to women.

The second factor responsible for changing the way in which clinical trials are viewed has been the HIV/AIDS pandemic, which has further politicised the field of clinical research. Patients with these conditions have campaigned for just allocation of access to research and have characterised clinical trials as treatment when there is no proven treatment for a medical condition (thereby further blurring the dichotomy between research and therapy, noted at the beginning of this chapter). Stimulated by these developments, patients with other diseases, notably breast cancer and Alzheimer's disease, and their families, have become more vocal about access to experimental drugs and treatments and have asserted the right to participate in trials. Consequently, being a research subject is no longer viewed as an unqualified sacrifice – rather it is seen as a potentially risky opportunity. The upshot is that researchers, long sensitised to the need for *protection of* research subjects, must now also focus on the need to *include* individuals and groups. All researchers should thus bear in mind the need for increased efforts to recruit certain populations, including patients with AIDS, minorities, the elderly and women. This constitutes one aspect of good experimental design of a research protocol, as well as fulfilling the general ethical obligation of fairness or justice.

12.4.6 Review of research and compensation

If a clinical trial is approved by a research ethics committee, then as we have seen, the conduct of that research is left up to the research team and there are limited possibilities for review. However, if a research subject is injured as a result of defective drugs or surgical appliances, they may be able to bring an action under the Consumer Protection Act 1987, arguing that a defective product was supplied. Although liability under the Act is strict, the real problem for a litigant taking action is the likelihood of researchers invoking the 'state of the art' defence, i.e. that any defects in the product were not ascertainable given the state of scientific knowledge when it was marketed. In all other cases where injury results from participation in a research project the only cause of action lies in negligence, but such an action would probably fail if a properly conducted research programme had been approved by an ethics committee and carried out in accordance with a responsible body of professional opinion [102].

Given the difficulties in pursuing a legal remedy for injury suffered as a result of participation in clinical trials, attention has focused on mechanisms for compensating those who suffer harm. There is no formal legal requirement that volunteers for research should be indemnified, although the Association of British Pharmaceutical Industry guidelines provide that where commercial companies sponsor research they should give contractually binding guarantees to healthy volunteers if they should be injured. However these guidelines are not mandatory [103]. In recognition of the inadequate protection given to participants in clinical research, the Pearson Commission recommended years ago that 'any volunteer for medical research who suffers severe damage as a result should have a cause of action, on the basis of strict liability, against the authority to whom he has consented to make himself available' [104]. However no government has taken action to implement this proposal [105]. The possibility of a major claim for compensation is particularly likely in the case of certain new technologies, where potentially very hazardous risks are difficult to estimate with any degree of certainty, as discussed in the following case study on xenotransplantation. The new European Union Directive on medicinal products, noted above, will require that ethics committees take into account the provision for indemnity or compensation in the event of injury or death when deciding whether to approve a clinical trial (Article 6 (h)).

A further source of controversy concerns the care provided in the aftermath of clinical trials. As noted above, one incentive to enrol in a clinical trial is the way it offers an avenue to high quality medical care, but this raises ethical issues about the care of patients once their participation in research is complete.

12.5   Case study – xenotransplantation

As new biotechnologies are developed, new ethical and legal dilemmas are raised for researchers. One area which potentially gives rise to huge concerns is that of xenotransplantation.

Xenotransplantation may be defined as the transplant of tissue between species. Most attention to date has centred on the transplant of whole animal organs (such as hearts, kidneys and livers) into humans. Biotechnology companies are currently breeding genetically engineered pigs, which are viewed as a likely source of these organs. The ethics and safety of xenotransplantation was considered in two major reports in the mid-1990s [106]. Both broadly concluded that xenotransplantation, using pigs, was an ethically acceptable solution to the chronic organ shortage, although it was not at that point safe to proceed to human trials given the incalculable risks posed.

The major risk identified is that diseases will spread from the pig source to the recipient and possibly the broader population. Notwithstanding such concerns, it is now clear that animal trials have progressed to the stage where there is an increased impetus towards permitting human trials. The decision to proceed to human trials would have to be approved by the Xenotransplantation Interim Regulatory Authority established on the recommendation of the Department of Health review of this technology (the Kennedy Report). However, it is envisaged that this body, and any subsequent statutory body which may be set up by legislation, would operate alongside existing LREC and MRECs, so that any decision in principle to authorise clinical trials will still require LREC/MREC approval.

Even if such approval is granted, questions remain concerning the role of health professionals involved in such trials. As with enrolment in most clinical trials, the crucial issue will be obtaining valid consent. However, xenotransplantation raises particular problems over and above the general difficulties of obtaining informed consent. In the first place, potential recipients of pig tissue are in an especially difficult situation, where it is questionable whether the decision to enter clinical trials actually represents an informed choice. If a particular class of patients realises that the only alternatives to enrolling in a potentially hazardous clinical trial are the slim chance of obtaining a suitable organ, or death, the likelihood is that they will be willing to take that risk regardless of the hazards it potentially creates for them or others.

Secondly, as an entirely new procedure, arguably it is not possible to assess the inherent risks with any degree of accuracy. In general, little is known about pig diseases, but the history of animal–human viruses lends plausibility to the view that xenotransplantation offers a unique opportunity for prion-type diseases to jump the species barrier. This is particularly so if source animals are genetically engineered with human genes. Two problems arise. The first is the practical difficulty posed by the Kennedy Report's suggestion that huge amounts of information would have to be given to research subjects. It is recommended that for an informed decision to be taken, potential recipients should be given information regarding the psychological and social effects of xenotransplantation as well as information about the source of tissue, breeding and genetic information, and animal suffering [107]. It is questionable how many patients are equipped to fully assimilate and evaluate such quantities of information.

A still more fundamental problem is whether individual recipients should be able to consent to a procedure which has the potential to unleash unsuspected hazards on the broader population. How should this sort of risk be explained to a potential participant in a clinical trial? A further issue is that, given these risks, those who enrol in the first trials, if they are authorised, must submit to surveillance and monitoring of their movements [108]. This gives rise to problems about how to present potentially very intrusive interferences with civil liberties (including the right to reproduce) to potential research subjects.

The case of xenotransplantation highlights the need for fuller consideration to be given to the adequacy of counselling and information provision when subjects are enrolled in clinical trials, especially where the research concerns new biotechnologies and there is no existing way of treating the disease [109]. This case study also raises concerns over how an effective system of scrutiny and accountability may be implemented, especially when a number of committees with potentially overlapping remits exist to regulate this procedure [110]. A final issue raised by xenotransplanatation is that, should the worst fears of its opponents be realised, a crucial factor yet to be addressed is who should bear the costs of compensating victims and paying for their health care, particularly if a major new disease is unleashed on the broader population.

12.6   Conclusions

As will be apparent from the above review, the law regulating nursing research is currently too vague and loaded in favour of the researcher. In particular there is an absence of clear guidance on consent and disclosure of risks; and too little has been done to ensure that research programmes are adequately monitored. Given this, it is especially problematic that no adequate arrangements exist to ensure compensation for research subjects if they are injured in the course of a clinical trial. Governments have consistently seemed disinclined to impose greater regulatory control in this area. However, there is now considerable impetus to ensure that good clinical practice is observed in the conduct of research. At the national level, the shortcomings revealed by the North Staffordshire Inquiry have resulted in proposals and subsequent guidance which should contribute towards the introduction of a more robust governance framework encompassing better monitoring and accounting procedures. The Griffiths Report highlighted the disparity between current best practice and the formal guidance available, which left considerable scope for individual latitude in how individual projects were managed. As a consequence it called for the development of formal guidance on research governance within the NHS, which should be issued to the NHS and to partners whose research it hosts [111]. This guidance has now been issued and aims to establish mechanisms to ensure the quality of clinical research [112].

The new guidance stresses the duties and accountability assumed by all NHS organisations before they agree to host any research, whether undertaken by its own employees or others. It emphasises the necessity for a favourable opinion by an appropriate ethical review committee (para. 2.22) and highlights the significance of informed consent, particularly in the case of research involving organs or tissue, which, as we have seen, has recently been especially contentious (paras 2.2.3–4). A particularly clear responsibility is placed on the named principal investigator in any project, who must apply for approval by a research ethics committee and retains responsibility for the scientific and ethical conduct of the research (para. 3.6.1). The need for systematic expert review of scientific evidence is also stressed (para. 2.3.1). This guidance also requires that organisations which employ researchers must be in a position to compensate anyone harmed, although only if such harm results from negligence (para. 2.6.2).

The North Staffordshire Inquiry also recommended that the Department of Health, professional and regulatory bodies should consult with a view to producing agreed guidance clarifying issues of consent for participation in clinical trials [113]. As we saw above, in the case of trials involving medicinal products, such changes are being imposed at European Community level, in recognition of variations in practice across member states. This is likely to presage future reforms. In the meantime, the onus is on researchers to be as truthful and clear as possible in their communications with patients about the risks and benefits of proposed research programmes.

12.7 Notes and references

1. DoH (2000) *Towards a Strategy for Nursing Research and Development: Proposals for Action*, Department of Health, London. p. 2; Kitson, A., McMahon, A., Rafferty, A. & Scott, E. (1997) On developing an agenda to influence policy in health related research for effective nursing: a description of a national R&D priority setting exercise. 2 *Nursing Times Research* 323.

2. DoH (1999) *Making a Difference: Strengthening the nursing, midwifery and health visiting contribution to health and health care.* Department of Health, London.

3. Fletcher, N., Holt, J., Brazier, M. & Harris, J. (1995) *Ethics, Law and Nursing*, p. 185. Manchester University Press, Manchester.

4. Fox, M. (1994) Animal Rights and Wrongs: Medical Ethics and the Killing of Non-human Animals. In Lee, R., Morgan, D. (eds) *Death Rites: Law and Ethics at the End of Life*, Routledge, London.

5. This has proven controversial in the context of suspected abuse of child patients by parents. For instance, in a review of research practices at North Staffordshire Hospital in the 1990s, considerable controversy was generated by covert video surveillance of parents suspected of abuse and whether this constituted a research programme. The Review Group recommended that the Department of Health should issue guidance to aid professionals in the identification of such abuse. See NHS Executive West Midlands Regional Office, *Report of a Review of the Research Framework in North Staffordshire Hospital NHS Trust* (The Griffiths Review), para 12.4.1. In this regard draft revisions to the CIOMS *International Guidelines for Biomedical Research Involving Human Subjects* (1993) propose that an ethical review committee must approve all research where there is an intention to deceive, and specify that the researcher must demonstrate that no other research method would suffice – see commentary on Guideline 10. The guidelines are currently subject to consultation – available from the Council for International Organisations of Medical Sciences (CIOMS) web-site www.cioms.ch/draftguidelines_may_2001.html (last visited 10 June 2001).

6. See McHale, J. & Fox, M. with Murphy, J. (1997) *Health Care Law: Text and Materials*, p. 593–5. Sweet & Maxwell, London.

7. This distinction was derived from earlier formulations of the Declaration of Helsinki – see Montgomery, J. (1992) Law and Ethics in International Trials, in *Introducing New Treatments for Cancer* (ed. C. Williams) Wiley, Chichester.

8. See McHale, J. & Fox, M. with Murphy, J. (1997) *Health Care Law: Text and Materials*, pp. 593–5. Sweet & Maxwell, London.

9. Whyte, R. (1994) Clinical trials, consent and the doctor–patient contract. *Health Law in Canada*, 15, p. 50.

10. See note 12 below.

11. For the full text of the current Declaration, see the following web-site: http://www.faseb.org/arvo/helsinki.htm (last visited 17 April 2001).

12. Although the Nazi and Japanese experiments during World War II overshadow all subsequent abusive medical research on humans, other infamous examples include the Tuskeegee experiments in 1932–1972 which used black males to determine the natural course of syphilis, even though the treatment had existed for centuries (see Jones, J. (1981) *Bad blood: The Tuskeegee syphilis experiment*, The Free Press, New York); experiments to test radiation as a therapy carried out in the US until the early 1970s (see McNeil, P. (1993) *The Ethics and Politics of Human Experimentation*, Chapter 1, CUP, Cambridge); and HIV research on prostitute women in the Phillipines in the 1980s (see Laurence, L., & Weinhouse, B. (1994/7) *Outrageous Practices: How Gender Bias Threatens Women's Health*, pp. 23–4, Rutgers University Press, New Brunswick). For

other examples, see British Medical Association (2001) *The Medical Profession & Human Rights: Handbook for a changing agenda*, Chapter 9, Zed Books, London.

13. Harris, J. (2000) Research on human subjects, exploitation, and global principles of ethics. In *Law and Medicine: Current Issues*, (eds M. Freeman & A. Lewis) Vol. 3, Oxford University Press, Oxford.
14. Royal College of Physicians (1996) *Guidelines on the Practice of Ethics Committees in Medical Research Involving Human Subjects*, 3rd edn, Royal College of Physicians, London.
15. Royal College of Nursing (1993) *Ethics Related to Research in Nursing*, Scutari Press, Harrow.
16. Department of Health (1991) *Guidelines to Local Research Ethics Committees*, The Stationery Office, London.
17. See Chapter V of the Convention for the articles governing scientific research. The full text of the Convention is available at http://www.coe.fr/eng/legaltxt/164e.htm (last visited 17 April 2001).
18. *Consent in the Criminal Law*, Law Commission Consultation Paper No. 139, paras. 8.38–8.52. The Stationery Office, London.
19. Brazier, M. (1992) *Medicine, Patients and the Law*, 2nd edn, p. 413. Penguin, Harmondsworth.
20. Miller, C. (1995) Protection of human subjects of research in Canada. *Health Law Review* 4, 8.
21. Berg, J.W. (1996) Legal and ethical complexities of consent with cognitively impaired research subjects: proposed guidelines. *Journal of Law, Medicine and Ethics*, 24, 18.
22. UKCC for Nursing, Midwifery and Health Visiting (1996) *Guidelines for Professional Practice*, para. 91.
23. McNeil, P. (1993) *The Ethics and Politics of Human Experimentation*, Chapter 1. CUP, Cambridge.
24. See Kennedy, I. (1989) The law and ethics of informed consent and randomized controlled trials. In (I. Kennedy) *Treat Me Right*, OUP, Oxford. Moreover, as discussed in Chapter 7A, even in the context of medical treatment, the *Sidaway* standard of disclosure seems to have been modified by subsequent cases to require much fuller answers to questions.
25. In 1965 the Saskatchewan Court of Appeal held that the subject should be informed of 'all the facts, probabilities and opinions which a reasonable man might be expected to consider before giving his consent'. See *Haluska* v. *University of Saskatchewan* (1965) 53 DLR 2d, 436, 444 per Mr Justice Hall.
26. See Montgomery, J. (1997) *Health Care Law*, pp. 343–5, OUP, Oxford; McHale, J. & Fox, M. with Murphy, J. (1997) *Health Care Law: Text and Materials*, pp. 574–5. Sweet & Maxwell, London.
27. For instance, Beecher has argued that the subject's truly informed consent cannot be obtained since the results of experiments are not known beforehand, so that there is no norm for the conduct of a 'pure scientific experiment' – see Beecher, H. (1970) *Research and the Individual: Human Studies* 5.
28. Bassiouni, M., Baffes, T. & Evrard, J. (1981) An appraisal of human experimentation in international law and practice: The need for international regulation of human experimentation. *The Journal of Criminal Law and Criminology*, 72(1597) 1611–2.
29. Tobias, J.S. (1997) BMJ's present policy (sometimes approving research in which patients have not given fully informed consent) is wholly correct. *BMJ*, 314, 1111.
30. McNeil, P. (1993) *The Ethics and Politics of Human Experimentation*, p. 135. CUP, Cambridge.
31. Medicines (Exemption from Licences) (Clinical Trials) Order 1995 (SI 1995/2808).

Medicines (Exemption from Licences and Certificates) (Clinical Trials) Order 1995 (SI 1995/2809). See further Mullon, K. (2000) *Pharmacy Law and Practice*, Blackstone Press, London, Chapter 4.

32. GPs failing to report drug side-effects. *Independent on Sunday* 15 April 2001.
33. Directive 2001/20/EC of the European Parliament and of the Council of 4 April 2001.
34. McNeil, P. (1993) *The Ethics and Politics of Human Experimentation*, p. 13. CUP, Cambridge.
35. Morehouse, R. (1994) Dilemmas of the clinical researcher: a view from the inside. *Health Law in Canada*, 15, 52–3.
36. Kennedy, I. (1989) The law and ethics of informed consent and randomized controlled trials. In *Treat Me Right* (I. Kennedy). OUP, Oxford.
37. See Fox, M. (1998) Research bodies: feminist perspectives on clinical research. In *Feminist Perspectives in Health Care Law*, (eds S. Sheldon & M. Thomson). Cavendish, London.
38. Katz, J. (1993) Human experimentation and human rights. *Saint Louis University Law Journal*, 38(7) p. 35.
39. Morehouse, R. (1994) Dilemmas of the clinical researcher: a view from the inside. *Health Law in Canada*, 15, 52. LREC guidelines state that the subject should be given an information sheet; Royal College of Physician guidelines suggest that she should be told the purpose, procedures, risk (including distress), benefits (including to others), informed that she may decline to participate or withdraw at any time and given a statement about compensation for injury. *Guidelines on the Practice of Ethics Committees in Medical Research Involving Human Subjects* (1996) 3rd edn.
40. See for example Bowden, P. (1997) *Caring: Gender-Sensitive Ethics*, Chapter 4. Routledge, London.
41. See footnote 5 above.
42. GMC, *Medical Research: The Role and Responsibilities of Doctors*, March 2001, available from www.gmc-uk.org/standards (last visited 17 April 2001).
43. MRC (1998) *Guidelines for Good Practice in Clinical Trials*, para. 5.4.6. Medical Research Council, London.
44. See para 22 of the Helsinki Declaration in the previous section of this chapter.
45. See McHale, J. (1993) Guidelines for medical research – some ethical and legal problems. *Medical Law Review*, 160, 167.
46. See, for instance, MRC (1998) *Guidelines for Good Practice in Clinical Trials*, p. 3. Medical Research Council, London.
47. Rawlings, G. (1992) Ethics and regulation in randomised controlled trials of therapy. In *Challenges in Medical Care* (ed. A. Grubb) pp. 41–2. Wiley, Chichester.
48. Oakley, A. (1990) Who's Afraid of the Randomized Controlled Trial. In *Women's Health Counts* (ed. H. Roberts). Routledge, London.
49. Fletcher, N., Holt, J., Brazier, M. & Harris, J. (1995) *Ethics, Law and Nursing*, p. 187. Manchester University Press, Manchester.
50. Tobias, J.S. (1997) BMJ's present policy (sometimes approving research in which patients have not given fully informed consent) is wholly correct. *BMJ*, 314, 1111.
51. Kennedy, I. (1989) The law and ethics of informed consent and randomized controlled trials. In *Treat Me Right* (I. Kennedy). OUP, Oxford.
52. See footnote 5 above.
53. Para. 9.3.5.
54. See further the discussion of whistleblowing in Chapter 8A.
55. In recognition of the fact that this is contrary to many national regulations, which allow for more liberal use of placebos in trials, the World Medical Association has acknowledged the need for further discussion of this issue and committed itself to a

follow up meeting within the next year on this matter. See WMA. Newsletter, April, 2001, available at http://www.wma.net/e/home.html (last visited 17 April 2001).

56. See footnote 5 above.

57. Bristol Royal Infirmary Inquiry, *The Inquiry into the management of care of children receiving heart surgery at the Bristol Royal Infirmary: Interim Report – Removal and Retention of Human Material*, May 2000; The Royal Liverpool Children's Inquiry, 30 January 2001.

58. Royal College of Pathologists (2000) *Guidelines for the Retention of tissue and organs at post-mortem examination*; Department of Health (2000) *Organ Retention: Interim Guidance on Post-mortem Examination*.

59. BMA (2001) *Interim BMA Guidelines on Retention of Human Tissue at Post-Mortem Examinations for the Purposes of Medical Education and Research*.

60. MRC (2001) *Human Tissue and Biological Samples for Use in Research: operation and ethical guidelines*. Medical Research Council, London.

61. MRC (2000) *Personal Information in Medical Research*, Principle 1. Medical Research Council, London.

62. See Central Office for Research Ethics Committees (COREC) at www.doh.gsi.gov.uk

63. Fox, M. & McHale, J. (1998) Xenotransplantation: The Ethical and Legal Ramifications. *Medical Law Review* 6, 42–61.

64. NHS Executive West Midlands Regional Office, *Report of a Review of the Research Framework in North Staffordshire Hospital NHS Trust*. See footnote 5 above.

65. See Neuberger, J. (1992) *Ethics and Health Care: The Role of Research Ethics Committees in the United Kingdom*. King's Fund Institute, London.

66. McNeil, P. (1993) *The Ethics and Politics of Human Experimentation*, p. 10. CUP, Cambridge.

67. McNeil, P. (1993) *The Ethics and Politics of Human Experimentation*, p. 110. CUP, Cambridge.

68. MRC (1998) *Guidelines for Good Practice in Clinical Trials*, Chapter 6 and Appendix 3. Medical Research Council, London.

69. Miller, C. (1995) Protection of human subjects of research in Canada. *Health Law Review*, 4, 9.

70. Protection of Human Research Subjects and Creation of NBAC, Exec. Order No. 12,975, 60 Fed. Reg. 52,063 (1995). See Mastroianni, A, and Kahn, J, "Remedies for Human Subjects of Cold War Research: Recommendations of the Advisory Committee" (1996) *Journal of Law, Medicine and Ethics* 24, 118–26.

71. See McHale, J. (1993) Guidelines for medical research – some ethical and legal problems. *Medical Law Review*, 160, 184–5.

72. UKCC (1996) *Guidelines for Professional Practice*, para. 82.

73. Neuberger, J. (1992). (See note 65).

74. Friedman, P.J. (1992) Mistakes and fraud in medical research. *Law, Medicine and Health Care*, 20, 17; Parrish, D.M. (1996) Falsification of Credentials in the Research Setting; Scientific Misconduct? *Journal of Law, Medicine & Ethics*, 24, 260.

75. Lock, S. (1996) *Fraud and Misconduct in Medical Research*, 2nd, BMJ Publishing Group, London.

76. Despite calls in the medical press to do so – see McHale, J. & Fox, M. with Murphy, J. (1997) *Health Care Law: Text and Materials*, pp. 593–5. Sweet and Maxwell, London.

77. Chalmers, I. (1999) Unbiased, relevant and reliable assessments in health care. *British Medical Journal*, 318, 1167.

78. See preamble to Directive 2001/20/EC of the European Parliament and of the Council of 4 April 2001, para. 3.

79. Family Law Reform Act 1969, section 8; *Gillick* v. *West Norfolk and Wisbech Area Health Authority* [1986] AC 112.
80. DoH Guidelines, 1991, para 4.1–2.
81. Para 4.4. See also Nicolson, R. (1985) *Medical Research on Children*. OUP, Oxford.
82. British Paediatric Association (1992) *Guidelines for the Ethical Conduct of Research Involving Children*. British Paediatric Association, London.
83. See footnote 5 above.
84. CIOMS Commentary on Guideline 14 (see footnote 5).
85. See McHale, J. & Fox, M. with Murphy, J. (1997) *Health Care Law: Text and Materials*, pp. 583–4. Sweet and Maxwell, London.
86. See footnote 5 above.
87. For the position in Scotland, see the Adults with Incapacity (Scotland) Act 2000.
88. *F* v. *West Berkshire Area Health Authority* [1989] 3 All ER 545; see further Chapter 7A.
89. See McHale, J. & Fox, M. with Murphy, J. (1997) *Health Care Law: Text and Materials*, pp. 589–93. Sweet and Maxwell, London.
90. Law Commission (1995) *Mental Incapacity*, Law Com. 231, paras 6.29–6.36.
91. Lord Chancellor's Department, *Who decides? Making decisions on behalf of mentally incompetent patients*, Consultation Paper, December 1997, para 5.41; LCD, *Making Decisions: The Government's proposals for making decisions on behalf of mentally incapacitated adults*, October 1999.
92. McHale, J. (1998) Mental incapacity: Some proposals for legislative reform. *Journal of Medical Ethics* 24, 322, 325.
93. Guideline 17 of the CIOMS guidance, currently under revision (see footnote 5 above) provides that 'Researchers and ethical review committees should ensure that prospective subjects who are pregnant are adequately informed about the risk and benefits to themselves, their pregnancies and their potential offspring'. However, it stresses that in principle there is no difference between this situation and the usual difficulty of making risk–benefit determinations for non-pregnant women, and that the ultimate decision is a matter for the woman.
94. DoH Guidelines, 1991, para 3.16.
95. Reported by The Associated Press, May 17, 2000, available on www.my.aol.com/news
96. MRC (2000) *Good Research Practice*, Medical Research Council, London.
97. Fox, M. (1998) Research bodies: feminist perspectives on clinical research. In *Feminist Perspectives in Health Care Law*, pp. 122–3. Cavendish, London.
98. DES was a drug first prescribed in America in 1943, in the hope that it would avert miscarriages. Its efficacy was challenged as early as 1953, and by 1971 the FDA had banned its use during pregnancy after substantial evidence that it was associated with high rates of cervical cancer in the daughters of DES users.
99. Department of Health Guidelines, para 4.5.
100. See further, Chapter 7.
101. Merton, V. (1993) The exclusion of pregnant, pregnable, and once-pregnable patients (aka women) from biomedical research. *American Journal of Law and Medicine*, 12, 369.
102. See further, Chapter 6.
103. On the limitations of these discretionary payments, see Barton, J.M. *et al.* (1995) The compensation of patients injured in clinical trials. *Journal of Medical Ethics*, 21, 166.
104. Royal Commission on Civil Liability and Compensation for Personal Injury, Cmnd 7054, 1978: para. 1341.
105. Gillon, R. (1992) No-fault compensation for victims of non-therapeutic research – should government continue to be exempt? *Journal of Medical Ethics*, 18, 59.

106. Nuffield Council on Bioethics (1996) *Animal-to-Human Transplants: the ethics of xenotransplantation*, Nuffield Council on Bioethics, London; *A report by the Advisory Group on the Ethics of Xenotransplantation* (1997) Department of Health, London (hereafter 'the Kennedy Report').

107. A report by the Advisory Group on the Ethics of Xenotransplantation (1997) (the Kennedy Report) para. 7.11. Department of Health, London.

108. UKIXRA United Kingdom Interim Xenoplantation Regulatory Authority (1999) Draft Report of the Infection Surveillance Steering Group of the UKIXRA.

109. The Kennedy report recommended that in the case of xenotransplantation it will be particularly important to establish a system of counselling which is independent of the transplantation team: para 7.13.

110. Fox, M. & McHale, J. (1998) Xenotransplantation: The Ethical and Legal Ramifications. *Medical Law Review* 6, 42–61.

111. Para. 4.1.4.

112. See Department of Health, *Research Governance Framework*, March 2001 (available from www.doh.gov.uk/research/rds/nhsrandd/researchgovernance.htm)

113. Para. 42.4.

The author of this chapter would like to thank Margaret Brazier, Kirsty Keywood and Jean McHale for their helpful comments.

B An Ethical Perspective – Nursing Research

Richard Ashcroft

Research is an essential element of innovation and quality improvement in health care. As such, it aims at something of great collective value. It can also be enormously personally rewarding to the researcher him or herself. For the 'subjects' or 'participants' in research, the research process can be beneficial for their health or their well-being, both through the intervention they receive as part of the research process, and through the fact of participating in the research process itself.

Research can, however, be pursued selfishly; it can cause harm or distress to subjects; it can be irrelevant, unoriginal, incompetently or fraudulently performed; and it can be exploitative.

There is therefore no question but that research is an ethically significant activity, and that any research project must be pursued in an ethically reflective way. Merely to say this is to skate over the complexities of doing so: the diversity of research methods, settings in which research can be pursued, purposes to which the results of research are put, people who do research and relationships between them. This chapter will present the elements of the ethics of research, illustrating these with examples. It will concentrate on two kinds of nurse (and midwife and health visitor) research activity: nursing research (research into the health care work and types of care and treatment that nurses do) and the work of research nurses (the role of the research nurse in clinical trials and other kinds of biomedical research). Nurses will also care for patients in clinical trials and other studies in which the nurse has no direct involvement, but for most purposes the ethical principles will be similar, since in all circumstances the nurse's primary responsibility is for the patient. What varies between the roles of nurses with care of patients in research, research nurses, and nursing researchers is the degree of responsibility for the research and control over it, and the kinds of dilemma that may arise.

12.8 The sources of nursing ethics

Ethical principles for professionals have a number of sources. These include:

- the law;
- professional codes of conduct;

- fundamental moral principles;
- the core values of:
    - the individual
    - the institution
    - the profession
    - society.

This list has no special order, as it is a matter of controversy which source of ethics is most reliable, and which takes priority. However, most of us would agree that nurses have a strong obligation to abide by, and work within, the law. The law does not determine precisely what is ethical, for instance many actions are lawful but possibly unethical, and some actions may be ethical without being lawful. Examples might include abortion and euthanasia – many people who think abortion ethical also think euthanasia ethical, while in law abortion is legal in many circumstances and active euthanasia is unlawful. Conversely, many people who think euthanasia is unethical also think that abortion is unethical.

The role of professional codes of ethics and conduct is in part to define the nature of the profession they regulate. They identify certain actions which might be permitted for lay people but are not permissible in nurses, and other actions which are permissible in nurses but not permitted for lay people. Codes set out the higher standards of competence, rights and duties which go along with being a nurse. Many of these rights and duties have an ethical character, but many are more in the nature of the requirements of professional etiquette.

In identifying the roles that the law, ethics and professional codes have for nurses and others, we must turn eventually to the ethical foundations of these codes – the fundamental principles and values which are meant to underlie these codes. An example of a fundamental moral principle is the principle of non-maleficence: individuals have a duty to refrain from harming others. This principle is particularly associated with the caring professions, but it is not specific to them alone. Rather, it has special importance for the caring professions simply because their patients or clients are particularly vulnerable, and thus at greater risk of being harmed, and because the skills and tools of the caring professions are particularly liable to being turned to harmful ends. However, saying that this principle is fundamental is not to say that it is absolute. Thus, certain actions do cause harm (e.g. venepuncture) but are justified by their being carried out with beneficent intentions (e.g. to provide pain relief). Hence, fundamental principles must be balanced against each other; in this case, non-maleficence is balanced with beneficence and with respect for autonomy (the individual must be asked for his or her consent).

The question of epistemology of values (how we know them) has exercised philosophers for generations. It appears in an interesting way in research ethics. Firstly, research ethics, like health care ethics generally, is a field which has experienced considerable historical evolution, as its principles have become more clearly articulated and ramified over time. The key scandals in the ethics of research always raise the question: did the responsible agents know that they were acting wrongly? Was it possible for them to know? Even if we can show that they did not and could not have known that they were in the wrong, we may perhaps argue that they are nonetheless culpable. Relatedly, the guilty individuals or institutions may insist that their critics and colleagues were just as guilty, and that they are unjustly escaping censure, or are being judged hypocritically. Exactly these arguments were used in their defence by the Nazi doctors at the Nuremberg Trial for instance.

The epistemology of values and the difficulty of balancing principles lead us to consider a problem which is much discussed in the nursing ethics literature: whether any principles exist, whether they are in any sense universal or objective, and whether the 'principles' approach is consistent with the orientation of caring which many argue is what typifies the nursing relationship. This is a large topic, which is beyond the scope of this chapter. However, for present purposes, it is important to distinguish between the genuine problems of knowledge and application of principles, and the relativist proposal that ethical principles are merely matters of stance and subjective attitude.

I suggest that moral relativism is neither a practical possibility – since in fact all nurses are regulated by a framework of law and by professional codes of conduct – nor a viable intellectual stance. Even 'situational' approaches, such as the 'ethics of care' approach, turn on judgements that certain values are non-negotiable. Where ethical approaches differ is generally in relation to how we know and apply values and principles to situations.

Epistemological questions arise in another context in research ethics, as we will consider in the next section.

12.9   Ethics and the design of research

It is commonly said that 'bad science is bad ethics'. Before we consider why this is so, we must understand better what is meant by 'bad science'. I propose the following definition as a description of science:

> Science is the activity of the disciplined, collective acquisition of reliable, generalisable knowledge; science is also the evolving set of outcomes of that activity.

The scientific activity includes a great range of methods, styles, techniques and practices, such that 'good' science is hard to define and perhaps amounts to nothing more than 'successful' science. Nevertheless, 'bad science' is easier to define. Bad science is 'science' which contradicts the very idea of science, as defined above. Hence, science which is methodologically ill-defined or likely to result in meaningless or unreliable data, unjustified knowledge claims, or no significant contribution to generalisable knowledge at all, is bad science. What is meant by 'generalisable' is somewhat controversial, but at least it requires the scientific experience to be communicable, that is, understandable by others and in some way usable by others. Science is about public knowledge, rather than some essentially private experience. This view applies as much to qualitative or action research as to quantitative research or other 'natural science' inquiry. Likewise, scientific research which is kept secret or is unreported breaches the requirement that science be a collective enterprise.

This account of bad science is meant to cover the whole range of scientific methods, from statistical analysis of large numerical data sets to qualitative research interviews. Translated into practical terms, some obvious recommendations come out:

- The study should start with a satisfactory literature review which permits the definition of the research question, in such way as to show that the question is important, it has practical relevance and we don't already know the answer to the question. No inquiry is so 'naïve' or 'novel' that it does not build in some way on previous work or on previously developed methods, and these debts need to be brought into view and analysed, so far as this is possible.
- The design of the study must be reliable and likely to answer the research question in such a way that the validity of the answer is determinate and the findings of the study are interpretable and applicable by other practitioners and researchers.
- The results of the study must be publishable and actually published, within a reasonable time from the completion of the study, even if negative, to permit other researchers and the public to learn from the study (including its weaknesses no less than its strengths). The publication should be a fair and accurate account of the research design and results. There is an equivalent duty on the editor of the journal or book and reviewers for the journal or book to give a fair and competent assessment of the article or chapter submitted for publication.

All of these recommendations are now included in the Declaration of Helsinki, which is the most important international ethical guideline regulating biomedical research. However, they are here restated in language which shows their applicability as widely as possible to the diversity of research methods used in nursing today, including qualitative and health services research methods.

Having defined 'bad science', it should be clear why 'bad science is bad ethics'. In the first place, research involves exposing patients or colleagues or other research subjects to the risks of the research. Hence, if this research is unlikely to produce reliable results, it is arguable that the subjects are exposed to risk without this in any way being balanced by the prospect of benefit to society. To the extent that participants are taking part with altruistic motives, bad research misrepresents itself as an opportunity to benefit others, when it has no prospect of doing so. As such, it could be seen both as an insult to the altruism of the participants, and as deception of them.

To the extent that the research offers some benefit to the participants in terms of access to new treatment, increased access to nursing or other health care services, or financial or other inducements, there is still an issue about the waste of resources bad research involves. Research always involves staff time and use of basic resources, even where there is no additional grant funding component. Hence, there is always an 'opportunity cost', as the economists say, involved in doing research. The opportunity cost of bad research is at least the opportunity of using staff and other resources more effectively, either in caring for patients or carrying out bona fide research, for instance. Research ethics typically ignores the ethical issues involved in resources and facilities management in the health services, but this is morally shortsighted.

12.10   The competence of the research staff and research governance

One important exception to the requirement that the research design be 'good' science appears to be research carried out as part of the researcher's own education or training. Does 'student research' have to be judged by standards as high as those of 'real' research? There are different schools of thought here, but in essence it comes down to how the researcher (student) wishes the research to be considered: is it an educational project, designed to instruct the student in research methods and management? Or is it primarily intended as research, i.e. an attempt to add to collective knowledge? If the latter, then the research standard applies. The project must be assessed as objectively as possible in the light of existing knowledge and standards of research method. If the former, then the project must meet a different, not necessarily a lower, standard.

The educational project must be evaluated as a project which aims to teach the student something about research method and management. As such, it must be evaluated in the same way that any educational intervention is – according to the aims and objectives of the teaching and the capacity this work has for permitting fulfilment of those aims and objectives. To some extent, these overlap with the aims and objectives of research; the best student research is often publishable in its own right. Moreover, at a certain standard, the appropriate educational aim is to produce work which can stand the rigours of objective peer review. This is certainly the case of work produced for masters degrees by research, and for doctoral research.

The moral issues involved in educational projects are not, finally, different to those involved in research projects: the subjects must be told of the aims of the research and what it is hoped to achieve. In educational projects, they must be told that this is to help the student learn – as when a student nurse takes part in ward rounds and clinical care of patients. In research projects, they must be told that this research will aim to add to knowledge. In either case, the patient's consent should be sought (where possible) and the risks and benefits of the research explained, and so on. What differs between the educational project and the research project is simply the explicit non-clinical aim of the activity over and above its clinical aim, if any.

Just as the standard of the design may vary in the research and educational contexts, so too may the standard of competence expected of the principal investigator. However, there are limits. In research projects, there is a clear obligation for the research undertaken to lie within the competence of the investigator (or investigating team together) to carry out the work. This is clearly true in clinical negligence terms, but even where the possible incompetence has no clinical consequences for the subject, the general obligation not to do 'bad science' entails the duty to carry out only such research as can be done competently.

When the investigator is carrying out an educational project, the competence requirement obviously varies somewhat. Additionally, innovative research may well involve pushing the boundaries of the investigator's competence. What these situations illustrate is that 'competence' is as much an institutional as an individual affair. In the cases of the student or inexperienced or methodologically innovative researcher, competence must be secured by appropriate supervision and support, clear lines of accountability and, where necessary, physical oversight of the research activity. The same rules as apply to the student or inexperienced nurse in a novel situation, apply also to the individual learning a new research technique. Here the emphasis must lie on 'appropriate' supervision – an otherwise experienced professional learning a new technique may not require the same kind of supervision as the greenhorn student. Nevertheless, a supervisory mechanism will be required. Supervisory mechanisms include piloting of the method, and peer review of the research design and of interim and final results, as well as more traditional means of educational supervision.

An important feature of supervision is that supervision is not identical to hierarchical reporting. So in a clinical team running a clinical trial, it may be that the principal investigator with overall responsibility for the trial, financially and administratively, is a new consultant physician. His or her research experience in this kind of clinical trial may be limited. The senior nurse on the team, acting as research nurse, may have considerable experience, however, even though from the point of trial management he or she reports to the principal investigator. (The Declaration of Helsinki requires any biomedical research project to be led by a physician, even if only nominally.) In this situation, it is clear that the 'supervisory' role may in reality fall to the research nurse, rather than the designated principal investigator.

Each individual member of the clinical team is thus responsible for his or her own tasks, as well as participation in the generic task of quality oversight of the project. Hence, in addition to each individual's competence (or 'supported competence' in the case of supervised work), there is 'team competence' – can this group function effectively as a team to ensure that the ethical and quality obligations to carry out the research to a certain standard are met? This is a very brief summary of the implications of 'research governance' or 'good clinical practice' for research and clinical teams.

12.11   Recruitment and consent

The voluntary informed consent of the individual research participant is essential. In certain kinds of research consent may be impossible (for instance research with babies or young children, or incapacitated subjects who are unable to give consent). In certain circumstances, consent may not be sought because the research project is of great collective importance, consent would be impractical, and the risk of harm to the participants is minimal. The details of these exceptions are complex, and cannot be covered here; the reader is referred to the excellent guidelines prepared by the UK Medical Research Council on research with the mentally incapacitated and on the use of personal medical information in research.

Consent is important because it respects the autonomy of individuals: their right to privacy, their right to determine what can be done to their bodies, and their right to choose whether or not to assist others in activities which may not benefit them directly. Justifications of departures from the consent standard may rest on legally shaky ground, but ethically two principles can be invoked. The first is that, in the case of individuals unable to consent by reason of lacking capacity to consent, medical and nursing innovations which will benefit them are required by the principle of beneficence. Research interventions which have a therapeutic component can directly benefit the individual, and enrolling an individual lacking capacity to consent would be justified by this. However, the principle of non-maleficence requires that their special vulnerability to harm and exploitation be noted, and special care be taken to minimise the possibility of harm to them. Here, arguably, the principle of respect for autonomy is replaced by a principle of respect for the dignity of the vulnerable person.

A second justification for research without consent is that, where the harm and inconvenience caused to the individual is zero or negligible, all of us have, other things being equal, a duty to benefit others (especially if that involves no cost to us) and participation in socially useful research is one way to do that. This might be held to be supplemented in the UK by a sort of political claim that we are all members of the National Health Service, and all benefit from it, and all have an interest in its development and management. Hence, informally we mandate it to carry out records based research and audit, without the necessity to obtain consent provided our privacy is protected. The former version is an argument from solidarity; the latter is an argument from social contract theory. But what is clear is that both arguments rest on a claim about the importance and utility of the research, a claim that the research is minimal risk and a claim that the rational individual would not object to their consent not being sought. All of these claims need proof in each situation, and the burden of proof lies with the researcher; these claims must be adjudicated by an independent research ethics committee.

A more troubling worry about consent is the extent to which research on patients involves people who may be emotionally vulnerable, who invest trust in health care professionals simply because they are professionals, or perhaps because they have come to like and rely on particular individual professionals. They may not distinguish between the individual's roles as carer and as researcher, or they may think that they must somehow 'please' the member of staff in order to maintain good relationships or access to care. While this is explicitly ruled out by the Declaration of Helsinki, and patients must be told that their care will not be compromised if they refuse, this is sometimes difficult for patients to believe or accept.

A particular difficulty arises where a clinical trial is being managed by a research nurse who is requested by the principal investigator to recruit and enrol individuals in the trial. Strictly speaking, the consent must be obtained by the individual responsible for prescribing the study treatment – normally the physician principal investigator. This raises more general issues about the roles and responsibilities of the different members of the clinical team, which is beyond the scope of this chapter.

12.12   Research and care

Ethically, the issue of most profound concern about research involving patients is how research and care roles conflict. While the actions performed may be consistent with good medical and nursing care for the individual patient, there does seem to be a conflict in orientation. Research aims to benefit the community, and it must be pursued with scientific, methodical rigour. Care for the sick and vulnerable aims at benefiting the individual and is essentially personal and non-universalisable. The very idea of 'methodical care' seems to be an oxymoron, yet is implicit in the collection of clinical data and carrying out of research procedures at regular intervals, especially in the context of busy hospital settings with the whole range of other clinical duties to be carried out, by the researcher or his or her colleagues.

What is at stake here is an ethical relationship between the patient and the professional caring for them, which depends on respect for the dignity and autonomy of the patient, and maintenance of the integrity and professionalism of the carer. This can be a difficult balance to strike and is particularly acute when we reflect on the idea of the nurse as patient's advocate. To some extent this is possible where the nurse is not the principal investigator, but it is very difficult to maintain this stance where the nurse is both patient advocate and advocate of his or her own research. The risk here is that the nurse uncritically assumes that his or her goals are shared by the patient, hence that advocating the research is advocacy of the patient's interests and views. The ethical concept of most importance here is the concept of 'virtue': the researcher must maintain the virtues of the health care professional (care for the well-being of others, integrity and responsibility, for instance) at the same time as the virtues of the researcher (scrupulosity, honesty and curiosity, for instance).

This balance can be struck by many remarkable individuals, but it is more important that it is struck at the level of institutions – individuals working in teams with a shared institutional culture. The trend toward quality improvement and 'research governance' in part marks this attempt to achieve an institutional balance; there is a cultural shift in the health service to see research and treatment as complementary activities, rather than activities in tension. A central question in research ethics today is whether this cultural shift is coherent, or whether it is a sort of institutional delusion.

12.13   Conclusion

Research will be an increasing part of the work of nurses in the coming years, and arguably this can only improve the care given by nurses. In this chapter I have described some of the ethical dilemmas that arise in research at a rather abstract and reflective level. As I point out at various places in this chapter, the growth in the role and importance of research outside of the narrow biomedical context which has historically shaped research ethics raises difficult philosophical and professional concerns, which guidelines alone will not solve. What is clear, however, is that attention to the core principles of good nursing – respect for the dignity and autonomy of patients, beneficence, non-maleficence, justice and integrity – will remain essential. The best research, and best practice in research, embodies and promotes these principles.

12.14 Acknowledgements

The author thanks Paul Wainwright and Heather Widdows for their helpful comments on drafts of this chapter.

12.15 Further reading

Handbooks

Baruch Brody (1998) *The Ethics of Biomedical Research*. Oxford University Press, Oxford.
Trevor Smith (1999) *Ethics of Medical Research: A Handbook of Good Practice*. Cambridge University Press, Cambridge.
Royal College of Nursing (1993) *Ethics Related to Research in Nursing*. Scutari Press, Harrow.

Principles of ethics

Donna Dickenson & Michael Parker (2001) *The Cambridge Medical Ethics Workbook*. Cambridge University Press, Cambridge.
Leslie Gelling (1999) Ethical principles in health care research. *Nursing Standard* 13(36), 39–42.
Raanan Gillon (1986) *Philosophical Medical Ethics*. John Wiley, Chichester.

Consent

Priscilla Alderson (1995) Consent to research: The role of the nurse. *Nursing Standard*, 9(36), 28–31.
Len Doyal & Jeffrey S. Tobias (eds) (2000) *Informed Consent in Medical Research*. BMJ Books, London.
Sarah Edwards *et al.* (1998) Ethical issues in the design and conduct of randomised controlled trials. *Health Technology Assessment*, 2(15), 1–128.

Recruitment

Richard Ashcroft *et al.* (1997) Implications of sociocultural contexts for ethics of clinical trials. *Health Technology Assessment*, 1(9), 1–65.
Richard Ashcroft (2000) Human research subjects, selection of. In *Concise Encyclopedia of Ethics of New Technologies* (ed. Ruth Chadwick) pp. 255–66. Plenum Press, San Diego.

Research management

Richard Ashcroft (2002) Ethical issues in outsourced clinical trials. In *Outsourcing Health Care Development and Manufacturing* (eds Roy Drucker & R. Graham Hughes) Interpharm Press, Englewood, Colorado.

Useful Links

All the organisations listed below produce useful publications. Please see the appropriate web page or write to them for a current publications' list.

Action for Victims of Medical Accidents (AVMA)
44 High Street
Croydon
CR0 1YB
www.avma.org.uk

Commission for Health Improvement (CHI)
10th Floor
Finsbury Tower
103–105 Bunhill Row
London
EC1Y 8TG
www.chi.nhs.uk

Department of Health
Richmond House
79 Whitehall
London
SW1A 2NS
www.doh.gov.uk

General Medical Council (GMC)
178 Great Portland Street
London
W1W 5JE
www.gmc-uk.org

The Health Service Ombudsman
15th Floor
Millbank Tower
Millbank
London
SW1P 4QP
www.ombudsman.org.uk

The Medical Defence Union
230 Blackfriars Road
London
SE1 8PJ
www.the-mdu.com

The Medical Protection Society (MPS)
Granary Wharf House
Leeds
LS11 5PY
www.mps.org.uk

National Institute of Clinical Excellence (NICE)
11 Strand
London
WC2N 5HR
www.nice.org.uk

The National Patient Safety Agency (NPSA)
Marble Arch Tower
55 Bryanston Street
London
W1H 7AJ
www.npsa.org.uk

Royal College of Nursing
20 Cavendish Square
London
W1M 0DB
www.rcn.org.uk

United Kingdom Central Council (UKCC)
23 Portland Street
London
W1B 1PZ
www.ukcc.org.uk

Table of Cases

The following abbreviations are used:

AC   Law Reports, Appeal Cases
All ER   All England Law Reports
BMLR   Butterworths Medico-Legal Reports
Ch   Law Reports, Chancery Division
CLR   Commonwealth Law Reports
CMLR   Common Market Law Reports
Cr App Rep   Court of Appeal Reports
DLR   Dominion Law Reports
ECJ   European Court of Justice
ECR   European Court Reports
ECtHR   European Court of Human Rights
Fam   Family Division Law Reports
FCR   Family Court Reports
FLR   Family Law Reports
KB   Law Reports, King's Bench Division
KIR   Knight's Industrial Reports
Lloyds Rep Med Lloyds List Medical Law Reports
LTL   Lawtel
Med LR   Medical Law Review
OR   Ontario Reports
PIQR   Personal Injuries and Quantum Reports
QB   Law Reports, Queen's Bench Division
SJ   Solicitors' Journal
TLR   Times Law Reports
WLR   Weekly Law Reports
WWR   Western Weekly Reports

Table of Statutes

Index